Derrida: *A Critical Reader*

Edited by
David Wood

BLACKWELL
Oxford UK & Cambridge USA

First published 1992

Blackwell Publishers
108 Cowley Road, Oxford, OX4 1JF, UK

3 Cambridge Center
Cambridge, Massachusetts 02142, USA

A CIP catalogue record for this book is available from the British Library.

Library of Congress Cataloging in Publication Data
Derrida: a critical reader/edited by David Wood.
p. cm.
Includes bibliographical references and index.
ISBN 0–631–16102–3 (alk. paper).—ISBN 0–631–16121–X (pbk. alk. paper)
1. Derrida, Jacques. I. Wood, David (David C.)
B2430.D484D477 1992
194—dc20
91–46355
CIP

Typeset in 10 on 12pt Plantin
by Hope Services (Abingdon) Ltd.

Printed and bound in Great Britain by Marston Lindsay Ross International Ltd, Oxfordshire

Contents

Notes on Contributors   vii

Acknowledgements   xi

Reading Derrida: an Introduction   1
David Wood

1 Passions: 'An Oblique Offering'   5
Jacques Derrida
Translated by David Wood

2 Elliptical Sense   36
Jean-Luc Nancy
Translated by Peter Connor

3 The Play of Nietzsche in Derrida   52
Michel Haar
Translated by Will McNeill

4 Responsibility with Indecidability   72
John Llewelyn

5 Mosaic Fragment: if Derrida were an Egyptian . . .   97
Geoffrey Bennington

6 Doublings   120
John Sallis

7 No More Stories, Good or Bad:
de Man's Criticisms of Derrida on Rousseau   137
Robert Bernasconi

8 Deconstruction, Postmodernism and Philosophy:
Habermas on Derrida   167
   Christopher Norris

9 Derrida and the Issues of Exemplarity   193
   Irene E. Harvey

10 Is Self-Consciousness a Case of *présence à soi?*
Towards a Meta-Critique of the Recent French
Critique of Metaphysics   218
   Manfred Frank
   Translated by Andrew Bowie

11 Is Derrida a Transcendental Philosopher?   235
   Richard Rorty

A Bibliography of the Works of Jacques Derrida   247
   Albert Leventure with Thomas Keenan

Index prepared by Iain Hamilton Grant   290

Notes on Contributors

Jacques Derrida
Professor at the Ecole des Hautes Etudes en Science Sociales, Paris. He holds
visiting professorships at the University of California at Irvine, and at Cornell
University.

David Wood
Director of the Centre for Research in Philosophy and Literature and Senior
Lecturer in Philosophy at the University of Warwick. He is the author of *The
Deconstruction of Time* (1988), and of *Philosophy at the Limit* (1990). He has
edited many books on various aspects of continental philosophy, including
Derrida and Différance (1988), *Writing the Future* (1990) and *Derrida,
Heidegger and Spirit* (1992).

Jean-Luc Nancy
Teaches philosophy at the University of Strasbourg. He is the author of *Le
partage des voix* (1982), *L'impératif catégorique* (1983), *L'oubli de la philosophie*
(1986), *Des lieux divins* (1987), *L'expérience de la liberté* (1988), *Une pensée
finie* (1991), *La communauté désoeuvrée* (1986) and *The Literary Absolute* (with
Philippe Lacoue-Labarthe) (1978, trans. 1988) and *Ego sum* (1979).

Michel Haar
Teaches philosophy at the University of Paris-Sorbonne. He is author of *Le
Chant de la Terre: Heidegger et les assises de l'Histoire de l'Etre* (1987), and
Heidegger et l'essence de l'homme (1990).

John Llewelyn
Recently Arthur J. Schmitt Distinguished Visiting Professor of Philosophy at Loyola University of Chicago and before that Reader in Philosophy at the University of Edinburgh. He is the author of *Beyond Metaphysics?* (1985), *Derrida and the Threshold of Sense* (1986) and *The Middle Voice of Ecological Conscience: A Chiasmic Reading of Responsibility in the Neighbourhood of Levinas, Heidegger and Others* (1991).

Geoffrey Bennington
Senior Lecturer in French at the University of Sussex. He is the author of *Sententiousness and the Novel* (1985), *Lyotard: Writing the Event* (1988), *Dudding: des noms de Rousseau* (1990), and (with Jacques Derrida) *Jacques Derrida* (1991). He is an editor of the Oxford Literary Review.

John Sallis
W. Alton Jones Professor of Philosophy at Vanderbilt University. His recent books include *Crossings: Nietzsche and the Space of Tragedy* (1991), *Echoes: After Heidegger* (1990), and *Spacings: Of Reason and Imagination* (1987). He is the founding editor of the journal *Research in Phenomenology* and the editor of *Deconstruction and Philosophy: The Texts of Jacques Derrida* (1987).

Robert Bernasconi
Moss Professor of Philosophy at Memphis State University. He is the author of *The Question of Language in Heidegger's History of Being* (1985), *Heidegger in Question* (1992) and *Between Levinas and Derrida* (1992), and editor (with David Wood) of *Derrida and Différance* (1989) and (with Simon Critchley) of *Rereading Levinas* (1991).

Christopher Norris
Professor of English at the University of Wales. He has written many books on Derrida and deconstruction, most recently *Derrida* (1987), *Paul de Man: Deconstruction and the Critique of Aesthetic Ideology* (1988), *Deconstruction and the Interests of Theory* (1988), *What is Deconstruction?* (with Andrew Benjamin) (1988) and *What's Wrong with Postmodernism?* (1990).

Irene Harvey
Associate Professor of Philosophy at Pennsylvania State University. She is the author of *Derrida and the Economy of Différance* (1986) and numerous articles on continental French thought.

Manfred Frank
Dean of the Philosophy Faculty at the University of Tübingen. His *What is Neostructuralism?* has recently appeared in English (1989).

Richard Rorty
Professor of Humanities at the University of Virginia. He is best known for his *Philosophy and the Mirror of Nature* (1979), *The Consequences of Pragmatism* (1982) and *Contingency, Irony, and Solidarity* (1989).

Albert Leventure
A writer. He was educated in London, Egypt and Oxford. He is currently writing two books: *Without Settlement* and *Insignia of the Plenum: the signature Derrida the proper name*.

Thomas Keenan
Teaches English at Princeton, and is the author of *Fables of Responsibility* (forthcoming). He has edited (with Werner Hamacher and Neil Hertz) Paul de Man's *Wartime Journals* and *Responses*. With Deborah Esch he is preparing two volumes of essays by Derrida: *Institutions of Philosophy* and *Negotiations*.

Acknowledgements

I would like to thank John Sallis, as editor of *Research in Phenomenology*, for permission to publish Jean-Luc Nancy's 'Elliptical Sense', which appeared in the 1988 issue, and I thank *Yale Journal of Criticism* for permission to reprint Richard Rorty's 'Is Derrida a Transcendental Philosopher?', which appeared in vol.2 (1989), pp. 205–17. I am grateful to Editions EHESS (Paris), to Faber (London) and to Minuit (Paris) for permission to quote passages from Malamoud and Benveniste respectively. I am also grateful to the translators of papers by Michel Haar (Will McNeill), Jean-Luc Nancy (Peter Connor) and Manfred Frank (Andrew Bowie) for their care and expertise, and for the assistance and advice of Will McNeill, Leslie Hill and Peter Larkin in translation of Jacques Derrida's 'Passions'. Special thanks go to Albert Leventure, whose bibliography of Derrida's own writing is a monument of dedication and attention to detail, and to Thomas Keenan, through whose generous additions, suggestions and corrections the bibliography verges on completeness (to date). An early version appeared in *Textual Practice*, Vol. 5, No. 1 (spring 1991) published by Routledge (London). I also owe a debt to the philosophical labour of Iain Grant in preparing the index to this book. Finally I would like to thank Jacques Derrida for agreeing to make an oblique entry into a collection of papers which, though they deal with various parts or aspects or dimensions of his work, are never quite *on* Derrida.

Reading Derrida: an Introduction
David Wood

There are philosophers, as yet untouched by Derrida's writing, who suspect (and hope) it can be subsumed under some ancient error, such as scepticism or irrationalism. Others moved to more serious engagement have judged it a repetition of dead-end themes in German idealism, a dangerous neo-Heideggerianism, or the revenge of literature against philosophy. Yet others have defended Derrida, at least in parts, as a quasi-transcendental philosopher strongly tied to the tradition, or, on the contrary, as a Socratic figure whose mission is to keep us honest by stirring the congealings of complacency. Derrida has inspired both anger and indifference. And his many enthusiastic imitators have been blind to the paradox that to imitate someone who is not an imitator is to miss what matters.

Artificial as are all periodizations, the reception of Derrida's writing could now be said to be in its third phase. At first, in the late sixties and early seventies, there was incredulity, enthusiasm and indifference. Since then there has been the staking out of positions, the adjustment of the theoretical landscape to the intruder's persistence. What began to emerge in the late eighties was a bevy of philosophers and literary theorists for whom Derrida's work aroused productive, but not uncritical, engagement.[1] Some, such as Habermas, who belongs to the second phase, had shot their bolt before this collection was conceived. Others, such as Lyotard, found their very proximity to Derrida too complex to disentangle. And this problem is one peculiarly faced by those I group in the third phase. What once seemed to be a philosophical reflex – marking out a critical distance from the philosopher or the position one is dealing with – is triply problematized in the case of Derrida. Derrida does not, typically, take up philosophical positions, traditional or otherwise. Nor does he ever unequivocally endorse the particular discourse he happens to be employing or engaged with. Finally, the kind of relationships that Derrida establishes with the texts he reads do not resolve themselves within, and indeed fundamentally problematize the idea of, a homogenous space in which critical distances can be measured and marked out. Of course, Derrida's readers are not *compelled* to confirm in their relation to him a certain non-positionality, or his discourse-provisionality, or the subtlety of his relation to the texts he reads. Both Habermas and Gadamer, for example, and in different ways, notably fail to do this.[1] Derrida's readers are free to read him as they will, but they may mistakenly believe that Derrida actually licenses such disregarding of an author's intentions. If this were true it would of course be irrelevant, because such readers should, to be consistent, care nothing for what Derrida licenses or does not license. But the belief that Derrida has no concern with authorial intentions is itself a misreading of his typical concern to play off such intentions against structural constraints that both limit and subvert authorial meaning. This is very clear in his early readings of Husserl, Saussure and Rousseau, and continues throughout his negotiations with Heidegger.

But there is another way of laying out the question of what we should permit ourselves when reading Derrida. We may suppose, for example, that Derrida's readings are *strong readings*, to be compared with with Heidegger's reading of Nietzsche, or Levinas's reading of Heidegger. And that Derrida's work implicitly licenses a similar response on the part of those with a powerful new agenda. Such a comparison, however, backfires. The paradox of *strong reading* is that it is strong precisely to the extent that it is not a reading, but the use of a sacrificial victim to exhibit one's own position. What we learn from Heidegger, curiously, is how *not* to read Nietzsche, and the importance of engaging with a thinker's relation to language–a dimension to which Heidegger ought to have been sensitive. What we learn from Levinas's reading of Heidegger is how *not* to allow the Other to speak. In lamenting the absence of the ethical in Heidegger, Levinas blinds himself to the fact that Heidegger *locates it elsewhere*. Those who would locate Derrida within a lineage of such strong readings do themselves a disservice. They also misunderstand the status of Derrida's readings. Deconstructions, allowing ourselves this word for temporary convenience, are not critical overcomings of texts, not summary executions, not *destructive* as such. They may indeed kill off certain existing mortifying tendencies of reading. But deconstructive readings do not conquer from the sky, they do not bring to a text concerns alien to its production and its structuration. Indeed they take a certain level of such concerns too seriously if anything.

I am claiming, then, that Derrida's own readings of others do not license a wanton disregard for the strategic dimension of his work on the part of his readers, either in the sense of license which would recommend such readings, or in the sense of giving him no defense against such readings.

Nor do his readings license the kind of strong reading with its own externally imposed programme. Derrida's angry response to those who *misread* both the purpose and the context of his essay 'The Last Word of Racism' was not, as some have thought, based on an illegitimately metaphysical standard of correctness.[2]

None of Derrida's readers is *required* to take on board the various dimensions of his writing that we have singled out. But not to notice the specificity of the relations he establishes to other texts, not to recognize that Derrida is elaborating *a new space of reading*, is surely to fail to address the real challenge (and seduction) of his work. The differences between, say, Gasché's articulation of Derrida's work as a theory of infrastructures (in *The Tain of the Mirror*), Llewelyn's drawing out of an ethics of responsibility, Nancy's evocation of the passion of the text and Sallis's account of Derrida's mimetic mechanisms are real enough. What unites them with the other contributors–Michel Haar, Geoffrey Bennington, Robert Bernasconi, Christopher Norris, and Richard Rorty, and what Manfred Frank so clearly resists–is an engagement with the expanded space of reading that Derrida's writing *exemplifies without fully determining* (a structure which takes us close to Irene Harvey's concerns). This space involves both the kind of features on which Gasché has concentrated–supplementarity, infrastructures and so on–which would suggest the possibility of something like a deconstructive logic, and the ethical space, the space of responsibility, which Llewelyn deals with here, and which Derrida is increasingly concerned to emphasize himself. We can *begin* to think the relation between the two by coming to think of deconstructive readings not as undermining a finished text, but as a responsiveness that re-engages with the conditions of a text's production, with the desire that philosophy (and perhaps all theory) articulates even when it is lost sight of. It might almost be worth the metaphysical overdraft required to say that Derrida is engaged in a theatrical re-animation of the textual space of philosophy's passion.

This, it may be said, is just more interpretation, just *my* reading. Well, it is not *just* that. It is at some level a selective principle by which the distinctiveness of this volume, this collection of Derrida's readers, is constituted. But is it more than that? Derrida's mode of engagement with the texts he deals with is not, it must be agreed, something that we are obliged to endorse. But that this is a distinctive and significant dimension of what Derrida is usually doing cannot seriously be ignored. It would be a very sad ontology of the text that demanded that every page be addressed, but did not concern itself with its levels, structures, strategies, spaces and passions. The papers in this volume are united not by their agreement with Derrida on how to address the space of philosophy's passion, but on the need to do so. The reader must decide whether the first paper can be exempted from this generalization, a paper in which Derrida brilliantly takes up the challenge of the impossible space prepared for him within this book.

NOTES

1 See, for example, *Deconstruction and Philosophy: The Texts of Jacques Derrida*, ed. John Sallis, Chicago: University of Chicago Press, 1987; *Derrida and Différance*, ed. David Wood and Robert Bernasconi, Evanston, Il: Northwestern University Press, 1988; Rodolphe Gasché, *The Tain of the Mirror*, Cambridge, MA: Harvard University Press, 1987; John Llewelyn, *Derrida on the Threshold of Sense*, London: Macmillan, 1986.

2 See Jurgen Habermas, *The Philosophical Discourse of Modernity*, Cambridge, MA: MIT Press, 1987, especially pp. 161–210; and Hans Georg Gadamer's contributions to *Dialogue and Deconstruction: The Gadamer–Derrida Encounter*, ed. Diane Michelfelder and Richard Palmer, Albany, NY: State University of New York, 1989. I discuss this latter debate in 'Vigilance and Interruption: Derrida, Gadamer and the Limits of Dialogue', in my *Philosophy at the Limit*, London: Unwin Hyman, 1990, chap. 7.

1

Jacques Derrida

Passions: 'An Oblique Offering'[1]

Let us imagine a scholar. A specialist in ritual analysis, he seizes upon this work, assuming that someone has not presented him with it (something we will never know). At any rate, he makes quite a thing of it, believing he can recognize in it the ritualized unfolding of a ceremony, or even a liturgy, and this becomes a theme, an *object* of analysis for him. Ritual, to be sure, does not define a field. There is ritual everywhere. Without it, there would be no society, no institutions, no history. Anyone can specialize in the analysis of rituals; it is not therefore a speciality. This scholar, let us call him an analyst, may also be, for example, a sociologist, an anthropologist, a historian, or, if you like, an art critic or a literary critic, perhaps even a philosopher. You or me. Through experience and more or less spontaneously, each of us can to some degree play the part of an analyst or critic of rituals; no one refrains from it. However, to play a role in this work, to *play a role* wherever it may be, one must at the same time be inscribed in the logic of ritual and, precisely so as to perform properly in it, to avoid mistakes and transgressions, one must to some extent be able to analyse it. One must understand its norms and interpret the rules of its functioning. Between the actor and the analyst, whatever the distance or differences may be, the boundary therefore appears uncertain. And always permeable. It *must* even be crossed at some point not only for there to be analysis at all but also for behaviour to be appropriate and ritualized normally.

But a 'critical reader' would quite properly object that not all analyses are equivalent. Is there not an essential difference between, on the one hand, the analysis of someone who, in order to participate *properly* in a ritual, must understand its norms, and an analysis which, instead of aligning itself with the ritual, tries to explain it, to give an account of its principle and of its purpose? Perhaps, but what is a critical difference? Because in the end if he is to analyse, read or interpret, the participant must also maintain a certain critical position. Even if his activity is often close to passivity, if not passion, the participant goes on to critical and criteriological acts: a vigilant discrimination is required from whoever, in one capacity or another, becomes an interested party in the ritual process (the agent, the beneficiary, the priest, the sacrificer, the property man, and even the excluded (the victim), the villain or the *pharmakos*, who may be the offering itself, because the offering is never a simple thing, but already a discourse, at least the possibility of a discourse, putting a symbolicity to work). The participant must make choices, distinguish, differentiate, evaluate. He must operate according to some *krinein*. Even the 'spectator', here the reader, in the volume or outside the volume, finds himself in the same situation in this respect. Instead of opposing critique to non-critique, instead of choosing or deciding between critique and non-critique, it is necessary, then, both to mark the differences between the critiques and on the other hand to situate the non-critical in a place which would no longer be opposed to, nor even perhaps exterior to, critique. Critique and non-critique are fundamentally the same.

Let us then imagine this work being proposed (delivered, offered, given) to a reader-analyst concerned with objectivity. This analyst may be among us: any recipient or sender of this book. We can imagine that without making available an unlimited credit to such a reader. At any rate the analyst (I choose this word, of course with the use that Poe made of it in mind)[2] would be sure, perhaps rashly, that he had come across the coded unfolding of a ceremony, an unfolding both predictable and prescribed. *Ceremony* is doubtless the most appropriate and the richest word to bring together all the aspects [traits] of the event. How could I, then, how could you, how could we, how could they, not be ceremonious? What exactly is the subject of a ceremony?

But it is here in the description and the analysis of ritual, in deciphering it or, if you prefer, in reading it, that a difficulty suddenly arises, a sort of dysfunctioning, what could be called a crisis. In short, a *critical* moment. Perhaps it would affect the very unfolding of the symbolic process.

What crisis? Was it predictable or unpredictable? and what if the crisis even concerned the very concept of crisis or of critique?

Some philosophers have got together or have been gathered together by academic and editorial procedures familiar to *us*. Emphasizing the critical determination (impossible because obvious, obvious to you, precisely) of this personal pronoun: who is 'us', who are we precisely? These philosophers, university academics from different countries, are known and nearly all know each other (here would follow a detailed description of each of them, of their type and of their singularity, of their sexual allegience–only one woman–of their national affiliation, of their socio-academic status, of their past, their publications, their interests, etc.). So, on the initiative of one of them, who cannot be just any one and someone whose interests are certainly not uninteresting, they agreed to get together and participate in a volume whose focus (relatively determinate, thus indeterminate, one could say secret up to a certain point—and the crisis remains too open to merit the name of crisis yet) will be such and such, (relatively determined, etc., relatively identifiable, in principle, by his work, his publications, his proper name, his signatures. 'Signatures' is perhaps best left in the plural, because it is impossible, at the outset, and even if legal, illegitimate, to preclude their multiplicity.) But if a critical difficulty arises in this case, one likely—but this is not yet certain—to put in difficulty the programmes of ritual or of its analysis, it does not necessarily have to do with the content, the theses, the positive or negative evaluations, most often infinitely overdetermined. It need not, in short, concern the quality of the discourse of this or that person, what they translate, or what they make of their relation to the title, to the pretext or to the object of the book. The critical difficulty concerns the fact that it has been thought necessary to ask, propose, or offer (for reasons which it is possible to analyse) to the supposed signatory of the texts which are the focus of the book ('me', surely?) the opportunity of intervening, as they say, of 'contributing', which means bringing one's tribute, but doing so freely, *in the book*. We will have something to say in due course about the extent of this freedom; it is almost the entire question. The editor of the work, head of protocol or master of ceremonies, David Wood, had suggested that the book might here even begin with a few pages of text which, without truly responding to all the others, could appear under the suggestive title of 'An Oblique Offering'. What? From whom? To whom? (More of this later.)

But straightaway, as we were saying, the unfolding of the ritual risks losing its automatic quality, that is to say, it risks no longer conforming to the first hypothesis of the analyst. There is a second hypothesis. Which? At a certain place in the system, one of the elements of the system (an 'I', surely, even if the I is not always, and 'without further ado',[3] 'me') no longer knows what it should do. More precisely it knows that it must do contradictory and incompatible things. Contradicting or running counter to itself, this double obligation thus risks paralyzing, diverting or jeopardizing the successful conclusion of the ceremony. But does not the hypothesis of such a risk *in going against* [*à l'encontre*] or on the contary *going along with* [*à la rencontre*] the desire of the participants, supposing that they had only one desire, lead on to suppose that there was a single desire common to all or that each had in himself only one non-contradictory desire? Because one can imagine that one or more than one participant, indeed the master of ceremonies himself, may somehow desire the failure of the aforementioned ceremony. More or less secretly, it goes without saying, and that is why we must *tell* the secret, not reveal it, and, with the example of this secret, pass judgement on the secret in general. What is a secret? Certainly, even if this work in no way corresponds to a secret ceremony, one may imagine that there is no ceremony, however public and exposed, which does not revolve around a secret, even if it is the secret of a non-secret, if only what one calls a 'secret de Polichinelle', a secret which is a secret for no one. On the analyst's first hypothesis, the ceremony would unfold normally, according to the ritual; it would achieve its end at the cost of a detour or of a suspense which not only would not have at all threatened it, but would perhaps have confirmed, consolidated, extended, embellished or intensified it by an expectation (desire, premium of seduction, preliminary pleasure of play, foreplay [*prélude*], what Freud calls *Vorlust*). But what would happen on the second hypothesis? This is perhaps the question that, by way of a reply and as a token of boundless gratitude, I would like to ask, I, in my turn, and in the first instance to all those who have generously brought their tribute [*apporter leur tribut*] to this work.

Friendship as well as politeness would enjoin a double *duty*: would it not precisely be to avoid at all cost, both the *language of ritual* and the *language of duty*? Duplicity, the being-double of this duty, cannot be added up as a 1 + 2, but on the contrary hollows itself out in an infinite abyss. A gesture 'of friendship' or 'of politeness' would be neither friendly nor polite if it were purely and simply to obey a ritual rule. But this *duty* to eschew the rule of ritualized decorum also demands that one goes beyond the very language of *duty*. One must not be friendly or polite out of duty. We venture such a proposition, of course, against Kant. Would there thus be a duty not to act *according to duty*, neither *in conformity to duty*, as Kant would say (*pflichtmässig*), nor even *out of duty* (*aus Pflicht*)? In what way would such a duty, or such a counter-duty, indebt us? According to what? According to whom?

Taken seriously, this hypothesis in the form of a question would be enough to give one vertigo. It would make one tremble, it could also paralyze one at the edge of the abyss, there where you would be alone, all alone or already caught up in a struggle with the other, an other who would seek in vain to hold you back or to push you into the void, to save you or to lose you. Always supposing–we shall return to this–that one ever had any choice in this matter. Because we already risk no longer knowing where the evidence could lead us, let us venture to state the double axiom involved in the hypothesis or in the question with which we inevitably had to begin. Doubtless it would be impolite to appear to be making a gesture, for example, by responding to an invitation, out of simple duty. It would also be unfriendly to respond to a friend out of duty. It would be no better to respond to an invitation or to a friend in conformity with duty, *pflichtmässig* (rather than out of duty, *aus Pflicht*, and we cite once more the *Groundwork for a Metaphysics of Morals* of Kant, our exemplary 'critical reader', indebted as we are, as his heirs, to the great philosopher of critique). That would indeed add to the essential failing [*faute*], one further shortcoming: to consider oneself beyond reproach by playing on appearances just where intention is in default. It is insufficient to say that the 'ought' ['*il faut*'] of friendship, like that of politeness, must not be the order of duty. It must not even take the form of a rule, and certainly not of a ritual rule. As soon as it yields to the necessity of applying the generality of a prescription to a single case, the gesture of friendship or of politeness would itself be destroyed. It would be defeated, beaten, and broken by the ordered rigidity of rules, or, put a different way, of norms. An axiom from which it is not necessary to conclude further that one can only accede to friendship or politeness (for example, in responding to an invitation, or indeed to the request or the question of a friend) by transgressing all rules and by going against all duty. The counter-rule is still a rule.

A critical reader will perhaps be surprised to see friendship and politeness regularly associated here, each distinguished, by a single trait, from ritualized behaviour. For whatever cultural tradition is linked to (Western or otherwise), the hypothesis about politeness and the sharp determination of this value relates to what enjoins us to go beyond rules, norms, and hence ritual. The internal contradiction in the concept of politeness, as in all normative concepts of which it would be an example, is that it involves both rules and invention without rule. Its rule is that one knows the rule but is never bound by it. It is impolite to be merely polite, to be polite out of politeness. We thus have here a rule–and this rule is recurrent, structural, general, that is to say, each time singular and exemplary–which prescribes action of such a sort that one not act simply by conformity to the normative rule but not even by virtue of the said rule, out of respect for it. *Let's not beat about the bush* [*N'y allons pas par quatre chemins*]: what is at issue is the concept of duty, and of knowing whether or up to what point one can rely on it, on what it structures in the order of culture, of morality, of politics, of law, and even of economy (especially as to the relation between debt and duty);[4] that is to say, whether and up to what point one can trust what the concept of duty lays down for all responsible discourse about responsible decisions, for all discourse, all logic, all rhetoric *of* responsibility. By speaking of responsible discourse on responsibility, we are *implying* already that discourse itself must submit to the norms or to the law of which it speaks. This implication would seem to be inescapable, but it remains disconcerting: what could be the responsibility, the quality or the virtue of responsibility, of a consistent discourse which claimed to show that no responsibility could ever be taken without equivocation and without contradiction? Or that the self-justification of a decision is impossible, and could not, a priori and for structural reasons, be absolutely answerable to itself?

We have just said: '*n'y allons pas par quatre chemins* [an almost untranslatable French expression which invokes the cross or the crucial, the crossing of ways, the four and the fork of a crossroad (*quadrifurcum*) in order to say: let us proceed directly, without detour, without ruse and without calculation]: *what is at issue* [*il s'agit de*] *is the concept of* (. . .) and *knowing whether* (. . .)'. What is implied by an expression of such an imperative order? That one could and one should tackle a concept or a problem frontally, in a non-oblique way. There would be a concept and a problem (of this or that, of duty, for example, it matters little for the moment), that is to say, something determinable by a knowing ('what matters is knowing whether') and which lies before you, there before you (*problema*), *in front of you* [in English in the original, Tr.]; from which comes the necessity to approach from the front, facing towards, in a way which is at once direct, frontal and head on [*capitale*], what is before your eyes, your mouth, your hands (and not behind your back), there, before you, like an *object* pro-posed or posed in advance [*pro-posé ou pré-posé*], a question to deal with, therefore quite as much a *subject* proposed (that is to say, surrendered, offered up: in principle one always offers from the front, surely? in principle). Continuing the semantics of *problema*, there would also be the question of an *ob-subject extended* like a jetty or the promontory of a headland [*cap*],[5] an armour, or protective garment. *Problema* also means, in certain contexts, the excuse given in advance to shirk or clear oneself of blame, but also something else that interests me. By metonymy, if you will, *problema* can come to designate that which, as we say in French, serves as a 'cover' when assuming responsibility for another or passing oneself off as the other, or while speaking in the name of the other, that which one places before one or behind which one hides. Think of the passion of Philoctetus, of Ulysses the oblique– and of the third, at once innocent witness, *actor*–participant but also an *actor* to whom it is given to play a role, instrument and active delegate *by representation*, that is the *problematic* child, Neoptolemus.[6] From this point of view responsibility would be *problematic* to the further [*supplementaire*] extent that it could sometimes, perhaps even always, be what one takes, not for oneself, *in one's own name* and *before the other* (the most classically metaphysical definition of responsibility) but what one must take for another, in his place, in the name of the other or of oneself as other, before another other, and an other of the other, namely the very undeniable of ethics. 'To the further [*supplementaire*] extent' we said, but we must go further: in the degree to which responsibility not only fails to weaken but on the contrary arises in a structure which is itself supplementary. It is always exercised in my name *as* the name of the other, and that in no way affects its singularity.

This singularity is posited and must quake in the exemplary equivocality and insecurity of this 'as'.

If the experience of responsibility could not be reduced to one of duty or of debt, if the 'response' of responsibility no longer appeared in a concept with respect to which we must 'know whether . . . '; if all this were to challenge the space of the *problem* and returned not only to within the pro-positional form of the response but even to within the '*question*' form of thought or language, and thus what is no longer or not yet problematic or questionable, i.e., critique, namely of the order of judicative decision, we could no longer, it would be *our duty above all* not to, approach in a direct, frontal *projective*, that is, thetic or thematic way. And this 'do not do it', this 'duty above all not to' which seems to give the slip to the problem, the project, the question, the theme, the thesis, the critique, would have nothing to do with a shortcoming, a lapse in logical or demonstrative rigour, quite the contrary (always supposing that the imperative of rigour is sheltered from all questioning–and if I may I would refer here to the account linking *stricture* and the Eucharist in *Glas*). If there was a shortcoming, and a shortcoming of justice as much as of reading, it would occur rather on the side where one would want to summon such a 'do not do it' 'duty above all not to' to appear before some philosophical or moral tribunal, that is to say, before proceedings both critical and juridical. Nothing would seem more violent or naive than to call for more frontality, more thesis or more thematization, to suppose that one can find a standard here. How can one choose between the economy or the discretion of the *ellipse* with which one credits a writing, and an *a-thematicity*, an insufficiently thematic explanation of which some believe it is possible to accuse a philosopher.

Instead of tacking the question or the problem head on, directly, straightforwardly, which would doubtless be impossible, inappropriate or illegitimate, should we proceed obliquely? I have often done so, even to the point of demanding obliqueness by name[7] even while acknowledging it, some might think, as a failure of duty since the figure of the oblique is often associated with lack of frankness or of directness. It is doubtless with this fatality in mind, this tradition of the oblique in which I am in some way inscribed, that David Wood, in order to invite me, encourage me, or oblige me to contribute to this volume suggested to me [*m'a offert*] that these pages be entitled 'An Oblique Offering'. He had even printed it beforehand on the projected Table of Contents of the complete manuscript before I had written a line of this text.[8] Will we ever know whether this 'offering' is mine or his? Who takes responsibility for it? This question is as serious and intractable [*intraitable*][9] as the responsibility for the name one is given or bears, for the name that one receives or the name that one gives oneself. The infinite paradoxes of what is so calmly called narcissism are outlined here: suppose that X, something or someone (a trace, a work, an institution, a child) bears your name, that is to say your title. The naive rendering or common illusion [*fantasme courant*] is that you have given your name to X, thus all that returns to X, in a direct or indirect way, in a straight or oblique line, *returns* to you, as a profit for your narcissism. But as you *are* not your name, nor your title, and as the name or the title does very well without you or your life, that is without the place towards which something could return–just as that is the definition and the very possibility of every trace, and of all names and all titles, so your narcissim is frustrated a priori by that from which it profits or hopes to profit. Conversely, suppose that X did not want your name or your title; suppose that, for one reason or another, X broke free from it and chose himself another name, working a kind of repeated severance from the originary severance; then your narcissism, doubly injured, will find itself all the more enriched precisely on account of this: that which bears, has borne, will bear your name seems sufficiently free, powerful, creative and autonomous to live alone and radically to do without you and your name. What returns to your name, to the secret of your name, is the ability to disappear *in your name*. And thus not to return to itself, which is the condition of the gift (for example, of the name) but also of all expansion of self, of all augmentation of self, of all *auctoritas*. In the two cases of this same divided passion, it is impossible to dissociate the greatest profit and the greatest privation. It is consequently impossible to construct a non-contradictory or coherent concept of narcissism, thus to give a univocal sense to the 'I'. It is impossible to speak it or to act it, as 'I', and as Baudelaire put it 'sans façon' [without ado; without ceremony]. This is the secret of the bow or of the instrumental string (*neura*) for Philoctetus, for the passion according to Philoctetus: the child is the problem.

On reflection, the oblique does not seem to me to offer the best figure for all the moves that I have tried to describe in that way. I have always been ill at ease with this word of which I have, however, so often made use. Even if I have done so in a generally negative way, to disrupt rather than to prescribe, to avoid or to say that one ought to avoid, that moreover one could not fail to avoid defiance or direct confrontation, the immediate approach. Confession or auto-critique, then: one has to smile at the hypothesis of the most hyperbolic *hybris*, namely the hypothesis that this whole 'critical' reader would add up to an 'autocritical reader' (whose auto?) which sustains itself and carries itself along, having in particular no more need of me for this purpose, no need of an I which itself needs no help from anyone else in asking itself all the questions or putting to itself all the critical objections that one could want. (In the syntax of 'X: a critical reader', it will moreover always be difficult to determine who is the reader of whom, who the subject, who the text, who the object, and who offers what–or who–to whom). What I would criticize in the oblique, today, is the geometrical figure, the compromise still made with the primitiveness of the plane, the line, the angle, the diagonal, and thus of the right angle between the vertical and the horizontal. The oblique remains the choice of a strategy that is still crude, obliged to ward off what is most urgent, a geometric calculus for diverting as quickly as possible both the frontal approach and the straight line: presumed to be the shortest path from one point to another. Even in its rhetorical form and in the figure of figure that is called *oratio obliqua*, this displacement still appears too direct, linear, in short economic, in complicity with the diagonal arc. (I think straight away of the fact that a bow [*arc*] is sometimes *stretched*; and again of the passion of Philoctetus; in French to say of a bow [*arc*] that it is stretched [*tendu*] can mean, in some contexts, that its string is taut and ready to propel the weapon, namely the deadly arrow, or that the bow is offered [up], given, delivered, transmitted (*handed on, over to?* [English in original, Tr.]). Let us therefore forget the oblique.

Is this a way of not responding to the invitation of David Wood and of all those whom he represents here? Ought I to respond to him? How is one to know? What is an invitation? What is it to respond to an invitation? To whom, to what, does this return, what does it amount to? [*à quoi cela revient-il?*]. An invitation leaves one free, otherwise it becomes constraint. But it must be pressing, not indifferent. Without such pressure, the invitation immediately withdraws and becomes unwelcoming. It must therefore split and redouble itself at the same time, at once leave free and take hostage: double act, redoubled act.

Whoever ponders the necessity, the genealogy and therefore also the limits of the concept of responsibility cannot fail to wonder at some point what is meant by 'respond', and *'responsiveness'* [English in original, Tr.], a precious word for which I can find no strict equivalent in my language. And to wonder whether to 'respond' has an opposite, which would consist, if commonsense is to be believed, in not responding. Is it possible to make a decision on the subject of 'responding' and of 'responsiveness'?

One can attend or participate today, in many different places, in a congenial and disturbing task: to restore morality and especially to reassure those who had serious reasons for being troubled by this topic. Some minds believing themselves to have found in Deconstruction ['*La Deconstruction*]', as if there were only one, a modern form of immorality, of amorality or of irresponsibility (etc.: a discourse too well known, I do not need to continue), while others, more serious, in less of a hurry, better disposed towards so-called Deconstruction, today claim the opposite; they discern encouraging signs and in increasing numbers (at times, I must admit, in some of my texts) which would testify to a permanent, extreme, direct or oblique, in any event, increasingly intense attention, to those things which one could identify under the fine names of 'ethics', 'morality', 'responsibility', 'subject', etc. Before reverting to not-responding, I would like to declare in the most direct way that if I had the *sense* of duty and of responsibility, it would compel me to break with both these moralisms, with these two restorations of morality, including, therefore, the remoralization of deconstruction which naturally seem to me more attractive than that to which it is rightly opposed, but which at each moment risks reassuring itself in order to reassure the other and to promote the consensus of a new dogmatic slumber. And it is so that one not be in too much of a hurry to say that it is in the name of a higher responsibility and a more intractable [*intraitable*] moral exigency that I declare my distaste, uneven as it may be, for both moralisms. Undoubtedly, it is always following the affirmation of a certain excess that I suspect the well-known immorality, indeed the denegating hypocrisy of moralisms. But nothing leads me to believe that the best names or the most suitable figures for this affirmation are ethics, morality, politics, responsibility, or the subject. Furthermore, would it be moral and responsible to act morally because one has a *sense* (the word emphasized above) of duty and responsibility? Clearly not, it would be too easy and, precisely, natural, programmed by nature (the well-known problem of 'respect' for the moral law in the Kantian sense, a problem of interest to me only for the disturbing paradox that it inscribes in the heart of a morality incapable of giving an account of being inscribed in an affect (*Gefühl*) or in a sensibility of what should not be inscribed there or should only call for the sacrifice of everything that would only obey this sensible inclination. It is well known that sacrifice and the sacrificial offering are at the heart of Kantian morality, under their own name (*Opferung, Aufopferung*); (cf., for example, Kant's *Critique of Practical Reason*, L. 1, ch. III. The object of sacrifice there is always of the order of the sensuous motives [*mobile sensible*], of the secretly 'pathological' interest which must, says Kant, be 'humbled' before the moral law; this concept of sacrificial offering, thus of sacrifice in general, requires the whole apparatus of the 'critical' distinctions of Kantianism: sensible/intelligible, passivity/spontaneity, *intuitus derivativus/ intuitus originarius*, etc.; the same goes for the concept of passion; what I am looking for here, passion according to me, would be a concept of passion that would be non-'pathological' in Kant's sense.)

All this, therefore, still remains open, suspended, undecided, questionable even beyond the question, indeed, to make use of another figure, absolutely aporetic. What is the ethicity of ethics?, the morality of morality? What is responsibility? What is the 'what is?' in this case?, etc. These questions are always urgent; in a certain way they must remain urgent and unanswered, at any rate without a general and rule-governed response, without a response other than that which is linked specifically each time, to the occurrence of a decision without rules and without will in the course of a new test of the undecidable. And let it not be said too precipitately that these questions or these propositions are *already* inspired by a concern that could by right be called ethical, moral, responsible, etc. I know that, in saying that ('And let it not be said too precipitately . . . etc.), one gives ammunition to the officials of anti-deconstruction, but all in all I prefer that to the constitution of a consensual euphoria or, worse, a community of complacent deconstructionists, reassured and reconciled with the world in ethical certainty, good conscience, satisfaction of service rendered, and the consciousness of duty accomplished (or, more heroically still, yet to be accomplished).

So the non-response. Clearly, it will always be possible to say, and it will be true, that non-response is a response. One always has, one always must have, the right not to respond, and this liberty belongs to responsibility itself, that is, to the liberty that one believes must be associated with it. One must always be free not to respond to an appeal or to an invitation – and it is worth remembering this, to remind oneself of the essence of this liberty. Those who think that responsibility or the sense of responsibility is a good thing, a prime virtue, indeed the good itself, are convinced, however, that one must always answer (for oneself, to the other, before the other or before the law) and that moreover a non-response is always a modality determined in the space opened by an unavoidable responsibility. Is there then nothing more to say about non-response? On it or on the subject of it, if not in its favour?

Let us press on and, in the attempt to convince more quickly, let us take an example, whether or not it is valid for the law. What example? This one. And certainly, when I say this very example, I already say something more and something else; I say something which goes beyond the *tode ti*, the this of the example. The example itself, as such, overflows its singularity as much as its identity. This is why there are no examples while at the same time there are only examples; I have said this often about many examples. The exemplarity of the example is clearly never the exemplarity of the example. We can never be sure of having put an end to this very old children's game in which all the discourses, philosophical or not, which have ever inspired deconstructions, are entangled even by the performative fiction which consists in saying, starting up the game again, 'take precisely this example'.

If, for example, I respond to the invitation which is made to me to respond to the texts collected here and which do me the honour or the kindness [*l'amitié*] of taking an interest in certain of my earlier publications, am I not going to be heaping up errors [*fautes*] and therefore conduct myself in an irresponsible way–by taking on false [*mauvaises*] responsibilities? What faults?

1) First of all, that of endorsing a situation, of subscribing to it and acting as if I found myself at ease in such a strange place, as if I found it normal or natural to speak here, as if we were sitting down at the table in the midst of twelve people who were speaking on the whole about 'me' or addressing themselves to 'me'. 'I' ['*Moi*'], who am both a twelfth insofar as I am part of a group, one among others, and already, being thus split or redoubled, the thirteenth insofar as I am not one example among others in the series of twelve. What would it look like if I supposed I could reply to all these men and this woman at the same time, or if I supposed I could *begin by replying*, thus disregarding the very scholarly and very singular strategy of each of these eleven or twelve discourses, at once so generous and so unselfsatisfied and so overdetermined? By speaking last, both in conclusion and in introduction, in twelfth or thirteenth place, am I not taking the insane risk and adopting the odious attitude of treating all these thinkers as disciples, indeed the apostles among whom some would be preferred by me, others potential evil traitors. Who would be Judas here? What is someone to do who does not want to be and who knows himself not to be (but how can one be sure about these things, and how can one extricate oneself from these matrices) either an apostle (*apostolos*, a messenger of God), or Jesus, or Judas? Because it dawned on me a little late, counting the number of participants gathered here, exactly twelve (who is still to come?), then noticing the words 'oblique offering' and 'passion' in his letter, that David Wood was perhaps the perverse producer [*metteur en cène*] of a mystery–and that in fact the 'oblique offering' which was no less his than mine had a flavour that was ironically, sarcastically, eucharistic (no vegetarian–there are at least two among the guests–will ever be able to break with the sublimity of mystical cannibalism): the 'this is my body which is given for you, keep this in remembrance of me', is this not the most oblique offering [*don*]? Is this not what I commented on all year long in *Glas* or in my last seminars on 'consuming the other' and the 'rhetoric of cannibalism'? All the more reason not to respond. This is no Last Supper [*Cène*], and the ironic friendship which brings us together consists in knowing this, while peering with a 'squinty eye' [English in original, Tr.] towards this cannibalism in mourning.

2) If I did respond I would put myself in the situation of someone who felt *capable of responding*: he has an answer for everything, he takes himself to be up to answering each of us, each question, each objection or criticism; he does not see that each of the texts gathered here has its force, its logic, its singular strategy, that it would be necessary to reread everything, to reconstitute the work and its trajectory, the themes and arguments of each, the discursive tradition and the many texts set to work, etc. To claim to do all this, and to do it in a few pages, would smack of a *hybris* and

a naivety without limit—and from the outset a flagrant lack of respect for the discourse, the work and the offering of the other. More reasons for not responding.

3) From these two arguments we can glimpse that a certain non-response can attest to this politeness (without rules) of which we spoke above, and finally to respect for others, that is to say, also to an exigency of responsibility. It will perhaps be said that this non-response is the best response, that it is still a response and a sign of responsibility. Perhaps. Let us wait and see. In any case, one thinks of that pride, that self-satisfaction, that elementary confidence which it would take to answer when a good education teaches children that they must not 'answer back' (at any rate in the sense and tradition of French manners) when grown-ups speak to them, they must not reproach them or criticise them, and certainly not ask them questions.

4) The overweening presumption from which no response will ever be free not only has to do with the fact that the response claims to measure up to the discourse of the other, to situate it, understand it, indeed circumscribe it by responding thus *to* the other and *before* the other. The respondent presumes, with as much frivolity as arrogance, that he can respond to the other and before the other because first of all he is able to answer for himself and for all he has been able to do, say or write. To answer for oneself would here be to presume to know all that one could do, say, or write, to gather it together in an intelligible and coherent synthesis, to stamp it with one and the same seal (whatever the genre, the place, or the date, the discursive form, the contextual strategy, etc.), to posit that the same 'I think' accompanies all my representations which themselves form a systematic, homogeneous tissue of 'theses', 'themes', 'objects', of 'narratives', of 'critiques', or of 'evaluations', a tissue which can be subjectivized and of which I would have a total and intact memory, would know all the premises and all the consequences, etc.; this would also be to suppose that deconstruction is of the same order as the critique whose concept and history it precisely deconstructs. So many dogmatic naiveties that one will never discourage, but all the more reason not to respond, not to act as if one could respond to the other, before the other, and for oneself. Someone will retort: indeed, but then this non-response is still a response, the most polite, the most modest, the most vigilant, the most respectful—both of the other and of truth. This non-response would again be a respectable form of politeness and respect, a responsible form of the vigilant exercise of responsibility. In any case, this would confirm that one cannot or that one ought not fail to respond. One cannot, one ought not to respond with nothing. The ought and the can are here strangely co-implicated. Perhaps. Let us wait and see.

Continuing these four preceding arguments, I would avoid errors (errors of politeness, moral errors, etc.) by not responding, by responding elliptically, by responding obliquely. I would have said to myself: it would be better, it is fairer, it is more decent, and more moral, not to respond. It is more respectful to the other, more responsible in the face of the imperative of critical, hypercritical, and above all 'deconstructionist' thought which insists on yielding as little as possible to dogmas and presuppositions. So you see–if I took heed of all these reasons, and if, still believing that this non-response was the best response, I decided not to respond, then I would run even worse risks.
Which ones?

1) To start with, the first injury or injustice: seeming not to take sufficiently seriously the persons and the texts offered here, to evince an inadmissible ingratitude and a culpable indifference.

2) And then to exploit the 'good reasons' for not responding to make use of silence in a way that is still strategic: because there is an art of the non-response, or of the deferred response which is a rhetoric of war, a polemical ruse. Polite silence can become the most insolent weapon and the most deadly irony. On the pretext of waiting to have read through, pondered, laboured to be able to begin to reply seriously (which will in fact be necessary and which could take forever), non-response as postponed or elusive response, indeed absolutely elliptical can always shelter one comfortably, safe from all objection. And on the pretext of feeling incapable of responding *to* the other, and answering *for* oneself, does one not undermine, both theoretically and practically, the concept of responsibility, which is actually the very essence of the *socius*?

3) To justify one's non-response by all these arguments, one can still refer to rules, to general norms, but then one falls short of the principle of politeness and of responsibility that we recalled above: never to believe oneself free of any debt and hence never to act simply according to a rule, in conformity to duty not even out of duty, still less 'out of politeness'. Nothing would be more immoral and more impolite.

4) Certainly, nothing would be worse than substituting for an inadequate response, but one still giving evidence of a sincere, modest, finite, resigned effort, an interminable discourse. Such a discourse would pretend to provide, instead of a response or a non-response, a performative (more or less *performante* [*literally: performing, also dynamic, effective*] and more or less metalinguistic) for all these questions, non-questions, or non-responses. Such an operation would be open to the most justified critiques, it would offer its body, it would surrender, as if in sacrifice, the most vulnerable body to the most just blows. Because it would suffer from a *double* failure, it would combine two apparently contradictory faults:

firstly the claim to mastery or to an overview [*survol*] (be it meta-linguistic, meta-logical, meta-metaphysical, etc.) and secondly the becoming-work of art (literary performance or performative, fiction, work), the aestheticizing play of a discourse from which one expects a serious, thoughtful or philosophical response.

So, what are we to do? It is impossible to respond here. It is impossible to respond to this question about the response. It is impossible to respond to the question by which we precisely ask ourselves whether it is necessary to respond or not to respond, whether it is necessary, possible or impossible. This aporia without end paralyzes us because it binds us doubly (I must and I need not, I must not, it is necessary and impossible, etc.) In one and the same place, on the same apparatus, I have my two hands tied or nailed down. What are we to do? But also how is it that it does not prevent us from speaking, from continuing to describe the situation, from trying to make oneself understood? What is the nature of this language, since already it no longer belongs, no longer belongs simply, either to the question or to the response whose limits we have just verified and are continuing to verify. Of what does this verification consist, when nothing happens without some sacrifice?

Among other things, to return to the start of the scene, we find that the analyst, the one to whom we have given the name, can no longer describe or objectify the programmed development of a ritual, still less of a sacrificial offering. No one wanted to play the role of the sacrificeable or of the sacrificer, all the *agents* (priests, victims, participants, spectators, readers) not only *refuse to act*, but even if they wanted to make the prescribed gestures they would find themselves brought to a halt when faced with these contradictory orders. And it is not only a religious sociality whose identity is thus menaced, it is a philosophical sociality, insofar as it presupposes the order (preferably circular) of the appeal [or the call: *appel*, Tr.], of the question and the response. Some will say that this is the very principle of the community which sees itself thus exposed to disruption. Others will say that the threat of disruption threatens nothing, that it has always been the instituting or constitive origin of religious or philosophical ties, of the social bond in general: the community lives and feeds on this vulnerability, and so it should. If the analyst in fact discovers limits to his work of scientific objectification, that is quite normal: he is a participant in a process which he would like to analyse, he can virtually play all the roles in it (that is to say, also to mime them).[10] This limit furnishes positively the condition of his intelligence, of his reading, of his interpretations. But what would be the condition of this condition? The fact that the *critical reader* [English in original, Tr.] is a priori and endlessly exposed to a *critical reading* [English in original, Tr.].

What could escape this sacrificial verification and so secure the very space of *this very discourse, for example*? No question, no response, no responsibility. Let us say that there is a secret here. *There is something secret. [Il y a là du secret].* We will leave the matter here for now, but not without some discussion of the apophatic[11] aspect of the essence and existence of such a secret. The apophatic is not here necessarily dependent on negative theology, even if it makes it possible too.

We speak of a secret without content, without content separable from its performative experience, from its performative tracing (we will not say from its performative *utterance* or from its *propositional argumentation,* and we will keep in reserve a number of questions about performativity in general).

Let us say therefore: *There is something secret [il y a là du secret].* It would not be a matter of an artistic or technical secret reserved for someone–or for several, such as style, ruse, the signature of talent or the mark of a genius, the know-how that is thought to be incommunicable, untransmittable, unteachable, inimitable. It would not even be a matter of that psycho-physical secret, the art hidden in the depths of the human soul, of which Kant speaks in connection with the transcendental schematism, and of the imagination (*ein verborgene Kunst in den Tiefen der menschlichen Seele*).

There is something secret. It would not be a question of a secret as a representation dissimulated by a conscious subject, nor moreover of the content of an unconscious representation, some secret motive that the moralist[12] or the psychoanalyst might have the skill to detect, or, as they say, to de-mystify. This secret would not even be of the order of absolute subjectivity, in the rather unorthodox sense, with respect to a history of metaphysics, that Kierkegaard gave to *existence* and to all that resists the concept or frustrates the system, especially the Hegelian dialectic. This secret would not belong to any of the stages (aesthetic, ethical, religious a or b) that Kierkegaard distinguishes. It would be neither sacred nor profane.

There is something secret. But to take account of what we have just suggested, the being-there of the secret belongs no more to the private than to the public. It is not a deprived interiority that one would have to reveal, confess, announce, that is, to which one would have to respond by accounting for it and thematizing it in broad daylight. Who would ever determine the proper extent of a thematization so as to judge it finally adequate? And is there any worse violence than that which consists in calling for the response, demanding that one *give an account of* everything, and preferably *thematically.* Because this secret is not phenomenalizable. Neither phenomenal nor noumenal. No more than religion, can philosophy, morality, politics or the law accept the unconditional respect of this secret. These authorities are constituted as authorities who may properly ask for accounts, that is, responses, from those with accepted responsibilities. No doubt they allow sometimes that there are conditional secrets (the secret of confession, the professional secret, the military secret, the manufacturing secret, the state secret). But the *right to secrets*, is in all these cases a conditional right. Because the secret can be shared there, and limited by given conditions. The secret becomes simply a problem. It can and must be made known under other circumstances. Everywhere that a response and a responsibility are required, the right to a secret becomes conditional. There are no secrets, only problems for those knowledges which in this respect include not only philosophy, science and technology, but also religion, morality, politics and the law.

There is something secret. [*Il y a du secret.*] It concerns neither that into which a revealed religion *initiates* us nor that which it *reveals* (namely a mystery of passion), nor a learned ignorance (in a Christian brotherhood practising a kind of negative theology), nor the content of an esoteric doctrine (for example, in a Pythagorean, Platonic or neo-Platonic community). In any case it cannot be reduced to these because it makes them possible. The secret is not mystical.

There is something secret. But it does not conceal itself. Heterogenous to the hidden, to the obscure, to the nocturnal, to the invisible, to what can be dissimulated and indeed to what is non-manifest in general, it cannot be unveiled. It remains inviolable even when one thinks one has revealed it. Not that it hides itself for ever in an indecipherable crypt or behind an absolute veil. It simply exceeds the play of veiling/unveiling, dissimulation/revelation, night/day, forgetting/anamnesis, earth/heaven, etc. It does not belong therefore to the truth, neither to the truth as *homoiosis* or adequation, nor to the truth as memory (Mnemosyne, *aletheia*), nor to the given truth, nor to the promised truth, nor to the inaccessible truth. Its non-phenomenality is without relation, even negative, to phenomenality. Its reserve is no longer of the intimacy that one likes to call secret, of the very close or very proper which sucks in or inspires [*aspires ou inspires*] so much profound discourse (the *Geheimnis* or, even richer, the inexhaustible *Unheimliche*).

Certainly, one could speak this secret in other names, whether one finds them or gives them to it. Moreover this happens at every instant. It remains secret under all names and it is its irreducibility to the very name which makes it secret, even when one makes the truth in its name [*fait la verité à son sujet*] as Augustine put it so originally. The secret is that one here calls it secret, putting it for once in relation to all the secrets which bear the same name but cannot be reduced to it. The secret would also be homonymy, not so much a hidden resource of homonymy, but the functional possibility of homonymy or of *mimesis*.

There is something secret. One can always speak about it, that is not enough to disrupt it. One can speak of it *ad infinitum*, tell stories[13] about it, utter all the discourses which it puts to work and the stories which it unleashes or enchains, because the secret often makes one think of these secret histories and it even gives one a taste for them. And the secret will remain secret, mute, impassive as the *chora*, foreign to every history, as much in the sense of *Geschichte* or *res gestae* as of knowledge and of historical narrative (*epistémè*, *historia rerum gestarum*), and outside all periodization, all epochalization.

It remains silent, not to keep a word in reserve or withdrawn [*en retrait*], but because it remains foreign to speech [*la parole*], without our even being able to say in that distinguished syntagm: 'the secret is that in speech which is foreign to speech'. It is no more in speech than foreign to speech. It does not answer to speech, it does not say 'I, the secret', it does not correspond, it does not answer [*répondre*]: either for itself or to anyone else, before anyone or anything whatsoever. Absolute non-response which one could not even call to account or for something on account [*acomptes*], grant indemnities, excuses or 'discounts'–so many ruses, always, to draw it into a *process* [*procès*] that is philosophical, ethical, political, juridical, etc. The secret gives rise to no *process* [*procès*]. It may appear to give rise to one (indeed it always does so), it may lend itself to it, but it never surrenders to it. The ethics of the discussion may always not respect it (according to me it owes it respect, even if this seems difficult or contradictory, because the secret is intractable [*intraitable*]), but it will never reduce it. Moreover, no discussion would either begin or continue without it. And whether one respects it or not, the secret remains there impassively, at a distance, out of reach. In this one cannot not respect it, whether one likes it or not, whether one knows it or not.

There is no longer time nor place.

A confidence to end with today. Perhaps all I wanted to do was to confide or confirm my taste (probably unconditional) for literature, more precisely for literary writing. Not that I like literature in general, nor that I prefer it to something else, to philosophy, for example, as they suppose who ultimately discern neither one nor the other. Not that I want to reduce everything to it, especially not philosophy. Literature I could fundamentally do without, and in fact quite easily. If I had to retire to an island, it would be particularly history books, memoirs, that I would doubtless take with me, and that I would read in my own way, perhaps to make literature out of them, unless it would be the other way round, and this would be true for other books (art, philosophy, religion, human or natural sciences, law, etc.). But if, without liking literature in general and for its own sake, I like something *about it*, and which above all cannot be reduced to some aesthetic quality, to some source of formal pleasure [*jouissance*], this would be *in place of the secret*. In place of an absolute secret. There would be the passion. There is no passion without secret, this very secret, indeed no secret without this passion. *In place of the secret*: there where nevertheless everything is said and where what remains is nothing–but the remainder, not even of literature.

I have often found myself insisting on the necessity of distinguishing between literature and belles-lettres or poetry. Literature is a modern invention, inscribed in conventions and institutions which, to hold on to just this trait, secures in principle its *right to say everything*. Literature thus ties its destiny to a certain non-censure, to the space of democratic freedom (freedom of the press, freedom of speech, etc.) No democracy without literature; no literature without democracy. One can always want neither one nor the other, and there is no shortage of doing without them under all regimes; it is quite possible to consider neither of them to be unconditional goods and indispensable rights. But in no case can one dissociate one from the other. No analysis would be equal to it. And each time that a literary work is censured, democracy is in danger, as everyone agrees. The possibility of literature, the legitimation that a society gives it, the allaying of suspicion or terror with regard to it, all that goes together–politically–with the unlimited right to ask any question, to suspect all dogmatism, to analyse every presupposition, even those of the ethics or the politics of responsibility.

But this authorization to say everything paradoxically makes the author an author who is not responsible to anyone, not even to himself, for whatever the persons or the characters of his works, thus of what he is supposed to have written himself, say and do, for example. This authorization to say everything (which, moreover, together with democracy, as the apparent hyper-responsibility of a 'subject') acknowledges a right to absolute non-response, just where there can be no question of responding, of being able to or having to respond. This non-response is more original and more secret than the modalities of power and duty because it is fundamentally heterogenous to them. We find there a hyperbolic condition of democracy which seems to contradict a certain determined and historically limited concept of such a democracy, a concept which links it to the concept of a subject that is calculable, accountable, imputable and responsible, one that has-to-respond, has-to-tell [*devant-répondre, devant-dire*] the truth ('the whole truth, nothing but the truth') before the law, having to reveal the secret, with the exception of certain situations that are determinable and regulated by law (confession, the professional secrets of the doctor, the psychoanalyst, or the lawyer, secrets of national defence or state secrets in general, manufacturing secrets, etc.) This contradiction also indicates the task (task of thought, also theoretico-practical task) for any democracy to come.

There is in literature, in the *exemplary* secret of literature, a chance of saying everything without touching upon the secret. When all hypotheses are permitted, groundless and *ad infinitum*, about the meaning of a text, or the final intentions of an author whose person is no more represented than non-represented by a character or by a narrator,[14] by a poetic or fictional sentence, when these are detached from their presumed source and thus remain *locked away* [*av secret*], when there is no longer even any sense in making decisions about some secret beneath the surface of a textual manifestation (and it is this situation which I would call text or trace), when it is the call [*appel*] of this secret, however, which points back to the other or to something else, when it is this itself which keeps our passion aroused, and holds us to the other, then the secret impassions us. Even if there is none, even if it does not exist, hidden behind anything whatever. Even if the secret is no secret, even if there has never been a secret, a single secret. Not one.

Can one ever finish with obliqueness? The secret, if there is one, is not hidden at the corner of an angle, it does not lay itself open to a double view or to a squinting gaze. It cannot be seen, quite simply. No more than a word. As soon as there are words—and this can be said of the trace in general, and of the chance that it is—direct intuition no longer has any chances. One can reject, as I have done, the word 'oblique'; one cannot deny the destinerrant indirection [*indirection destinerrante*: see Derrida's *The Post Card: From Socrates to Freud and Beyond*, trans. Alan Bass, Chicago: Chicago University Press, 1987 (*La carte postale: de Socrate à Freud et au-delà*, Paris: Flammarion, 1980.) Tr.] as soon as there is a trace. Or, if you prefer, one can only deny it.

One can stop and examine [*arraisonner*] a secret, make it say things, make out that [*donner a croire*] there is something there when there is not. One can lie, cheat, seduce by making use of it. One can play with the secret as with a simulacrum, with a lure or yet another strategy. One can cite it as an impregnable resource. One can try in this way to secure oneself a phantasmatic power over others. That happens every day. But this very simulacrum still bears witness to a possibility which exceeds it. It does not exceed it in the direction of some ideal community, rather towards a solitude without any measure common to that of an isolated subject, a solipsism of the *ego* whose sphere of belonging (*Eigentlichkeit*) would give rise [*lieu*] to some analogical appresentation of the *alter ego* and to some genesis constitutive of intersubjectivity (Husserl), or with that of a *Jemeinigkeit* of *Dasein* whose solitude, Heidegger tells us, is still a modality of *Mitsein*. Solitude, the other name of the secret to which the simulacrum still bears witness, is neither of consciousness, nor of the subject, nor of *Dasein*. It makes them possible, but what it makes possible does not put an end to the secret. The secret never allows itself to be captured or covered over by the relation to the other, by being-with or by any form of 'social bond'. Even if it makes them possible, it does not answer to them, it is what does not answer. No *responsiveness* [English in original, Tr.]. Shall we call this death? Death dealt? Death dealing? I see no reason not to call that life, existence, trace. And it is not the contrary.

Consequently, if the simulacrum still bears witness to a possibility which exceeds it, this exceeding remains, it (is) *the* remainder, and it remains such even if one precisely cannot here trust any definite witness, nor even any guaranteed value to bearing witness, or, to put it another way, as the name suggests, the history of any *martyr* (*martyria*).

That remains, according to me, the absolute solitude of a passion without martyr.

NOTES

1 I would like to thank Leslie Hill, Peter Larkin and Will McNeill for their considerable help in uprooting errors and suggesting numerous felicitous phrasings and construals. Without their help this translation would have betrayed considerably greater linguistic eccentricity. [Tr.].

2 What does *the narrator* suggest on the subject of the analysis and the analyst in *The Purloined Letter* but especially in the first pages of *The Murders in the Rue Morgue*? To give the greatest sharpness to the *un-rulebound* concept of the analyst, he suggests that the latter would have to proceed beyond calculation, and even without rules: 'Yet to calculate is not in itself to analyze [. . .] But it is in matters beyond the limits of mere rules that the skill of the analyst is evinced. He makes, *in silence* [my emphasis, JD], a host of observations and inferences. So, perhaps do his companions [. . .] It will be found, in fact, that the ingenious are always fanciful, and the truly imaginative never otherwise than analytic.' See Edgar Allan Poe, *Poetry and Tales* (New York: Library of America), pp. 388–9. In *The Purloined Letter* (op. cit., pp. 691–2), Dupin quotes Chamfort and denounces as 'folly' the *convention* by which mathematical reason would be '*the* reason *par excellence*', and as a perfectly *French* 'scientific trickery' the application of the term 'analysis' only to 'algebraic operations'. Note already, since this will be our theme, that these exchanges between the narrator and Dupin take place *in secret*, in a 'secret place'. Like them, with them, we are '*au secret*' [isolated, shut away, Tr.], as we say in French, and 'in the secret', which does not mean that we know anything. It is at least and precisely what the narrator, in a form written and published by Poe, *tells* (us): twice the secret is *told* (even the address supplied: 'at an obscure library in the rue Montmartre', then 'in a retired and desolate portion of the Faubourg St Germain', then 'in his little back library, or book closet, No 33, Rue Dunôt, Faubourg St Germain' (op. cit., p. 680) without for all that the same secret ever being penetrated at all. And this is because it is all a matter of trace, both in the trace of discourse, and in the discourse of inscription, of transcription or, if one wishes to follow convention, of writing, both in the writing of literature, and in the literature of fiction, both in the fiction of narration, and placed in the mouth of a narrator, to whom, for all these reasons, nothing requires us to give credit. That a secret can be announced without being revealed, or, alternatively, that the secret is manifest, this is what there is [*il y a*] (*es gibt*) and will always remain to translate, even here, etc.

3 'Je fus profondément intéressé par sa petite histoire de famille, qu'il me raconta minutieusement avec cette candeur et cet abandon—ce sans-façon du *moi*—qui est le propre de tout Français quand il parle de ses propres affaires.' (Edgar Allan Poe, 'The Murders in the Rue Morgue', trans. Baudelaire in the latter's *Oeuvres Completes: Histoires Extraordinaires* (Paris: Louis Conard, 1932), p. 6). ('I was deeply interested in the little family history which he detailed to me with all the candor which a Frenchman indulges whenever mere self is the theme' [Edgar Allen Poe, op. cit., supra p. 400].) Is it enough to speak French, to have learned to speak French, to be or to have become a French citizen to appropriate for oneself what is, according to Baudelaire's translation, so strictly personal—a translation more appropriating than appropriate—'le propre de tout français' [the property of all French people]?

4 One ought not to have [*On devrait ne pas devoir*], even for reasons of economy, to dispense with here [*faire ici l'economie de*] a slow, indirect, uncertain analysis of that which, in *certain* determined linguistic and cultural regions [*aires*] (*certain*, hence not all nor all equally), would root duty in debt. Even before getting involved in that, we cannot detach ourselves from a feeling, one whose linguistic or cultural conditioning is difficult to assess. It is doubtless more than a feeling (in the most common sense of the term, that of the sensibility or the 'pathological' of which Kant spoke), but we keenly *feel* this paradox: a gesture remains a-moral (it falls short of affirmation of an unlimited, incalculable or uncalculating giving, without any possible reappropriation, by which one must measure the ethicity or the morality of ethics), if it was accomplished out of *duty* in the sense of 'duty of restitution', out of a duty which would come down to the discharge of a debt, out of such a duty as having to return what has been lent or borrowed. Pure morality must exceed all calculation, conscious or unconscious, of restitution or re-appropriation. This feeling *tells* us, perhaps without *dictating* anything, that we must go beyond duty, or at least beyond *duty as debt*: duty owes nothing, it must owe nothing, it ought at any rate to owe nothing [*le devoir ne doit rien, il doit ne rien devoir, il devrait en tous cas ne rien devoir*]. But is there a duty without debt? How are we to understand, how to translate a *saying* which tells us that a duty ought to prescribe nothing [*un devoir doit ne rien devoir*] in order to be or to do what it should be or should do, namely a duty, its duty? Here a discrete and silent break with culture and language announces itself, and it is, it would be, *this* duty.

But if debt, *the economy of debt*, continues to haunt all duty, then would we still say that duty insists on being carried beyond duty? And that between these two duties no common measure should resist the gentle but persistent imperative of the former? Now, who will ever show that this haunting memory of debt can or should ever cease to disturb the feeling of duty? Should not this disquiet predispose us indefinitely against the good conscience? Does it not dictate to us the first or the last duty? It is here that conscience and etymologico-semantic knowledge are indispensable, even if as such they must not have the last word? We must be content *here* with indicative references (*here* provides the rule: a place, a certain limited number of pages, a certain time, a *deadline* [English in original, Tr.], yes, time and space ruled by a mysterious ceremony). One would have to cross-reference between them, and try, if possible, to link them up in a network. One very accidental trajectory would follow the movements back and forth [*aller et retours*: also 'return tickets'; 'outgoings and returns' would perhaps capture a more financial idiom, Tr.], for example, between the determination of duty in *The Critique of Practical Reason* or *The Foundations of the Metaphysics of Morals*, the determination of debt and of culpability in the Kantian metaphysics of law, the meditation of *Being and Time* on the call [*Ruf*] and on originary 'Schuldsein' [being-guilty], and (for example) the Second Essay of [Nietzsche's] *The Genealogy of Morals* on 'guilt' ('Schuld'), 'bad conscience' ('*Schlechtes Gewissen*') and the like ('*und Verwandtes*') in which Nietzsche begins (section 2) by recalling 'the long history of the origin of *responsibility*' ('*die lange Geschichte von der Herkunft der Verantwortlichkeit*' and asks (section 4) whether 'these genealogists of morality had ever had the faintest suspicion that, for example, the central moral concept of "guilt" (*zum Beispiel jener moralische Hauptbegriff "Schuld"*) draws its origin from the very material concept of "debt" ("Schulden")'. In the same movement, Nietzsche recalls (section 6) the cruel aspect (*Grausamkeit*) of 'old Kant's' categorical imperative. Freud would not be far away, the Freud of *Totem and Taboo* on the religions of the father and the religions of the son, on the origin of remorse and of the moral conscience, on the sacrifices and the puttings to death that they require, on the accession of the confraternal law (let us say, of a certain concept of democracy).

Accidental back and forth movements [*aller et retour*, see above, Tr.], comings and goings, then, between all these already canonical texts and meditations of a type apparently different but in fact very close–and closer to our time, for example, the most recent proposals of Emile Benveniste (*Le vocabulaire des institutions indo-européennes* (I) (Paris: Minuit, 1969), ch. 16: 'Prêt, Emprunt et Dette', pp. 185–6. [*Indo-European Language and Society*, trans. Elizabeth Palmer, Coral Gables (Miami: University of Miami Press, 1973), ch. 16: 'Lending, Borrowing and Debt', pp. 148–9]) or of Charles Malamoud (*Lien de vie, noeud mortel: les représentations de la dette en Chine, au Japon et dans le monde indien*, Paris: EHESS, 1988). Two quotations will explain better, if more obliquely, the direction which I ought to pursue here, but cannot. One from Benveniste (op. cit., trans. Elizabeth Palmer, pp. 148–9), the other from Malamoud (op. cit., pp. 7, 8, 13, 14). Each quotation finds ample expansion, of course, in the work of these two authors.

Benveniste: The sense of the Latin *debeo* 'owe' seems to result from the composition of the term *de* + *habeo*, a compound which is not open to doubt since the Latin archaic perfect is still *dehibui* (for instance in Plautus). What does *debeo* mean? The current interpretation is 'to have something (which one keeps) from somebody': this is very simple, perhaps too much so, because a difficulty presents itself immediately: the construction with the dative is inexplicable, *debere aliquid alicui*.

In Latin, contrary to what it might seem, *debere* does not constitute the proper expression for 'to owe' in the sense of 'to have a debt'. The technical and legal designation of the 'debt' is *aes alienum* in the expressions 'to have debts, to settle a debt, in prison for debt'. *Debere* in the sense of 'to have debts' is rare, it is only a derived usage.

The sense of *debere* is different, although it is also translated by 'to owe'. One can 'owe' something without having borrowed it: for instance, one 'owes' rent for a house, although this does not involve the return of a sum borrowed. Because of its formation and construction, *debeo* should be interpreted according to the value which pertains to the prefix *de*, to wit: 'taken, withdrawn from'; hence 'to hold (*habere*) something which has been taken from (*de*) somebody'.

This literal interpretation corresponds to an actual use: *debeo* is used in circumstances in which one has to give back something belonging to another and which one keeps without having literally 'borrowed' it: *debere* is to detain something taken from the belongings or rights of others. *Debere* is used, for instance, 'to owe the troops their pay' in speaking of a chief, or the provisioning of a town with corn. The obligation to give results from the fact that one holds what belongs to another. That is why *debeo* in the early period is not the proper term for *debt*.

On the other hand, there is a close relation between 'debt', 'loan', and 'borrowing', which is called *mutua pecunia*: *mutuam pecuniam solvere* 'pay a debt'. The adjective *mutuus* defines the relation which characterises the loan. It has a clear formation and etymology. Although the verb *muto* has not taken on this technical sense, the connexion with *mutuus* is certain. We may also cite *munus* and so link up with an extensive family of Indo-European words which, with various suffixes, denote the notion of 'reciprocity' [. . .] The adjective *mutuus* indicates either 'loan' or 'borrowing', according to the way in which the expression is qualified. It always has to do with money (*pecunia*) paid back exactly in the amount that was received.

Malamoud: In the modern European languages to which we have just alluded, there appears to be a direct relationship between the forms of the verb '*devoir*', which deal with obligation properly speaking or with obligation as probability, and those which mean 'being in debt [*dette*]'. This relationship appears at one time in the fact that 'duty [*devoir*]' used absolutely is the equivalent of 'being indebted, being in debt', with, when appropriate, a substantive complement indicating what the debt consists of ('I owe [*dois*] a hundred francs'); at other times, in the very name of debt, which, in a more or less perceptible fashion for the speaker who is not an etymologist, derives from the verb '*devoir*' [should, ought, must: Tr.]: the debt, is what is '*dû*' [owed, due], what is carried into 'debit', the French term '*dette*' [debt] derives from the Latin *debitum* which itself, past participle of *debere* '*devoir*', is used in the sense of 'debt'.

In debt are combined duty and fault [*faute*; also lack]: a connexion for which the history of the Germanic languages provide evidence: the German *Schuld* means both 'debt' and 'fault' [*faute*], and *schuldig* means both 'guilty' and 'debtor'. But *Schuld* derives from the Gothic *skuld* which itself is connected with a verb *skulan* 'to have an obligation', 'to be in debt' (it translates, in the Gospel, the Greek verb *opheilō*, which has these two acceptations) and also 'to be at fault'. On the other hand, from the same Germanic radical *skal, but with another treatment of the initial letter, derives the German verb *sollen* 'should (do)' [*devoir* (*faire*)] and the English *shall* which, although enjoying a specialist usage today in the expression of the future, meant, at a much older stage of the language, '*duty*' in the full sense.

Groups of this type, more or less dense, more or less articulated, appear in a great number of Indo-European languages. They do not always delineate the same configurations, and each particular situation would demand a careful study. [. . .] the linguistic analyses of Jacqueline Pigeot for Japanese, of Viviane Alleton for Chinese, show, with all the requisite nuances, that the sphere of moral debt is clearly distinct from that of material debt, and that neither is connected with the morphemes corresponding to the word '*devoir*' [ought/should] as an auxiliary of obligation or of probability. The configurations that we notice in the languages that we have mentioned cannot be detected either in Japanese or Chinese. It is not quite the same for Sanskrit: there is no word '*devoir*' in Sanskrit, and there is no etymological connection between the different names for moral obligation and the name of debt. On the other hand, debt, named by a term which refers just as well to economic debt (including that which results from borrowing money with interest) as it does to moral debt, is presented, in Brahmanism, as the prototype and the principle by which debts are explained. [. . .] However, the notion of '*créance*' [belief, credence, credit also debt, claim!, Tr.] can also lend itself to polysemic games: one only has to recall that in French '*croyance*' [belief] and '*créance*' are originally one and the same word, that in German *Glaübiger* means both '*croyant*' [believer] and '*créancier*' [creditor]. But the connection between '*faire crédit*' [to give credit] and '*croire*' [believe] is less fecund, ideologically, than that which binds '*devoir*' [duty/ought] to '*être en dette*' [being in debt]. [. . .] That man according to Brahmanism, is born 'as debt', that this debt is the mark of his mortal condition does not mean that human nature is determined by original sin. As the Sanskrit word ṛna, '*dette*', can sometimes be coloured by '*faute*' [fault, lack], the German philologists of the last century, influenced perhaps by the ambiguity of the word *Schuld*, as both 'debt' and 'fault', suggested making ṛna derive from the same Indo-European radical as Latin: *reus* 'accused', 'culpable'. The etymology is erroneous, as would be a similarity between fundamental debt and original sin. Debt is neither the sign nor the consequence of a fall, nor, moreover, of any such occurrence. It does not result from a contract, but directly places man in the condition or the status of debtor. This status itself is made concrete and is diversified in a series of duties or of partial debts, which are invoked, in the Hindu Laws, to justify the rules of positive law which organise the administration of material debt. [. . .] The most concrete example, and if we may say so, the best illustration of this 'connection and drawing together [*colligence*] of heaven and earth' which would be debt, was provided for us by Hou Ching-lang, who shows us excellently how man buys his destiny by pouring into the celestial treasury the bad money of a true sacrifice.

5 On this 'problematic' of the semantic configuration of *cap*, of *capital*, of the *capital*, of *front* (in the double sense of 'front'–for example, a military front or '*faire front*' [to face someone] as in *affrontement* [face, brave, tackle], or *confrontation* [confrontation]– and the prominence of the face, the *forehead* [English in original, Tr.]), of the frontal and of the frontier, I would refer the reader particularly to my *L' autre cap*, followed by *La démocratie ajournée* (Paris: Minuit, 1991, to be published in English translation by Indiana University Press).

6 The child is the problem. As always. And the problem is always childhood. Not that I am distinguishing here, as we used to do in my student days, and in the tradition of Gabriel Marcel, between *problem* and *mystery*. The mystery would rather depend here on a certain problematicity of the child. Later I will try perhaps to distinguish the *secret* both from the *mystery* and the *problem*. In the Sophoclean tragedy which bears his name, Philoctetus makes this supplementary use of the word *problema*: the substitute, the deputy, the prosthesis, whatever or whoever one *puts forward* to protect oneself while concealing oneself, whatever or whoever comes in the place or in the name of the other, delegated or diverted responsibility. It is at this moment when, abandoned by his friends after a serpent bite had left a fetid wound on his body, Philoctetus still keeps the secret of the Heraclean bow, an invincible bow from which he will be temporarily separated. Right now, he is in need of both the weapon and the secret. Acting always indirectly, after many detours and stratagems, without ever facing him [*faire front*], Ulysses gives the order that the bow be seized. Philoctetus accuses, protests or complains. He is astonished at the *offerings*, he no longer recognizes a child and bewails his hands: 'Hands of mine (*O kheires*), quarry of Odysseus' hunting now suffer in your lack of the loved bowstring. You who have never had a healthy thought nor noble, you Odysseus, how you have hunted me, how you have stolen upon me with this boy [Neoptolemus] (. . . *labôn problema sautou paidia* . . .) as your shield, because I did not know him that is no mate to you but worthy of me [. . .] now to my sorrow you have me bound hand and foot, intend to take me away, away from this shore on which you cast me once without friends or comrades or city, a dead man among the living. [. . .] To you all I have long been dead. God-hated wretch, how is it that now I am not lame and foul-smelling? How can you burn your sacrifice to God if I sail with you? Pour your libations? This was your excuse for casting me away.' (1008–35; tr. by David Grene in *The Complete Greek Tragedies*: Sophocles II, ed. David Grene and Richard Lattimore, New York: Washington Square Press, 1967).

7 I have made use of the word 'oblique' very often, too often and for a long time. I no longer remember where, nor in what context. In *Marges* certainly (the '*loxos*' of *Tympan*) and in *Glas*, in any case. Very recently, and in a very insistent way. In 'Force of Law: The "Mystical Foundation of Authority"' (in 'Deconstruction and the Possibility of Justice', *Cardozo Law Review*, Vol. 11, Nos. 5–6 (1990), pp. 928, 934, 944–7, *et passim*), in *Du droit à la Philosophie* (Paris: Galilée, 1990), especially pp. 71 ff). On the oblique inclination of *clinamen*, cf. 'Mes chances: au rendez-vous de quelques stéréophonies épicuriennes', in *Confrontation* (Paris, 1988) (previously published in English in *Taking Chances*, Johns Hopkins University Press, 1984).

8 Without asking his approval, I think I may quote certain fragments of the letter which he wrote to me on 28 May 1991. I leave it to the reader to decide how far this letter (including the entry for 'Oblique' from the *Oxford English Dictionary* which did not fail to accompany the consignment) will have prescribed the logic and the lexicon of this text. Perhaps I had already, again, uttered the word 'oblique' in the course of an earlier conversation to which David Wood was thus referring. Fragments to share out, therefore, in the course of the ceremony, and David

ventures to speak of 'passion', as he ventures elsewhere, calling up the shade of Mark Antony, to distinguish (perhaps to associate, *aut . . . aut* or *vel*) 'to praise' and 'to bury' ('Its remit, he says of the book, is neither to praise nor to bury Derrida, but . . . ' (but what, exactly?). Here then the fragment of the letter of 28 May 1991, and his 'germ of a passion': 'Dear Jacques, As you will see, I have taken you at your/my word, using my phrase "an oblique offering" to describe what you agreed would be the only appropriate mode of entry into this volume. It is hardly surprising, perhaps, that the *most* oblique entry into this collection of already oblique offerings would be the most vertical and traditional auto-critique, or confession, or levelling with the reader (see e.g. S. Kierkegaard's "A First and Last Declaration" at the end of *Concluding Unscientific Postscript*: "Formally and for the sake of regularity I acknowledge herewith (what in fact hardly anyone can be interested in *knowing*) that I am the author, as people would call it of . . . " [. . .] This (and the whole sequence of thematizations of the interleavings of texts that you have offered us) suggests to me that the problem of an oblique entry might not simply be a problem, but a stimulus, the germ of a passion. Obviously, I would be equally happy (?) with something not yet published in English that would *function* in this text in an appropriate way: as a problematizing (or indeed reinscription) of the very idea of critique, as a displacement of the presumed subject of the collection ("Derrida"), as something that will *faire trembler* [French in the original, an allusion to Derrida's use of this expression in *De la grammatologie* [1967], Ed.] the 'on' of writing *on* Derrida.'

The allusive reference to Kierkegaard is very important to me here, because it names the great paradoxical thinker of the imitation of Jesus Christ (or of Socrates)–and of the secret.

9 If elsewhere it has often forced itself upon me, the French word *intraitable* is doubtless difficult to translate. In a word it can mean [*dire*] at one and the same time 1) what cannot be *traitè* [treated, dealt with] (this is the impossible, or the inaccessible, it is also the theme of an impossible discourse: one would not know how to *thematize* it or to formalize it, one would not know how to treat it [*en traiter*]); and 2) something whose imperative rigour or implacable law allows for no mercy and remains impassive before the required sacrifice (for example, the severity of duty or the categorical imperative). Which is as much as to say that the word *intraitable* is itself *intraitable* (for example, untranslatable)–and this is why I said that it had forced itself on me.

10 Other titles for this aporetic paradox: *mimesis*, mimicry, imitation. Morality, decision, responsibility, etc., require that one act without rules, and hence without example: that one never imitates. Mime, ritual, identifying conformity have no place in morality. As far as simple respect for the law is concerned, as for the other, is not the first duty to accept this iterability or this iterative identification which contaminates the pure singularity and untranslatability of the idiomatic secret? Is it by chance that, touching on this logic, Kant quotes, but *against the example*, the very example of passion, of a moment of the sacrificial passion of Christ who provides the best example of what it is necessary not to do, namely to offer oneself as an example. Because God alone, the best and only possible example? remains, in Kant's eyes, invisibly secret and must himself put his

exemplary value to the test of moral reason, that is to a pure law whose concept conforms to no example. The reference to Mark X, 17, and to Luke XVIII, 18, lies behind the passage in Kant's *Foundations of the Metaphysics of Morals* which comes not long after the condemnation of suicide ('to preserve one's life is a duty', '*sein Leben zu erhalten, ist Pflicht*', Section 1, ed. de Gruyter, Bd. IV, p. 397 [see the translation by Lewis White Beck, New York: Bobs-Merrill, 1959, p. 14]; it is, in short, what one would like to reply to someone who invites you, directly or indirectly, to commit suicide or to sacrifice your own life): 'Nor could one give poorer counsel to morality than to attempt to derive it from examples (*von Beispielen*). For each example of morality which is exhibited to me must itself have been previously worthy to serve as an original example, i.e. as a model (*ob es auch würdig sei, zum ursprünglichen Beispiele, d.i. zum Muster, zu dienen*). By no means could it authoritatively furnish (offer, *an die Hand zu geben*) the concept (*den Begriff*) of morality. Even the Holy One of the Gospel must be compared with our ideal of moral perfection before He is recognized as such: even He says of Himself, "Why call ye me (whom you see) good? None is good (the archetype of the good, *das Urbild des Guten*) except God only (whom you do not see)." But whence do we have the concept of God as the highest good? Solely from the idea of moral perfection which reason formulates a priori and which it inseparably connects with the concept of a free will. Imitation has no place in moral matters, and examples serve only for encouragement (*nur zur Aufmunterung*). That is, they put beyond question the practicability of what the law commands, and they make visible that which the practical rule expresses more generally. But they can never justify our guiding ourselves by examples and our setting aside their true original (*ihr wahres Original*) which lies in reason' (pp. 408–9; Eng. trans., p. 25). Elsewhere, in connection with the imperative of morality (*Imperatif der Sittlichkeit*): 'But it must not be overlooked that it cannot be shown by any example (*durch kein Beispiel*) (i.e. it cannot be empirically shown) whether or not there is (*ob es gebe*) such an imperative' (p. 419; Eng. trans., p. 37). This is a most radical claim: no experience can assure us of the 'there is' at this point. God himself cannot therefore serve as an example, and the concept of God as sovereign Good is an idea of reason. It remains that the discourse and the action (the passion) of Christ demonstrates *in an exemplary way*, singularly, *par excellence*, the inadequacy of the example, the secret of divine invisibility and the sovereignty of reason; and the encouragement, the stimulation, the exhortation, the instruction (*Aufmunterung*) is indispensable for all finite, that is to say, sensory, beings, and for all intuitive singularity. The example is the only visibility of the invisible. There is no legislator that can be figured [*figurable*] outside reason. Put another way, there are only 'figures of the legislator, never any legislator *proprio sensu*, in particular any legislator to sacrifice (Moses, Christ, etc.). But no finite being will ever provide an economy of these figures, nor of *mimesis* in general, nor of anything that iterability contaminates. And passion is always a matter of example.

On the motives which act in secret (*insgeheim*), duty, sacrifice, example, and respect, it is necessary above all to return, of course, to the third chapter of [Kant's] *Critique of Practical Reason* ('The Motives of Pure Practical Reason').

Over ten years ago, I dedicated a seminar to this text and to these questions and I hope one day to publish certain transcriptions of it.

11 *Apophasis*: [1657] 'a kind of an Irony, whereby we deny that we say, or do that which we especially say or do' *Oxford English Dictionary* (Tr.).

12 *Geheimnis, geheim*. It is precisely in respect of duty that Kant often evokes the necessity of penetrating behind secret motives (*hinter die geheimen Triebfedern*), to see if there might not be a secret impulse of self-love (*kein geheimer Antrieb der Selbstliebe*) behind the greatest and most moral sacrifice (*Aufopferung*), the sacrifice that one believes can be achieved properly by duty (*eigentlich aus Pflicht*), by pure duty (*aus reiner Pflicht*), when one accomplishes it in a manner solely in conformity to duty (*pflichtmässig*). This distinction is equivalent in Kant's eyes to that which opposes the letter (*Buchstabe*) to the spirit (*Geist*), or legality (*Legalität*) to moral legislation (*Gesetzmässigkeit*) (cf. further the beginning of ch. 3 of the *Critique of Practical Reason*). But if, as Kant then recognized, it is 'absolutely impossible to establish by experience with complete certainty a single case' in the world in which one could eliminate the suspicion that there is a secret (that is to say, that which would allow us to distinguish between 'out of duty' and 'conforming to duty'), then the secret no more offers us the prospect of some interpretation [*déchiffrement*], even infinite, than it allows us to hope for a rigorous decontamination between 'in conformity with duty' and 'out of pure duty'. Nor to finish with *mimesis* whose principle of iterability will always connect the constitutive *mimesis* of one (the 'in conformity with duty', *pflichtmässig*) to the non-mimesis constitutive of the other ('out of pure duty', *aus reiner Pflicht*), as non-duty to duty, non-debt to debt, non-responsibility to responsibility, non-response to response. The de-contamination is impossible not by virtue of some phenomenal or empirical limit, even if indelible, but precisely because this limit is not empirical; its possibility is linked *structurally* to the possibility of the 'out of pure duty'. Abolish the possibility of the simulacrum and of external repetition, and you abolish the possibility both of the law and of duty themselves, that is, of their recurrence. Impurity is principally inherent in the purity of duty, i.e., its iterability. Flouting all possible oppositions: *there* would be the secret [*là serait le secret*]. The secret of passion, the passion of the secret. To this secret that nothing could confine, as Kant would wish, within the order of 'pathological' sensibility, no sacrifice will ever disclose its precise meaning. Because there is none.

13 In this paragraph I have translated *histoire* mostly as *story* (though *history* was usually also possible) except in those cases where *history* was clearly more appropriate (Tr.).

14 I attempt elsewhere this 'de-monstration' of the secret in connection with Baudelaire's *La fausse monnaie* (in *Donner le temps*, 1: *La fausse monnaie*, Paris: Galilée, 1991). As for the *exemplary* secret of literature, allow me to add this note before concluding. Something of literature will have begun when it is not possible to decide whether, when I speak of something, I am indeed speaking of something (of the thing itself, this one, for itself) or if I am giving an example, an example of something or an example of the fact that I can speak of something, of my way of speaking of something, of the possibility of speaking in general of something in

general, or again of writing these words, etc. For example, suppose that I say 'I', that I write in the first person or that I write a text, as they say 'autobiographically'. No one will be able seriously to contradict me if I claim (or hint by ellipsis, without thematizing it) that I am not writing an 'autobiographical' text but a text *on* autobiography of which this very text is an example. No one will seriously be able to contradict me if I say (or hint, etc.) that I am not writing about myself but on 'I', on any I at all, or on the I in general, by giving an example: I am only an example, or I am exemplary. I am speaking of something ('I') to give an example of something (an 'I') or of someone who speaks of something, or gives an example of an example. What I have just said about speaking on some subject does not require utterance [*la parole*], i.e., a discursive statement and its written transcription. It is already valid for every trace in general, whether it is pre-verbal, for example, for a mute deictic, the gesture or play of an animal. Because if there is a dissociation between myself [*moi*] and 'I' ['*moi*'], between the reference to me and the reference to (an) 'I' through the example of my 'I', this dissociation, which could only *resemble* a difference between 'use' and 'mention' [both in English in original, Tr.], is still a pragmatic difference and not properly linguistic or discursive. It has not necessarily to be marked *in* words. The same words, the same grammar can satisfy two functions. Simultaneously or successively. No more than in irony, and other similar things, does the difference between the two functions or the two values need to be thematized (sometimes it *must not*–and that is the secret), neither explained earnestly, nor even marked by quotation marks, visible or invisible, or other non-verbal indices. That is because literature can all the time play economically, elliptically, ironically, with these marks and non-marks, and thus with the exemplarity of everything that it says and does, because reading it is at the same time an endless interpretation, a pleasure [*jouissance*] and an immeasurable frustration: it can always mean, teach, convey, more than it does, or at any rate something else. But I have said, literature is only exemplary of what happens everywhere, each time that there is some trace (or grace, i.e., each time that there is something rather than nothing, each time that *there is* (*es gibt*) and each time that it gives [*ça donne*] without return, without reason, freely) and even before every *speech act* [English original, Tr.] in the strict sense. The 'strict' sense is moreover always extended by the structure of exemplarity.

I am always speaking about myself, without speaking about myself. This is why one cannot count the guests who speak or who squeeze round the table. Are they twelve or thirteen, or more or less? Each can be redoubled ad infinitum.

As this last note is a note on the first notes to which it could respond, I will allow myself to add here: it is owing to this structure of exemplarity that I can say: I can speak of myself without ado [*sans façon*: also directly, without ceremony], the secret remains intact, my politeness unblemished, my reserve unbreached, my modesty more jealous than ever, I am responding without responding (to the invitation, to my name, to the word or the call [*appel*] which says 'I'), you will never know whether I am speaking about myself, about this very self, or about other self, about any self or about the self in general, whether these statements concern [*relèvent de*] philosophy, literature, history, law or any other identifiable institution; not that these institutions can ever be assimilated, but the distinctions to which they lend themselves become rigorous and reliable, statutory and stabilizable (through a long history, certainly) only so as to master, order, arrest this turbulence, to be able to make decisions, to be able *tout court*. It is of this, and for this, that literature (among other things) is 'exemplary': it always is, says, does something other, something other than itself, an itself which moreover is only that, something other than itself. For example or *par excellence*: philosophy.

Translated by David Wood

2

Jean-Luc Nancy

Elliptical Sense

I have never written on Jacques Derrida–neither on his body nor on his work. I did once address myself to the voice or trace of 'duty' in his thought, but I have never, as one says, 'written on' his thought or proposed a reading of his work. This is understandable; there is too great a proximity between us, and I have often written in the space of this proximity, and by means of it. This does not mean that our thinking always converges or that there is only a complicity between us. There is something of an *ellipsis* in our proximity–or rather, our proximity resides in this very ellipsis. This ellipsis is, in fact, and we will come back to this, what falls short of being identical, and, more precisely, what falls short of being circular. This lack of circularity, this gap which postpones the infinite return of the identical to itself, is also what governs the rapport between Derrida's text entitled 'Ellipsis' and Jabès' book 'on' which, it appears, it is written[1].

If I now choose to write 'on' Derrida, or if I feign to do so, it is not because the ellipsis of the proximity has been effaced. On the contrary, it is because the desire (no doubt long held) has come to me to trace its movement. A *'freundliches Geschick'*, as Hegel says, a 'happy fate', gives me the opportunity to do so, in the form of an invitation from Rodolphe Gasché to come here to speak[2]. Since the law of genre here is to speak 'on' a text by Derrida, I knew right from the start that I would speak on 'Ellipsis'. (One can easily imagine how 'to speak on ellipsis' might be a statement or a concept of Derrida himself.) I knew this, first, out of a kind of affection. Then I realized that this very brief text, no doubt the briefest of Derrida's texts which we might call 'properly theoretical', describes elliptically the entire orbit of his thought. It does not however close it off; it describes the doubling and the displacement of the ring by means of which this orbit, like that of the earth and of all thought, does not remain identical to itself. And finally, because of this, I realized that writing on ellipsis would not exactly require me to write 'on Derrida' (commenting on him, analysing him, discussing him)–and so I won't do this: this is and this is not a preterition–but requires, rather, accompanying the movement or the movements of the ellipsis for no other reason, in sum, than the pleasure of repetition. So the desire which came to me was nothing other than the desire for this pleasure (or perhaps, more simply, the taste for this pleasure), nothing other, in a sense, than the pleasure of friendship. But this is perhaps never far from the work of thinking, or from the *philo*-sophies.

I

For Kant, a pleasure that we no longer perceive is at the origin of thought. This is why thought is 'originally impassioned', as 'Ellipsis' puts it. The trace of this pleasure can be found in all philosophy. It is the pleasure of the origin itself: the satisfaction or the joy of discovering the source, the principle or the centre; or, more exactly: the satisfaction or the joy which the origin experiences in finding itself, in originating from itself in itself. This is also properly the act of thinking which Kant calls *transcendental*: reason discovering itself as the principle of its own possibilities. We will have more to say about the transcendental, around which Rodolphe Gasché has organized this colloquium. Let us say for the meantime that 'Ellipsis', writing as it does on the origin and on writing as the 'passion of the origin', is in a transcendental position or at least seems to be in such a position.

It is this position which gives us the condition of possibility, which is not itself the origin (and this ellipsis or eclipse of the origin in the Kantian 'condition of possibility' is beyond doubt what sets in motion all of modern thought), but which forms, on the contrary, the condition of possibility of the origin itself, or again, the condition of possibility of *meaning* or *sense*, if the origin is by definition the origin of meaning, which is to say nothing less than meaning itself, 'all meaning', '*tout le sens*', as is written in 'Ellipsis'. (This is the only mention of meaning or sense in the entire text: what is at stake is nothing less than 'all meaning'). The condition of possibility of the origin or of meaning is called *écriture*. *Ecriture*, 'writing', is not the vehicle or the medium of meaning, because, were this the case, it would not be its condition of possibility. Writing here does not refer to Jacques Derrida's writing, which communicates to us the meaning and the logic of a certain discourse on the origin, on meaning and on writing. This writing is not that of the *book*, which this text concludes and closes; rather, it is this very writing itself; there is no other. There are not two writings, the empirical one and then the transcendental one; there is a single 'transcendental experience' of writing. But it is precisely this experience which attests to its non-self-identity; in other words: the experience of that which can never be the object of any experience. (This is perhaps the only *experience* in the full sense or meaning of the word.)

Thus writing is said to be the *'passion de l'origine'*, 'passion of and for the origin'. This passion does not arise at the origin: it is the origin itself. The origin is a passion, and therein resides meaning, 'all meaning'; this is what makes sense, *'tout le sens'*. All meaning is always passion, in all the senses of this word 'meaning'. (Hegel knew this; for him the double meaning of 'sense' was the crux and the passion of the *aesthetic* in general, and hence also of writing in its rapport with philosophy.) What makes sense about meaning is that it senses itself making sense. In meaning, it is not that something *has* a meaning (the world, existence or Derrida's discourse); it is that meaning apprehends itself as and in making sense. (To sense the meaning or the sense, to *touch* its 'meaning-being', which itself has no meaning–this is Derrida's passion. I will speak on nothing else than that.) This apprehending implies that meaning must repeat itself, not by being stated or given twice in identical fashion, as is the case in the 'reissuing of a book', but by opening in itself the possibility of relating to itself in the 'referral of one sign to another', which is also the route to the re-cognition of meaning as meaning. Such is the passion: meaning, to be or to make sense, has to repeat itself in another sense of this word, its primal sense; that is, it has *to make repeated demands on itself*. It has to think on itself 'anew' (but it is in this 'anew' that everything begins; the origin is not the new, but the 'anew'); it has to place demands on itself, to appeal to itself, to beseech itself, to entreat itself, to implore itself; it has to want itself, to desire itself, to seduce itself as meaning. Writing is nothing other than the continued demand of meaning for itself. Meaning calls for more meaning just as, for Valéry, in poetry 'it is the meaning which calls for more form'. And, in effect, this is the same thing. Meaning is lacking to itself; it misses itself; and this is why 'all meaning is altered by this lack'. Writing is the outline of this altering. This outline is 'in essence *elliptical*' because it does not come back full circle to the same.

But *nothing* is strictly or properly altered. There is no first meaning which a second writing would then come along to divert and upset, dooming it forever to lament its infinite loss or painfully to await its infinite reconstitution. 'All meaning is altered', *'tout le sens est altéré'*: what this says first of all is that meaning is *thirsty*, *altéré*. It thirsts after its own lack; that is its passion. (And this is also Derrida's passion for language; in the word *'altéré'* and in the *altered* word, the word thirsty for change, we might say, an ellipsis of meaning is what makes the meaning, and the excess of meaning.) Meaning thirsts for its own *ellipsis*, for that which hides it, eludes it, which silently lets it pass. What is passed over in silence in all meaning is the meaning or the sense of meaning. But there is nothing negative in this, nor anything truly silent. For nothing is lost, and nothing is silenced. Everything is said; and, like every philosophical text, this text says everything about the origin and announces the origin; and it bespeaks itself as the knowledge of the origin. ('*Ici*', 'here', is the first word of the text, and later on we read 'we now know'.) Everything is said here and now; all meaning is proffered even in this writing. No thinking thinks more economically–or less passionately– than this: than thinking everything and all at once. Thus the text proclaims itself, or the general orbit around which it gravitates, to be nothing less than a 'system', *the* system in which the origin itself 'is only a function and a locus'.

Writing is the passion of this system. The system, in general, is the adjoining which holds together the articulated parts; and, more precisely, in the philosophical tradition it is the way the organs of the living (body) are conjoined; it is their life or Life itself (this life which, according to Hegel, is characterized essentially by sense in that it senses and senses itself making sense). The adjoining of writing is the 'binding joint' of the book, or its life. The life of the book is played out–it is 'in play' and 'at stake'–not in the closed book, but in the open book 'between the two hands which hold the book'. The *maintenant*, the now or present-at-hand, is articulated in the *mains tenant*, the hands holding the book. The holding hands multiply that which is presently at hand; they divide its presence, making it plural. These are 'our hands': there is no longer a singular *I* which we find proffered here, but the proliferation and the articulation of a *we*. This joining goes beyond the adjoining of the living reader. It prolongs and exceeds him. Reading as such does not imply a *living* reader though, nor does it presume him dead. He or that which has the book, now, in hand, is a system whose systematicity differs from itself and defers itself. What Derrida names 'the difference within the now of writing' is itself the 'system' of writing in whose heart the origin is inscribed only as a 'locus'. *Différance* is nothing other than the infinite repetition of meaning, which does not consist in its duplication or in a way of always distancing itself to infinity, but which is rather the grounding of meaning, which is to say the absence of a ground, which destines it to be that which it *is*: its own *différance*. If meaning had a ground, if it did not (have to) call and name itself, it would have no more meaning than the immanence of water in water or stone in stone or the closed book in the book never opened. *Différance* is bidding, appeal, request, seduction, imploring, supplication. *Différance* is passion.

With a jolt–for it is a jolt, the jolting of the origin by the origin itself–'the joining is a fracturing'. Thus the system really is a system, but a system of fracturing. This is neither the negative of the system nor a system in reverse.

The fracturing does not break the joint: in repetition 'nothing has budged' (says the text), or else the joint has always already been broken in itself, as such, and in sum by itself. That which joins divides; that which joins together is divided. Fracturing is not the other of joining; it is the *heart* and the *essence* of it. It is the exact and infinitely discrete limit *upon* which the joint is articulated–the book in one's/our hands, and the fold of the book in the book. The heart of the heart is always a beating, and the essence of essence consists in the withdrawal of its own existence.

It is this limit for which passion calls; it is this to which it appeals: the limit of that which, to be itself and to be present to itself, does not come back to itself; the circle which misses itself: ellipsis. Meaning is elliptical when it does not come back to itself: meaning which, as meaning, does not link up with its own meaning or rejoin it by repeating itself, appealing again and again to its limit as to its essence and its truth–then coming back to itself as to this passion.

To appeal to the limit is not to undertake the conquest of a territory. It would not extend, nor would it pretend, to the appropriation of the boundaries. For when the boundaries are appropriated, there is no longer a limit. But to solicit the limit *as such* is to demand that which cannot be appropriated. It is to demand the infinite exposition of that which takes place on the limit, the yielding to this spaceless space which is the limit itself: it *has* no limits, nor does it have an infinite spatiality, and therefore it is not even 'finite' but the end or finitude itself. Writing does not *have* any limit, but it *is* the endless inscription of the end itself.

Such is the last page of the book, the last line of the text–which is what the book, the text, never stops demanding, calling for and seducing. The text– every text–closes around the opening of its own appeal. The ellipsis of 'Ellipsis' links up with itself and wraps up a book within the difference of its own circularity. On the last line Derrida inscribes the last words of a quotation from Jabès. It is a signature: 'Reb Dérissa'. The whole meaning of the text will have been altered by this play. It will have become the thirst, the passing for setting into play the *I* (*de mettre en jeu le je*).

The closure of the text is the quotation of the other text; the quotation of the text is like a signature. The signature marks the limit of signs: it is their event, the property of their advent, the origin or the sign of the origin, or the origin itself in the form of a singular sign, which no longer signs. Even here, however, the singularity itself is double. The signature is *altéré*, it thirsts for change: it thirsts for itself as the origin of the text. Derrida is changed by his own thirst for himself. It is an exhorbitant thirst, the thirst of one who has already drunk, the thirst of drunkenness. Derrida is a drunken rabbi. The mastermind commanding the system of the text confides his own name to a double (itself unreal: the text reminds us that Jabès' rabbis are 'imaginary').

The double substitutes a double *s*–'disseminating letter', Derrida will later write–for the *d* in the *da* of Derrida: an elsewhere in the guise of a *here*, a fictional being in the guise of a *Dasein*, or existence. Dérissa touches the limit 'with an animal-like, quick, silent, smooth, brilliant, slippery motion, in the manner of a fish or a serpent', as the text says of the book insinuating itself 'into the dangerous hole' of the centre, to fill it in.

But it is just playing: yes, it's a laugh. A laugh breaks out here, the laughter of the ellipse bursting open like a mouth around its double foci, Derrida and Dérissa. The origin is laughing. There is a transcendental laugh, and at several points the text insists on a certain 'joy' of writing. What is a transcendental laugh? It is not the obverse of the sign or value accorded to serious matters, which thinking, necessarily, reclaims. It is knowledge of a condition of possibility which gives nothing to know. There is nothing comic about it: it is neither nonsense nor irony. This laugh does not laugh *at* anything. It laughs at nothing, for nothing. It signifies nothing, without however being absurd. It laughs at being the peal of its laughter, we might say. Which is not to say that it is unserious or that it is painless. It is beyond all opposition of serious and non-serious, of pain and pleasure. Or rather, it is at the juncture of these oppositions, at the limit which they share and which itself is only the limit of each one of these terms, the limit of their signification, the limit to which these significations, as such, are exposed. One could say, in another language, that such a limit, as the place where pain and pleasure partake each of the other, is a place of the sublime. I prefer to say, in a less aesthetic language, that it is a place of exposition.

There is a joy, a gaiety even, which has always stood at the limit of philosophy. It is not comedy or irony or the grotesque or humour (though it also perhaps mixes together all these significations). But it is also the ellipsis of all these '*comiques significants*' (to use Baudelaire's expression), and this belongs to that 'strange serenity' that the text has named. In this serenity knowledge lightens itself of the weight of knowledge, and meaning knows itself–or senses itself–as that extreme lightness which characterizes the 'exit from the identical' which 'thinks and weighs' ('*qui pense et pèse*', says the text) the book as such. This play on thinking and weighing (*penser et peser*) speaks of thought as a measuring and a weighing. Here the book, or its joining, is measured and weighed. But even here, where something is actually said, and said in the meaningful play of a slippage of the *etymon*, even this says nothing. It appropriates nothing of the *etymon*; it appropriates not one originary property of meaning. Thought will not let itself be weighed; weight will not let itself be thought. There is only the lightness of laughter, this minute, infinite lightness which does not laugh *at* anything, let me say once more, but which is itself the lightening of meaning. No theory of comedy or of the joke has been able to master it. Here is theory laughing by itself at itself–or, better, if this is not a laughter *at* anything, here is laughter as the joyful *différance* of theory. Derrida is always laughing.

The 'lightening of meaning' is not brought about by meaning casting overboard its ballast, the better to engage in unbridled debauchery. Meaning lightens itself and laughs, *as meaning*, at the cutting edge of its appeal and its repeated demand for meaning. It lightens itself by having its limit as a resource and having *for sense or meaning* the infinity of its own finitude.

This meaning, this meaning of 'all meaning', this totality of meaning made up of its own altering, this totality whose whole being-total consists in not letting itself be totalized (but in being totally exposed) is something which is all too hastily translated into 'wordplay', into an acrobatics or mirror-game of language. So, the in-significant (or hyper-significant?) enormity of the ellipsis of Derrida in Dérissa defies wordplay itself. But we would be no less wrong to try to 'sublate' this play in language–in the manner of Hegel, who sublates everything in a play on the word 'sublate'. There is no spirit or wit *of* language or in language, origin of words and before words, which the 'living word' could bring to its presence. It is infinitely lighter, and more serious: *the language is alone*, and this is what the word *écriture* means (what remains of language when it has laid down its sense, having confided it to the living and silent voice).

'The language is alone' does not mean: this alone exists, as is believed naively and imperturbably by those who denounce as 'philosophy imprisoned in language' all thinking which does not offer them–that is, which does not *name* for them . . .–a slice of life and the 'meaning' of the 'concrete'. What this means, on the contrary, is that language is not an existence, nor is it existence. But it is its *truth*. Which means that if existence is the sense or meaning of being, and the being of meaning or sense, language *alone* marks it *as its own limit*. There is only language for the 'there is' of whatever it happens to be, for that 'there is' which transfixes us, fills us with wonder, anguishes us, for that 'there is' which 'is *there* but *out there, beyond*'. This 'there is' is presence itself, experienced presence, next to our hands and from now on–but the *there* of 'there is' (the *y* of 'il *y* a') will not let itself be situated either 'here' or 'out there' or elsewhere or nearer in some interiority. *There* 'signals' there where there no longer is any sign–save the repetition of the demand, from sign to sign, towards the limit where existence is exposed. The *there* is infinitely light; it is a joining and a fracturing; it is the lightening of every system and every cycle, slender limit of writing. There one touches upon presence which is no longer present *to itself*–but is repetition and supplication of presence coming. 'The future is not a future present', and this why 'beyond of the closure of the book is not to be awaited'. This means that it is to be called forth, on the limit. The appeal, the repeated demand, the joyful supplication is: 'that *everything comes* there'; the passion of writing is impassioned by nothing other than this.

II

In the 'there is' of existence and in that which 'comes there' to presence, what is at stake is being and the sense or meaning of being. In its two great philosophical formulations, the transcendental has included a notion of putting in reserve, a withdrawing of being. For Aristotle, being is that which keeps itself in reserve, on this side and beyond the multiplicity of categories (predicates or transcendentals) by which it can be expressed πολλαχῶς, 'in various ways'. And Kant's transcendental substitutes a knowledge of the only conditions of possibility of experience for knowledge of the being offered in this experience.

When the question of the meaning of being was reinforced in philosophy–or on its limit–it was not in order to break into the transcendental, to track it down, transcend it and penetrate its reserve. But it was, with Heidegger, to inquire into this *retreat* itself as the essence and the meaning of being–Being: that which is nothing of all which is, but that whose stakes are set and determined by existence. Thus considered, the opposition or the complementarity of the transcendental and the ontological lost all pertinence. What was needed was quite another ontology or, rather, quite another transcendental or, again, nothing of the kind, but an ellipsis of the two; an ellipsis of transcendental and ontological; neither the withdrawal of Being nor its given presence; but this presence itself, Being itself, and, as Being, exposed in a trace or as a tracing: withdrawing the presence, but presenting the withdrawing, in its property of being non-presentable–which is *the* absolute property or the property of the absolute. Tracing is the event, the advent and the material existence (the *Ereignis*, perhaps) of such a property.

The question of writing–as the question of the letter of meaning and of the meaning of the letter (or as the question of a body of language lost on the limit of language itself)–re-inscribes the question of the meaning of being: ellipsis of being and of the letter (*de l'être et de la lettre*). What does this re-inscription of the question bring about? What happens when, as happens here–in the text–one assigns to the origin a 'being-written' and a 'being-inscribed'? There is no question of responding to such an inquiry right now: its scope would take us beyond the dimensions of a lecture and probably also beyond our chances for reading Derrida or for writing 'on' him, 'on' this writing which still writes, which is always thirsting for change, and particularly when still writing 'on' Heidegger. But perhaps we can say this much: in the ellipsis of being and the letter, Being (capital B) no longer or at least not only withdraws into the heart or into the space of its difference from being (*Sein und Seiende*). If at one time this difference could be taken as *central* (has in fact been so taken, and up to what point, by Heidegger himself?), it certainly no longer can be. It is itself differ*ant*. It withdraws still further into itself and from then still calls itself back. Its retreat is even more withdrawn than any assignation to 'ontico-ontological difference' could ever leave it, and it is altogether yet *to come*, indeed more so than any statement could say. Derrida will write later (in *Of Grammatology*, p. 23) that 'within the decisive concept of the ontico-ontological difference, *all is not to be thought in one go* [*tout n'est pas à penser d'un seul trait*].' More than 'one-go'–more than one *trait* or *ductus* (if we can choose, as G. Bompiani suggested to me, this Latin translation by the paleographic word *ductus*, meaning each of the several lines used to trace one letter – more than one *ductus* means all together the multiplication of the *ductus*, the fracturing of it, and also, as the very condition of those events, the effacing of the *ductus*, less than one *ductus*, its effacing into its own ductility (not unlike, perhaps, the tracing and effacing of everything in the *khŏra* of Plato). The sense or meaning of the ontico-ontological difference is neither *to be* this difference nor to be *this* or *that*–but its meaning is in its having a *to come*, in its advent, or, rather, to be only in a *coming* which would be equal to the infinite retreat it at the same time traces and effaces. It is 'there', but 'out there', as is stated at the end of 'Ellipsis'.

Perhaps we have to say that there is nothing beyond being, by definition, and that this marks an absolute limit. But an absolute limit is seen as a limit with no outside, a frontier without a foreign country, an edge without an external side. It is therefore no longer a limit, or it is the limit *of nothing*. Such a limit therefore would always be expanding; it would be an expansion without limits, but the expansion of nothing into nothing, if being itself is nothing. This expansion is a digging without end or limit, and the digging is writing, 'a void which re-empties itself' runs the quotation from Jean Catesson in 'Ellipsis'. Thus this void digs its own abyss *and* brings itself to light. Writing is the excavator digging a cave deeper than any cave philosophy has ever dreamed of, a bulldozer and a Caterpillar to break up the whole terrain, passion's machinery, mechanical passion, a mechanical machination. The machine digs to the centre or to the very bowels, the guts. The guts are the altered void. The machine works by a gutting, which is itself hysterical. This hysteria in writing would bring to light, to an unendurable light, by a genuine simulacrum of disemboweling and parturition, that limit of being which no bowel contains. Writing goes to it with a passion and to the point of exhaustion.

But writing does not *do* anything; it rather lets itself be done by a machination which always come to it from beyond it, from being's passion in being nothing, nothing but its own difference to come, and which always comes *there*, there where out there is there.

This also means that, as with the question of writing, the question of the meaning of being is altered *as* question, can no longer appear as a *question*. A question presupposes some meaning and aims to bring it to light in the answer. But here meaning is only presupposed as the call to meaning, the meaning which has no meaning, of calling to meaning: the ellipsis which never links up, but which calls (the 'open mouth', then, in which ellipsis itself and its geometry are eclipsed). To a call, no 'answer' answers; but rather a coming, a coming through to presence. In Heidegger, *Ereignis* names the advent of presence in its appropriation. *Ecriture* would be the ellipsis of the present in the advent itself, that ellipsis of the present *in which* the event takes place–taking place with no other place than the displacing of all 'natural place and centre' (in the text), the spacing of the place itself, of 'the trace' and of 'our hands'. But writing, on the limit which is its own and where it *is* not *itself*, would not even *say* this. It would not substitute affirmation (or denial) for the question. It would not substitute anything for anything; it would not effect any transformation, no re-elaboration or re-evaluation of discourse. In a sense, an exorbitant sense–the ellipsis of ellipsis itself–Derrida's philosophy does not exist, nor does Derrida's thinking. Moreover, this would be his passion: to eclipse thinking in writing. No longer to think, to come and to let come. The meaning of being differing from itself, differing from its own difference, and calling to itself, in the letter of meaning, would be no longer even Derrida's discourse, or anyone else's. It would be that which *comes* to all discourse, in all discourse, at its fractured joint, without this coming ever being arrested *there*–being, on the contrary, always coming and advent. What is *to come* (*qu'est-ce que venir, et jouir? qu'est-ce que la joie?*)–what is joy? This is no longer a *question*. this is precisely *to come*, to come to the limit, and the limit of coming as its infinite finitude.

(As to what it comes to and where it comes from, this is still less discourse, nor is it writing–writing is the coming, and its call. What it is, is all the rest, all meaning or sense of all the rest: what we call the world, history, chance, the body, the senses, work, the work of art, the voice, the community, the city, techniques, passion, again passion.) (Within this rest could also be the gods, if gods were not gone–but there are their empty places.)

III

Let's go back; let's repeat the text again; let's go back to the other extreme of ellipsis, take up the altered ring at its beginning, insofar as a ring has a

beginning. 'Here or there, we have discerned writing'–everything is there, in
one blow, in this lapidary *incipit* whose affirmation or affirmativity rests on
a discrete prosody (*here* we should re-read the sentence, properly scanned). *Ici
ou là / nous avons / discerné / l'écriture.* Everything is there in a passion of language
which has overcharged with meaning this simple sentence, so anodyne,
which has saturated with harmony this very brief monody to the point that
somewhere, at some discrete place, it alters itself, fissures, and cracks
noiselessly. Derrida-Dérissa will always have a devouring thirst for language,
and he will always passionately endeavour to make it crack.

'Here or there'. The first words of the text produce a *mise en abîme* both of
the book it closes and of this text itself. What *has been* done (discerning
writing) has been done right here and *is* therefore being done right here and
now. It is done; a discovery has taken place; a principle has been laid down–
this *incipit* is a conclusion, the systematic conclusion of the book–but it is
here, under our very eyes, between our hands, and it never ceases to be at
stake, still and most especially when it is written 'here'. It is not a 'past
present'; it is the passing of the present of writing, the coming into presence
of that which *is* not *present*. (What comes to or into presence does not *become*
present. It does not cease to *come*, and *where* it comes is still a limit. Presence
itself is nothing but limit. And limit itself is nothing but the unlimited
coming to presence–which is also the unlimited *present* [as a gift] of the
presence, or its offering: for the presence is never *given*, but always *offered* or
presented, which means *offered to* a decision [our decision] to receive it or not.)

And the *here* immediately redoubles: it is here *or* there. *There*, the *there*,
will come at the end of the text, and it in turn will redouble: 'there, but out
there', '*là, mais au-delà*'. Here or there: already the two foci of the text,
already the ellipsis. It's all there. A few years later, at the end of another text,
commenting on the form and forgery of his own signature, Derrida will write
that he signs 'here. Where? There'. '*Here*' takes itself out of its own place,
and *there is always out there*.

And so it is already time to inscribe an ellipsis right here–as the title has
already done–or more exactly, the ellipsis of ellipsis. For Derrida has
omitted, following the stylistic or rhetorical use of the word 'ellipsis', to make
explicit the meaning of this word. He will inscribe it in Greek, and he will
elliptically attach to it the double value of lack and decentring. He will not
say that ellipsis (like eclipse) has an *etymon* the idea of fault, of failing to be
precise or exact. The geometric term 'ellipse' was first of all the name given to
figures which lacked identicality, before being used (by Apollonius of Perga,
in his treatise on *Conics*) in the sense familiar to us as that which is missing in
a circle and as that which doubles the property of the constant radius of the
circle into the constancy of the sum of two distances which constantly vary.
All of this, together with a whole structural, historical, rhetorical, and

literary analogy of ellipsis and ellipses, has itself been subject to an ellipsis. But it is not just a matter of the specular play of the abyss. In being called 'Ellipsis' (and not simply being entitled 'On Ellipsis') and in its display of abysmal speculation (itself simple, infinitely simple), the text says or it writes or it ellipses something else as well, something we cannot know. It lets us know that we are truly missing something, probably many things, and at the same time: for example, an identity *between* Dérissa and Derrida; for example, 'that other hand', pointed to and shown to be invisible, unnamable—and those little dots which follow after it . . . serpent's hand or fish . . . (For example also: that Jacques Derrida himself does not remember exactly what has been the origin of this text, 'Ellipsis', or how and why it came at the end of this book, as the only unpublished text of the book. A text coming from nowhere, going to nowhere—but closing a book.) *Ellipse*, therefore, is as well a title as the ellipsis of a title or of any title. *Ellipse* does not *entitle* the text, but *names* it, as text, as altered ring (*Ellipsis*: the transcendental of the text, and [and as] the ellipsis of any transcendental.)

But let us take another example, and the first one, 'here or there': an ellipsis of place, the ellipsis of two foci neither of which can centre the text or localize the writing which has been discerned. In the 'here or there', it is the suspension, the hesitation, the beating of the *or* which really counts: this *or* which never says *where* writing is or when or wherefore. 'Here or there' is without definite place, and it is also 'sometimes, at moments, from time to time, and therefore 'by chance, by accident, fortuitous'. Writing only lets itself be discerned by chance. Even the cool calculations of writing we see Derrida engage in here—meticulous and unflinching reckonings, hot on the trail of the dissemination of meaning—even these calculations (and, to tell the truth, these calculations more than anything else) are given up to the hazards of language. Here-or-there language might lend itself to the game or impose it. If the circle of meaning did link up, the game would take place everywhere or nowhere (and the meaning would do so also). The game of sense includes the hazardous ellipsis of its own rules. Neither the '*mise en abîme*' nor the obvious literality makes the sense of the text. Only the ellipsis does it, which means: the sense itself *as* ellipsis, as not being circular, not moving around and towards a centre, but coming endlessly to the limit—here or there— where the presence ellipses the meaning by coming to its own sense. This sense is the *joy*—the pleasure and the pain—*to come* [*la joie (la peine) de jouir*] to presence or to be *exposed* to it behind or beyond any meaningful presence or present. This is, therefore, to take place where the place is the limit of the place itself: taking place out of place, here or there.

What takes place or has taken place is a discerning, that is to say, a fine, penetrating insight. A clear-sighted glance has managed to slip itself into writing, across 'labyrinth' and 'abyss', 'plunging into the horizontality of a pure surface which represents itself from detour to detour' (as in the text). (For where else is writing to be discerned if not here next to its 'grapheme'?) In the interstices of 'deconstructed' discourse, a more insightful theory has seen what has never before been seen: a classic *incipit* of the philosophical text. But to discern also means only to glimpse or to make out; it is to see, but barely, or to guess. The *theorein* has been reduced to an extremity, to a remnant in the half-light–to a vision of the 'vigil' and not of the midday.

'We have discerned': we have divided off from a *cerne*, which in French is the contour and particularly the ring of fatigue surrounding tired eyes; thus we have divided off from two *cernes*, tracing the contour and the division, the division as contour. (The next sentence will 'outline' this 'division' [*partage*], and the 'division' will itself 'divide': separation and communication, exchange and isolation.) We have traced the limit of writing *as* limit. We have written writing–it can't be seen at all; it is written; it is traced and consequently effaced before the eyes of him who would try to look. But its effacement is its repetition; it is its demand and its calling forth; 'all meaning' traverses it, always coming from elsewhere, from nowhere, always coming elsewhere, and nowhere, offering itself to us while at the same time stealing us away from ourselves.

But who is this 'we'? This *we* which has or have discerned writing is both the modest authorial *we* and the *we* of his majesty the Philosopher. But it is also our *we*: the 'we' of a community within history. 'We' bespeaks the historicality in discerning writing. This is a discerning which is as recent as the line which, in modern times–let us say from Benjamin to Blanchot– maps out a certain chapter or a certain graph of writing whose philosophical inscription Derrida has assumed and assured. Derrida will later relate back to Plato this division between the book and the text: Ellipsis of the Occident.

The transcendental experience is right here. In this *incipit* there is in fact nothing which does not bear the stamp of the empirical: the uncertainty of place and time, history and discerning. The *incipit* puts the origin and principle of the system on the register of the empirical. It not only opens up the discourse on writing, but it already begins it (begin' is, as it should be, the second to the last word in the text); it begins it with an irrepressible empiricalness by writing it. Thus the transcendental experience of writing is not the 'transcendental experience' described by Husserl. Husserl's transcendental experience was a 'pure experience', which reduced and purified empiricalness. Here experience is impure, and this is indeed why neither the concept of experience, if this supposes at least some elaboration on the experiential level, nor the concept of the transcendental (which is always the concept of a knowledge which, as a condition of possibility, is *a priori* pure) can be considered as adequate.

Experience is to be expressed or thought rather as 'wandering' and 'adventure' and as the '*danse*' named in the text and, in short, as passion itself: the passion of sense. What would make for a 'condition of possibility' here–and (or) an ontology–would be on the order of passion, if passion has an order. But passion always is destined towards the impossible. It does not transform the impossible into the possible; it does not master it; it is rather dedicated to it; it expresses itself in it, passive on the limit where the impossible comes–that is, where *everything* comes, where all meaning comes, and where the impossible itself cannot be touched, even though one *touches its limit*.

The impossible is the centre, the origin and the meaning. Ellipsis is the ellipsis of the centre, its lack, its fault, and the exposing of its 'dangerous hole' into which 'the anxious desire of the book' tries to 'insinuate itself' (in the text). But when it insinuates itself it discovers–or it discerns–that it has plunged into nothing other than 'the horizontality of a pure surface'. The circle makes a hole; ellipsis makes a surface. Touching the centre, one touches writing. All of meaning is altered–but what glides along the surface (brilliant, slippery fish) and what plunges into the hole, would these not be the same . . . the same which is always altered, tirelessly, *all* of *meaning* again? Is it the same machine which digs, fills in and retraces anew?

Undoubtedly it is the same. (Has there ever been more than one passion, more than one anguish, more than one joy–even if this unicity is in essence plural? The passion of the centre, of touching and tampering with the centre, of the touch of the centre, this has always been Derrida's passion–the passion of philosophy *and* the passion of writing: the one and the other, passion of and for writing, and the one in the other, and one by the other; accomplice one to the other, thrown or plunged, in the passion of touching language, as he will repeat later; to touch language, to touch the tongue, to touch the trace, to touch its effacement; to touch what moves and vibrates in the 'open mouth . . . '; to touch the ellipsis itself–and to touch ellipsis itself inasmuch as it touches, as an orbit touches an extremity of a cosmological or occular system; strange orbital touch: touching the eye, the tongue, language, the world; at its centre, in the guts.

It is the same passion: *to discern* is to see and to trace; it is to see or to trace, there where the *cernes*, the rings, touch–between the eyes. It is the limit of vision and the limit of touch. To discern is to see what differs to the touch. To see the centre differing: the ellipsis. There is in all discerning a certain narrowing: the eyes tighten up to the extreme; sight becomes sharper and more strangled (if sight can be strangled, if it has a throat). There are always, in hysteria, two hands clenched around the book. He did always clench his hands around the book.

It is the system again. It is the will of the system. (But what is will? Who knows it, or thinks he knows it? Does will not differ in its essence?) It is the will to touch that hands touch, through the book and by the book–skin in between, always, but that our hands touch. It is also perhaps, only half in jest, will's touch: to touch oneself outside of oneself ('to be by one's representations the cause of the reality of these same representations'–Kant). It is writing; it is love; it is meaning.

Sense *is* touching. What is transcendental, or ontological, in meaning is touch: the obscure, the impure, the untouchable touch, 'quick, silent, smooth, brilliant, slippery, in the manner of a serpent or a fish', even more than hands, the surface of the skin, skin repeating itself–here or there. He did ellipse the skin. But this is because there is no such thing as *the* skin. It is missing, always fainting, and this is how it covers, it unveils and it offers: always a fainting fit of sense, always an ellipsis, there where meaning advenes. It is the passion for a skin for writing on: 'a thousand prints on our skin'. He writes endlessly onto his own skin, hand to hand, *corps à corps, à corps perdu.*

IV

This '*corps perdu*', this lost body, is the passion of writing. Writing can only lose the body. When it touches it, it loses the touch itself, the sense of touching. When it traces it, it effaces it. But this body is not lost into a simple 'physical' or 'concrete' exteriority. It is lost for all manners of metaphysical presence, material and spiritual. If writing does lose it, it is because it inscribes its presence beyond the metaphysical presence, beyond its different ways and their oppositions. To inscribe presence is not to present it or to signify it; it is to let come that which presents itself only on the limit where the inscription withdraws itself. Derrida–under the name of Derrida or under some alteration of this name–did endlessly inscribe this presence of the lost body. He did not deal with language in order to make some new power arise, to organize some new system or disposition of the meaning. On the contrary, he always did play–he did put on the stage and at stake–*the body which is lost on the limit of all language*, the foreign body which is the body of our foreignness.

This is why this body is lost even for the discourse of writing and of deconstruction of metaphysics, inasmuch as it is a discourse. But the experience named 'writing' *is* this violent exhaustion of discourse where 'all the sense' is altered–not altered in another meaning or in the other of the meaning, but into this body, into this flesh which is all the resource and all the fullness of sense or meaning, although it is neither its origin nor its end.

This body is material and singular–it is also the very body of Jacques Derrida–but it is material in a singular way: one cannot present it as a 'matter'. Its presence is the presence of the unavoidable withdrawal of writing, where it can be nothing but its own ellipsis, here or there, out of there.

There, out of there—out of 'Derrida' himself, although here (on his body or on his text)—philosophy has materially budged or moved, which means that our history has moved. It has inscribed something which does no longer belong to any of the possible transformations either of the ontological or of the transcendental (although one can always bring its discourse back to such transformative operations). Philosophy did make a thin, discrete, powerful and trembling moving: the moving of a lost body presented on the limit of language. This body is made of flesh, gestures, forces, passions, techniques, powers, impulses; it is dynamic, energetic, economic, politic, sensuous, aesthetic—but it is no one of those meanings as such. It is the presence which *has* no meaning, but which *is* the sense, or its ellipsis.

Derrida 'himself'—or his ellipsis—is a singularity of this body, a singular hystery of it and an offering of it, crazy with its presence, crazy with laughter and anguish on the always retraced limit where its own presence does not stop to come—*à corps perdu*—discrete, powerful, trembling like any future.

Translated by Peter Connor

NOTES

1 Derrida's text 'Ellipsis' appeared as chapter 11 of *Writing and Difference* [1967], trans. Alan Bass, (Chicago: Chicago University Press, 1978). [Editorial note]

2 This paper was originally presented to the Collegium Phenomenologicum organized by Rodolphe Gasché in Perugia, Italy in 1987, in the presence of Derrida. [Editorial note].

3

Michel Haar

The Play of Nietzsche in Derrida

It is difficult for us today, finding ourselves in an uncertain post-Heidegger era, to assess what we owe to the immense work of Jacques Derrida. In the first place, undoubtedly–apart from his unequalled example of a faultless precision and patience in reading–for having *re-opened* the Heideggerian questions, for having given them a new lease of life. And then for having shown, beyond what was foreseeable, in a free, delightful and sovereign manner, that this re-opening signified a 'repetition' of these questions *at the expense of language again*, with semantic and syntactic transplants, cuttings, breaches and unexpected proliferations. In philosophy, no one has gone so far in this Joycean struggle with the angel of discourse.

Among the questions re-opened, we find that of Nietzsche's inscription in metaphysics. Nietzsche, as Derrida reads him and resuscitates him in his own writings, incontestably exceeds the over-simplified schema of 'inverted Platonism' within which Heidegger was sometimes content to confine him. If ever a philosopher was able to 'dance with the pen', to solicit concepts, to make them shake and vacillate so as to set their traditional weight back into play, to awaken the 'aphoristic energy' of language; if ever a philosopher was able to re-read, to put a shine on the imperceptible erasure of inscriptions, and to circumscribe, sometimes daringly, sometimes with prudence, the stubborn precariousness of Being in view of tribunals older and more straightforward than it and resistant to it (the 'gift' ['*don*'], the 'yes', the 'come' ['viens']), if ever a philosopher could pierce below it as the Necessity, eternally adhering to the concept, of language itself–it is undoubtedly the author of *Of Grammatology*.

However, this proximity to Nietzsche is so radical–sometimes to the point of identification: *Philosophizing with a hammer*[1]–that it poses difficulties. No one would think of saying that Derrida is Nietzschean. His whole phenomenological know-how–the analysis of temporality and temporalization that the word *différance* comprises–as well as the Heideggerian de-struction of metaphysics, distances him decisively from the Nietzschean *physics* of forces, and further still from a philosophy of life and the cosmos. And yet, there can be no doubt that he has *a debt of thought* with regard to Nietzsche. Who is Nietzsche for Derrida? How, despite the distance separating him from Nietzsche, can he take him as a screen, a forerunner and sometimes a mouthpiece for himself?

Since the lecture *La différance*, through *Spurs* and *Otobiographies* up to more recent writings, Nietzsche has been more than a privileged reference or one of the four great names thanks to which the Derridian web has been woven. He is more than an inspiration, a model or a resource. Whereas Freud, Levinas, and especially Heidegger, are, to a greater or lesser degree, convicted in turn of belonging to metaphysics, Nietzsche alone, if not absolutely spared, is, as we shall see, at least subtly accommodated. The unique and inordinate privilege accorded him over a period of more than twenty years obviously stems not from the frequency of citations or the range of texts commented on, but from a certain position of inviolability and of overhang. In the face of this *authority* alone the ruthless and omnivocal cutting edge of deconstruction turns away, the omnipresent suspicion becomes suspended, and the *Stimmung* of questioning, prudent or distrustful, changes into an elation of reading. It is only in the context of his readings of Nietzsche that we find the expression *affirmative . . . deconstructive interpretation*.[2] The painstaking care with which Heidegger is cited to the letter, put into question, kept close hold on, driven into a corner, taken at his word, contrasts with the generous and liberal, easy-going and quasi-ethereal use made of Nietzsche. Whereas the former is suspected of bringing back and perpetuating the proper, essence, and the 'metaphysics of presence', the latter is granted his innocence from the start. He would indeed have given in to a certain naivety with respect to the words of the tradition, whence a pretence of absolute dependence with respect to metaphysics. Yet *his writing*, its disruptive play, saves him straightaway, wrests him from the reductive grid of the Heideggerian interpretation.

Thus somehow opening up an unlimited future trust in the *Nietzschean text*, Derrida prefers–at least in his first writings–to borrow grand motifs from it, themes, a program, an overall orientation:

> Radicalizing the concepts of *interpretation, perspective, evaluation, difference . . .* Nietzsche, far from remaining simply (with Hegel and as Heidegger wished) within metaphysics, would have contributed a great deal to the liberation of the signifier from its dependence or derivation with respect to the logos and the related concept of truth or primary

signified, in whatever sense that is understood. Reading, and therefore writing, the text, *would* for Nietzsche be 'originary' operations.[3]

Why these conditionals, this doubt, this apparent hesitation: *would have contributed . . . , would* for Nietzsche be . . . ? [my emphasis]. Is it a matter of not 'identifying' too closely with Nietzschean positions? The assurance drawn from the model of Nietzschean writing is thus veiled by the insertion of a 'perhaps', which bears witness to a strange restraint on the verge of the most unambiguous affirmation with respect to giving oneself free rein. Let us cite a few of these 'perhaps':

> Perhaps, therefore, rather than protect Nietzsche from the Heideggerian reading, we should offer him up to it completely, underwriting that interpretation without reserve . . . [4]
> This is perhaps what Nietzsche wanted to write and what resists the Heideggerian reading: difference in its *active* movement–what is comprehended in the concept of 'différance' without exhausting it . . .[5]
> [A question in passing: how can a textual difference 'comprehend', embrace a *difference of forces*? *Is the text stronger than the force?*]
> The eternal return always involves differences of forces that perhaps cannot be thought in terms of being . . . [6]

The 'perhaps' in these three cases concerns the *validity* of the Heideggerian reading. It is completely right . . . if one abstracts from the manner in which Nietzsche has written what he has written, from *his style*–which is impossible!

Thus from the beginning the doubt was only apparent, and moreover will become progressively effaced; hence no more 'perhaps' in *Spurs*, where the question of being, or that of essence (can the two be identified?), is deliberately submitted to the 'more powerful question of propriation' as 'sexual operation', an indecidable exchange of give and take. It is *submitted* and inscribed, without ambiguity, into this process 'older' than it: the '*coup de don*', in this 'donation-that-keeps-itself' that would be the feminine donation.

From the beginning, therefore, the doubt is victoriously relegated, by way of a series of affirmations resting on an almost tangible and factual primary elementary certainty: the *Nietzschean text*. 'Nietzsche has *written* what he has written. He has written that writing–and first of all his own–is not originarily subordinate to the logos and to truth.'[7] No citation at this decisive point; while a few lines lower, on the subject of the 'logos of being', the Heideggerian expression is scrupulously cited: 'Thought obeying the Voice of Being' (why all these capitals?), and is immediately convicted of belonging to pure auto-affection and to the pure self-presence of a non-worldly 'transcendental signified'!

Is it certain that for Nietzsche writing is not subordinated, indeed as rigorously as possible, to a '*truth*'? Why the absence of *Auseinandersetzung* with the Nietzschean doctrine on the origin of language (is it so evidently false as not to merit examination?), and the silence regarding the clearly affirmed and thematized subordination of writing with respect to *spoken* language? Can it be that the Nietzschean text states the contrary of its philosophical *thesis*?

THE ORIGINARY DOUBLE TRUTH OF LANGUAGE

For the *non-subordination of writing* is, from a thetic and thematic point of view, explicitly rejected. Writing, like style, is submitted to an 'extra-moral' *originary truth*. Nietzsche, as we know, in *Truth and Lie in the Extra-moral Sense* (1873), as in numerous very late fragments (1888), maintains that every word, every concept is well and truly derived. Not from the intra-linguistic play of signifiers, but from an *intuition*, an 'image', that is, from a sensible impression or a 'nervous excitation', born of our *perceptive* encounter with a singular object. Every concept results, he claims, from a conventional, 'gregarious' 'metaphor', that is, from an 'arbitrary transposition' that has *forgotten* 'the unique, wholly individualised original experience to which it is indebted for its emergence . . . '[8]

The concept is formed 'from a *forgetting* of things distinct'. 'Only . . . the forgetting of that primitive world of metaphor . . . '[9] allows one to arrive at logical and conceptual 'truth', namely postulating *the identity* of what is non-identical. Nietzsche's constant position is that language ensues from a prelinguistic experience commanding it and to which it is unknowingly subordinated: this experience is in essence 'aesthetic' or rather 'artistic', it is a fictional process. This originary process–which is *the logos and the truth of the artistic will to power*, deeper than the will as pseudo self-identity or than the scientific logic of 'identical cases'–without knowing it governs the language which turns back *against it*. Language revolts against the sensible, Dionysian truth which nonetheless governs it throughout the originary fictional process. It is founded on an exhaustion or abandonment of the force of images and affects which is socially useful for the needs of communication. Language is the *tomb of force*: 'The grand conceptual edifice displays the rigid regularity of a Roman *columbarium*':[10] all language is a code, a 'language encoded with affects', but this code is a distant, weakened echo of precisely the 'originary melody of pleasure and displeasure'[11] and of general affects (sensations, emotions, feelings). This music, anterior to the musical art, is none other than the internal rhythm or the pulsations of the primitive will where pleasure and pain initially and perpetually cross and mix.

This other original truth of language, its musical truth, is not in contradiction to its 'metaphoric' truth: it is equally a prelinguistic logos, an artistic logos. Spoken and written language is moreover an impoverished, that is, formal and luminous Apollinian analogy of the noctural Dionysian depth where the original melody of pleasure and displeasure is played out. The essence of language is founded on a double entropy or on a double dissimulation: that of sensation and that of the musical affect. It exteriorizes

> an original depth which our *gaze* cannot attain.[12] *Language*, as the organ and symbol of appearances, can simply never turn the most intimate depth of music outwards . . . [13]

In spite of this impotence of language to 'translate' the fluctuations of affective intensity, its relaton to the origin is a relation of *analogy in the sensible* or of *symbolization*. It is not the Platonic-Schopenhauerian relation of reproduction or copy. Every language possesses a specific musicality. Thus, Nietzsche suggests, English and German have more tone, more tonic accent than French, which is flatter, more monochord, less melodious. Every language has its rhythm, its scansion, its harmony, its breath, its vital, almost biological equilibrium, its own 'metabolism'.[14]

However, 'the tonal background would go beyond this specificity, would be the same in all men', would constitute 'a general foundation comprehensible beyond the diversity of languages'.[15] This dream of pre-Babelonian universality is founded on a *relative* Cratylism of the linguistic *sound*. Just as the *sign aspect* of language is indeed *totally* arbitrary, as a result of the *complete leap* which each time implies a total 'metaphoric' transport (first from the sphere of sensory excitation to that of the image, then from that of the image to the concept), so its *symbolic aspect*, in a way that is certainly non-adequate, merely analogical and proportional, or *partial*–via the play of vowels and consonants, via accent, via tone, via cadence too–carries the echo of the prelinguistic melody, of the melody of affects. However, this music *itself*, as primitive image, is always already lost. Equally, there is a rupture, but not a complete leap, between the *unarticulated* sound silently vibrating in the depths of the original will and the vocal sound that is always integrated into a mimic, into gesture, a sound articulated by the movements of the mouth and of the vocal organs, instantaneously echoed in the tympan of the one speaking. In accordance with this schema, every language is founded on an entropy, on a loss of force and 'aesthetic' creativity, on a forgetting of the natural art which, without our knowing it, maintains the fictional constitution of conceptual universality and of interchangeable abstract meanings. In spite of this forgetting, and in it, language bears traces of its double origin of melody and image. Words rest on effaced images, but only in part. They allow an almost muted, twisted, attenuated and scarcely recognizable echo to resonate, an echo of what Nietzsche calls *the music of the heart* or, less lyrically, *the life of drives*. In any case, Nietzsche firmly insists that the word is above all symbol.[16] It symbolizes affects, just as in Aristotle, except for the distinction that *affects* must be understood as 'corporeal states' which have a hold over inanimate life. In the word there survives a trace of experience, of *corporeal experience*.

WRITING AS THERAPY OF LANGUAGE

This is why the musical and intuitive *intensity* in general that language by its essence loses can–up to a certain point–be *symbolically* restituted to it by writing. Writing, and above all the aphorism, can reverse the entropy of language, heal its congenital illness, go back to its double source. There is certainly a Nietzschean philosophy of writing, but it isn't exactly the one attributed to him by Derrida. For style as defined by Nietzsche does not amount to an entirely intra-linguistic 'play' (*the advent of writing is the advent of play*,[17] *systematic play of differences*,)[18] and especially does not amount to an absence of origin and absence of foundation. The world for Nietzsche is not a *groundless chess board*. The *chaos of forces*, another name for cryptic phusis, sustains and maintains man. Language for Nietzsche is not a supremely embracing and indefinitely postponed horizon, nor a game producing metaphysical oppositions. Nor is there for him anything 'pre-originary' that is 'inscribed', that would be textual, in whatever sense this is understood. Nor any omnidirectional play, able to move in any direction. Despite the plurality of perspectives, there is indeed always an ascending or descending direction of the will, a choice between the point of view of logic (gregarious) and that of art (solitary). Language, the play of language, namely the style, are for him *equivalents of a living body*.

To *communicate* a state, an inner tension of pathos by signs, including the *tempo* of these signs–such is the meaning of every style.[19]

Which state is communicated by style? The 'aesthetic state', that is, a state of the body, or a certain state of equilibrium or non-equilibrium of forces constituting it, always in a harmonious struggle, but also an *affective tonality*, a *Stimmung*.

The best style consists in creating the *Stimmung* most welcome to a reader.[20] Aim: give a reader such an elastic *Stimmung* that he stands on tiptoe.[21]

Make the reader feel like dancing. Writing does not in the first place, and perhaps not at all, aim at communicating some conceptual content, ideas, but at suggesting via a certain arrangement of words that sonorous machine pregnant with ideas that constitutes a *Stimmung*.

What is most comprehensible in language is not the word itself, but the tone, the intensity, the modulation, the tempo with which a series of words is pronounced–in short, the music behind the words, the passion behind this music, the person behind this passion, thus everything that cannot be *written*. This is why it has nothing to do with literature.[22]

Contempt, then, for writing, which has always already lost the effervescence, the effusion, the incantation, the singular vibration of a spoken word.

The aesthetic state possesses an overabundance of *means* of communication . . . –It is the source of languages. It is there that languages had their birth: the language of sounds just as the languages of gestures and looks. It is always the richest phenomenon that constitutes the beginning: the powers of we civilized people are reductions of richer powers. Yet even today we hear with our muscles, we even still read with our muscles . . . One never communicates thoughts, one communicates movements to oneself, mimical signs, which are *reinterpreted* as thoughts . . . [23]

Nietzsche, just like Plato and Rousseau–in an entirely metaphysical manner–theoretically conceives of writing qua style as a pale imitation, an attenuated replica or copy (*Abbild*) of the aesthetic state, of *Stimmung* and of gestures, of the live voice and of the present 'passion', which is to say, of the deployment of energy of someone speaking. Writing, in a word, would only be the *image* of a force.

One must first know precisely: 'It is in such and such a manner that I would pronounce that and *would provide an oral exposition* of it' before daring to write. Writing should be an imitation [*Nachahmung*]. Because he who writes *lacks* many of the means available to a lecturer, he should in a general way take as his model a very *expressive* style of oral exposition: the copy [*Abbild*] of this, what is written, will necessarily seem much more pale [*blässer*] in every way.[24]

All writing would run, breathless and exhausted, after the living archetype of the voice. All writing would be anaemic . . . And yet: *I only like that which is written with one's blood.* Writing has the means (undoubtedly an instrumental conception of language, Heidegger would say) to remedy its native consumption, to revive and invigorate this languid pallor so pleasing to gregarious people. Yet it can do so thanks to a strategic operation, thanks to a conscious calculation.

The *intensity*, the force spontaneously lacking in language, can be breathed into it by a will to write, by a calculated concentration of words, a work of the higher rationalism of the artistic will to power. In order to repair the loss of energy due to reduction to the 'identical case', one must *desire to be cunning with language*, so as to thwart and disarticulate the codes. This voluntarist therapeutics can be a shock therapy. The Nietzschean poetics of writing, poetics of diversion and of parody, of aphorism and of fragment–whose density and heuristic segmentation are sought after as such–this hyperconscious and hypercalculated politics of severity towards language Derrida makes his own, without at all assuming the Nietzschean motifs, without in the least adhering to Nietzsche's fundamental thesis. The aphorism, for Derrida, is 'the form of the written': *All writing is aphoristic.* Thus he also fails to accompany language towards that which lies beyond the condensed and the fragmentary, towards its other tone, that of song, lyricism or dithyramb, or again that of the hymn or *Lied*, as in *Zarathustra* (*Lieder* of the night, of the dance, of the grave. Song of melancholy. Drunken song):

Sing! Speak no more!–Are not all words made for those of gravity? Do not all words lie to he who is light! *Sing! Speak no more!* (Song of the Seven Seals, §7)

The aphorism is not the most intense level of language. The supreme level is the song, the hymn, the dithyramb. The aphoristic fragmentation undoubtedly marks a higher intensity of writing than the discursive style of critical analysis that dominates, for example, in the *Untimely Meditations* and in the *Genealogy of Morals*.

Written and spoken language is incurable. The 'wisdom of the bird' is to sing. This ultimate Nietzschean misology, this recourse to song, to the higher intensity of the hymnal word–which *sings* the yes, without worrying about the no–this return to song, not to the primitive melody itself, but to its echo–this Derrida cannot accept. Why? Undoubtedly because a writing still more intense and more affirmative than the aphorism, a writing founded not on the giving [*donation*] of a horizon, but of *Stimmung*, is, at the same time as absolute youth, as the supreme regeneration and the most powerful resourcing of language–the abolition of its *meaning*! A writing that lets itself be possessed by a *Stimmung* no longer controls its effects very well. Its finality is no longer that of meaning, but the unconceptualizable melody of affects, a thought of the body, whose symbolization flows back infinitely towards its unsayable 'physical' source.

A HYPER-NIETZSCHEAN STRATEGY

If Derrida passes over the genealogy of words and of style in silence, remains quiet on this doctrine of the origin of poetry which is unacceptable to him, he borrows from Nietzsche two elements of a strategy which is in no way Heideggerian: that of the *reversal* of metaphysical oppositions, and that of a *severity*, or sometimes—in *Glas*—of a cruelty with regard to language. This strategy is hyper-Nietzschean, for in both cases it goes to the extreme. The reversal leads to an abyssal destabilization. The play or *fire of words* proceeds to the point of their sacrificial consummation, whereas Nietzschean writing, which is certainly not tender with language—which does not *let it be*, as the other would say—does not go so far as the 'bloody' dislocating of words, as the *carnage of language*,[25] as the *ekpyrosis* of the text.

Without any doubt—Derrida has explained himself clearly on this point—the reversal could not be frontal. To execute a reversal of fronts would be to repeat the inadequate operation of the reversal of Platonism. In order to reverse metaphysics as a 'system of oppositions' (soul/body, good/evil, intelligible/sensible, speech/writing), it is not enough to invert it, as this keeps the whole oppositional structure intact. Yet nor can one naively attempt to oppose metaphysics as a whole to a non-metaphysics. (Who has done this? Certainly not Heidegger.) Derrida rightly underlines the fact that there are no concepts which *in themselves* would be metaphysical, that is, outside the textual fabric within which and thanks to which they are operative. He writes:

> There is no such thing as a 'metaphysical concept'. There is no such thing as a 'metaphysical name'. The metaphysical is a certain determination or direction taken by a chain. One cannot oppose it to a concept, but to a process of textual labor and another enchaining.[26]

To oppose without re-creating a term-for-term opposition: such would be a fine strategy. The movement consists in reversing at the same time as displacing, in reversing *obliquely*.

> To luxate the philosophical ear, to set the *loxos* in the *logos* to work, is to avoid frontal and symmetrical protest, opposition in all forms of *anti-*, or in any case to inscribe *antism* and reversal . . . [27]

Deconstruction prefers to *inscribe* a loxic (*loxos* means oblique, but also equivocal), that is, obliqueness, equivocality, indecidability into the logic of reversal. It thereby reverses the traditional oppositions while transporting them toward their undecidable limits so as ultimately, if not to neutralize them, at least to thwart their functioning as a restoration of the proper and of essence.

> Deconstruction . . . must, by means of a double gesture, a double science, a double writing, practise a *reversal* of the classical opposition *and* a general *displacement* of the system.[28]

Now every metaphysical opposition (is there any other kind?) implies not a simple face to face of two terms, 'but', writes Derrida in a very Nietzschean fashion, 'a *hierarchy* and an order of subordination'.[29]

To deconstruct means in the first place to *reverse a hierarchical order*, the order of that which commands (the principle, the *arche*) and of that which obeys (the consequence); it means to show who is the true master of the game. However, in this thinking who, or what, is master of its own game, if not language itself?

This programme of inversion which defocalizes an oppositional structure and makes it excentric is brilliantly executed in *Plato's Pharmacy*. There Derrida does not, like Nietzsche, reverse the Platonic opposition while remaining within it, by raising one of the terms to the top and lowering the other. He reverses and displaces the order of dependence of *the whole of the system* with respect to what Platonism considers to be a derived term, the *pharmakon*, writing. Derrida reverses the order of derivation, the relation between 'the originary' and the derived. Plato presents writing as remedial poison, a pseudo-remedy against forgetting, a poison because it distances us from the presence of the idea or of the thing itself. Now Derrida tries to show conversely that it is the *pharmakon*, the possibility of repetition of the same which is the origin of the *episteme*. The dialectic of weaving between the same and the other would be a *pharmakon inverted*, denied, forgotten. Although Derrida refrains from re-establishing the originary in its plenitude since writing has neither unity nor simplicity nor identity (*The pharmakon has no ideal identity*),[30] he nevertheless presents it as a *matrix* or a productive medium:

the prior medium in which differentiation in general is produced, along with the opposition between the eidos and its other.[31]

Writing constitutes the medium in which opposites are opposed . . . [32]

Contradictions and pairs of opposites are lifted from the bottom of this diacritical reserve of différance.[33]

Pharmaceutical writing would be the 'foundationless fund', without fundamental depth–a fund 'older' than the elements in opposition–where '*the dialectic comes to draw its philosophemes*'.[34]

Just as clearly, in a more recent text, the *chôra* in the *Timaeus* is interpreted not as a 'physical' *place*, but as the obscure presentiment of the necessary return towards the pure 'matrix' of metaphysical dualisms, their 'receptacle', language–whose 'pre-originary' Necessity 'sustains philosophy . . . *precedes* . . . the image* of the oppositions (the intelligible and the sensible)'.[35] It would thus be oppositions that would constitute the *image* (my emphasis) of a Model that could not be figured, incapable of presentation, pre-eidetic: language!

If this thesis is confirmed, established–if not in an irrefutable manner (this would once more boil down to the old logic!), but in an uncircumventable way–why is it then necessary abyssally to ruin, twist and consume the words themselves, since the abyssal ruin of the matrix of language will take care of dissolving them by dissolving the oppositions of which they are captive? If it is not the concept in itself which produces the philosopheme, but the function of the coupling and web of oppositions, why is it necessary to do violence to, to consume, to reduce to fire and ashes these unfortunate atoms of language denuded of power? Are they, in spite of everything, bastions, centres of resistance that perpetuate 'philosophical autism'? 'To luxate, to tympanize philosophical autism is never an operation *within* the concept or without some carnage of language.'[36]

If, for example, the 'soul' (*psyché*!) can become reborn, can say itself anew in a new text–perhaps as 'presence' or 'good' (who knows?):

Es ist die Seele ein Fremdes auf Erden,

why this mutilation and especially these 'fires of words'? Why:

Consume signs right down to their ashes, but first and more violently, with an irritated verve, dislocate verbal unity . . . a ceremony both joyful, irreligious and cruel (let them dance with the pieces)?[37]

Is not 'ceremony', this sacrificial rite, this *inverted* ceremonial expiatory destined not for some resacralization, but to desacralize the word? Innumerable examples: the 'origin-arily' [*originaire-ment*], the 'crack [*fellure*] of identity', 'the gallows [*la potence*] of the text' in *Glas* where a cruel and sombre game, a funereal ritual, stripped of all joyful dancing, is celebrated with great pomp. Who has laughed over the 'galactic'? Desacralize the Name, the Author. Hegel is dead: glued, glazed in his phoneme GL–by a glottal strangulation–an old imperial eagle glutted, englossed in his glory. So be it. Who has the key to this parade of parody, so little Dionysian? For what is one playing? Who is playing with what here? What makes language play and regulates its play? And this 'play': what does it mean?

THE ATTEMPTED EQUIVALENCE BETWEEN TEXT AND FORCE: THE CONCEPT OF 'WORLDLY PLAY'

For the motif of play, everywhere at work in Derrida's text, has a *very wide range*, perhaps too much so. It is the equivalent of writing–'writing is the play in language'[38]–maintaining itself below or beyond metaphysical oppositions. Older and more auroral than the latter, 'the concept of *play* . . . announces, on the eve of philosophy and beyond it, the unity of chance and necessity in calculations without end.'[39] In other words, play is the auto-computation of words, without finality, putting into play and perhaps thwarting all the obligatory oppositions. Play would be the strange place where metaphysical oppositions are produced. The equivalent of 'différance', play 'is (then) no longer simply a concept, but the possibility of conceptuality, of a conceptual system and process in general.'[40] Play is the non-'originary' origin, the erased origin of conceptual differences in general. Therefore, 'negatively', play is equivalent to an absence, the absence of a founding origin, the absence of foundation, the absence of principle: 'One could call *play* the absence of the transcendental signified as limitlessness of play . . . [41] On the positive side, this play would cross, somehow envelop and exceed the question of being, since it is 'not a play *within the world*',[42] not an ontic play, but 'a trace whose play transports and encloses the meaning of being': the 'play of the trace (. . .) has no meaning and is not'. Finally, the motif of play summons two more major equivalences, one historial, the other non-historial: the entire epoque ('It is in this age that it can be called the play of the trace'),[43] for this epoque is that of unlimited play in which onto-theology vacillates and becomes dispersed; and the world in its entirety ('it is . . . the *play of the world* that must first be thought, before attempting to understand all the forms of play in the world').[44]

Let us pause at this one expression: 'play of the world'. It undoubtedly comes from Nietzsche. One citation among others:

The imperious play of the world mixes being and semblance . . . [45]

And it can also be found in Heidegger, in *The Principle of Reason*, following a reference to the play of the 'Aion' in Heraclitus, as another name for the ontological difference:

> Why does the great Child that Heraclitus saw in the *Aion* play, the child who plays in the Play of the world? He plays because he plays.[46]

Derrida does not conceal this encounter, and refers in a note to this passage in Heidegger, and even to Fink (*Play as symbol of the world*). He affirms: 'these themes obviously refer us back to Nietzsche.'[47] Undoubtedly. There is nothing to object to here. The 'theme' is so well known. So much so that, surprisingly, Nietzsche's very statement on Heraclitus is quoted at the end of the reading of *Numbers*, and without the author being mentioned at all. For: 'the world is Zeus's play or, in physical terms, the play of fire with itself. The One is at the same time the Multiple in this sense alone.'[48] There follows this sole elliptical and sibylline remark:

> Fire always plays with fire.

What world, what fire, what play? This appropriation of Nietzsche by no means follows of its own accord. Leaving aside Heidegger and Heraclitus, what essentially distinguishes play in Nietzsche, what makes the 'play of the world' possible is an over-abundance of plastic forces, *a surplus of force*.[49] All play is the exercise, the deployment of a 'drive of play' (*Spieltrieb*), an expression borrowed from Schiller, but reintegrated into the physics of the will to power. 'It is the incessantly reawakened drive of play that calls new worlds to life.'[50] Play is not, symbolically, a play of signifiers, but a manifestation of force. The world 'plays', it has play, it is not tensed or coiled upon itself; it pulsates, contracts and expands, propels and expels. The 'fire' is not a verbal holocaust–nor pure *Lichtung* as Heidegger understands it–but for Nietzsche 'the living fire', the burning, invisible harmony which incessantly unites creation and destruction in the world as a work of art that produces itself.

> Thus the eternally living fire plays, like the child and the artist, thus it builds and destroys, in all innocence . . . and this play is the Aion playing with itself.[51]

The play of the world in Nietzsche is cosmological. It belongs to *Phusis*. Its attributes of 'eternity' and 'innocence' signify that it is not subject to a 'moral', that is, anthropocentric teleology.

However, although devoid of teleology, the drive of play is commanded and orientated by a force or a complex of forces which is essentially extra-linguistic. Is there room for such a force, or for force in general in Derrida?

'Force itself is never present; it is only a play of differences and quantities',[52] he writes. Certainly force is not a substance, a quality indefinitely overshadowed. Can it for all that, as Hegel's thinking of understanding wrongly believes, be integrally reduced to its phenomenal effects? On one occasion Derrida has indeed rightly emphasized and regretted the lack of any thought of force in Husserlian phenomenology: 'One would seek in vain a concept in phenomenology which would allow one to think intensity or force.'[53] And above he had even excellently affirmed: 'Force is the other of language without which language would not be what it is.' (!) This critique–of Nietzschean inspiration–could moreover also be applied *mutatis mutandis* to Heidegger, who reduces *phusis* to *aletheia*, to an un-concealment, without inquiring concerning the force necessary to operate the opening and *keep* the 'clearing' open. Despite this penetrating insight, the Derridean analysis of force nevertheless dismisses at once any secret belonging to force, annuls and expressly rejects the possibility of an enveloped, concealed 'physical' density, of a retreat or a 'crypt' *within* force.

'Force is not darkness, and it is not hidden under a form for which it would serve as substance, matter or crypt.'[54] Incontestably. Yet does the critique of force as substance in the metaphysical sense or even as 'subsisting entity' entail the refusal of envelopment, of invisibility, and especially of the *reserve* proper to every force? A force which would only have the series of its effects at its disposal, which would have no 'surplus' with respect to what it manifests in exerting itself, would be dead in advance, would be exhausted. There is no force without some accumulation or potential of force, without an élan and a thrust–features manifested not directly, but indirectly by the said 'effects', which do not 'effect' a void. Force always does only that of which it is capable; but its effectiveness and its power belong to the order of the possible, not that of an incessant and groundless actualization.

The idea of an unfathomable, non-founding, non-fundamental depth, the idea of an elemental resource of the world, of an active latency which would be neither 'matter' nor 'nature', nor even 'flesh', of a sustaining basement which would not be an absolute base, the idea of a base [*assise*] freely springing forth which, however, would be neither 'origin' nor 'cause' of historical figures, in short, the Greek concept of *physis* and the Heideggerian concept of 'earth'–that 'ungraspable flow' which closes in on itself again, but which supports us, gives us direction at first, high and low, full and penetrating–this concept seems to be foreign to Derridean thinking. An Apollinian thinking if there is such a thing, inscribed upon the forgetting of its anchor [*ancre*], upon the forgetting of the black ink [*encre*] of its graphic.

No alien force, no force of phusis, of earth, of body or of *Stimmung* drives or animates the play of writing. Yet this play is not 'without why'. What sets the chain of signifiers in motion does not possess any 'cosmic' or 'phusical' character. On no account is it a play of the world. It is solely the 'logic of the supplement', namely an indefinite process of substitutions or permutations. ('I define writing as the impossibility of a chain arresting itself on a signified that would not relaunch it, so as to have already put itself in the position of the signifying substitution.')[55] The word 'signifier' finds itself put in question, for it finds itself deprived of its logical opposite. The movement of signifiers is incessantly cast and recast only by the absence of a transcendental signified that could halt the play. The absent signified, or the impossible and mythical full presence, in its constant escaping and vertiginous slipping away, is the fictive *primum movens* of the chain. The *unlimited* play signifies that there is neither presence nor absence which *would hold* and precede the play. Neither within nor without, since there is no 'outside the play'. (Is a kind of play from which one cannot exit still play? How did 'we' enter it?) Does not its unlimited nature impart to play an unreal character, a phantasmatic one that cannot be localized? Play slides on the spot in a non-place without borders or density. 'There is no maintaining, and no depth to, this bottomless chessboard on which being is put into play.'[56] The unlimited nature of play frees a space-time without base [*assise*] or ballast, necessarily levelled-out and one-dimensional in its multilateral character, an extra-flat landscape. How can the unlimited transcendental play be the opposite of an empirical play which, if we believe Huizinga (*Homo ludens*, p. 29), is always by essence strictly limited in time and in space?

How, in this absolute ludism, are we to conceive of a site, a situation, a place? The brilliant definition of *place* given by *Schibboleth* is strictly relational, a 'relation to', a configuration produced by code and by convention: a place *without earth*.

> By place, I understand equally the *relation to* [my emphasis] a border, the country, the house, the threshold, as well as every site, every situation in general, in terms of which on a practical, pragmatic level contracts are made between alliances, codes and conventions are established which give meaning to the *insignificant* [my emphasis], institute passwords, bind language to what exceeds it, make language into a moment of gesture and step, secondarise it or 'reject' it so as to find it again.[57]

The place, if it is not a said place, would therefore be insignificant as such. But how would we move towards a meaning if it were not sketched in advance in the things themselves? Everything would be arbitrary, convention.

Certainly the text of codes and alliances, of passwords, can 'make a world', that is, institute a microcosm, a local system or a play of references signifying itself. But how is this play *attached* to an earth? *Where* does this world maintain itself? Does it provide its own 'dimension'?

The text itself is not a place, is not an earth. We do not walk on texts. We are not borne by them. The paths and routes are planted upon an earth, shaped by it as much as by human labour, an earth without which places would be as abstract as points on a geographical map. A place lives according to *phusis* (knows the seasons, the climates and the skies), and thrives as historial . . . A text can neither live nor body forth (*leben* and *leiben*), nor even be, that is, temporalize *itself*.

Is not the 'play of the world' reduced to a purely formal worldhood, to an abstract network of relations? As Heidegger wrote in *Sein und Zeit*, one can certainly formally grasp the complex of references constituting worldhood as significance (*Bedeutsamkeit*) in terms of a system of relations (*Relationssystem*). 'But one must note that such formalisations level off the phenomena to the point where their proper phenomenal content is lost.'[58]

A world which would be constituted only by references would no longer have a *place* to be. The 'inscription' of world in a place is not a graphic and linguistic relation, but a physical insertion. As such it cannot be formalized, always partly concealed in the *Lethe* of earth which makes it possible. What is a world without earth, without base [*assise*], without hidden roots, absolutely incapable of becoming unconcealed? Less than a *no-man's-land*, as much as a geometric space or a territory arbitrarily charted on paper: merely a formal system, a *generalized graphic*.

The dissemination or seminal dispersion that propels and diffuses the signifier, engaging the movement of *spectral errancy of words*, is not engendered by an exterior force, by an authority anterior or ulterior, superior or inferior to the world of signifiers, but by the sole *logic of supplementarity*. We are dealing with a pure Apollinianism haunted by its missing foundation which it goes without. The supplement is called 'overabundant' not because it is 'superfluous', but on the contrary because it is luxuriant, proliferating to try in vain to fill an unfillable loss, to plug the void of the absent origin. By way of a pseudo-filling the supplement replaces the irreplaceable absence of originary presence. The word is the curate of nothing. The terms exhaust themselves and are relentlessly reborn, untiringly tire, for this play: to substitute for what they cannot make appear, full presence, substance, the subject, the centre, being. Play in Derrida is the index of the generalized transcendental illusion, the index of the absence of any truth, metaphysical or not. The index of an immense disillusion, or of a disgust or rage, or an unbearable irritation. It is the critical point at which patience turns to impatience:

–There is no *aletheia*, only a wink of the hymen.[59]
–It's in the cursed name of truth that we have become lost, in its name
alone, not for truth itself, if there were any, but for the desire for truth
(. . .) without getting a single step closer to any truth, whatever it
might be.[60]
–An apocalypse . . . without truth.[61]

From the beginning Nietzsche has been marked out as a transgression
outside the 'house of being', suspected of being a captive of metaphysics.
This exit would be what will later be called a 'beyond being', which is already
a beyond the text! This transgression which 'burns' the text *will be* (it is in the
future) dance, festival, forgetting, erasure of play. For it is said with respect
to the Overman: 'He burns his text and erases the traces of his steps (. . .)
He will dance, outside the house, this "active forgetting" and this cruel feast
. . . '[62] It is again under the sign and under the invocation of Nietzsche that
not one, but several breakaways beyond or on this side of, *outside* the closure
of play are announced. This happens prudently, by way of small, successive
touches, in the most recent writings. Not all these breakaways are inspired by
Nietzsche. Some come from Heidegger himself: the unfathomable character
of the *gift* [*don*], of every gift, of every sending, even 'empirical'; or from
Levinas or Blanchot: an elementary gesture of speech coming from the other,
the 'come' ['viens'], would be older than being. Would the imperative/
affirmative 'come' addressed to me by the other and especially by the other
woman be anterior or exterior to the opening of being and to the space of
meaning? The 'come' in its absolute singularity, double as well: from you to
me or from me to you, 'calls beyond being',[63] or 'beyond good and evil',[64]
and from an unimaginable anteriority calls starting from a *tone*, in a *tone*, that
is, a *Stimmung* which on its own *makes* the call, *makes sense*. 'The difference is
tonal.'[65] The tonal difference would be older than the question of being.
Certainly. It comes from *phusis* of which every *Stimmung* is the repercussion.[66]
    Yet several of these breakaways are Nietzschean: the *affect* ('beyond
calculation') and the laugh,[67] the question *who*,[68] the great *yes*.[69] Play cannot
stop. In itself it is *irresponsible*. Yet is there really a play in itself? Does not
every referential structure inevitably include at least one reference to a
Dasein in the first place, that is, to a transcendence? Always, somewhere,
someone may respond in person: yes, that is destined for me. Otherwise the
movement of references of references would be a circle of circles turning
about itself, or else the uncertain expansion of a uniform dispersion, a
metaphysical absolute or a bad infinity. Derrida has not always believed in
the necessity of this *pre-ethical responsibility*, in the necessity of a *yes*; or has
not always said so. 'The discourse on being supposes the responsibility of the
yes: yes, what is said is said, I respond or there is a response to the
interpellation of being, etc.'[70]

So be it, but what yes is this? Is it the yes of a dialogue (the yes, says Derrida, can only call to another), or is it as in Nietzsche the pure yes, the cosmic, Panic yes, the self-affirmation of the world, the unlimited *Yeah and Amen*? The yes, says Derrida, necessarily comes back to itself, refers back to itself: 'a reference of itself to itself which at the same time *never leaves itself and never happens to arrive.*'[71] Here we have finally left the play of references, the initial position of a 'structure of generalised reference'.[72] But this yes, again ambiguous, congeals, becomes immobilized, surprised by its audacity, as if it were afraid to recognize . . . *its force.*

It, however, is the fire ever reborn from its ashes, the gift [*don*] that expends and maintains itself, tearing from us the ecstatic yes. It is the rhythm or pulsation of *phusis* that anticipates and calls every word spoken, carries away and exceeds all language, like the murmur of the beaches, the rustling of the forests and the soul of the wind, and like the song of the earth.

NOTES

1 Expression cited without quotation marks, which Derrida adopts as his own. *Marges de la Philosophie* (Paris: Minuit, 1972), p. III; trans. Alan Bass, *Margins of Philosophy* (Chicago: University of Chicago Press, 1982), p. xii. [*Margins*].

2 *Eperons: les styles de Nietzsche* (Paris: Flammarion, 1978), p. 28; trans. Barbara Harlow, *Spurs: Nietzsche's Styles* (Chicago: University of Chicago Press, 1979), p. 37.

3 *De la grammatologie* (Paris: Minuit, 1967), pp. 31–2; trans. Gayatri Spivak, *Of Grammatology* (Baltimore: Johns Hopkins University Press, 1976), p. 19. [*OG*].

4 Ibid.

5 Ibid., p. 206; trans., p. 143.

6 *L'oreille de l'autre* (Montreal: VLB, 1982), p. 65; trans. Peggy Kamuf, *The Ear of the Other* (New York: Schocken, 1985), p. 46.

7 *OG* pp. 32–3; trans., p. 19.

8 Trans. Donald Breazeale in *Philosophy and Truth* (Atlantic Highlands, NJ: Humanities, 1979), p. 83.

9 Ibid., p. 86. I emphasize *forgetting*.

10 Ibid., p. 85.

11 *Kritische Studienausgabe* (*KSA*), Bd. 7, p. 361.

12 I emphasize *gaze*.

13 *The Birth of Tragedy* (1872), trans. W. Kaufmann (New York: Vintage, 1966), p. 55.

14 *Beyond Good and Evil* (1886), trans. W. Kaufmann (New York: vintage, 1966), section 28.

15 *KSA*, Bd. 7, p. 361.

16 Ibid., pp. 360–9.

17 *OG*, p. 16; trans., p. 7.

18 *Margins*, p. 11; trans., p. 11.

19 *Ecce Homo* (1988), trans. W. Kaufmann (New York: Vintage, 1968), 'Why I write such good books', section 4.
20 *Nachlass*, Kröners Taschenausgabe, I, p. 191.
21 Ibid., p. 188.
22 Ibid., p. 190–1.
23 *KSA*, Bd. 13, p. 296.
24 *Nachlass*, op. cit., p. 191.
25 *Margins*, 'Tympan', p. VII; trans., p. xv.
26 *La dissémination* (Paris: Seuil, 1972), p. 12; trans. Barbara Johnson (Chicago: University of Chicago Press, 1979), p. 6. [*Diss*].
27 *Margins*, 'Tympan', p. VII; trans., p. xv.
28 *Margins*, p. 392; trans., p. 329.
29 Ibid.
30 *Diss.*, p. 144; trans., p. 126.
31 Ibid.
32 *Diss.*, p. 145; trans., p. 127.
33 Ibid.
34 Ibid.
35 'Chora', in *Poikilia: études offertes à Jean-Pierre Vernant* (Paris: EHESS, 1987), p. 292.
36 Note, *Margins*, p. XV.
37 *Ecarts* (Paris: Fayard, 1973), p. 311.
38 *OG*, p. 73; trans., p. 50.
39 *Margins*, p. 7; trans., p. 7.
40 Ibid., p. 11; trans., p. 11.
41 *OG*, p. 73; trans., p. 50.
42 Ibid.
43 *Margins*, p. 23; trans., p. 22.
44 *OG*, p. 73; trans., p. 50.
45 *The Gay Science* (1882), trans. W. Kaufmann (New York: Vintage, 1974), 'Songs of Prince Vogelfrei'.
46 *Der Satz vom Grund* (Pfullingen: Neske, 1986), p. 188.
47 *OG*, p. 73, n. 1; trans., p. 50, n. 14.
48 *Diss.*, p. 406; trans., p. 365.
49 *The Will to Power* (1883–8), trans. W. Kaufmann and R. Hollingdale (New York: Vintage, 1968), section 797.
50 *KSA*, Bd. 1, p. 833.
51 Ibid.
52 *Margins*, p. 18; trans., p. 17.
53 *L'écriture et la différence* (Paris: Seuil, 1967), p. 46; trans. Alan Bass, *Writing and Difference* (Chicago: University of Chicago Press, 1978), p. 27.
54 Ibid., p. 45; trans., p. 28.
55 *Positions* (Paris: Minuit, 1972), pp. 109–10; trans. Alan Bass (London: Athlone, 1972), p. 82.
56 *Margins*, p. 23; trans., p. 22.

57 *Schibboleth: pour Paul Celan* (Paris: Galilée, 1986), p. 54.
58 *Being and Time* (1927), trans. J. Macquarrie and E. Robinson (Oxford: Blackwell, 1967), pp. 121–2.
59 *Diss.*, p. 293 trans., p. 261.
60 *La carte postale de Socrate à Freud et au-delà* (Paris: Aubier-Flammarion, 1980), pp. 91–2.
61 *D'un ton apocalyptique adopté naguère en philosophie* (Paris: Galilée, 1983), p. 95. [*D'un ton*].
62 *Margins*, p. 163; trans., p. 136.
63 *D'un ton*, p. 94.
64 Ibid., p. 95.
65 Ibid., p. 93.
66 As Heidegger indicates in *Vom Wesen des Grundes*, p. 52, n. 55, in: *Wegmarken*, 2. Auflage, p. 154.
67 *Ulysse gramophone* (Paris: Galilée, 1987), p. 51.
68 *D'un ton*, p. 77.
69 *Ulysse*, pp. 108–9.
70 Ibid., p. 132.
71 Ibid., p. 133.
72 *Margins*, p. 25; trans., p. 25.

Translated by Will McNeill

4

John Llewelyn

Responsibility with Indecidability[1]

> There is even a more radical responsibility before questions, on the subject of ethics for example, that are not intrinsically ethical. (Jacques Derrida, *Altérités*)

The topics–or utopics–of responsibility and undecidability have been prominent in Derrida's writings from the beginning. Perhaps it is because the second of them is treated more explicitly than the other in his earlier publications, for instance in his Introduction to Husserl's 'The Origin of Geometry', that in his more recent ones express attention is given increasingly to the first, though Husserl's obsession by 'radical responsibility' is also already treated at some length in the Introduction (HO 38(52)).[2] Derrida is no less aware than are some of his critical readers that undecidability is *prima facie* incompatible with responsibility. The one seems to exclude the other. How can we respond responsibly to a question unless there is a criterion, rule or law by reference to which the validity of the answer can be judged? Surely, we cannot. How can a response to a command be responsible and taken seriously unless it is guided by a determinate criterion, principle or law? Surely, it cannot, unless it is in this sense critical, as defined by *krinò*, to divide and decide.

I

Despite what some of his readers have too quickly concluded, Derrida is not (in principle?) against (the) law:

I see well the risk there is, I wouldn't say in going beyond law, which I believe to be impossible . . . but in subordinating law. What I am saying here is not said against law in the ethical sense of the term. (A 72)

Nonetheless, wherever we find him using-or-mentioning principles we also find him busy demonstrating that what is allegedly a first principle is never really first. This is the revised version of Husserl's 'principle of all principles'. This is the law of all law.

'Necessarily', 'law', 'never', 'all'? By what right, it must be asked, does Derrida use these expressions? Is he not entitled to use them only if they are used in inverted commas–mentioned, not used, or, if used, used with a trepidation to mark which inverted commas, 'scare quotes', should also be used? At the very least, should he not admit that inverted commas are there invisibly? But, will not his response be, where is 'there'? Alongside a token of the word? That cannot suffice. Because Derrida's general practice is being called into question, because what is being challenged is what he is meaning to say when he lays down the law about the law of the law, our concern must be with the word as type. Only thus can what is being challenged be what he says or what he means to say. His words and what he says with them cannot be unrepeatable. So the 'there' is wherever he or anyone else says what he means to say, in the space of statements, propositions or thoughts.

What Derrida means to say is that, although someone can mean what he says and say what he means, and although we can understand him when he does so, his doing so and our understanding him are possible only by the grace of the repeatability of marks or sounds in circumstances which we cannot predict. Such successful communication occurs, as it does more often than not, because we have acquired a mastery of words. However, that mastery is for any given speaker or community of speakers counterpoised against and sometimes unbalanced by a mastery that words have over us. The most familiar experience of this shortfall in our power over words is the so-called unintended pun, the pun we discover we have made after we have uttered it. Derrida, following Freud, wonders whether such puns are as unintended as they seem. He also observes that the punster is someone who turns the lucky find into an opportunity to enjoy and enjoy showing off a particular linguistic gift. Hence, if that is what it is to pun, there are no puns in *Glas*. If that is what it is to 'make' a pun, there are no puns in *Glas* since *Glas* is an analysis of the formation and deformation rules of puns and other suchlike displays of verbal wit. Note the conditionality of this statement made by Derrida in *Glassary* (17–18).[3] It is designed to open the question of the relationship of the making of a statement to the making of a pun, or, more precisely–since one can be making a statement in making a pun and vice versa–it is designed to test that assumption that the pun is sheer free play with no other motivating force than the pleasure of exhibiting one's verbal address or *Geschicklichkeit*, as we may provisionally say.

However, even after all of Freud's labours to demonstrate that the mechanisms of what we call abnormal behaviour are operative in what we call normal everyday life, it still has to be asked how an analysis of puns and other tricks with words can tell us something general about language, its use and its users. If playing with words is ploying with words, we can see through the joke once we have tracked the deception to its source. Take the one about the pub-sign painter who made a mess of a job by putting commas between Fox and and and and and Goose. To turn this apparent gibberish into good sense all we need do is insert some inverted commas. The addition of inverted commas also straightens out the sense of the piece of advice we are being given when we are told 'Wenn Sie brauchen gebrauchen, müssen Sie brauchen mit zu gebrauchen, sonst brauchen Sie brauchen überhaupt nicht zu gebrauchen'. As Hegel asks the defender of sense-certainty, we just need to ask our adviser to write it down employing the conventional signs to distinguish the mention of an expression from its use or at least to indicate this distinction by varying the tone of his voice or by raising his fingers, as is sometimes done when a speaker wants his audience to remark the quotation-marks that he has in his script. These examples are made-up. How can our views of natural language functioning as it does in ordinary everyday life be upset by a set-up? Or by a send-up, a carrécature, of the Le Carré style of spy story like Tom Stoppard's where

> In the beginning the idea was that if they thought Purvis was their man, they would assume that the information we gave Purvis to give them would be the information designed to mislead, so they would take that into account and thus, if we told Purvis to tell them we were going to do something, they would draw the conclusion that we were not going to do it, but as we were on to that, we naturally were giving Purvis genuine information to give them, knowing they would be drawing the wrong conclusions from it . . . ?[4]

Can these double takes and double binds be resolved? One might think that precisely because the examples we have given are fictions nothing could be easier. All we have to do is ask the author to work out from the *dénouement* of his story what the characters in it decided as a matter of empirical or literary fact. But this does not show that the author or his story can provide us with a decision procedure by which undecidability can be avoided. It shows only that decisions can be made that leave an undecidability in its unlocatable place. Decisions can be made by tossing coins, but not all the coins in the vaults of the Royal Mint will resolve a double bind.

II

Other ways of deciding some classes of apparent undecidability have been proposed. One such proposal is Russell's theory of types–a 'theory', it should be noted in passing, which is no less a prescription for practice. Now many of Derrida's examples of undecidables appear to be of the sort for which Russell's theory would offer the most appropriate solution. Like the semantic paradoxes generated by 'This sentence is false' and '"Heterological" is heterological', they involve self-reference and the dyad mention-use. To avoid the paradoxes to which sentences like these give rise, all it seems necessary to do is decide to prohibit self-reference by ordering classes and propositional functions hierarchically according to the arguments they can take and by asserting that no propositional function can meaningfully take itself as argument. Hence both the statement that a class is a member of itself and the statement that a class is not a member of itself will be neither true nor false, but meaningless. However, as F. P. Ramsey observes, although the theory of types thus formulated may serve to protect a logical or mathematical system from the paradox of the class of all classes which are not members of themselves, this is so only because in the absence of such protection the contradiction would occur inside the system and so would show that there is something wrong with it.[5] On the other hand, of the paradoxes which are not as he sees them internal to a mathematical or logical system, since they invoke the empirical notions of language or symbolism or thought, we are not at liberty to say that they can be prevented by noting that a propositional function cannot significantly take itself as argument; for the paradox may arise because there is something wrong with our beliefs about these empirical notions.

Ramsey is perhaps too sanguine in his belief that a mathematical and formal system can be protected in this way. Does the idea of such a system make sense in isolation away from the non-formal language in terms of which it is set up and understood? If not, it may be vulnerable to the paradoxes that crop up in that non-formal language, the so-called semantic paradoxes. Whichever of the two kinds of paradoxes we have in mind, the theory of types, at least in the informal formulation Ramsey gives it, succumbs to semantic paradoxicality. For if the assertion of the theory of types itself refers to all assertions, it refers to itself. If a qualifying clause is embedded in it purporting to exclude itself from the range of its reference, it refers to itself in excluding itself from its range of reference; it includes itself in excluding itself.

Ramsey is not sanguine enough, however, in his belief that non-formal discourse cannot be protected from paradoxes simply by pointing out that a proposition or propositional function cannot significantly take itself as argument. We can agree with this denial and go on to assert positively that propositions outside formal logical and mathematical systems can refer to themselves while retaining significance, and this significance is not restricted merely to the meanings of the words in the sentence or sentences in which they are affirmed. An example of this maybe is the quotation from Francis Ponge analysed by Derrida in 'Invention de l'autre':

> Par le mot *par* commence donc ce texte
> Dont la première ligne dit la vérité,
> Mais ce tain sous l'une et l'autre
> Peut-il être toléré?

> With the word *with* then begins this text
> Of which the first line tells the truth,
> But this foil beneath the one and the other
> Can it be tolerated?

This is a text that refers to itself. Since 'text' is what Ramsey calls a semantic term, any paradox to which this self-reference may give rise will not be a paradox of the kind peculiar to a mathematical or logical calculus. That this is so is confirmed by Derrida's statement in the Introduction to *Parages* that the undecidables analysed in the pieces collected under that title and elsewhere are not of the kind that may be anticipated in a calculus (P 15). This statement taken in isolation echoes Ramsey's optimism over our ability to separate mathematical and logical systems off from non-formal discourse and any paradoxes that may arise there. Such optimism about this separability assumes a greater degree of optimism than we are perhaps entitled to about our ability to distinguish the analytic from the synthetic. However, earlier in his Introduction to *Parages* Derrida has agreed that there is at least an indirect and analogical relation between the paradoxes of set theory and the paradoxes of which he treats (P 12), and that he is alert to the problems posed by forms of optimism analogous to Ramsey's is already made plain by his comments in his Introduction to *The Origin of Geometry* on Husserl's handling of the distinction between what is intra-mathematical and what is not (HO 38ff. (52ff.)).

Are the paradoxes of which Derrida treats to be included in the set which Ramsey calls semantic? Is the par-adox Derrida cites from Ponge and re-cited above, if we may take that as an example? That at least an analogical relationship between them can be expected is suggested by the fact already mentioned that Ponge's and Derrida's text makes use of the semantic notion of text. This expectation is strengthened by the further fact that this text talks about truth. Semantic paradoxicality is an undecidability as to which, if either, of the values True and False, Yes and No, should be ascribed to a given statement. But of particular interest in the Ponge case is that instead of an undecidability as to the truth-value of a given statement there is an undecidability as to what act is being performed in making the statement in question. The second line claims that what the first line says, namely that this text begins with the word 'with', is true. What makes it true, however, is not some independent state of affairs constated by this statement. What makes the statement true is the making of the statement itself. Rather as of 'I am making a statement' or *cogito ergo sum* we may ask whether it is constative or performative and find it not at all easy to decide, so with 'With the word *with* then begins this text'. Derrida says that it is both performative and constative. It is performative in the sense that it produces, institutes or invents the state of affairs, namely a text's beginning with the word 'with'. On the other hand, this practical producing is performed at one and the same stroke or in one and the same breath as the theoretical constatement. Ponge's lines, constructed in strict conformity with the conventions of grammar and syntax, deconstruct two contrasts made by some proponents of the theory of speech acts, the contrast between constative and performative speech acts and the contrast between use and mention. We cannot decide whether Ponge's text is performative as opposed to constative, and this is because we cannot decide for every word in it whether it is mentioned or used. Our endeavours to decide this are foiled by the tin or silver retina backing of the looking glass in which the first 'with' in the sentence looked at as performatively producing a state of affairs is reflected in the same sentence looked at as constating that state of affairs, and thus becomes second because there will be no sentence or text produced in which it can be truly reported that it begins with the word 'with' until this report is made.

The point here is not that constative statements are *made* and are for that reason performative. Whatever may be the case with other proponents of the theory of so-called speech acts, the deeds done with words that primarily interest John Austin are not necessarily acts of speech or writing as such in the way that any employment of words is the performance of an act, a locutionary act, whether this be merely the utterance of phonemes (a 'phonetic' act), the utterance of phonemes belonging to and as belonging to a vocabulary, according to grammatical conventions, with a certain tone of voice, etc. (a 'phatic' act), or also the performance of a phatic act in which the constituents are given sense and reference (a 'rhetic' act). He introduces the word 'performative' because although the word 'operative' as used by lawyers covers what he has in mind, they use it in other senses as well. A performative utterance as understood at least in Austin's consideration of the subject early on in *How to Do Things with Words* is one that is 'operative' in the sense appropriate to that part of a legal instrument which, unlike its preamble, effects a transaction, brings about a conveyance or a bequest or, more ceremonially, a marriage, a baptism or the opening of a new town hall, by using certain forms of words in certain appropriate circumstances. This is part, but only part, of the explanation for Derrida's fondness for the word *effet*, as in the title of the series in which some of his own writings appear, *La philosophie en effet*. From those writings, for instance those collected in that series under the titles *Psyché: inventions de l'autre* and *Parages*, it is plain that Derrida does not limit the label 'performative' to utterance that are operative in the legal or quasi-legal sense for which Austin at first reserves the word. As with *effet* in the title of the series, 'performative' gets used not just for a putative kind of utterance, but also for a style of philosophizing, a practice which calls for analytic labour, experiments on given texts that test their mettle in a fashion not utterly remote from what goes on in a laboratory where apparatus is set up and experiments are performed. Derrida does not agree with Heidegger that in doing science you cannot as such be doing any philosophical thinking, a view Derrida challenges on the grounds that it depends on notions of science and thinking that fail to recognize that the constitutive laws of both of these are derivatives of deconstitutive laws whose workings are displayed by the science of graphematics, which is a science of the impossible conditions of the possible. Among the findings with which Derrida's performative philosophizing with a *hama* comes up (see below) is that performative and constative utterances, as some speech-act theoreticians purport to define them, do not constitute two distinguishable classes. This is what Austin himself eventually comes to suspect, but his reasons for doing so are different from Derrida's reasons for questioning whether the distinction can be maintained.

Austin's *Kehre*, assuming that it is not just a pedagogical device, comes about after the failure of a dogged attempt to discover either a semantic or a simple or complex grammatical or verbal criterion that would mark off performative from constative utterances. The semantic test would demarcate the performative from the constative on the grounds that utterances of the latter but not of the former kind are true or false. This test does not work, he says, because on the one hand questions of fact have to be answered before we can be in a position to appraise the fairness, validity, etc. of advice, warnings, arguments and other utterances we would not be inclined to call constative. This is a bad argument because there being questions of truth and falsity to be answered before we can properly appraise a piece of advice, warning or an argument does not imply that the advice, warning or argument can, without raising eyebrows, be called true or false–even if, as a matter of fact, since advice (*avis*) can be information or an observation offered as counsel, there may be nothing odd in saying at least of a piece of advice that it is true or false. However, this last fact, if it is one, supports Austin's main point. And this is supported by the second part of his argument, a mirror image of the first, that the terms of appraisal we naturally use of utterances we would not be inclined to regard as constative, terms like 'good', 'bad', 'valid', 'fair', are terms we quite naturally use of utterances we would regard as typically constative or descriptive. 'France is hexagonal' is a good, bad or rough description, rather than true or false. (Still, 'France is roughly hexagonal' is true, isn't it?)

Of the various grammatical or verbal hypotheses Austin puts through the hoops, the most promising to his mind is the proposal that a performative utterance either is or is expressible in the form 'I x that . . . ', 'I x to . . . ' or 'I x', where x is a grammatically present indicative active verb, and where to make an utterance of one of these forms in certain circumstances (for example, I own a watch when I say 'I bequeath my watch . . . ', I am the Lady Mayoress or some such authorized personage when I say 'I declare this building open') is thereby to x. Because 'I state . . . ' passes this test, Austin comes round to offering it not as a way of demarcating performatives from constatives, but as a way of making explicit the illocutionary force of an utterance, that is, the act that is performed in making it. We must therefore give up the idea of a dichotomy of performative and constative utterances each with sufficient or sufficient and necessary defining conditions. We must turn instead to the task of drawing up a genealogy of speech acts related only by family resemblances allowing one kind of speech act to overlap another. This overlap permits not only the same sentence to be employed on different occasions in what before his *Kehre* Austin distinguishes as performative and constative utterances (H 67). It would seem to permit this on one and the same occasion. '"I class" or perhaps "I hold" seems in a way one, in a way the other. Which is it, or is it both?' (H 68). 'With the word *with* begins then this text.' Which is it, or is it both? We can now see how different are the considerations leading Austin to admit that an utterance may be simultaneously constative and non-constative from those leading Derrida to affirm a simultaneity in his citation from Ponge. Austin's reasons have to do with the semantic property of open texture. Derrida's are such as to disrupt, as Einstein did, the very notion of simultaneity. The 'open texture' of the Ponge sentence, its sponginess, is such that the simultaneity, without being altogether abandoned, is holed by an altertaneity, by the different occasion marked by the 'then' and tol(le)d by Ponge's *donc*, which is not only chronological and campanological, but at the same time a logical 'therefore' related by more than a family resemblance to the *ergo* of Descartes and the *igitur* of Mallarmé and others. The combination of both illocutionary forces in one syllogism is more than the psyche can bear. The psyche—which is also a revolving cheval mirror such as might reflect the *Psyché* that in the verso running head of the collection of that name at the same time reflects the title of one of the essays it collects–is split. The 'at the same time' (*hama*) of the flip between the performative or constative citation and the constative or performative recitation is not the 'at the same time' of the classical formulation, criticized by Kant, of the principle of non-contradiction which permits that both *p* and not-*p* may be true provided that they are asserted of different respects and different times. The strange logic of the relation between the two faces of the mirror exceeds classical logic. Its non-Euclidean space-time is the space-time of the eyelid of the momentary ironic wink (*Augenblick, clin d'œil*) which, in blacking out the light of day, thereby effects a syncope in which the 'hereby' implicit in 'Par le mot *par* donc commence ce texte' vanishes into the otherwhere and otherwhen of a dislocated, allotemporally illocutive otherwise said.

III

There is something eccentric about the example of otherwise saying with which we have been occupied up until now. Surely (*ergo* unsurely, for, as Derrida remarks, 'surely' is a sure sign that one is unsure) the undecidability it exemplifies is overdetermined in comparison with the examples of undecidability that suffice in some of Derrida's other writings to demonstrate the dividedness of the moment? To shake our confidence in the self-containedness of an act of speech is it not enough to have our attention drawn to the necessary possibility of the whole and any part of what we say being said again, by someone else or by ourselves? Nothing is said unless it can be resaid. Its identity as something said consists in the possibility of its being said on a different occasion by the speaker or writer or someone else, for instance the reader of a note he/she wrote, who may be the same person as the author. This is a necessary feature of language. But is it the feature that Derrida has uppermost in his mind? If it is, it is what has been uppermost in the minds of all those philosophers before him who have distinguished universals or concepts from particulars falling under them and linguistic tokens from types. One of the aims of Derrida's philosophical or so-called non-philosophical text works against its own assumption that the repeatability implied in the notions of the universal, the concept, the type, the class, meaning and the notion is at least in principle delimitable, where by this is meant that a line can be drawn defining the logical or semantic space occupied by these notions, even if this definition may often have to be less strict than a specification of necessary and sufficient conditions. Derrida tries to show that delimitations have a tendency to become de-limitations. The question we are now asking is whether, in order to show this, he has to come up with paradoxes as mind-boggling as the one to which we have confined our attention so far, the one from Ponge. That paradox has us turning in a circle, it would seem, with no hope of breaking out, whereas for Derrida (*pace* Heidegger, *Being and Time*, p. 153) what is decisive is to break out of the circle: *Das entscheidende ist . . . , aus dem Zirkel heraus- . . . zukommen*–or, more exactly, what is decisive is to realize that the circle is inscribed in an ellipse. This sense of claustrophobic aporia is not diminished by the words of 'Limited Inc a b c . . . ', 'There would thus be two speech acts in a single utterance. How is this possible?' (G2 215), the tone of which words might seem to suggest that the occurrence of two simultaneous speech acts in one utterance is impossible, notwithstanding the suggestion that this is possible which appears to be made in the words cited above from Austin. Of course, tones of voice and appearances, like duck-rabbits, depend on how we hear or see what surrounds them, for the surroundings are also internal to the figure of which they are the ground. So when we pan out from the words we have cited from Austin and Derrida they may come to make on us the opposite impression to that which they made in close-up. Let us now take into account another aspect of the Ponge text.

The Ponge text is entitled 'Fable'. A fable, from *fari*, to speak, is a fabulation, a fabrication, a fiction, even a fib, a 'story': the Ponge paradox could turn out to be a liar paradox of sorts. So Ponge's fable, one might say, bears to statements of fact a relation similar to that in which stand the formal logical and mathematical systems we touched on earlier. Hence anyone who was worried by the paradox Derrida elicits from that text can stop being so worried. He/she need not feel, as Frege did on learning of Russell's paradox, that the entire world is crumbling around him/her. There are more things on earth than literary fictions, so, it would seem, those other things, like well-behaved school-children sitting up properly in the class where they belong, could be kept quite safe from the dizzying dilemmas contrived in literary artefacts. What would Derrida say about this sigh of relief?

The title of the Ponge piece, 'Fable', is but one of the many devices indicating a literary genre. In 'The Law of Genre' Derrida cites other ways in which this indication is made. 'A Novel' or 'A Play' on the cover or the title page serve the same purpose. So too does the line length or verse form in the case of a poem. The mark of a literary genre may be fairly complex, and especially in modern writing the genres may be more or less artfully mixed. After granting that this indicator of genre may not be explicitly before the mind of the author or the reader and may even be at variance with the genre as stated in or under the title or elsewhere, Derrida writes: 'If I am not mistaken in saying that such a trait is remarkable, that is, noticeable, in every aesthetic, poetic or literary corpus, then consider this paradox . . . ' (G7 185 and 212). If I am not mistaken, Derrida believes that he is not mistaken. A page earlier he says unreservedly: 'this re-mark . . . is absolutely necessary for and constitutive of what we call art, poetry or literature'. That is what interests him at this point. And all he says at this point about other kinds of text is that it is always possible for them to bear such a mark, whether they be oral texts, like a speech for the defence in a court of law, or written, like an editorial in a newspaper. Whereas the literary text is necessarily re-marked, other kinds of text are necessarily re-mark-*able*. Note therefore that there still seems to be a loophole through which we can evade the apparently paralyzing dilemma of 'Par le mot *par* . . . '. Derrida seems to be interested so far only in a special theory of undecidability, one concerned with literary texts. 'What interests me' at this stage, he stresses, is a paradox resulting from the fact that all literary texts carry a genre-marker. Note secondly, therefore, that whatever this paradox may turn out to be, it too may be avoidable if Derrida is mistaken in his belief, asserted here without argument, that what for simplicity's sake we are calling literary texts must have such markers. Must he not prove this if we are to be bound to accept his paradox? Whether or not he must is something we shall find out in finding out what this paradox may be.

The paradox is that at the very same moment that the mark of the genre of a literary text marks off that genre it marks itself off from the genre. Russell proposed that the paradox of the class of all classes not belonging to themselves should be avoided by a theory of types from which it follows that no class can belong to itself. Derrida's paradox of the genre-clause has to do not solely with class inclusion and class membership or participation, so the theory of types is of no avail to avoid it. The paradox of the genre-clause has to do with the distinctive feature marking the membership of a text in a genre, for example, the explicit proclamation 'A Novel', 'Fable' or *Un récit*, as on the cover and elsewhere of Maurice Blanchot's *La folie du jour*, or the less explicit traits which amount to declarations in which the text mentions itself, such as 'Hey presto, I am a poem'. This prosopopoeic mention is not poetic.

To anticipate the objection (to which we shall return) that the titular or subtitular announcement of the genre of a text does not even begin to look like a part of the text itself, consider just the features, for instance, the rhyming or rhythmic character of the lines or the tone of voice in which the lines are read, that vindicate the classification of the text as a poem but would usually be presumed to disqualify its classification as a piece of philosophic or scientific prose. These marks tell us 'This is a poem' and so, like an operative clause in a legal instrument, constitute the texts membership of that particular genre. However, because remarks like 'This is a poem' are not poetic, at one and the same time they exclude the text from its genre. The text both belongs and does not belong. The condition of its possibility is at the same time the condition of its impossibility.

But, it must be asked, is a mark or index of the genre of a text a part of the text itself? If it is not at least partly a part of it we shall be without a clue as to whether the text is to be taken as a literary product or as a piece of philosophical or scientific prose.

But, it must also be asked, what about 'I am prose', which seems to be a bit of unpoetic prose? And what about 'I am taxonomic' or 'This (this taxonomic text) is taxonomic'? Do not these belong to the genre of text they mention and do not the texts they mention belong entirely to themselves, without any disruptive residue? Not if we accept that these markers are makers, that is to say, operatively constitutive in their function, as signalled (operatively?) by their allowing themselves to incorporate a 'Hey presto', 'voilà' or 'hereby'.

But now it must be asked whether such recognizably operative markers do not belong fairly and squarely, *carrément*, within the class of the text whose class they define in the case where the text is operative. In that case do not both the constituting marker and the text constituted by it belong to the class of operative texts without not belonging to it? What casts doubt on this is the fact that for our classificatory purposes the marker which makes or constitutes the text a text of its kind is required at the same time to make a statement constating that kind. Hence the text's kind is deconstituted. Let us name this predicament the paradox of quasi-analysis.

The paradox of quasi-analysis is distantly related to the paradox of analysis provoked by the philosophy of G. E. Moore. According to the paradox of analysis an analysis of a statement is trivial if the sentence expressing the analysing statement means the same as the sentence expressing the statement analysed, and incorrect if it does not. The remoteness of the relationship of this paradox to the paradox of quasi-analysis is due to the fact that the latter excludes the possibility of a division down to self-contained logical elements and includes a pragmatic element, the illocutionary deed done in saying the words, which confers upon the paradox of quasi-analysis a kinship with another notion germane to the philsophy of G. E. Moore, the notion of pragmatic or, as Austin has since taught us to say, performative contradiction. If the paradox of quasi-analysis may be looked on as a hybrid of Moorish and Austinian lines of thought, it should not be overlooked that it also has a connection with the predicament that confronts Heidegger and Levinas among others: how to combine the prose of the lecture which talks about its topic with the poetry without which there would be no topic to be talked about and threatened. Where, if anywhere, do *poiesis*, *praxis* and *theoria* meet? That is one of the topics or utopias in plotting the geography of which Derrida discovers the paradox of quasi-analysis.

What are we to make of this paradox? Does not Derrida make too much of it? Would it not dissolve if he made less of the vagueness of the idea of telling, took this idea less literally? We can sex chickens by their distinctive features without those features literally telling us 'I am a male', so is it not only in a manner of speaking, a *façon de parler*, that the verse form, metre and rhymes tell us 'I am a poem', even if we can allow that the title or subtitular gloss 'Poem' may say this? Surely it is only the chicken sexers and the literary theorists who say something here, not the shape of the sexual organs or the length of the text's lines. The degree of relevance of this objection depends in part on whether it is legitimate to draw an analogy with non-literary classification according to gender in view of the fact that Derrida's analysis in 'The Law of Genre' begins with, even if it is not ultimately confined to, the question of classification according to literary genre. The relevance of this objection decreases dramatically if, as idealists of one stripe or another and non-idealists like Heidegger have in their different ways held, we cannot make sense of the notion of something's constituting the membership of a class and the notion of something's being of this or that gender independently of the notion of beings who are users of and used by language through which and through whom constitution itself is constituted–and deconstituted, Derrida would have us add. Assuming that Derrida, with this important supplement, shares this point of departure, as is implied, for example, by his remark 'the things themselves are marked in advance by the possibility of fiction' (G2 243), it makes little difference whether we say prosopopoeically that the verse form or rhyme says unpoetically 'I am a poem' or say prosaically, as in a lecture, that on the basis of the verse form or rhyme we say 'This is a poem'. In either case we are left with the problem how to understand the relationship between what is taken to make something a member of a class and our making about it the statement that it belongs to that class. That is to say, we are left with the paradox of quasi-analysis.

What difference does the paradox of quasi-analysis make as regards our purposes here? The Ponge paradox seemed to be an especially special and eccentric case in so far as it looked as though its apparently sheerly aporetic and negative outcome had no stultifying implications for our thinking about what is beyond the range of such artfully devised examples. Now, however, we have been given reason to believe that we have to say goodbye to the possibility of classification across the entire field of literature, to give it up as lost, *en faire son deuil*. As far as literature is concerned, all genre suffers from a congenital degenerative disease. We are listening to the death knell of classification in this field, the *glas* of the class of its classes. Its field is a field of burial. The only firm ground left to stand on can be that of its complementary class, the class of non-literary texts of which Derrida states at one point of 'The Law of Genre', it will be recalled, that it is not what at that point interests him.

What was it that at that point did not interest him? Whatever was to be opposed to the literary genre, for example, the mode *récit*, which Gérard Genette considers to be a category not of literature but of the anthropology of verbal expression. Derrida unravels and reravels Blanchot's '*récit*' *La folie du jour* with a view to questioning whether we or Genette understand what we mean by a mode and, more generally, what we are doing when we distinguish literary texts and their genres from other texts. For any text is haunted as much as any other by the possibility of its becoming literature–'The Bible as Literature', for example. It is not only such parts of the Bible as the Psalms and the Song of Solomon that are susceptible to being read as literature; so too are those parts that started off as factual genealogical records of the tribes of Israel, as factual in intent as, to give another example, the Anglo-Saxon Chronicle. Of course, what is at stake here is the very idea of example. If the class falls so does the case or example that falls under it. We now see why we had to be so cagey earlier on in our employment of this word 'example', and why Derrida refers so frequently to what is an example 'maybe', *peut-être*. *Peut-être* may be construed as Derrida's graft on to the *Seinkönnen* of *Being and Time*, the concept onto which, after writing that book, Heidegger himself grafts the concept *Vermögen*. The possibility denoted by Derrida's *peut-être* shares with Heidegger's *Seinkönnen* at least the negative characteristic of not being a potentiality whose actualization is the unfolding of a definable self-contained essence. But if it is not what expresses itself with the analytic necessity of a Leibnizian essence, neither is its realization the sheerly empirical contingency of a historical event that befalls something from outside. The possibility of this *peut-être* is the necessary contingency that the so-called normal, standard or paradigm case, for example, the statement of fact, may turn out to be abnormal, non-standard, parasitized, fictive or fake, and vice versa. *Peut-être*, intrinsically, the insider has it in him/her to be an outsider and the outsider to get outside his/her disreputable, pocket-picking, unself-contained self to be acknowledged as an honest citizen. Apropos: 'Purvis was acting, in effect, as a genuine Russian spy in order to maintain his usefulness as a bogus Russian spy.' 'Apropos: in what sense did Nixon pretend to be Nixon, President of the United States up to a certain date? Who will ever know this, in all rigour? He himself?' (G2 251).

Peut-être is one of the marks of the deconstructive genre, as too are 'almost', 'not quite' and 'up to a certain point'. It is the mark that commemorates and announces the deconstruction of deconstruction. So are we to put the flags at half-mast or hoist them to the top of the pole? We began by supposing that the cancer could be contained, because its victims seemed to be only eccentric fictions. Then we discovered that any fictions are vulnerable, any literature, if we agree with Derrida that every literary genre has a mark, however complex and unobvious it may be. Should we agree with this? I am inclined to think that we should, because not only is literature man- or woman-made; so too are literary theory, criticism and rhetoric which see to it that its subject matter gets classified, however much overlap there may in some cases have to be. Anyway, it is enough that a putatively non-literary text be capable of becoming literary. That is also enough to diminish our confidence in the sharpness of the distinction between the literary and the non-literary, and so to dampen our hope of stopping the degenerative rot.

IV

Sursum corda. The degeneration of classification is also its regeneration. When in the Pro-verb of *Glassary* Derrida calls what is going on in *Glas* analysis we can see this as a name for the renaming and reclassification to which the law of law gives rise. Searle is right to say, as Derrida says, that a distinction must be made between citation in which quotation-marks are used and whatever it is that Derrida means by the iteration which makes citation possible. But further distinctions must be made between such citation and citation in which the quotation-marks are mentioned or quoted. And still further distinctions must be made among the varieties of mention and use, and their subvarieties or, rather, grafts. Thus do our ears get finer. The tain of the mirror is corroded by iterability, by the remarkability of the mark. However, the mirror can be retained so as to reflect with greater power of resolution, that power thanks to which things are called by their names, and called to be renamed interminably. Iterability is not an it or a namable being. Beyond the opposition of being and non-being, and beyond the ontological difference, iterability defeats the inclination of the *es* of *es gibt Sein* and the *ça* of the unconscious to become reified. A quasi-transcendental rather than a transcendental condition, iterability is a condition not simply of the possibility of class as effect but also of its impossibility as a logically self-contained entity. For according to the generalized law of genre, every class is necessarily outside itself, declassified by the very condition of its identity, deconstructed by its own structure.

Nevertheless, to reiterate, deconstruction is an affirmative force, trans-structuration, *perestroika*, invention of the other, its own other included, as displayed in the history of its many pseudo-names: différance, supplement, *pharmakon*, *hymen*, restance, trace, archi-writing . . .

theography

(neither just title or subtitle nor text or subtext as opposed to it).

Iterability is another name for what theology calls God (Ps 561). Not 'the church's one foundation' and older than 'the old old story' of hymnography, not quite the creative spirit or the maker of the new, iterability's entitlement to be compared with the incomparable and uncompèrable God of negative theology is considered in 'Comment ne pas parler' (1986). This essay takes further the question raised in the Différance essay (1968) of the distance between graphematic alterity and the *totaliter aliter* of so-called negative onto-theology. It is also, in passing, a comment on the theory of placing, exemplification and classing which Austin outlines in 'How to Talk–some simple ways', though Derrida's essay (whose title could be translated perhaps as 'How not to talk–some not so simple ways' or 'How to undo things with-or-without ("*sans*") Words') does not mention Austin's piece or its author. Austin is more than mentioned in 'Signature Event Context'. Not every reader of this piece notices however that God gets more or less of a mention there. As 'Limited Inc a b c' points out, the title of the penultimate section of 'Sec' (what sort of a mention or use is this, and is it a different sort from *Sec?*) mentions or uses or abuses the title of Descartes' penultimate Meditation, before going on to a series of *Objections et réponses*. Descartes' title, 'On the Essence of Material Things; and once more of God, that He Exists', *De essentiâ rerum materialum; et iterum de Deo, quod existat*, is parodied as 'Parasites, Iter, Of Writing: That It Perhaps Does Not Exist', where the English translation of Derrida's parasitizing traduction of Descartes, *Les parasites. Iter, de l'écriture: qu'elle n'existe peut-être pas*, demolishes the pyramid of *essentiâ*, as the French already does, though the circumflex accent of its *être* re-erects the resting place which commemorates the loss of a disseminative letter and the death of the metaphysical being of matter and its sustaining God. It also loses the suggestion that writing and the God inscribed in it are perhaps feminine. On the other hand, it gains the hint of a promise or a threat that it may remain to be discovered that our path leads nowhere in particular, *partout et nulle part*, to no decidable site, and that the It of iteration is not an identifiable item and *idem* but paradoxically participates in the indefiniteness of the status of the definite article-cum-pronoun in what Derrida calls Jean-Luc Marion's 'magnificent title' *Dieu sans l'être* (Ps 540). Without being the God of 'negative' theology, without being the being of the God of onto-theology, the theographematic heir and ancestor of God, far from being a *Dieu sans lettre* is not just, as Bishop Berkeley and others say, the Author of the book of nature set for humanity to read, but is already Text inventing Him-Her-It-self and the other. God of the old, old story becomes Archi-Secretarial scriptance of a still older story, becomes without quite being and without quite becoming either a being or a non-being.

Despite the magnificence of the title of this book, in his earlier publication *L'idole et la distance* Marion does not allow sufficiently for the supplementary logic Derrida ascribes to the little (dis)connecting word *sans*. The 'negativity without negativity' (Ps 575) of the withoutness intended in Derrida's

Blanchotian employment of *sans* means that it is misleading to say, as Marion does, that the writing of différance 'contests' the ontological difference or tries to 'pass beyond' it (I 292, 293), hence commits itself dialectically to the ontological difference no less than does Levinas who, according to Marion, simply inverts the order of priority Heidegger gives to being over beings, a judgement that Levinas contests. This is in both cases to suppose that the first step is the only one each of them makes. It is to forget that in the case of both Levinas and Derrida the first step is first only pedagogically. It is not true here that the first step is the only step that counts, for when the second step has been taken it takes with it the firstness of the other. This is the nature of the negativity of the *pas*. The trace will have retraced the distance covered by the first step before it was ever made. Therefore perhaps both Levinas and Derrida are asking the question that Marion poses as follows: 'Would distance overstep the ontological difference and Being that figures metaphysically in it, hence also their idol, not in leaving it, but in remaining in it—as not remaining in it?' (I 294). This sounds very like the question Levinas asks at least in *Totality and Infinity*. And it is not difficult to hear this question being asked in a Derridian tone of voice so long as allowance is made for the paradoxicality of the class inclusion 'exemplified' earlier in this essay and quite felicitously captured, if that is not too strong a word, in Marion's ruptured (self-de-constructing?) phrase *y demeurant–comme n'y demeurant pas*.

Marion's second objection is that Derrida facilitates the passage to a différance beyond onto-theology by drawing 'an astonishing equivalence' between onto-theology, 'negative theology' and philosophy (I 293, 318–19). Marion aims to show that so-called negative theology, in particular that of the (according to some authorities pseudonymously named) Pseudo-Dionysus, can be rescued from this equation, thereby opening up room for a non-idolatrous because non-ontological God. He believes that this room is left by what he calls, with Kierkegaardian and Barthian overtones, Levinas's 'vertical' alterity, the infinite alterity of Autrui. Can we not now say that this room is left also by the 'horizontal' alterity of différance, in so far as we are entitled to rename it theographematics on the basis of the remark in 'Comment ne pas parler' (Ps 561) that the talking or 'parlance' (*langage*) has already begun without us, in us, before us, that it is what theology calls God and that we are and will have been obliged to speak?

In view of what is up to a certain point a Heideggerian element in the ancestry of this remark, one cannot avoid wondering whether Derrida would be able to imagine a dialogue arising from it involving himself analogous to the one that, in the last few pages of *De l'esprit*, he imagines Heidegger having with persons whom we may call, remembering again the above-mentioned historical objections and replies, diverse theologians. What would Derrida say to these theologians? This question is particularly relevant to the second of Marion's objections. A clue to what Derrida might say is provided by his comment that what he sees as Heidegger's attempt to save Trakl's conception of *Geist* from a Christian interpretation is prejudiced by an extremely narrow conception of Christianity (E 178). Does Derrida think this undermines or reinforces the theologians' right to say, as they do in his not entirely imaginary conversation, that Heidegger, with the help of his poets, is putting into words what they, diverse Christian, maybe Jewish and even Muslim theologians, have been trying to say all along? *De l'esprit* refuses to conclude. And its readers must make do with a long-range forecast of how the breezes of *ruah*, *pneuma* and *spiritus* eventually may blow. That forecast will have to recognize that Heidegger's later thinking follows two paths. It has no 'common root', or if it has it is one that is twofold. There are at least two Heidegger mark IIs. There is the one who says that *Geist*, of which he finally brings himself to write without the inverted commas that earlier protected him from it, is the 'common root' of *spiritus*, *pneuma* and (on second thoughts) *ruah* from which these subsequently spring. This is the Heidegger of the origin. Then there is the Heidegger of what is heterogeneous to the origin, heterogeneous perhaps both because it is at the origin and although it is at the origin (E 177). Derrida says that in his outlining of these two paths he is highlighting 'what, I imagine at least, can still tell us something about *our* steps, of a certain crossing of *our* paths. About an *us* who are maybe not given'. Would the theologians who in the *Zwiesprache* with Heidegger welcome his word *Zuspruch* as another name for God be equally welcoming to Derrida's theographematics? This depends on their belief as to how well Heidegger's word is translated by Derrida's word *provocation* and, no less, on how they translate the word 'translation'.

V

Provocation provokes us to return to the beginning and before. Before the question with which this text failed to begin. Before the question, to provocative address. In the *Grundbegriffe der Metaphysik* (1929–30) Heidegger thinks of *Zusprechen* still as true or false affirmation, opposing it to true or false denial, and opposing both to the prior possibility of the neither true nor false and of the both positive and also negative (§ 73). This possibility, he says, is what puts us on the way to understanding the essence of logic, not, as Aristotle and he himself in *Being and Time* had supposed, the true affirmative proposition. Does this put us on the way to understanding why Derrida begins his texts again and again by citing not just literary fictions, but mind-boggling paradoxical ones, like 'Par le mot *par . . .* '? Of the dozens of sting-rays Derrida nets, one of the most numbing is the behest of the angel of the Revelation whose logic is explored in 'D'un ton apocalyptique . . . ': 'Seal not the sayings of the prophecy of this book.' If the sayings are not sealed, that is, signed or endorsed, this saying is endorsed, and if it is, it isn't. We do not know what to do or say. Now being told something that tells us that we do not know what to do or to say could well have the perlocutionary effect that we reflect on fundamentals. That is to do something, and to do it is to shoulder a fundamental responsibility. This is a Socratic way of bringing out the tie between responsibility and undecidability. A semantic or pragmatic paradox that helps us see more particularly the Derridian way of conceiving this tie is the one unfolded from the title of his earlier-mentioned essay 'Comment ne pas parler'.

In addition to reminding us that there are several monstrous species of sting-ray, species to which they do not quite belong, the words 'Comment ne pas parler' take us further through the looking glass of language than do the words from Heidegger just paraphrased. They not only take us to the undecided alethic modes true-or-false, true-and-false, and the undecided assertive modes, affirmation-or-denial, affirmation-and-denial, that are modes of the powers (*Vermögen*) that are prior to and enabling conditions of the decided values truth, falsity, affirmation and denial ascribable to (con)statements. They bring to our attention that also on the scene is performance or production, whether we think of this in the way Austin comes to think of it in the later parts of *How to Do Things with Words*, as an illocutionary act of which constating is one kind, or in the way Derrida continues to do, as a non-constative act. Heidegger himself takes a step in this direction in 'The Nature of Language' (1957–8). Early in these lectures Heidegger wonders whether they should be entitled 'The Nature (?)–of Language?' in order to indicate that the nature of language and of nature and the language of 'nature' and of 'language' are being put into question. The experimentally inserted question-marks are removed, however, when it emerges that the question itself, the point of departure of *Being and Time*, is discovered to be a point of departure only in the *ordo inveniendi*. On the page on which Heidegger admits that this idea of adding question-marks was not such a good one after all, and that they should be crossed out, *gestrichen* (which is not quite the same as removed), he explains that this is because to think is to listen to language. We must let language avow its nature to us, *uns zusprechen*. This *Zusprechen* is the enabling condition of the *Zusprechen* of which Heidegger writes nearly thirty years earlier in the *Grundbegriffe der Metaphysik*. There it is affirmation as opposed to denial. Here it is affirmation presupposed by such assertive acts: unassertive affirmation that is the affirmation not of language users but of language itself. Heidegger speaks of this *Zuspruch* also as *Zusage*, promise.

Derrida says yes to this, up to a certain point. Hear hear, he says, *ouï ouï, oui oui*. Before I can ask 'Comment ne pas parler?' I am already engaged in language. *Langage* is *l'engage*. The words 'Comment ne pas parler', with the question-mark not inserted, mark my pre-predicative predicament of being already provoked by the quasi-transcendental double affirmation between any 'I' who says yes, for example Derrida or Nietzsche, and the quasi-transcendental absolute performative yes inscribed in it as *l'engage* is performed in *langage*. The say-so of my *dire oui* is predicated upon the hear-say of an unpredicative *ouï-dire*.

Why yes only up to a certain point? Perhaps because of the first path Derrida discerns *du côté de chez* Heidegger. And because of Heidegger's inclination to think that that first path and the second have a common source or *souche*. And because of the reliance Heidegger puts on reliance, *Verlässlichkeit*, in 'The Origin of the Work of Art' and other writings dating from the 1930s, of which Derrida writes in *La vérité en peinture*, *De l'esprit* and other pieces, anticipating some of the stories told in the Farias affair.[6] Also in *De l'esprit* however, as we saw, Derrida states that there is a crossing of Heidegger's two paths. Further, no one has been more insistent than he on the revolution that takes place in Heidegger's thinking between *Being and Time* and 'Time and Being' when attention moves not only from *Dasein* to *Sein*, but to *Ereignis, es gibt* and (the focus of our own attention now) *Zusage* and *Zuspruch*. It is not without significance that Derrida's partial endorsement of parts of what Heidegger writes about promise and engagement, shifting the force of this last word from what it was made to mean in France immediately after the Second World War, is given in paragraphs of the essay 'Nombre de oui' following some paragraphs on Eckhart's notion of *Gelāzenheit*. Heidegger's adaptation of this notion must be such as to let it be without (*sans?*) *Seinlassen* being any longer at its base. Heideggerian ontological responsibility must falter and give way, *il faut*, to responsibility otherwise said.

If Heidegger's paths cross each other, Derrida says, they also cross ours. The '*us* who are maybe not *given*' includes Derrida and Levinas. And their paths cross, as Levinas says at the end of the essay on Derrida entitled 'Tout autrement':

> The ridiculous ambition to 'improve on' a true philosopher is certainly not part of our aim. To cross him on his path is already a good thing and is probably exactly what meeting in philosophy means. In stressing the primordial importance of the questions Derrida puts we have wanted to express the pleasure given by an encounter at the heart of a chiasmus. (N 89)

And here is one way in which Derrida returns the compliment, without it being necessary to give Levinas's name:

Command or promise, this injunction engages (me) in a rigorously
asymmetrical fashion even before I have managed, myself, to say *I* and
to sign such a *provocation*, in order to reappropriate it and reconstitute
symmetry. That attenuates my responsibility not one whit. On the
contrary. There would be no responsibility without this *prevenience* of
the trace, and if autonomy were primary or absolute. Autonomy itself
would not be possible, nor respect for the law (the sole 'cause' of this
respect) in the strictly Kantian sense of these words. To escape this
responsibility, to deny it, to attempt to efface it by means of an absolute
retreat, I must countersign it again or already. When Jeremiah curses
the day he was born, he must once more or already *affirm*. (Ps 561–2).

Derrida and Levinas also complement each other. The analysis of the pun
that, in the Proverb for *Glassary*, he says he is doing in *Glas* and elsewhere is
not analysis in the usual sense of division down to simples. It is quasi-analysis
the end of which is after a fashion a beginning, but a beginning that has
already begun (Ps 648). The complexity of the crossing of the traces of
Derrida and Levinas and Heidegger is the complexity of the crossing of
responsibility or obligation or religion in Levinas's non-dogmatic sense with
the undecidable double bind. It obliges us to ask, for example, how pre-
predicative affirmation stands to the *Verlässlichkeit* of what Derrida calls
Heideggerian hope, how both of these relate to the religious faith that
according to Heidegger is not compatible with thinking, and whether
Derrida's response to Heidegger and to Heidegger's question *Was heisst
Denken?* is that a certain faith, *foi*, without any assumptive act of
commitment, and religious only in Levinas's sense, is necessary, *inévitable-
ment*, as the last word of *De l'esprit* affirms, if we are to respond responsibly: a
certain loyalty, *loi, une certaine fidélité à la venue, chaque fois, de l'autre
singulier* (A 71), an already pledged, affirmed, 'Come', a *Bienvenue* that
'marks in itself neither a desire, nor an order, nor a prayer, nor a request',
but crosses the grammatical, linguistic, semantic and pragmatic categories
(F 476). It binds us to ask at least this: what happens where the professedly
'horizontal' other of Derrida meets Levinas's 'vertical' *Autrui*? What or who
takes precedence when their unparallel lines meet at Infinity? Derrida writes:

> Suppose a first *yes*, the archi-original *yes* that engages, promises,
> acquiesces before all. On the one hand, it is originarily, in its very
> structure, a reply. It is *from the beginning second*, coming after a request, a
> question, or a *yes*. On the other hand, as engagement or promise, it must
> *at least* and in advance bind itself to a confirmation in a neighbouring *yes*.
> *Yes* to the neighbour(ing), otherwise said to the other *yes* that is already
> there and yet remains to come. *Oui au prochain, autrement dit à l'autre
> oui qui est déjà là mais reste pourtant à venir.* (Ps 648–649)

There is no comma after the words *autrement dit* here. Even if there were, we should still be bound to ask: does the 'prochain' say a who or a what? A sayer or a constative said? Neither or both? Neither and both? Or a constative performative saying, *dire*, that is other than either? In any case, the *in-venire* of the other is the invention *of* the other where the genitive is both subjective and objective and where the invention is at the same time advent and address, the *Geschick* of a *Geschenk* that is never an entirely present gift, never an entirely given present, but always promised, presently to come. So maybe we have here yet another undecidability, another not-quite-either-and-not-quite-both, to add to the manifold overlapping quasi-classes of undecidability of which this essay has only begun to sketch the (u)topography: illocutionary undecidability as to the performative or constative status of a speech act (for example, 'Par le mot *par* . . . '); alethic undecidability as to the truth or falsity of a constatation (for example, a Gödelian sentence, 'This sentence is false', 'This is a poem'); semantico-pragmatic undecidability as between the affirmation and denial of apparent contra-*dictory* responses to a question (for example, 'Comment ne pas parler?'); pragmatico-semantic undecidability as between responses to a command (for example, 'Seal not . . . '); undecidability as to genre (for example, *Glas*, *Feu la cendre* and the dangerous liaisons of *La carte postale*), as to style (for example, *Spurs*), as to tone of voice (Hölderlin: *Wechsel der Töne*) or gesture or both (for example, the *chanson de geste* of 'D'un ton apocalyptique . . . ', especially F 476–7: 'the difference between one "Come" and another . . . is tonal. . . . It is the gesture in the utterance (*parole*), that gesture which does not allow itself to be recaptured by the–linguistic, semantic or rhetorical–analysis of an utterance.' Compare Austin's reference (H 74 and 76) to the difficulty of reproducing tone and gesture analytically, a difficulty to which Derrida's style of quasi-analytic negotiation may be seen as an inevitably interminable, hence both unsuccessful and maybe at the same time and for the same reason up to a point successful, response; and so on.

None of these quasi-classes of undecidability implies irresponsibility, notwithstanding the suspicions to the contrary expressed in the first paragraph of this essay. Undecidability increases responsibility in that it obliges us to make finer and finer distinctions–for example, as we have seen, between quasi-kinds of undecidability and, as we shall begin to see in a moment, between classes and quasi-classes of responsibility–and to recognize that the order of priority of classes, for example, that between human beings and chimpanzees, is no more grounded in the nature of things than is the distinction between the nature of things and culture or convention. Older than nature and culture or convention is the immemorial trace inviting and welcoming alterity, calling for the responsiveness of a responsibility *towards* without which the responsibilities *for* of my station and its duties are irresponsible. The price of justice is indeed eternal vigilance, but the recollection of pre-judicial undecidability prevents the vigilance of blind justice turning into the vigilantism of the totalitarian *polis* and its panoptical police which insist either that a distinction is guillotine-sharp or that where there appears to be a difference there is monolithic continuity.

Undecidability is not exclusively opposed to responsibility any more than is seriousness to frivolity or necessity to chance—or responsibility to an essential pre-ethical irresponsibility, a pre-requisite of ethical responsibility: for there is an 'essential irresponsibility of the promise and response' in that these are not made unless made in the language of the other, a language for which I lack full responsibility, because it is a language I cannot make entirely my own (P 197–8). As Derrida writes in 'La guerre de Paul de Man', precisely because the experience of undecidability seems to make responsibility impossible, the one calls for the other and the other for the one. Responsibility is beyond being. It cannot be. It can only be denied. But to deny it is to affirm it (M 210, CI 639; Ps 561). In his demonstrations of how entrenched hierarchical oppositions within nature and without (The Great Chain of Being) reconstrue themselves, theographematic undecidability, the *coup de Dé-ité*, is shown to be not the sworn enemy of responsibility, but pre-ontological and pre-ethical responsibility's inseparable friend. If Searle, Austin, Derrida, Levinas *et al* belong to a *Société à responsabilité limitée*, Sarl, and if in the deconstruction of the *archè* one does not make a choice (Gr 91 (62)), this does not mean that anything goes. It means that the range of choice over which we can be either ethically responsible or ethically irresponsible is opened more widely than we are normally allowed to discover when we take up our position on the apparently 'firm ground of prejudice', to use Austin's phrase, that supports a certan metaphysical conception of conception, classification and critique. The quirky quasi-French spelling of the word by which quasi-transcendental undecidability is alluded to in the title of this essay marks not only the difficulty of deciding whether a title is outside or inside its text. It not only names what the text is about. It is also operative within it, performing a deconstrual of the simply negative and oppositional 'un-', de-capitating both capitation and decapitation. It de-marcates it and effaces it by tracing it back to a mark which is not exclusively negative or privative but is at the same time an 'in' (*donc dans*). Where responsibility is responsibility to the singularity of the other, respect for whom and for which must not be sacrificed to respect for the universality of the law, that is to say, where responsibility is critical co-respondence of reflective judgement and determinant judgement, *responsabilité limitée* is at the same time *responsabilité illimitée*. Therefore indecidability is not necessarily without responsibility, for, indecidably limited and unlimited, *before* the law in both senses, responsibility within decidability is responsibility with indecidability.[7]

NOTES

1 For special assistance in the preparation of this essay I thank Nelly Demé, Howard Llewelyn, Howell Oakley and David Wood.

2 Publications referred to by abbreviation in the text are as follows:

A Jacques Derrida and Pierre-Jean Labarrière, *Altérités* (Paris: Editions Osiris, 1986).

CI 'Like the Sound of the Sea Deep Within a Shell: Paul de Man's War', trans. Peggy Kamuf, *Critical Inquiry*, 14 (1988), 590–652.

E Jacques Derrida, *De l'esprit* (Paris: Editions Galilée, 1987).

F Philippe Lacoue-Labarthe and Jean-Luc Nancy, eds. *Les fins de l'homme à partir du travail de Jacques Derrida* (Paris: Editions Galilée, 1981).

G2 *Glyph* 2 (Baltimore and London: Johns Hopkins University Press, 1977).

G7 *Glyph* 7 (Baltimore and London: Johns Hopkins University Press, 1980).

Gr Jacques Derrida, *De la grammatologie* (Paris: Editions de Minuit, 1967); *Of Grammatology*, trans. Gayatri Chakravorti Spivak (Baltimore and London: Johns Hopkins University Press, 1974).

H John Austin, *How to Do Things with Words*, ed. J. O. Urmson (Oxford: Clarendon Press, 1962).

HO Edmund Husserl, *L'origine de la géométrie*, trans. with an introduction by Jacques Derrida (Paris: Presses Universitaires de France, 1962); Jacques Derrida, *Edmund Husserl's Origin of Geometry: an Introduction*, ed. David B. Allison, trans. John P. Leavey, Jr. (New York: Nicolas Hays; Brighton: Harvester, 1977).

I Jean-Luc Marion, *L'idole et la distance* (Paris: Grasset, 1977).

M Jacques Derrida, *Mémoires pour Paul de Man* (Paris: Editions Galilée, 1988).

N Emmanuel Levinas, *Noms propres* (Montpellier: Fata Morgana, 1976).

P Jacques Derrida, *Parages* (Paris: Editions Galilée, 1986).

Ps Jacques Derrida, *Psyché: Inventions de l'autre* (Paris: Editions Galilée, 1987).

3 John P. Leavey, Jr., *GLASsary* (Lincoln and London: University of Nebraska Press, 1986).

4 Tom Stoppard, *The Dog it was that Died and other Plays* (London and Boston: Faber and Faber, 1983), p. 44. Read on. The plot thickens.

5 F. P. Ramsey, *The Foundations of Mathematics* (London: Kegan Paul, Trench, Trubner, 1931), p. 20.

6 Victor Farias, *Heidegger et le nazisme* (Lagrasse: Verdier, 1987). See also Hugo Ott, *Martin Heidegger: Unterwegs zu seiner Biographie* (Frankfurt-am-Main, New York: Campus Verlag, 1988).

7 For amplification of what is said here on responsibility, classification, judgement and criticism, see Jacques Derrida, 'The Politics of Friendship', *Journal of Philosophy*, 85 (1988), 632–48, and 'Force of Law: The "Mystical Foundation of Authority"', *Cardozo Law Review*, 11 (July–August 1990), 919–1046. See also John Llewelyn, *The Middle Voice of Ecological Conscience: a Chiasmic Reading of Responsibility in the Neighbourhood of Levinas, Heidegger and Others* (London: Macmillan; New York: St Martin's Press, 1991), especially chap. 4, 'Critical Responsibility', and the Postface.

5

Geoffrey Bennington

Mosaic Fragment: if Derrida were an Egyptian . . .

'To Onias High Priest, greeting. A document has come to light which shows that the Spartans and the Jews are kinsmen descended alike from Abraham.' (Bernal, p. 110)

It was also at about this time that Hekataios of Abdera set out his view that the traditions of the Egyptian expulsion of the Hyksos, the Israelite Exodus and that of the Danaos' landing in Argos were three parallel versions of the same story. (Bernal, p. 109)

Has then the master-hand indeed traced such a vague or ambiguous script in the stone that so many different readings of it are possible? (Freud 14, 258)

Jewgreek is greekjew: but greekjew is Egyptian.

Hieroglyphs and pyramids, Thoth and Isis, colossi and the Sphinx: Egypt repeatedly returns to haunt Derrida's writing. From the two (or three) great Plato readings to the two great Hegel readings, via discussions of Freud and Warburton,[1] Egyptian motifs regularly appear at important moments in the texts. What is the place of 'Egypt' in deconstruction? Is there any sense in insisting on Derrida, greekjew or jewgreek, as North African, analogically 'Egyptian'?

Consider this example. If one says 'Moses did not exist', this may mean various things. It may mean: the Israelites did not have a *single* leader when they withdrew from Egypt–or: their leader was not called Moses–

or: there cannot have been anyone who accomplished all that the Bible
relates of Moses–or: etc. etc.

It is only by hearsay that you will get to know about psychoanalysis
. . . Let us assume for a moment that you were attending a lecture
not on psychiatry but on history, and that the lecturer was telling
you of the life and military deeds of Alexander the Great. What
grounds would you have for believing in the truth of what he
reported? At first glance the position would seem to be even more
unfavourable than in the case of psychoanalysis . . . but nevertheless I cannot think you would leave the lecture-room in doubts of
the reality of Alexander the Great. . . . The outcome of your
examination would undoubtedly be reassuring in the case of
Alexander, but would probably be different where figures such as
Moses or Nimrod were concerned. (Freud 1, 42–3)

– We may say, following Russell: the name 'Moses' can be defined by
means of various descriptions. For example, as 'the man who led the
Israelites through the wilderness', 'the man who lived at that time and
place and was then called "Moses"', 'the man who as a child was taken
out of the Nile by Pharaoh's daughter' and so on. And according as we
assume one definition or another the proposition 'Moses did not exist'
acquires a different sense, and so does every other proposition about
Moses.– And if we are told 'N did not exist', we do ask: 'What do you
mean? Do you want to say . . . or . . . etc.? (Wittgenstein, §79)

Given the manifest impossibility of considering Derrida's work to be
straightforwardly 'philosophical', and the no less manifest impossibility of
locating it philosophically as some 'regional' discourse (perhaps within the
human sciences), how are we to place his writing, once the rather silly
temptation to write it off as literature has been resisted? I recall two now
traditional ways of viewing Derrida's work: the one as Hegelian in spite of
itself, the other as anti-Hegelian. The second has noticed Derrida's
'definition' of deconstruction in *Positions*, as the systematic interruption of

a little later, Egyptian hieroglyphy will provide the example of what
resists the movement of the dialectic, history, logos (M, 96; cf. GL, 352a)

the Hegelian *Aufhebung* (POS, 55), and talks easily of deconstruction not
liking, criticizing or attacking such things as totalization and absolute
knowledge. This seems to leave Derrida in the position of sifting through the
dustbins of metaphysics for remainders and left-overs discarded by the
tradition or not assimilable by its digestive system. Whence the fact that
Derrida does not 'do' philosophy, but 'reads' it–there being no better

occupation for a philosopher once the 'closure of metaphysics' has been named. The other description suggests that as philosophy has always in fact proceeded by appropriating what was previously marginal or external to it (and Derrida himself opens *Margins* with a description of philosophy behaving in precisely such a manner (M, I)), then deconstruction is still a totalizing philosophy blind to its own Hegelianism, still a metaphysics, a particularly perverse strategy aiming to legitimate an essentially traditional continuation of a discipline which should nowadays be doing something quite different. Apparently contesting Hegelianism, deconstruction has in fact found a way of playing an interminable game with it, which it is desperately important not to seem to have won, at risk of having to accept the end of any 'foundationalist' philosophy, and therefore the uselessness of such erudite questioning of it. In spite of its apparent modernism or even post-modernism, deconstruction would on this view be an essentially conservative ruse the better to legitimate an antiquarian attachment to the history of philosophy. The point to be made against deconstruction would not be that

It seemed to me that I had been transported into a country far away from this country, into an age remote from this age, that I stood in ancient Egypt and that I was listening to the speech of some highpriest of that land addressed to the youthful Moses.

one should simply 'turn the page' of philosophy (cf. ED, 421–2), but that it is possible to get on philosophically without suffocating in the library of the Western tradition: it is possible, on this view, to get through one's mourning for metaphysics and get on with some philosophy, instead of trying all ways ('demi-deuil' and the rest) to justify what is essentially a melancholic attachment to dead problems and ambitions.[2]

Naturally enough, the ease with which these alternative views can be constructed suggests that there is something wrong here. After the fashion of the Kantian antinomies, it is easy to see apparently convincing arguments on both sides of the question, and to formulate something like the 'interests of reason' in the conflict. My purpose here is to maintain something of a Kantian rather than a Hegelian flavour to the way of formulating such problems, but to attempt to escape such antinomies, not of course by choosing one alternative over the other, nor by taking the Kantian route of sharpening up the distinction between phenomena and things in themselves, but by recasting the antinomy in terms of Jew and Greek, and by suggesting a non-dialectical way out through the suggestion that Derrida is neither Jew nor Greek, but 'Egyptian', in a non-biographical sense to be explored.

From that moment–how can I say it–I felt as displaced in a Jewish community, closed unto itself, as I would in the other (which they used to call 'the Catholics'). The suffering eased in France. At nineteen I naively believed that anti-Semitism had disappeared, at least where I was living then. But, during my adolescence, and that was the real tragedy, it was there for everyone else (because there was everyone else, which was perhaps just as much a determining factor: you see, we give in to a certain kind of facility or curiosity by selecting this sequence of events; why involve me in that side of things?). A paradoxical effect, perhaps, of this bludgeoning was the desire to be integrated into the non-Jewish community, a fascinated but painful and distrustful desire, one with a nervous vigilance, a painstaking attitude to discern signs of racism in its most discreet formations or in its loudest denials. Symmetrically, oftentimes, I felt an impatient distance with regard to various Jewish communities, when I have the impression that they close in upon themselves, when they pose themselves as such. From all of which comes a feeling of non-belonging that I have doubtless transposed . . . (Bernasconi, 75)

Recent work on Derrida suggests, if only through the considerable explanatory power of a term such as 'quasi-transcendental',[3] the interest of elaborating a Kantian-critical filiation for deconstruction. It seems important to maintain the importance of such a filiation, despite the relatively small place Kant occupies in Derrida's published work, if only to complicate the almost automatic tendency to place Derrida in a supposedly phenomenological or hermeneutical 'tradition' usually associated with Hegel, Husserl and Heidegger (cf. Kearney, 109). One fruitful way of approaching Derrida's evident interest in the relation between Kant and Hegel is that suggested

For we are indeed dealing here with the imagination, that is the agency in which are blurred or cancelled all the Kantian oppositions regularly criticized by Hegel. We are here in that zone–let's mark it with the title 'Critique of judgement'–where the debate with Kant looks most like an explication and least like a break. But it is also for convenience that we here oppose development to displacement. We should also have to reconsider this couple of concepts. (M, 90–1)

[The *pharmakon*] is, rather, the anterior milieu in which differenciation in general is produced . . . this milieu is *analogous* to that which later, after and according to the philosophical decision, will be reserved to the transcendental imagination . . . the element of the *pharmakon* is the site of combat between philosophy and its other. Element *in itself*, if one can still say that, *undecidable*. (D, 144, 158)

Occupying the **middle** [milieu] in the succession of the types of writing, the hieroglyph, as we shall see, is also the elementary milieu, the medium and general form of all writing. (SCR 23)

in *Glas*, where the Kantian position, at least as Hegel construes it, is consistently linked with that of the Jew. It is hard not to want to pursue the possibilities of an at least analogical relation in which Hegel is the Greek to Kant's Jew, and therefore to Derrida himself, and to extend that analogy to the perhaps more vexed question of Derrida's relationship with Levinas the Jew (against whom Derrida has said he never feels he has any objections (A, 64)) and Heidegger the Greek (without whose work Derrida has said none of his own thinking would have been possible (POS, 73)). It is not hard to construct an essentially 'Jewish' Derrida, not only on the basis of a vaguely 'talmudic' feel to his interminable commentaries and glosses,[4] but in a more fundamental way, to do with a sense that Derrida's is, for example, a thinking of a law which is given, which *il y a*, pre-ontologically, not for understanding so much as for negotiation, with no *telos* of comprehension or absolution. There is some comfort in a scenario which would attempt to appropriate Derrida for a Jewish thought opposed to (or at least not assimilable by) a supposed tyranny of the Greek *logos*, a thinking of the Law not to be absorbed by a thinking of Being, a thinking of justice which would not be (subordinate to) a thinking of truth, an archi-original passivity or passibility which precedes and undermines all claims to mastery, etc.

Hegel places the Jew under the sign of a cutting: cut from mother nature after the flood (GL, 52a ff), breaking from and opposing the life of community and love with Abraham, self-condemned to wandering in the desert away from any fixed domicile, marking this cut with the sign of circumcision (GL, 58a ff), the better to remain bound to the cut itself, subjected as a finite being to the cut-off infinite of a jealous God. The attempt to secure his own finite mastery leaves the Jew in the grip of mastery by an infinite he can never understand, plunged in finitude, in matter. The Jew is alienated, in touch not with a transcendent truth but with a quasi-transcendence which can only take the (formless) form of a command and of a law one cannot understand—which cannot therefore be rational—but which is suffered, without mediation, in its letter rather than its spirit (GL, 72–5a). Kant, structurally speaking, occupies the place of the Jew in Hegel (GL, 47a):

And it seemed to me that I heard the voice of that Egyptian highpriest raised in a tone of like haughtiness and like pride. I heard his words and their meaning was revealed to me.

Kant's autonomy, for example, the obedience to the 'ought' of the moral law, merely interiorizes the absolute heteronomy of the Jewish God, and is therefore no autonomy at all, but, on Kant's own terms, pathological (GL, 80–1). Just like the Jews, Kant remains caught in the oppositional thinking of the understanding, stuck between a formalism of the law and an empiricism of events. By claiming to fix the boundaries of what a finite subjectivity can know, Kant prevents all knowledge of the infinite to which he thus remains enslaved.

Imagine first, then, that Derrida is Kant: but not so much the Kant of the Enlightenment, as Hegel's Kant (or Hölderlin's Kant, 'The Moses of our

> But when I make a statement about Moses,–am I always ready to say: By 'Moses' I understand the man who did what the Bible relates of Moses, or at any rate a good deal of it. But how much? Have I decided how much must be proved false for me to give up my proposition as false? Has the name 'Moses' got a fixed and unequivocal use for me in all possible cases?–Is it not the case that I have, so to speak, a whole series of props in readiness, and am ready to lean on one if another should be taken from under me and vice versa? (Wittgenstein, § 79)

nation')[5]–yet not quite Hegel's Kant, but a Hegel's Kant whose YHWE is Hegel. Here then is Derrida, Jewish, condemned to the interminable elaboration of a law always in retreat and mystery, jealous of its truth that we can never know, but whose traces we can follow, at best, never arriving at a present perception or an experience (GL, 299–300a). By following the tracks of what should be *another* Hegel (another reading of metaphysics), a Hegel who says something other than what Hegel says, Derrida, himself become Hegel's shadow or double, has made Hegel his doubly mysterious God, hiding all the better for pretending to appear in the light. In spite of all of Hegel's efforts to overcome the cut, Derrida will have insisted on cutting him from himself, cutting himself from him, and therefore stays, fascinated, in the effort to show that Hegel is the fascinated one, still attached to the very thing (the cut) from which he tried to cut himself. Show that Hegel never really escaped from Judaism by making him your YHWE. Striving for finite mastery of the letter of philosophy, enslave yourself to the infinite you admit you cannot understand. Whence deconstruction's vertigo, fascination and repulsion, nomadic wandering in the desert, failure to announce any truth or promise any knowledge:

> The city and the desert, which are neither countries nor landscapes nor gardens, lay siege to Jabès's poetry and ensure for his cries a literally infinite echo. City and desert at once, that is Cairo from which comes Jabès, who as we know, also had his departure from Egypt. The dwelling built by the poet with his 'daggers stolen from the angel' is a

light tent made of words in the desert where the nomadic Jew is struck by infinity and letter. Broken by the broken Law. Divided in himself–(the Greek language would no doubt tell us a great deal about the strange relationship of the law, of wandering and non self-identity, about the common root–*nemein*–of sharing, of nomia and of nomadism). (ED, 105)

Unfortunately, I do not feel inspired by any sort of hope which would permit me to presume that my work of deconstruction has a prophetic function. But I concede that the style of my questioning as an exodus and dissemination in the desert might produce certain prophetic resonances. It is possible to see deconstruction as being produced in a space where the prophets are not far away. But the prophetic resonances of my questioning reside at the level of a certain rhetorical discourse which is also shared by several other contemporary thinkers. The fact that I declare it 'unfortunate' that I do not personally feel inspired may be a signal that deep down I still hope. It means that I am in fact still looking for something. So perhaps it is no mere accident of rhetoric that the search itself, the search without hope for hope, assumes a certain prophetic *allure*. Perhaps my search is a twentieth century brand of prophecy? But it is difficult for me to believe it. (Kearney, p. 119)

Hegel's Kant, Hegel's Moses: proposing to the Jews in Egypt an unintelligible liberation in a rhetoric so abstract and forced, a writing so artificial and full of tricks, that it is like a foreign language (GL, 67a)–a writing analogous to the tabernacle, mere construction of bands, empty inside, signifier without signified, nothing at its centre (GL, 68a).

And yet what could be more Greek than the Derrida of 'Violence and Metaphysics', defending Heidegger against Levinas, insisting on the absolute necessity of speaking alterity in the language of the Greek *logos*, claiming thereby that if Jewish thought is other than Greek thought, it can nonetheless not be absolutely external to it, but folded back in via the non-dialectical figure of invagination, non-identical same which is not different from *différance*, but the *milieu* of history in general. Derrida cannot be Hegel's Kant, nor Hegel's Jew, nor Hegel's Moses, if all his thought is concerned to show the incoherence of any absolutized cut or separation: so far, for example, from attempting to salvage absolute difference from Hegel's description, Derrida agrees with Hegel to the extent that *différance* must be thought of as the name for the impossibility of difference ever being absolute or pure (cf. ED, 227, n1).

And in fact the comfort of a 'Jewish' reading can hardly fail to be disturbed by Derrida's relation in general to Heidegger, still apparently too Greek for such thinking–and we can suggest quite confidently that any attempt to make Derrida *essentially* a Jewish thinker will always end up finding that he is somehow not Jewish enough, still too Greek (but the problem is that the attempt to find Derrida 'essentially' Jewish is already a Greek gesture: the Jewish reading is a Greek reading). Whence the disturbance caused by some of his comments on the recent Heidegger and De Man 'affairs'.[6] We need to look for something 'before' the opposition of Greek and Jew: but we need to beware any tendency to call that 'before' *mythos* or 'sophistry', for example, for, as Derrida shows in 'La pharmacie de Platon', 'mythos' is itself a philosophical concept, determined only from the point of view of *logos*, and 'sophistry' too is a Platonic concept, marking as much an inseparability as a rupture:

> Can we set off in search of another guarding, once the pharmaceutical 'system' constrains not only, in one and the same hold, the scene of the *Phaedrus*, the scene of the *Republic* and the scene of the *Sophist*, Platonic dialectics, logic and mythology, but also, it appears, certain non-Greek structures of mythology? And if it is not certain that there is any such thing as non-Greek 'mythologies', for the opposition *mythos/ logos* only ever has its authority *after* Plato, to what general and unnamable necessity are we referred? In other words, what does Platonism as repetition signify? (D, 194)

In proposing 'Egypt' as one name of that 'unnamable necessity', we are not naming any thing, any place or any date. If the question 'what is . . . ?' is dated (SCH, 30–31), and dated as 'later' than 'Egypt', we cannot ask 'what is Egypt?'.[7]

> Once again I am prepared to find myself blamed for having presented my reconstruction . . . with too great and unjustified certainty. I shall not feel very severely hit by this criticism, since it finds an echo in my own judgement. I know myself that my structure has its weak spots, but it has its strong points too. On the whole my predominant impression is that it is worth while to pursue the work in the direction it has taken. (Freud 13, 281)

Jewgreek is neither Greek nor Jew, nor greekjew as mix or *Aufhebung*. I call the non-teleological becoming Greek of the Jew, or the non-originary having-been-Jew of the Greek, 'Egypt': always left, never left, that 'veille du

Why will you Jews not accept our culture, our religion and our language? You are a tribe of nomad herdsmen; we are a mighty

people. You have no cities nor no wealth: our cities are hives of humanity and our galleys, trireme and quadrireme, laden with all manner merchandise furrow the waters of the known globe. You have but emerged from primitive conditions: we have a literature, a priesthood, and agelong history and a polity.

platonisme' which Derrida mysteriously suggests might also be the 'lendemain du hegelianisme' (D, 122–3)

> While I consider it essential to think through this copulative synthesis of Greek and Jew, I consider my own thought, paradoxically, as neither Greek nor Jewish. I often feel that the questions I attempt to formulate on the outskirts of the Greek philosophical tradition have as their 'other' the model of the Jew, that is, the Jew-as-other. And yet the paradox is that I have never actually invoked the Jewish tradition in any 'rooted' or direct manner. Though I was born a Jew, I do not work or think within a living Jewish tradition. So that if there is a Judaic dimension to my thinking which may from time to time have spoken in or through me, this has never assumed the form of an explicit fidelity or debt to that culture. In short, the ultimate site (*lieu*) of my questioning discourse would be neither Hellenic nor Hebraic if such were possible. It would be a non-site beyond both the Jewish influence of my youth and the Greek philosophical heritage which I received during my academic education in the French universities. (Kearney, p. 107)

The subaltern and supplementary god of writing and supplementarity is an Egyptian god (D, 96–107). Thot supplies and supplants, repeats and contests the sun-god, Rê or Amon or Osiris. Thot is the ungraspable god of death, of calculation, of ruse, of history, of the plurality of languages, of the game, with no fixed character or place, a principle of mobility and (therefore) of subversion in the pantheon of the gods, a mediator who merely simulates mediation, unreliably, with no eschatological resolution as the horizon of his manoeuvres.

> Jewish consciousness is unhappy consciousness and *The Book of Questions* is its poem; inscribed in the margin of the phenomenology of spirit along with which the Jew wants to go only a little way, without eschatological provision, so as not to limit his desert, close his book and scar over his cry. (ED, 104)

It is true that I interrogate the idea of an *eschaton* or *telos* in the absolute formulations of classical philosophy. But that does not mean I dismiss all forms of Messianic or prophetic eschatology. I think all genuine questioning is summoned by a certain type of eschatology, though it is impossible to define this eschatology in philosophical terms. (Kearney, p. 119)

Freud, hesitant and a little embarrassed, wants to suggest that Moses was perhaps an Egyptian. First of all, the name 'Moses' looks like an Egyptian

> There is a well-known comic anecdote according to which an intelligent Jewish boy was asked who the mother of Moses was. He replied without hesitation: 'The Princess.' 'No', he was told, 'she only took him out of the water.' 'That's what *she* says', he replied, and so proved that he had found the correct interpretation of the myth. (Freud 1, 195).

name, a suffix meaning a child, usually attached to the name of the god who gave the child. Among Freud's examples are 'Amen-mose' and 'Thoth-mose' (Freud 13, 244–5), and later he suggests 'Tuthmosis' may have been the name (Freud 13, 301). One of the reasons for Freud's hesitation is the fear of being 'classed with the school men and Talmudists who delight in exhibiting their ingenuity without regard to how remote from reality their thesis may be' (Freud 13, 254). And how are we to reconcile the rigid monotheism of Mosaic religion with the distressing plurality and confusion of the Egyptian gods, all identified with each other (thus Amen and Rê, gods of Thebes and Heliopolis)

You pray to a local and obscure idol: our temples, majestic and mysterious, are the abodes of Isis and Osiris, or Horus and Ammon Ra. Yours serfdom, awe and humbleness: ours thunder and the seas. Israel is weak and few are her children: Egypt is an host and terrible are her arms. Vagrants and daylabourers are you called: the world trembles at our name.

in a mass from which only Osiris emerges, himself sun-god for Derrida, god of death for Freud? (Freud 13, 256).

Osiris, killed in a plot with the participation of Thoth–who later changes sides, supports Osiris–and whose wife, Isis, finds all the pieces of his dismembered body except the penis (D, 102; TA, 43–57). Isis is the veiled goddess, Nature, the figure of the enigma for Hegel, who goes with a mysterious inscription, and a sun: ' . . . the fruit of my flesh is Helios' (GL, 357a), and is, too, in Kant's pamphlet against the mystagogues, the figure of their relation with the wisdom they claim to sense but cannot show (TA, 44ff). Elsewhere, Kant says that the inscription on the temple of Isis ('I am all that is, has been and will be, and no mortal has lifted my veil', quoted by Hegel as symbol of the enigma, as the being-enigma of the enigma (GL, 357a)) is perhaps the most sublime (EC, 73). But there is a risk of emasculation, of a castration of reason by the mystagogues, partisans of the veil that can above all not be lifted.

God of the sun: god of death. The sun is death, however, insofar as looking directly at it brings mortal blindness: cf. especially D, 93–4, 192; M, 289. Life as the economy of death begins in the turning away from this blinding presence.

> But it is precisely the *sight* of the chieftain that is dangerous and unbearable for primitive people, just as later that of the Godhead is for mortals. Even Moses had to act as an intermediary between his people and Jehovah, since the people could not support the sight of God; and when he returned from the presence of God his face shone . . . (Freud 12, 158).

Exodus, XXXIV, 30: 'And when Aaron and all the children of Israel saw Moses, behold, the skin of his face shone; and they were afraid to come nigh him'. A different interpretation of this passage has Moses not shining, but wearing a bull's mask, with horns:[8] whence the iconographical tradition of the horned Moses, as in Michelangelo's statue.

> **He spoke on the law of evidence . . . of Roman justice as contrasted with the earlier Mosaic code, the *lex talionis*. And he cited the Moses of Michelangelo in the Vatican . . .**
>
> He said of it: *that stony effigy in frozen music, horned and terrible, of the human form divine, that eternal symbol of wisdom and prophecy which if aught that the imagination or the hand of sculptor has wrought in marble of soultransfigured and soultransfiguring deserves to live, deserves to live.* (Joyce, 140–1)

Frozen music. Schönberg in 1933: 'My Moses is like Michelangelo's, if only in appearance. He is not at all human' (Wörner, p. 42).

We know the story. There was a monotheistic religion among the Egyptians, under Akhenaten, a religion of the sun or the sun-god, based in On (Heliopolis, city of the sun, to which Plato made a trip, perhaps (D, 96–7 n12)), and in emulation of which the priests of Hermopolis, city of the secret, of Hermes (who is not other than Thoth), invented a cosmogony in which Thoth played the leading part (cf. D, 102–3 n26 for the possible relations with the Greek *logos*, and the *Sophia* of the Alexandrian Jews). The religion of Aten, new sun-god, persecutes that of Amun, old sun-god in the polytheistic pantheon, and forbids any representation of the god other than that of the sun. Moses preserved the cult by leaving Egypt on Akhenaten's death and the persecution of his religion, having made his followers adopt the Egyptian custom of circumcision. Circumcision, Freud says later, 'has repeatedly been of help to us, like, as it were, a key-fossil' (Freud 13, 279).

> 'the conclusion of my study, which was directed to the single aim of introducing the figure of an Egyptian Moses into the nexus of Jewish history.' (Freud 13, 293) Like a circumcisor's knife. 'If all poets are Jews, they, the poets, are all circumcised or circumcisors.' (SCH, 100)

Later, the religion of YHWE is founded by *another* Moses, and picks up the Egyptian part of the story, including circumcision.

> The text, however, as we possess it today, will tell us enough about its own vicissitudes. Two mutually opposed treatments have left their traces on it. On the one hand it has been subjected to revisions which have falsified it in the sense of their secret aims, have mutilated and amplified it and have even changed it into its reverse; on the other hand a solicitous piety has presided over it and has sought to preserve everything as it was, no matter whether it was consistent or contradicted itself. Thus almost everywhere noticeable gaps, disturbing repetitions and obvious contradictions have come about—indications which reveal things to us which it was not intended to communicate. In its implications the distortion of a text resembles a murder: the difficulty is not in perpetrating the deed, but in getting rid of its traces . . . I am aware that a method of exposition such as this is no less inexpedient than it is unartistic. I myself deplore it unreservedly. Why have I not avoided it? The answer to that is not hard for me to find, but it is not easy to confess. I found myself unable to wipe out the traces of the history of the work's origin, which was in any case unusual . . . I determined to give it up; but it tormented me like an unlaid ghost. (Freud 13, 283; 349)

Cut circumcision from its Egyptian origins—which will return to haunt us—by claiming that YHWE had already introduced it with Abraham. But this is a 'clumsy invention' says Freud, for then a Jew transported into Egypt would have had to recognize all Egyptians as his brothers in the covenant, and it is precisely this that was to be avoided (Freud 13, 285).

> In the *Timaeus*, the old Egyptian priest taught Solon that they, the Greeks, resort to myth only because they have no writing to preserve the memory of the city through its recurrent catastrophes. But the

Egyptians have guarded that memory in the hypomnemic form denounced in the *Phaedrus* (CH, 283–4). 'The people who had come from Egypt had brought writing and the desire to write history along with them; but it was to be a long time before historical writing realized that it was pledged to unswerving truthfulness. To begin with it had no scruples about shaping its narratives according to the needs and purposes of the moment, as though it had not yet recognized the concept of falsification. As a result of these circumstances a discrepancy was to grow up between the written record and the oral transmission of the same material–*tradition*. What had been omitted or changed in the historical record might very well have been preserved intact in tradition. Tradition was a supplement but at the same time a contradiction to historical writing. (Freud 13, 310–1)

YHWE, volcano-god: 'an uncanny, bloodthirsty demon who went about by night and shunned the light of day' (Freud 13, 273). 'Coarse, narrow-minded . . . violent and bloodthirsty' (Freud 13, 290).

Moses, murdered by 'his' people, the fate of all legislators. Biblical style from Freud, explaining the inexplicable (cf. PRE, 116): 'There came a time when people began to regret the murder of Moses and to seek to forget it' (Freud 13, 288–9). Strange link: in regretting one cannot forget, in trying to forget one never stops remembering. Killing keeps alive the better. Incorporation according to Abraham and Torok, who also treat the organism as a hieroglyphic text, part of what Derrida calls a 'general hieroglyphics' (F, 38–9; 58–9):

A suspicion even arises that the Israelites of that earliest period–that is to say, the scribes of Moses–may have had some share in the invention of the first alphabet. [Note: If they were subject to the prohibition against pictures they would even have had a motive for abandoning the hieroglyphic picture-writing while adapting its written characters to expressing a new language] (Freud 13, 283).

Jean-Jacques Rousseau, trying to theorize the most Greek of Greek states as

The only reason for doubting that [Plato's] *Republic* was based on Egypt is the fact that he does not say so in the text. This omission, however, has an ancient explanation. As his earliest commentator, Krantor, wrote within a few generations of Plato:

Plato's contemporaries mocked him, saying that he was not the inventor of his republic, but that he had copied Egyptian institutions. He attached so much importance to the mockers that he attributed to the Egyptians the story of the Athenians and the Atlantines to make them say that the Athenians had really lived under this regime at a certain moment in the past.

[. . .] Thus, for Plato, if one wanted to return to the ancient Athenian institutions, one had to turn to Egypt. In this way he resembled Isokrates, who both called for a Panhellenic combination of Athens and Sparta and extolled the Egyptian constitution that was a purer version of the Lakedaimonian one. *The deeper they went towards the true Hellenic roots of Greece, the closer they came to Egypt.* One reason for this was that both Isokrates and Plato maintained that the great lawgivers and philosophers like Lykourgos, Solon and Pythagoras had all brought back Egyptian knowledge. (Bernal, pp. 106–8)

absolute autonomy, ends up reduced to bringing in a legislator to make his state whole and repair its necessarily flawed sovereignty. The law was to be generated by the purely immanent reflection of the general will upon itself: but this can never quite be achieved. The citizen was to give himself the law (and thus, in Hegelian terms, become properly human: cf. GL, 40a). Enter the legislator, essentially a foreigner (for if the law did not come from elsewhere, then it could indeed be generated autonomously, but the legislator is made necessary only by the failure of any such generation). As the legislator is a necessary moment of the foundation of any state whatsoever, and as this must therefore be true of *the first state* too, then the legislator is in essence not so much an empirical foreigner as a figure of absolute exteriority: the state constitutes its 'inside' only by bringing into its centre this element of an absolute outside, which it will never quite manage to absorb–this (empty) central exteriority is the (place of the) law. The legislator speaks a language incomprehensible to those for whom he legislates: only his law will make the people capable of understanding his law. In the absence of

Moses is said to have been 'slow of speech': he must have suffered from an inhibition or disorder of speech. Consequently, in his supposed dealings with Pharaoh, he needed the support of Aaron, who is called his brother. This again may be a historical truth and would make a welcome contribution to presenting a lively picture of the great man. But it may also have another and more important significance. It may recall, slightly distorted, the fact that Moses spoke another language . . . ' (Freud 13, 272).

understanding, the legislator must act violently, illegally, to get the law accepted: he pretends it was given by God. In the absence of understanding,

What must be received to make free choice possible cannot have been chosen, except after the event. In the beginning was violence (Levinas, p. 82).

the people cannot know that this is the legislator and not a charlatan–what indubitable signs could there be of a real legislator? 'The great soul of the Legislator is the true miracle which must prove his mission' (*Social Contract*, Book II, Chapter VII). But Rousseau knows very well that there are no indubitable signs, that nothing can prove a miracle to be a miracle, that in the moment of his coming, the legislator always might be a charlatan, and may well not know himself which he is. Rousseau offers a second criterion which

Discussing religious doctrine in the *Lettres écrites de la montagne*, Rousseau argues as follows, in a way which is strictly applicable to the situation of the legislator: God has distinguished his envoys with a number of signs which make them recognizable for what they are to all; these signs are 1) the nature of the doctrine they profess–this is the surest sign, but accessible to very few people (and has been ruled out in the case of the legislator in advance–we have seen that the people cannot understand the law when it is given); 2) the character of the envoy himself: 'This is the sign which strikes above all good and righteous people who see truth everywhere they see justice, and hear the voice of God only in the mouth of virtue. This characteristic still has its truth, but it is not impossible for it to mislead, and there is nothing prodigious about an imposter tricking good people, nor about a good man tricking himself, led on by the ardour of a saintly zeal that he takes for inspiration'; 3) The production of miracles. But miracles cannot be essential, for a) until we know all the laws of nature, we cannot be certain that a given phenomenon breaks them miraculously; b) even if there are real miracles, it is impossible to distinguish them with certainty from false or merely apparent miracles: 'When Aaron cast his

Aaron: In Moses' hand a rigid rod: this, the law.
In my own hand the most supple of serpents: discretion [*Klugheit*; prudence]. (*Moses and Aaron*, Act 1, Scene 4; Wörner, p. 141)

rod before Pharaoh it was changed into a snake, the magicians cast their rods too and they were changed into snakes. It does not matter whether this change was real in both cases, as Scripture says, or whether only Aaron's miracle was real and the magician's trick [*prestige*] was merely apparent, as some Theologians claim; this appearance was exactly the same . . . Now men can only judge miracles through their senses, and if the sensation is the same, the real difference, which they cannot perceive, is nothing to them. thus the sign, *qua* sign, proves no more on one side than on the other, and in this the Prophet has no advantage over the magician. . . . When Moses changed water to blood, the Magicians changed water to blood; when Moses produced frogs, the Magicians produced frogs. They failed with the third plague; but let us stay with the first two which God himself had made proof of divine power. The Magicians also produced that proof.

As for the third plague that they were unable to imitate, it is hard to see what made it so difficult, to the point of marking *that the finger of God was there*. Why could they who could produce an animal not produce an insect, and how could they not produce lice, having produced frogs? . . . The same Moses, instructed by all these experiences, orders that if a false Prophet comes to announce other Gods, that is a false doctrine, and if this false prophet authorises what he says by predictions or successful wonders, one must not listen to him but put him to death. So true signs can be used to support a false doctrine; a sign in itself proves nothing' (Rousseau III, 745–6).

can no longer help the people faced with a possible legislator: after the event (for this is an event), we can know from the longevity of the legislator's institution whether or not he was a real legislator or only a charlatan:

Any man who can engrave tablets of stone, or buy an oracle, or feign a secret commerce with some divinity, or train a bird to speak in his ear, or find other crude means of tricking the people. He who knows only that much might even gather by chance a troop of lunatics, but he will never found an empire, and his extravagant work will soon perish with him. Vain wonders [*prestiges*] form a transient bond, but only wisdom makes it durable. Judaic law which still subsists, the law of the son of Ismael which for ten centuries has ruled half the world, still today announce the great men who dictated them; and while proud philosophy or blind partisan spirit sees in them only happy impostors, the true politician admires in their institutions that great and powerful genius which presides over durable institutions.

We must not conclude from all this with Warburton that politics and religion have for us a common object . . . (Rousseau III, 384)

(This is of course the same Warburton whose writing on hieroglyphs and dream-interpretation is the subject of Derrida's 'Scribble', and an extended discussion in 'Freud et la scène de l'écriture': Derrida introduces Warburton in connection with the second of two popular methods of dream-interpretation he is rejecting before presenting his own sample analysis–the first of these methods, that of 'symbolic' interpretation, is illustrated by Freud (Derrida does not mention this) with the example of Joseph interpreting Pharaoh's dream (Freud 4, p. 170): it is of course the success of Joseph's interpretation which leads eventually to the prosperous establishment of the Jews in Egypt prior to their oppression, and liberation by Moses.)

In opening remarks to Rousseau's *Considérations sur le gouvernement de Pologne* (III, 956–7) Moses is the first named of three figures described by Rousseau as the three principal legislators of the ancient world (the other two being Lycurgus and Numa Pompilius). In a fragment which Rousseau's editors entitle 'Des Juifs', Moses appears dominant: 'The

> The Jews in the wilderness and on the mountaintop said: **It is meet to be here. Let us build an altar to Jehovah.** The Roman, like the Englishman who follows in his footsteps, brought to every new shore on which he sets his foot (on our shore he never set it) only his cloacal obsession. He gazed about him in his toga and said: **It is meet to be here. Let us construct a water-closet.**
> [. . .]
>
> Moses, Moses, king of the jews,
> Wiped his arse in the Daily News
> (Joyce, 132, 443)

Jews give us this astonishing spectacle: the laws of Solon, Numa, Lycurgus are dead, those of Moses which are much older live on still. Athens, Sparta and Rome have perished and have left no more children on the earth. Sion destroyed has not lost its children; they are preserved, they multiply, they spread throughout the world and always recognize each other, they mix with all peoples and never become part of them; they no longer have leaders and are still a people, they have no land and yet are still citizens.' (Rousseau III, 499) But this is further complicated in another very ambivalent fragment, which reads as follows in its entirety:

'What are you doing among us, O Hebrew, I see you here with pleasure; but how can you find pleasure here, you who despised us so strongly, why did you not remain among your people.

You are mistaken I come among my own. I have lived alone on earth, among a numerous people I was alone. Lycurgus, Solon and Numa are my brothers. I have come to rejoin my family. I have come at last to taste the sweetness of conversing with my kind, of speaking and being heard. It is among you illustrious souls, that I have come at last to enjoy myself [*jouir de moi*],

you have changed greatly in tone, in feelings and ideas . . . '. [crossed out words in the manuscript suggest a 'dialogue des morts' scenario for this dialogue, with the 'Hebrew', presumably Moses, arriving no doubt in the Underworld].

Hegel: in its letter, Mosaic law looks very like the laws of Solon and Lycurgus–but its spirit is different: or rather, it has no spirit (GL, 74a).

But we know from elsewhere in Rousseau that the duration of a political institution is not in fact indubitable proof of its quality (just as any sign of the genuineness of the legislator is necessarily open to the possibility of counterfeiting, so a durable state may always be a mere simulacrum of a good

> The rabbis whose words you quote are charlatans. (Jabès, quoted ED, 112)

one). Legislator and charlatan thus remain radically undecidable: it is in fact perfectly in the logic of Rousseau's argument to say that Moses might still (have) turn(ed) out to be a charlatan after all. Hegel: the Jew cannot become a citizen, cannot have true State laws (GL, 72aff); Hegel again: Thoth is reputed to be the first legislator (M, 117).

This situation is generalizable: not only can the logic of the legislator be

> The philosopher is not an artificer in the field of reason, but himself the lawgiver of human reason. (Kant *Critique of Pure Reason*, A839; B867)

> The legislator is a writer. (D, 129)

extended to that of Jean-Jacques Rousseau,[9] but to writing and thinking in general. Any event of thought, insofar as it is an event and not simply a programmed repetition, involves this undecidability and temporal *après-coup*, and the incidence of absolute exteriority I have here described with the help of Rousseau's political thinking.[10] A traditional description would no doubt call this event something like 'inspiration', or communication from the muse, and link it to poetry. But nothing in the description we have given can justify any such simple regionalization. For Derrida, this is philosophy:

> With this distinction between the empirical and the essential, a limit is blurred, that of the philosophical as such, the philosophical distinction. Philosophy then finds itself, *finds itself again* [*se trouve, se retrouve*] in the *parages* of the poetic, or even of literature. It finds itself again for

the indecision of this limit is perhaps what most provokes it to thought. It finds itself again, it does not necessarily lose itself as is thought by those who, in their tranquil credulity, believe they know where this limit passes and hold themselves on it fearfully, ingenuously (though not innocently), devoid of what one must call *philosophical experience*: a certain questioning crossing of limits, insecurity as to the frontier of the philosophical field–and especially the *experience of language*, always as poetic or literary as philosophical . . . (SCH, 80)

Transfer this set-up to the domain of academic discipline, and it is no surprise that Martin Bernal, for example, arguing against what he sees as the systematic repression of the Afroasiatic and more especially Egyptian roots of Ancient Greece, finds himself in the situation of the legislator, coming from outside and potentially condemned to expulsion. Fundamentally new approaches tend to come from outside, says Bernal, acutely aware that this privilege brings with it the equally fundamental uncertainty as to whether the outsider isn't just a 'crank'. Academics, says Bernal, academically nervous of his own 'amateur' status, quite typically accept that their discipline was founded by amateurs (as it necessarily must have been, insofar as what counts as a 'professional' in this sense can be determined only after that foundation, which is constitutively illegitimate), but reject any new input from the amateurish outside, just as Moses, once accepted as legislator, orders the putting to death of any new aspirant arrivals. Founders of discourse, as Foucault would call them (imprudently making of them a modern phenomenon, but giving Freud as a major example), are always as Moses, or Thoth, *before* Pharaoh. Israel in Egypt, Egypt in Israel. 'It is honour enough to the Jewish people that they could preserve such a tradition and produce men who gave it a voice–even though the initiative to it came from outside, from a great foreigner. . . . Unluckily an author's creative power does not always obey his will: the work proceeds as it can, and often presents itself to the author as something independent and even alien' (Freud 13, 292; 350).

And yet [Freud] was also Moses, giving the law of psychoanalysis, restraining his wrath in the face of the unbelievers who attacked him from all spheres of the Gentile academic society to which he so desperately desired to belong. (Handelman, p. 133)

In the centre, Moses, the Jew, dispossessed of his identity, barred, castrated, become Egyptian again, oscillating between the all-power of the legislator and the fault or parapraxis of a man who lets drop the tables of the law . . . If one turns the pages of *Moses* . . . , one can read between the lines the epic of a legendary city whose Nile is called

Danube and whose Egyptian hero is a Moravian Jew. (Roudinesco, I, 88, 100)

We are certainly getting ahead; if I am Moses, then you are Joshua and will take possession of the promised land of psychiatry, which I shall only be able to glimpse from afar . . . (Freud to Jung, 17/1/1909)

Freud too, naturally, is Moses. Mosaic, capital M, from Moses: small m, from Greek *mousa*, Muse.

To my critical sense this book, which takes its start from the man Moses, appears like a dancer balancing on the tip of one toe. If I could not find support in an analytic interpretation of the exposure myth and could not pass from there to Sellin's suspicion about the end of Moses, the whole thing would have had to remain unwritten. In any case, let us now take the plunge. (Freud 13, 299)

As pirouette, the dance of the hieroglyph cannot fully be played out inside. Not only because of the 'real space, or the stage', not only because of the point which pierces the book's page or image, but above all because of a certain lateral displacement: turning incessantly on its point, the hieroglyph, the sign, the cipher leaves its here, as though mocking, always here in passing from here to there, from one here to another, inscribing in the *stigmè* of its here the *other* point towards which it continuously moves, the other pirouette which, in each volt, in the flight of each tissue, instantaneously remarks itself. Each pirouette is, then, in its turning, only the mark of another pirouette, entirely other and the same. (D, 271–2)

But, ladies and gentlemen, had the youthful Moses listened to and accepted that view of life, had he bowed his head and bowed his will and bowed his spirit before that arrogant admonition he would never have brought the chosen people out of their house of bondage nor followed the pillar of cloud by day. He would never have spoken with the Eternal amid lightnings on Sinai's mountaintop nor ever have come down with the light of inspiration shining in his countenance and bearing in his arms the tables of the law, graven in the language of the outlaw.

Suppose I give this explanation: 'I take "Moses" to mean the man, if there was such a man, who led the Israelites out of Egypt, whatever he was called then and whatever he may or may not have done besides.'–But similar doubts to those about 'Moses' are possible about the words of this explanation (what are you calling 'Egypt', whom the 'Israelites' etc.?). [. . .]

The sign-post is in order–if, under normal circumstances, it fulfils its purpose. (Wittgenstein, §87)

That is oratory, the professor said, uncontradicted.

NOTES

References in the text are to the following:

Bernal, Martin, *Black Athena: the Afroasiatic Roots of Classical Civilisation* (London: Free Association Books, 1987).

Bernasconi, Robert, and Wood, David, ed., *Derrida and Différance* (Warwick: Parousia Press, 1985).

Derrida, Jacques,

(A) *Altérités* (with Pierre-Jean Labarrière) (Paris: Osiris, 1986).

(CH) 'Chora', in *Poikilia: études offertes à Jean-Pierre Vernant* (Paris: EHESS, 1987).

(CP) *La carte postale de Socrate à Freud et au-delà* (Paris: Aubier-Flammarion, 1980).

(D) *La dissémination* (Paris: Seuil, 1972).

(EC) 'Economimesis', in *Mimesis des articulations* (Paris: Aubier-Flammarion, 1975).

(ED) *L'écriture et la différence* (Paris: Seuil, 1967).

(EP) *Eperons: les styles de Nietzsche* (Paris: Flammarion, 1978).

(F) 'Fors: les mots anglés de Nicolas Abraham et Maria Torok'. Foreword to Nicolas Abraham and Maria Torok, *Cryptonomie: le verbier de l'homme aux loups* (Paris: Aubier-Flammarion, 1976).

(GL) *Glas* (Paris: Galilée, 1974).

(GR) *De la grammatologie* (Paris: Minuit, 1967).

(M) *Marges de la philosophie* (Paris: Minuit, 1972).

(POS) *Positions* (Paris: Minuit, 1972).

(PRE) 'Préjugés: devant la loi', in Lyotard et al., *La faculté de juger* (Paris: Minuit, 1985).

(PS) *Psyché: inventions de l'autre* (Paris: Galilée, 1987).

(SCH) *Schibboleth: pour Paul Celan* (Paris: Galilée, 1986).

(SCR) 'Scribble'. Préface à *l'Essai sur les hiéroglyphes de Warburton* (Paris: Aubier-Flammarion, 1978).

(TA) *D'un ton apocalyptique adopté naguère en philosophie* (Paris: Galilée, 1983).

(UG) *Ulysse gramophone* (Paris: Galilée, 1987).

(VEP) *La vérité en peinture* (Paris: Flammarion, 1978).

(VP) *La voix et le phénomène* (Paris: PUF, 1967).

Freud, Sigmund, *The Pelican Freud Library*, vols. 1, 4, 12, 13, 14.

The Freud-Jung Correspondence (London: Picador, 19XX).

Handelman, Susan, 'Reb Derrida's Scripture', in *The Slayers of Moses* (Albany: State University of New York Press, 1982).

Joyce, James, *Ulysses* (Harmondsworth: Penguin, 1960).

Kearney, Richard, *Dialogues with Contemporary Continental Thinkers* (Manchester: Manchester University Press, 1984).

Levinas, Emmanuel, *Quatre lectures talmudiques* (Paris: Minuit, 1968).

Roudinesco, Elisabeth, *La bataille de cent ans: histoire de la psychanalyse en France*, Vol. 2 (Paris: Seuil, 1986).

Rousseau, Jean-Jacques, *Oeuvres complètes*, ed. Gagnebin and Raymond, 4 vols. to date (Paris: Gallimard, 1959–).

Wittgenstein, Ludwig, *Philosophical Investigations* (Oxford: Blackwell, 1953).

Wörner, Karl, *Schönberg's 'Moses and Aaron'* (London: Faber, 1963).

1 Referring to 'La Pharmacie de Platon', D, 71–197; the opening of 'La Double Séance', Ibid., 201–318; CH; 'Le puits et la pyramide', M, 81–127; the left-hand column of Glas; 'Freud et la scène de l'écriture', ED, 293–340; 'Scribble (pouvoir-écrire)', introduction to Patrick Tort, ed. William Warburton, *Essai sur les hiéroglyphes* (Paris: Aubier-Flammarion, 1977), 7–43.

2 This view is to be found in whole or in part in quite disparate places: see, for example, Vincent Descombes, *Le même et l'autre: quarante-cinq ans de philosophie francaise (1933–1978)* (Paris: Minuit, 1979) and *Grammaire d'objets en tous genres* (Paris: Minuit, 1983); Jean-François Lyotard, *Economie libidinale* (Paris: Minuit, 1974), pp. 12 and 305; some of this attitude to deconstruction is still in evidence in Lyotard's *Heidegger et 'les juifs'* (Paris: Galilée, 1988), pp. 119, 122–3.

3 The term is most consistently and fruitfully exploited by Gasché, and although Derrida had used the term intermittently before the publication of Gasché's book, he appears to have used it more regularly since. See, for example, CP, 430; GL, 227a; PS, 220, 593, 641–2; UG, 116, 141; cf. the use of 'simili-transcendental' in GL, 340a. Cf. my discussion of this and other terms in Gasché in 'Deconstruction and the Philosophers (the very idea)', *Oxford Literary Review*, 10 (1988), 73–130.

4 See, for example, Susan Handelman, *The Slayers of Moses: the Emergence of Rabbinic Interpretation in Modern Literary Theory* (Albany: State University of New York Press, 1982). Despite the considerable interest of Handelman's book, her readings of Derrida, which have him 'gleefully proclaiming a new liberation', and generally advocating 'freeplay', are seriously insufficient.

5 I am grateful to Diane Morgan for drawing this reference to my attention.

6 This aspect of the problem is brought out most clearly by Lyotard, in *Heidegger et 'les juifs'* (Paris: Galilée, 1988), especially pp. 119ff, and, for the supposed 'missing' of the essential character of Jewish thinking in Heidegger, 'Le temps aujourd'hui', in *L'inhumain* (Paris: Galilée, 1988), pp. 69–88 (p. 88); ['Time today', translated by Geoffrey Bennington and Rachel Bowlby, *Oxford Literary Review*, 11 (1989), 3–20].

7 Add Egypt to the list of 'things' evading the question 'What is . . . ?' in Derrida:

see, for example, D, 169, 203, 253; EP, 57, 92; GL, 47a; GR, 31, 110; SCH, 30; UG, 122; VEP, 24; VP, 26.

8 Cf. J. R. Porter, *Moses and Monarchy: a Study in the Biblical tradition of Moses* (Oxford: Blackwell, 1963), p. 20.

9 For a more detailed account of the legislator in Rousseau, see my *Sententiousness and the Novel: Laying Down the Law in Eighteenth-century French Fiction* (Cambridge: CUP, 1985), pp. 166–71. For the generalization of this argument, see my *Dudding: des noms de Rousseau* (Paris: Galilée, 1991).

10 In some work in progress, I try to derive a similar description from Kant's political writings, in preparation for an analogical transfer of this structure to Kant's philosophy as a whole. On this reading, exorbitant absolute exteriority just is Reason.

6

John Sallis

Doublings

Erst der Mensch verdoppelt sich so, das Allgemeine für das Allgemeine zu sein. (Hegel, *Enzyklopädie*, Zusatz 1 to §24)

One cannot (therefore) have begun.

For one will always only have begun again, redoubling what will always already have commenced.

Redoubling–the word is itself double, saying again in its prefix the repetition, reproduction, that is said in *doubling*. Its sense too is double: it means both to double and to double again–hence, a doubling itself subject to doubling, reiterable without a controlling limit, doublings. As in the exhortation that Shakespeare has Gaunt deliver to Bolingbroke:

> And let thy blows doubly redoubled
> Fall like amazing thunder. . . .[1]

Doubly redoubled: the phrase itself doubles what *redoubled* alone (in its double sense) already says, thus both saying and enacting doublings.

To begin will always be (or prove to have been) redoubling–which is to say no beginning at all.

Even for Socrates, paradigmatic figure of the beginning of philosophy. He (too) must redouble his effort and can begin only by beginning again, by setting out on a δεύτερος πλοῦς. His final discourse, spoken in the face of death, recounts his redoubling turn to discourse, his recourse to λόγοι. The turn traces out the scene on which the history of metaphysics will be played out. For it is a turn away from the blinding vision of origin: Socrates will 'be careful not to suffer the misfortune that befalls people who look at and study the sun during an eclipse. For some of them ruin their eyesight unless they look at its image [εἰκών] in water or something of the sort.' A turn, then, to images. And yet, also a turn to λόγοι: 'I thought of that danger, and I was afraid my soul would be blinded if I looked at things [τὰ πράγματα] with my eyes and tried to grasp them with any of my senses. So I thought I must have recourse to λόγοι and examine in them the truth of beings [τῶν ὄντων τὴν ἀλήθειαν].'[2] Both the discourse that follows in the *Phaedo* (which interprets the recourse as issuing in ὑπόθεσις) as well as those around the centre of the *Republic* that are linked most closely with the pivotal discourse of the *Phaedo* serve to demonstrate that the recourse to λόγοι is nothing but a way of redoubling the drive to origin, of posing in every instance the thing itself (τὸ πρᾶγμα αὐτό)[3] as εἶδος and thus (re)launching the advance towards the originals. It is thus anything but simply a recourse to images, and one soon realizes that a redoubling haunts that very turn with which philosophy would begin. The turn is, at the same time–in Greek one would say, more appropriately, ἅμα–both originary, releasing an advance towards the origin, *and* regressive, directing one back to the images through which, if not among which, one would advance only by a kind of double vision. Thus, the double turn both directs one towards the origin and opens the space of the difference between the εἴδη and the things of sense. In turn, the εἴδη will only double in a sense, in sense itself, in sense as such, the things of sense, doubling thus the very sense of sense, establishing the limits that delimit (almost) the most gigantic of spaces, the scene of every γιγαντομαχία περὶ τῆς οὐσίας.

After Nietzsche–if not already in the Platonic inscription of the ἐπέκεινα τῆς οὐσίας (which fathers images–doubles–of itself), to say nothing of the χώρα (the mother of images, the virtually unspeakable condition of doublings)–one can no longer–that is, it turns out that one never could–be assured of controlling this doubling, of limiting it by referral to the delimiting origin. For when the true world finally becomes a fable, it is not only the (no longer) true origin that is set adrift but also the very doubling of sense. Now writing, whose very sense is in a sense to double sense, cannot but drift as on the open sea, on beyond 'the land of truth', on beyond that 'island, enclosed by nature itself within unalterable limits', out upon 'the wide and stormy ocean'.[4]

As if, again, on a δεύτερος πλοῦς. But now still more openly exposed to doublings. A writing amidst doublings.

Which is to say (also) a writing of–in the double sense of the genitive–a certain release of mimesis, a writing that would exceed the interpretation of mimesis that, inscribed in the Platonic texts, has governed, among other things, the history of the relationship between philosophy and literature. Even in the Platonic interpretation, mimetic doubling involves a mechanism that foils any effort at controlling inscription, except perhaps one that would itself double textually (as in certain dialogues) the very logic that the mechanism releases. In its very simplest schema this 'sort of logical machine'–as Derrida calls it in 'The Double Session'–consists in the following: mimesis both furthers and hinders the disclosure of the thing itself, disclosing the thing by resembling it but obscuring it by substituting a double in place of it.[5]

Another, related mechanism is outlined in one of Derrida's discussions of Saussure in *Of Grammatology*.[6] The discussion belongs to that moment of double reading in which one undertakes to expose a certain doubling interior to the text itself, a doubling by which the metaphysical solidarities that are marked undergo a certain destabilization. The solidarity in question is phonocentrism, the subordination of writing to speech. For Saussure this subordination is secured within the order of mimesis as representation: 'Language [*Langage*] and writing are two distinct systems of signs: the second *exists for the sole purpose* of representing [*représenter*] the first' (G 46; C 45–Derrida's emphasis). Writing would thus be related to human speech in the global sense (*langage*) as outside to inside. Since writing is 'foreign to the internal system' (G 50; C 44), it is to be excluded from the field of linguistics, spoken language alone constituting the object of that science. Thus would linguistics be rigorously delimited: 'External/internal, image/reality, representation/ presence, such is the old grid to which is given the task of outlining the field of a science' (G 50). Thus, in turn, is marked the solidarity of Saussurian linguistics with one of the oldest chains of metaphysical concepts. What produces a certain doubling back over this mark is Saussure's inability simply to disregard writing: 'Thus, although writing is foreign to the internal system, it is impossible to disregard a process by which language is continually represented [*figurée*]' (C 44). Writing cannot be disregarded because, even if properly outside, it is not in fact simply outside but has always already contaminated spoken language, invading the interior and usurping the role that belongs properly to spoken language. Saussure cannot but denounce this inversion of the natural relationship and propose to protect speech from the violent intrusion of writing, to restore thus the natural relationship. What is especially to be denounced is the usurpation: writing (a mere representation, an image, of speech) becomes so intertwined with speech (the presence, the reality, the original) that there is an inversion, a perversion, in which it comes to seem that speech is an image of writing. In place of the rigorous distinction between the original reality and the representational image, there is a mingling of image with original, a confusion that Saussure can only denounce as a dangerous promiscuity– dangerous because it obscures the origin, dividing it from itself. Hence the mechanism:

> There is no longer a simple origin. For what is reflected is split *in itself* [*se dédouble en soi-même*] and not only as an addition to itself of its

image. The reflection, the image, the double, splits what it doubles [*Le reflet, l'image, le double dédouble ce qu'il redouble*]. The origin of the speculation becomes a difference. What can look at itself is not one; and the law of the addition of the origin to its representation, of the thing to its image, is that one plus one makes at least three. The historical usurpation and theoretical bizarreness that install the image within the rights of reality are determined as the *forgetting* of a simple origin. (G 55)

Determined as (merely) a forgetting of a simple origin, this mechanism by which the double splits, and thus redoubles, that of which it is the double–this doubling operation is also determined by Saussure as catastrophe or monstrosity. Derrida cites from the *Course in General Linguistics*: 'Language [*La langue*] is independent of writing' (C 45); and then, assuming (one of) the voice(s) of Saussure, he continues:

such is the truth of nature. And yet nature is affected–from without–by an overturning that modifies it in its interior, denatures it, and obliges it to deviate from itself. Nature denaturing itself, deviating *from itself*, naturally gathering its outside into its inside, is *catastrophe*, a natural event that overturns nature, or *monstrosity*, a natural deviation within nature (G 61).[7]

Thus catastrophe, monstrosity, within the very order of mimesis, released by the very logic of such doubling. Or rather, what–within a certain interpretation of mimesis, within *the* interpretation of mimesis that both governs and is governed by metaphysics and its history–can only appear as catastrophic, as monstrous.

Writing as catastrophic doubling. Writing of monstrous doubling–again in the double sense of the genitive.

How, then, is a δεύτερος πλοῦς to be undertaken again? How is the turn that is inscribed in the Platonic texts (most succinctly in the pivotal discourse of the *Phaedo*) to be reinscribed in a writing of monstrous doubling. No doubt, by remarking the metaphysical inscriptions, submitting those texts to a double mark, a double reading and writing.[8] Among those inscriptions there is one that enjoys a certain privilege: a privilege, to be sure, with respect to Derrida's own itinerary, but also a certain limited privilege in principle. For in his readings of the Husserlian texts[9] what Derrida undertakes to demonstrate–or at least to begin to confirm–is 'that the recourse to phenomenological critique is the metaphysical project itself, in its historical achievement and in the purity, yet now restored [*seulement restaurée*], of its origin' (V 3). What Derrida submits to double reading in *Voice and Phenomenon* is a decisive reinscription of the beginning of metaphysics, a redoubling that would restore the original precisely in the double. Thus it is that, while proposing to relate his texts by way of a strange geometry that would allow them to be, for instance, stapled in the middle of each other, he grants nonetheless that 'in a classical philosophical architecture *Voice* [*and Phenomenon*] would come first [*en premier lieu*]'.[10]

The voice is the pivot on which Derrida's text turns. It is what would empower speech, what would grant to expression the capacity to become transparent, self-effacing, in such a way as to allow the expressed meaning to present itself in its pure ideality. Thus would expression be differentiated from mere indication, which would always remain outside this sphere of pure diaphaneity. Thus would Husserl, within the limits of the affinity of this differentiation to the Aristotelian differentiation between speech and writing, also authorize the classical concept of writing as the visible-spatial doubling of speech–even if less dogmatically than Saussure, even if also finally, in 'The Origin of Geometry', uncovering a decisive (and disruptive) connection between writing and ideality.[11] On the other side, Husserl would protect the ideality of meaning from all empirical contamination, rigorously differentiating expression from sense experience, marking them as distinct strata and precisely thereby undertaking to control the doubling that now comes to double the Platonic turn.

Everything depends, then, on the reduction that Husserl attempts to carry out in the first chapter of the First Logical Investigation. Here it is a matter of the reduction of indication: beginning–though in a sense also not beginning, in more than one sense–with the general concept of sign, Husserl's analysis generates a series of 'essential distinctions' by which what is non-essential, merely indicative, is separated off from the concept of meaningful sign, from expression, which through the reduction thus comes to be circumscribed in its essence. The reduction is in effect–or, rather, in its intended effect–an eidetic reduction of language.

And yet, Husserl evades the beginning; he begins, not at the beginning, but only at a point where a doubling has already come into play and produced a differentiation. Derrida notes that Husserl foregoes taking up the question of the sign *in general*, that he limits himself to the observation that every sign is a sign for something, without enquiring about what it means to be a sign for something. Instead of beginning at the beginning by asking 'What is a sign in general?' Husserl proceeds almost immediately to the radical dissociation between two kinds of signs, to the heterogeneity between expression and indication (*Ausdruck, Anzeige*). Derrida notes too that this move may be regarded as an operation of that same logocentric orientation that in general leads Husserl to subordinate the reflection on signs to logic and to undertake such reflection only within his *Logical Investigations*: Husserl's logocentrism would divert his analysis too quickly, dogmatically, in the direction of logical, meaningful signs, that is, expressions. Yet, on the other hand, Derrida hastens to add, Husserl's strategy can also be regarded as the very opposite of dogmatism, as a kind of critical vigilance. Specifically, it can be regarded as his refusal to introduce some presumptive–that is, presupposed–comprehension of the concept of sign in general. Thus, Husserl would in effect have foregone assuming that there is *a* concept of sign, capable then of being divided into two different kinds of signs; he would in effect have left open the possibility of there being two irreducible concepts improperly attached to the same word. Thus, there would prove to have been a curious complicity between Husserl's logocentrism and his critical vigilance: led by his logocentric orientation to seek the essence of sign in expression and meaning, he would precisely thereby have been drawn away from positing a presumptive general concept of sign. An even more critical vigilance could then also have been brought into play, one that would put the very question into question. For if one were to ask '*What is* a sign in general?' one would have presumed by the very form of the question that it is a matter of asking about the truth or essence of the sign–that is, one would not have asked whether a sign is such a thing as can have an essence. Is it perhaps the case, on the contrary, that essence and truth are first made possible by signs and language? In this case the classical question ('What is . . . ?' 'τί ἐστι . . . ?') could not but be interrupted: 'For if the sign in some way preceded what one calls truth or essence, there would be no sense in speaking of the truth or the essence of the sign' (V 26).

Derrida's reading retraces the Husserlian text, attempting–in the words of a contemporaneous interview–'to think the structured genealogy of its concepts in a manner most faithful, most interior';[12] yet, at the same time, drawing out what is implicit in those concepts, it would submit that text to the double mark, marking those points at which the text diverges from itself, at which one may use 'against the edifice the instruments or stones available in the house'.[13] *Of Grammatology* provides a more precise, more nuanced statement of what deconstruction would venture:

> Within the closure, by an oblique and always perilous movement, constantly risking falling back within what is being deconstructed, it is necessary to surround the critical concepts with a careful and thorough discourse, to mark the conditions, the medium, and the limits of their effectiveness, to designate rigorously their relationship [*appartenance*] to the machine whose deconstruction they permit; and, by the same stroke, designate the crevice through which the yet unnameable glimmer beyond the closure can be glimpsed. (G 25)

Let me recall–ever so briefly–the course of the reading in which Derrida doubles deconstructively the Husserlian reduction of indication.

The first stage of the reduction corresponds to the distinction between meaningful signs and indicative signs, between expression and indication. Husserl grants that normally meaningful signs are bound up (interwoven, entangled–*verflochten*) with indicative signs; or rather, since the difference proves quickly to be more functional than substantial (V 20), it turns out that most signs function in both ways, that in most signs the two functions are interwoven. Nonetheless, Husserl insists that the entanglement (*Verflectung*) of meaningful signs in an indicative function is not essential: in solitary mental life (*im einsamen Seelenleben*) meaningful signs function without indicating anything. It is clear initially that with this distinction Husserl intends to mark the difference between linguistic signs (speech–*Rede*) and non-linguistic signs. And yet, as Derrida's reading underlines, the boundary shifts in the course of Husserl's development of the distinction, indeed to such an extent that the very sense of the distinction changes. The shift is most conspicuous in Husserl's relegation of certain aspects of speech to the side of indication, for example, in his formulation, 'facial expressions [*Mienenspiel*] and the gestures that involuntarily accompany speech without communicative intent' (L II/1: 31). To an extent the exclusion of these aspects from the sphere of expression is determined by their lack of fusion with the meaning-intention. What for Husserl seems most decisive is their involuntary character, their lack of intention; and indeed whatever falls outside the voluntary, animating intention he will exclude from the sphere of expression. Derrida marks the scope of this exclusion: it includes 'facial expressions, gestures, the whole of the body and of mundane inscription, in a word the whole of the visible and spatial as such'. For: 'Visibility and spatiality as such could only lose the self-presence of will and of the spiritual animation that opens up discourse' (V 37). Clearly, then, it is no longer a matter of a distinction between the linguistic and the non-linguistic but rather of a distinction within language: 'For all these reasons, the distinction between indication and expression cannot rightfully be made as one between a non-linguistic and a linguistic sign. Husserl traces a boundary that passes, not between language and non-language, but within language in general, between the explicit and the non-explicit (with all their connotations)' (V 39). The distinction is, within language, between the voluntary, transparent, self-present, and the involuntary, external, non-self-present, that is, between the pure spiritual intention (*la pure intention spirituelle*), the pure animation by *Geist*, and those aspects of speech that involve visibility and spatiality, the bodily aspects, as it were, of speech.

Thus, the reduction of indication would enforce an assimilation of language to voluntary, self-present intentional *Leben*. It would place the essence of language on the side of the spiritual, enclosing it in the citadel of

Geist, securing it from intrusion from without. However problematic both *Leben* and *Geist* remain in Husserl's text.

The second stage of the reduction is addressed to what Husserl circumscribes as the most pervasive indicative function. This function, the intimating function (*die kundgebende Funktion*) or simply intimation (*Kundgabe*–Derrida translates: *manifestation*), is so pervasive as to be interwoven in all communicative speech: it is that function that serves to indicate to the hearer the 'thoughts' of the speaker; that is, in Husserl's formulation, intimation provides a sign 'for the sense-giving psychic experiences of the speaker, as well as for the other psychic experiences that belong to his communicative intention' (L II/1: 33). For Husserl it is of utmost consequence to distinguish this intimating function from the meaning function. It is, then, precisely this distinction that the second stage of the reduction would enforce.

The turn to intimation serves to show that the reduction is not a matter simply of excluding whatever belongs to the visible-spatial order. Derrida identifies what it is, instead, that determines the reduction: 'One approaches here the root of indication: there is indication whenever the sense-giving act, the animating intention, the living spirituality of the meaning [*vouloir-dire*], is not fully present' (V 41). It is just such full presence that is lacking in facial expressions and gestures, which retain a coefficient of externality, of non-presence. The lack is more radical in the case of the meaning-intention of another person: the lived experience of the other is radically non-present. Derrida concludes:

> The notion of *presence* is the nerve of this demonstration. If communication or intimation (*Kundgabe*) is essentially indicative, it is because we have no originary intuition of the presence of the other's lived experience. Whenever the immediate and full presence of the signified is concealed, the signifier will be of an indicative nature . . . . All discourse, or rather, everything in discourse that does not restore the immediate presence of the signified content, is inexpressive. (V 43)

What determines the reduction is the privilege accorded to presence: any moment of discourse that does not present the signified content, any moment that is irreducible to the self-present intention, is inexpressive, that is, indicative.

In order to maintain the integrity of expression, its essential distinctness from indication, it is imperative that Husserl demonstrate that speech in solitary mental life is free of intimation. His most decisive argument in this regard is the following: 'In a monologue words can perform no function of indicating the existence of psychic acts, since such indication there would be quite purposeless. For the acts in question are themselves experienced by us at that very moment [*im selben Augenblick*]' (L II/1: 36–37; cited in V 54). Whatever one might suppose to be intimated in speech in solitary mental life would in fact be experienced at that very moment, in the same moment, so that intimation would be superfluous, utterly without purpose (*ganz zwecklos*). Within the moment there would be no difference to be mediated by intimation, within the *Augenblick* no alterity to be bridged by an indicative function: 'The present of self-presence would be as indivisible as a *blink of the eye*' (V 66).

Husserl cannot but exclude also the articulated sound-complex and of course the written sign, thus distinguishing essentially between the sensible sign and those acts by which expression is more than mere uttered sounds, the acts by which something is meant. Such is the third stage of the reduction. Here again the reference to speech in solitary mental life plays a crucial role. For in monologue the sensible sign itself undergoes a kind of reduction: one speaks to oneself *in silence*. Not that words disappear entirely: one could hardly conceive an expression in which words would be utterly lacking. Husserl's recourse puts into play–without further question–a very old opposition: 'In phantasy a spoken or printed word floats before us, though in truth it does not at all exist' (L II/1: 36). Thus is the sensible sign reduced: as mere imagined word it is assimilated to the self-present intention, while as sounded it is consigned to indication. Despite Husserl's aim of delimiting pure expression as the very essence of meaningful signification, his analysis leaves intact only the ephemeral images of words, their imaginary doubles, and displaces their originals (what one would call the real signs) to the side, the outside, of indication, thus setting the originals outside what would be the very domain of origin: 'For it is clearer and clearer that, despite the initial distinction between an indicative sign and an expressive sign, only an indication is truly a sign for Husserl' (V 46).

The deconstructive doubling is thus such that, on the one hand, it (re)traces the Husserlian text from within, thinking the structured genealogy of its concepts in such a way as to show that the production of the essential distinctions is in effect an eidetic reduction of language, a reduction governed by the privilege of presence; while, on the other hand, it underlines that the pure expression to which language would be reduced would be only a silent soliloquy from which all real signs would have been banished, so that the effect of the Husserlian reduction would be finally to repress the sign, redoubling the metaphysical subordination of the sign to a domain of self-presence that would essentially precede all operation of signs.

Here one can begin to discern in the Husserlian project not just a reinscription of the metaphysical project in general but specifically a redoubling of the turn that marks the beginning of metaphysics. For in the reduction to a domain of pure self-present expression prior to all operation of signs, Husserl would in effect have carried out a turn to λόγοι that, as in the beginning, would serve to redouble the drive to origin. The question is whether this domain can remain intact in its pre-linguistic integrity; or whether the turn–this moment of logocentrism–will not be (re)diverted to an operation of signification from which *Bedeutung*, thus adrift, would never be free. Such a diversion is broached in deconstruction as a turn to writing, to a writing that would no longer be the mere image of speech but rather its monstrous double.

Yet, the δεύτερος πλοῦς is not only a turn to λόγοι but also a doubling that matches meaning and sense, a doubling of the sense of sense. In its Husserlian reinscription this doubling appears as a parallelism between expression (purified of indication) and sense (experience). To the reduction of signification to pure expression Husserl would add a second reduction: the reduction of pure expression to an unproductive medium that would merely reflect the pre-expressive stratum of sense, of perception. Derrida's reading is concerned to mark the condition that makes this reduction possible, the condition that allows expression to be regarded as merely reflecting the pre-expressive stratum, as merely doubling in the order of ideality the stratum of sense experience. Such doubling requires that expression re-create at its proper level the presence and self-presence allegedly characteristic of the pre-expressive level of sense: 'the medium of expression must protect, respect, and restore the *presence* of sense, *both* [*à la fois*] *as the object's being before us*, open to view, and *as proximity to self in interiority*' (V 83). What makes such restoration of presence possible is the essential connection of expression to the voice. It is the voice that preserves presence and thus lets the ideal meaning be immediately present:

> This immediate presence results from the fact that the phenomenological 'body' of the signifier seems to fade away at the very moment it is produced. It seems already to belong to the element of ideality. It phenomenologically reduces itself, transforming the worldly opacity of its body into pure diaphaneity. This effacement of the sensible body and its exteriority is *for consciousness* the very form of the immediate presence of the signified. (V 86)

In the voice the signifier effaces itself for the sake of the presence of the signified meaning; such effacement is possible only because the signifier never really escapes self-presence, because in the voice self-presence is preserved: 'When I speak, it belongs to the phenomenological essence of this operation that *I hear myself at the same time* [*je m'entende dans le temps*] that I speak' (V 87).

Again–as with the purposelessness of indication in silent monologue–it is a matter of a certain self-coincidence in the order of time, a matter of a sameness of time, that would give one back to oneself in the very unity of that moment in which one would reach out. Because the unity of the moment authorizes both reductions, it is also what determines the Husserlian reinscription of the Socratic turn.

Thus, it is on the question of time that the Husserlian project in a sense–in its doublings of sense and of the sense of sense–runs aground and prompts another δεύτερος πλοῦς that would be more openly exposed to doublings, a writing amidst doublings. For what Derrida marks in the Husserlian analysis of time, what he marks as working against the classical orientation of that analysis in a way that turns it against itself, is precisely a doubling that disrupts the unity of the moment.

Derrida's reading of the Husserlian analysis of time is even more explicitly double than his reading of the reduction of indication. On the one hand, he marks the point by which Husserl's entire analysis is inseparably linked to the metaphysical privileging of presence; that point is precisely the now-point, the punctual moment. Though Husserl grants that the now cannot be isolated as a pure stigmatic moment, as a simple point, this admission does not at all prevent its determination as a point from functioning constitutively in the analyses. Though indeed there is a certain spread from the now-point into the immediate, retended past and into the immediate, protended future–

> This spread is nonetheless thought and described on the basis of [*à partir de*] the self-identity of the now as point, as 'source-point'. In phenomenology the idea of originary presence and in general of 'beginning', 'absolute beginning', *principium*, always refers back to this 'source-point'. . . . Despite all the complexity of its structure, temporality has a nondisplaceable center, an eye or living core, the punctuality of the actual now. (V 69)

It is to this punctual–and, as such, self-identical–now that Husserl appeals in the phrase '*im selben Augenblick*', by which he would demonstrate the purposelessness of intimating indication in silent monologue. It is to this self-same now that he appeals also in conjoining, by the phrase *dans le temps*, speaking with hearing oneself, conjoining them into that self-presence of the voice that would make of expression an unproductive medium merely reflecting the pre-expressive stratum of sense. Not that Husserl is in error in making this appeal: on the contrary, he is proceeding from the most secure of grounds. He is moving within the very element of philosophy: such coincidence of intuition and presence as would be the originary as such, the originary from which every as such would be determined, the ἀρχή:

Moreover, within philosophy there is no possible objection concerning this privilege of the present-now. This privilege defines the very element of philosophical thought, it is evidence itself, conscious thought itself, it governs every possible concept of truth and of sense. One cannot cast suspicion upon it without beginning to get at the core of consciousness itself from a region that lies elsewhere than philosophy, a procedure that would remove every possible *security* and *ground* from discourse. (V 70)

Derrida proposes that–on the other hand–it is precisely Husserl's own analyses that serve to cast such suspicion and to disrupt the discourse on–the discourse of–the self-identical present. What those descriptions demonstrate is that the present is essentially, constitutively, connected to the immediate past (by retention) and the immediate future (by protention):

One then sees very quickly that the presence of the perceived present can appear as such only insofar as it is *continuously compounded* with a nonpresence and nonperception, with primary memory and expectation (retention and protention). (V 72)

This is to say that a nonpresence is admitted into the sphere of what would be originary presence, expanding the point, which it would come to constitute precisely in disrupting its punctuality. Thus, the self-identity of the present could no longer function as a simple origin (as present origin or originary present) but would rather be *produced* through a certain compounding of presence and nonpresence, of impression and retention, of impression and protention. Hence, the very constitution of the now, the moment, takes place as a doubling of the previous nows (or the nows to come) in the present now, that is, as retention (or protention); and as a doubling, an unlimited repetition, of the now as such, in its ideality, as the ideal form of presence. This double doubling in which time is constituted, produced–Derrida will call it *différance*–is thus more originary than the present: it is–'if one can use this language without immediately contradicting it and erasing it–more "originary" than the phenomenologically originary itself' (V 75). It will always already have introduced alterity into the moment, disrupting the '*im selben Augenblick*' and the '*dans le temps*', thus disrupting too the parallelism of indication/expression/sense that would be erected on the ground of that unity. When time begins, a monstrous doubling will already have begun; and it is only by repressing such catastrophe that one can be assured of controlling the doubling of sense marked by the Socratic turn. Deconstruction would release the monster from the cave and begin to write amidst doublings.

The stratification will be ruined, its schema disrupted, the schema that comes to govern and structure almost the entire programme of phenomenology from *Ideas* on, a schema with a strong affinity to the classical schema stemming from Aristotle's *On Interpretation*, in which writing, like indication for Husserl, is determined as an outside of speech, as doubling it in the visible order. For the Husserlian schema, which would determine the orders of indication, expression, and sense as distinct, parallel strata, requires precisely those reductions–the reduction of indication and the reduction of expression to an unproductive medium–that are shown by Derrida's reading to rely on the unity, the self-identity, of the present. As soon as the appeal to the self-presence of the '*im selben Augenblick*' is interrupted by the deconstruction of the Husserlian time-analysis, the distinctness and parallelism between indication and expression is ruined: indication–especially in the form of intimation–cannot be kept out of expression, not even in silent monologue. Correspondingly, as soon as the appeal to the '*dans le temps*' that would unite speaking with hearing-oneself-speaking is interrupted, the reduction of expression to an unproductive medium that would merely image sense–in a doubling both controllable and thematizable as such (*Experience and Judgment* would broach such a thematization)–is likewise ruined.

What is at issue at both levels is self-affection. There is no disputing the uniqueness of the voice as a form of self-affection: one can hear-oneself-speak 'without passing through an external detour, the world, the non-own [*non-propre*] in general' (V 88). There is marked contrast, for instance, with seeing oneself or touching oneself, for in these instances the exterior belongs inseparably to the field of the self-affection; whereas the voice in its purity would return one to oneself this side of any exteriority, fashioning a sphere of self-doubling that would open only upon meaning in its ideality, upon the universal (*das Allgemeine*):

> As pure self-affection, the operation of hearing-oneself-speak [*s'entendre-parler*] seems to reduce even the inward surface of one's own body; in its phenomenon it seems capable of dispensing with this exteriority within interiority, this interior space in which our experience or image of our own body is spread forth. This is why hearing-oneself-speak is experienced as an absolutely pure self-affection, in a self-proximity that would be the absolute reduction of space in general. It is this purity that makes it fit for universality. (V 88–9)

For Derrida there is no question of retracting the results of Husserl's minute, rigorous, and quite novel analyses: the uniqueness of the voice and its distinctive capacity for universality is to be acknowledged. Derrida insists even that vocal self-affection is 'no doubt the possibility for what is called *subjectivity* or the *for-itself*', that, even further, 'the voice *is* consciousness' (V 89). Yet, because the voice is submitted to time, to the production that cannot but introduce alterity into the moment, vocal self-affection cannot be–despite its capacity to reduce exteriority–a matter of pure undivided hearing-oneself-speak. Alterity will always already have been operative in the production of vocal self-presence, dividing one from oneself in advance of the very production of oneself, of subjectivity, of consciousness. In vocal self-affection it is not as though there is first a being (the self, subjectivity, consciousness), which then comes to affect itself through the circuit of hearing-oneself-speak. There (is) the (movement of) self-affection–the parentheses marking here the erasure that writing amidst doublings must bring into play. It is from the differential operation of self-affection that the self-coherent self, the self itself, would be produced:

> The movement of *différance* is not something that happens to a transcendental subject. It produces the subject. Self-affection is not a modality of experience that characterizes a being that would already be itself (*autos*). It produces the same as self-relation within self-difference, the same as the non-identical. (V 92)

The production of time is also a matter of self-affection. Referring to Heidegger's analysis in *Kant and the Problem of Metaphysics*, Derrida writes: 'The "source-point", the "originary impression", from which the movement of temporalization is produced [*à partir de quoi se produit* . . .] is already pure self-affection' (V 93). The structure of this self-affection, of the production of time, of temporality, is not only complex but also such as to interrupt the very language that the analysis nonetheless requires, thus also such as to demand, then, a different writing, a writing of difference, a writing amidst doublings. The analysis extends that of the retentional and protentional structures and involves–to proceed very schematically–three points. First: temporality is *pure production*. There is not some being in which temporality would then come to be produced: there (is) simply production of temporality without any being in which it would inhere. Second: the now, the 'originary' impression, *engenders itself*. It is not produced by any being, not produced by anything. Such is its 'absolute novelty': to be engendered by nothing, to engender itself without having somehow been there in advance of the self-affective engendering. If one steadily erases (unsaying in the very saying) such locutions as 'being there' ('there is') and 'in advance', one may say: the now produces itself in a doubling in which there is no original in advance of the double it produces. Third: this self-engendering doubling is (also) a self-differing, that is, the now doubles itself in such a way as to become a not-now to be retained in another now. Thus Derrida refers to–

the process by which the living now, producing itself by spontaneous generation, must, in order to be a now, be retained [*se retenir*] in another now. . . . Such a process is indeed a pure self-affection in which the same is the same only in affecting itself from the other [*s'affectant de l'autre*], only by becoming the other of the same. This self-affection must be pure, since the originary impression is here affected by nothing other than itself, by the absolute 'novelty' of another originary impression that is another now. (V 94–5)

Because the production of time is pure self-affection (the double doubling of self-differing self-engendering), all language, taking its resources from beings, fails to say such doublings otherwise than by metaphor:

But one has always already drifted into ontic metaphor. . . . The word 'time' itself, as it has always been understood in the history of metaphysics, is a metaphor that *at the same time* [*en même temps*] both indicates and dissimulates the 'movement' of this self-affection. (V 95)

This peculiar metaphoricity, this transfer between being and time, is decisive for writing amidst doublings.

The double doubling of temporality and its redoubling in the sphere of the voice disrupt, then, the Husserlian schema that would determine the orders of indication, expression, and sense as distinct, parallel strata, that is, as simple, controlled doubling:

Also, just as expression does not come to be added like a 'stratum' to the presence of a pre-expressive sense, so likewise the outside of indication does not come to affect accidentally the inside of expression. Their intertwining [*Verflechtung*] is originary. (V 97)

Between the orders of sense, expression, and indication the doublings of time and the voice would release: doublings. Thus would be prompted a δεύτερος πλοῦς as writing amidst doublings, writing those doublings as, for instance, *la différance*, as *le supplément d'origine*, but also as *mimesis* and as *doublings*. Perhaps, most notably, as the doublings of *Geist*: the doublings by which spirit is haunted by spirit and ventriloquized by a phantom whose separation from what would be spirit itself cannot be secured and controlled,[14] almost a parody of spirit's return to itself. Such writing amidst doublings one could call ghost writing.

NOTES

1 Shakespeare, *Richard II*, act 1, sc. 3, lines 80–1.
2 Plato, *Phaedo*, 99 d–e.
3 Plato, *Epistle* VII, 341 c.
4 Kant, *Kritik der reinen Vernunft*, A 235/B 294–5.
5 Derrida writes that 'the whole history of the interpretation of the literary arts has moved and been transformed within the diverse logical possibilities opened by the concept of *mimesis*. These are numerous, paradoxical, and disconcerting enough to have released a very rich combinatorial system.' Derrida adds a note outlining this logic in two propositions and six possible consequences, and concludes: 'this schema . . . forms a sort of logical machine; it programs the prototypes of all the propositions inscribed in Plato's discourse as well as in that of the tradition' [*La Dissémination* (Paris: Éditions du Seuil, 1972), 213]. The simple schema that I suggest here is discussed in *Delimitations: Phenomenology and the End of Metaphysics* (Bloomington: Indiana University Press, 1986), chap. 1.
6 *De la Grammatologie* (Paris: Éditions de Minuit, 1967)–references indicated in text by G. Saussure, *Cours de linguistique générale* (Paris: Payot, 1980)–references indicated in text by C.
7 Saussure offers several examples of such inversion, such monstrosity: 'But the tyranny of the letter goes even further. By imposing itself upon the masses, it influences and modifies language. This happens only in very literary languages where written texts play an important role. Then visual images lead to wrong pronunciations; such mistakes are really [*proprement*] pathological. This happens often in French. Thus for the surname *Lefèvre* (from Latin *faber*) there were two spellings, one popular and simple, *Lefèvre*, the other learned and etymological, *Lefèbvre*. Because *v* and *u* were not distinct in the old system of writing, *Lefèbvre* was read as *Lefèbure*, with a *b* that had never really existed in the word and a *u* that was the result of ambiguity. Now the latter form is actually pronounced' (C 53–4). Citing this passage, Derrida asks: 'Where is the evil? . . . And what has been invested in the "living word" that makes such "aggressions" of writing intolerable? What investment begins by determining the constant action of writing as a deformation and an aggression? What prohibition has thus been transgressed? Where is the sacrilege? Why should the mother tongue be protected from the operation of writing?' (G 61). Saussure predicts that such violence exercised by writing upon speech will only increase in the future: 'It is probable that these deformations will become ever more frequent and that the silent letters [*les lettres inutiles*] will come more and more to be pronounced. In Paris one already pronounces the *t* in *sept femmes*; Darmesteter foresees the day when one will pronounce even the last two letters of *vingt*–truly an orthographic monstrosity' (C 54).
8 'This structure of the *double mark* . . . works the entire field within which these texts move. This structure itself is worked in turn: the rule according to which every concept necessarily receives two similar marks–repetition without identity–one mark inside and the other outside the deconstructed system, should give rise to a double reading and a double writing' (*La Dissémination*, 10).

9 Primarily *La Voix et le phénomène: Introduction au problème du signe dans la phénomènologie de Husserl* (Paris: Presses Universitaires de France, 1967)–references indicated in text by V. Edmund Husserl, *Logische Untersuchungen* (Tübingen: Max Niemeyer, 1968)–references indicated in text by L.

10 *Positions* (Paris: Éditions de Minuit, 1972), 13.

11 See Introduction to Husserl's *L'Origin de la géométrie* (Paris: Presses Universitaires de France, 1962), 83ff.

12 *Positions*, 15.

13 *Marges de la philosophie* (Paris: Éditions de Minuit, 1972), 162.

14 See *De L'esprit: Heidegger et la question* (Paris: Galilée, 1987), esp. 66.

7

Robert Bernasconi

No More Stories, Good or Bad: de Man's Criticisms of Derrida on Rousseau

'A story? No. No stories, never again.' (Blanchot, *La folie du jour*)

I

'I have never known how to tell a story.'[1] Derrida begins his *Memoires for Paul de Man*, written and delivered shortly after de Man's death, with the complaint that he lacks the gift of narration. In the course of the lectures that follow, he describes some techniques he has developed in order to cope with this handicap. So, for example, he asks if narrative is possible, admitting that he poses the question in part in self-defence in the face of his deficiency (M 10). Another ruse he admits to employing is that of borrowing stories from mythology. Hence the appeal to Mnemosyne, Lethe, Atropos, Clotho and Lachesis (M 86).

The consequences of Derrida's disability reflects itself in his having to renounce telling the story of who and what brought him to America (M 11). It would have been the story of how deconstruction was transplanted to the United States, a story which intertwined Paul de Man and Jacques Derrida in their mutual friendship and collaboration. And the story would have to have concentrated on the relation between literature and deconstruction because it was among literary critics, rather than among philosophers, that Derrida first found a large audience in the United States. Not that the transposition of deconstruction to America can be understood as its transference from philosophy to literature: in America deconstruction has often been understood as putting the distinction between philosophy and literature in question.[2] And in an autobiographical statement, which approximates to a somewhat punctuated narrative of his intellectual life, Derrida insists that the question 'what is literature?' was his original question. The question of literature not only organizes his first attempts to identify his thesis topic, but returns in later works, albeit with the classical form of the interrogative, the 'what is . . . ?', now submitted to scrutiny.[3] Nevertheless, the patronage of de Man was important both in helping to establish Derrida's new audience and in directing that audience to read Derrida in a certain way. This was done not only in the classrooms at Yale, but also in de Man's chapter on Derrida in *Blindness and Insight*. De Man introduces Derrida's work as 'one of the places where the future possibility of literary criticism is being decided'.[4] In the light of the devoted following both men have accumulated, it is perhaps somewhat ironic that one of the contrasts de Man draws between Rousseau and Derrida is that the former is more radical and mature because 'he cuts himself off once and forever from all future disciples' (BI 140).

In any event, de Man, notwithstanding his debts to Derrida, is no disciple. In *Memoires for Paul de Man* Derrida acknowledges the critical edge of de Man's essay on *Of Grammatology*. He writes, ' . . . never has any criticism appeared to me so easy to accept as that of Paul de Man in "The Rhetoric of Blindness". None has ever given me so much to think about as his has, even if I did not feel I was in agreement with it; though I was not simply in disagreement with it either' (M 126). What was the criticism or criticisms that Derrida found so easy to accept? What was so thought-provoking about de Man's essay? And how does one accept a criticism and yet situate it beyond both agreement and disagreement? In what follows I shall use de Man's criticisms of Derrida to explore the difficulties of criticizing Derrida in general.

The prime difficulty is that Derrida has not left the practice of critique untouched. It is not only that one does not often find in his work the diminishing kind of objections which have been the common stuff of philosophy for much of its history. Derrida had learned from Heidegger and Levinas other possibilities of approaching texts that depart from traditional models, albeit, and I shall be more specific later, he more carefully circumscribes his relation to the texts upon which he comments than they do. In 'Violence and Metaphysics' Derrida describes their approach as follows: 'In the style by which strong and faithful thought is recognised (this is Heidegger's style, too), Levinas respects the zone or layer of traditional truth; and the philosophies whose presuppositions he describes are in general neither refuted nor criticised.'[5] In these terms Levinas's treatment of Heidegger would have to be regarded as an exception, conventional in its polemic. Not that Derrida renounces all criticism of the conventional kind either. He is in no position to write, 'I have never known how to issue a refutation, indulge in critique, or engage in polemic', in quite the way in which he says 'I have never known how to tell a story'. But criticism has never been his principal activity. Nor does it organize his relation to the texts upon which he writes. What is Derrida's relation to critique?[6]

One can read the title of the present volume, *Derrida: A Critical Reader*, in the usual way as offering a series of critical interpretations of Derrida. De Man's 'The Rhetoric of Blindness' would be an appropriate starting-point for an essay in such a volume because de Man provides one of the first detailed *critiques* of Derrida in English. And yet, in order to sustain his critique, de Man assimilates Derrida to traditional models and casts him in the role of a critical reader of Rousseau, without posing the question of whether he conforms to that role. Insofar as my essay raises this question, it might belong better in a volume with the interrogative title *Derrida: A Critical Reader?*, where the contributors would no longer be assigned the task of criticizing the thinker to whom the volume is dedicated, but where the nature of criticism is found to have been put in question by that thinker. 'Critique', 'criticize' and 'criticism' are not particularly common words in Derrida's texts and when they are used they are usually employed in a conventional sense.[7] Nevertheless, one could read much of Derrida's work as being concerned with the question of the possibility, impossibility and redetermination of critique.

Of Grammatology is unique among Derrida's works, to the best of my recollection, for presenting itself specifically as an exercise in critical reading and an examination of what that involves. In the preface, Derrida says of the second part, 'although I have no ambition to illustrate a new method, I have attempted to produce, often embarrassing myself in the process, the problems of critical reading'.[8] And later, in a section entitled 'The Exorbitant: Questions of Method', Derrida describes how a writer writes in a language and logic which is discourse cannot dominate absolutely. The task of a critical reading is understood to be that of 'producing' the relationship between what the writer commands and what he does not command of the patterns of the language that he uses.[9] Such a production must take more risks than a 'respectful doubling commentary', which simply reproduces the text. Nevertheless, doubling commentary has its place in a critical reading because, without it, 'critical production would risk developing in any direction at all and authorize itself to say almost anything'. Recently, Derrida has issued the clarification that what he 'perhaps clumsily' called 'doubling commentary' was '*already* an interpretation', reflecting 'the relative stability of the dominant interpretation (including the "self"-interpretation) of the text being commented upon'.[10] The role of doubling commentary in critical reading was therefore, at least in part, to understand 'what interpretations are probabilistically dominant and conventionally acknowledged to grant access to what Rousseau thought he meant and to what readers for the most part thought they could understand, in order, second, to analyse the play or relative indetermination that was able to open the space of my interpretation, for example, that of the word *supplément*.'[11] De Man praises Derrida's chapter on method in *Of Grammatology* as 'flawless in itself' (BI 139), but it is questionable whether in his interpretation of Derrida he was sufficiently attentive to the discussion of critical reading to be found there.

II

'The Rhetoric of Blindness' was the seventh chapter of de Man's *Blindness and Insight*. In 1977, five years after its original publication, it was reprinted as 'On Reading Rousseau'.[12] The second version shows some changes over the first, but these are mainly determined by the circumstances of its republication. The first twelve paragraphs, more than seven pages, including an epigraph from Nietzsche, are omitted from the 1977 version, as are some explicatory footnotes.[13] Neither Derrida nor Rousseau are mentioned by name on these pages, but it is important for understanding de Man's approach to them to appreciate that the recurrent pattern which he finds from studying figures as varied as Lukacs, Blanchot, Poulet and the American New Critics is that 'all these critics seem curiously doomed to say something quite different from what they meant to say' (BI 105–6). That formulation is a careful echo of a phrase in Derrida to which de Man returns throughout his essay, as I shall in mine. A further two paragraphs and part of a third are moved from early on in 'The Rhetoric of Blindness' and placed at the end of 'On Reading Rousseau'.

It is in one of the omitted paragraphs that de Man poses the question that governs his presentation of Derrida: 'Is the blindness of these critics (those already dealt with earlier in the volume) inextricably tied up with the act of writing itself and, if this is so, what characteristic aspect of literary language causes blindness in those who come into close contact with it?' (BI 106). Other passages, to be found in both versions, reiterate the point. For example, *Of Grammatology* is described as 'an exemplary case of the interaction between critical blindness and critical insight . . . as a necessity dictated and controlled by the very nature of all critical language' (BI 111). Such passages provide some indication of the larger context to which de Man's reading of Derrida belongs, although that context will not be investigated here for the simple reason that the present essay is largely concerned with de Man's essay only for the light it throws on Derrida.

De Man treats *Of Grammatology* almost exclusively as a 'commentary on Rousseau' (BI 111). He discusses only the final three chapters and so examines Derrida as a reader rather than as a philosopher or, more generally, a theoretician. De Man's decision to focus on only one of Derrida's readings is to be preferred to the practice of those commentators who rely almost exclusively on Derrida's programmatic statements. Nevertheless, the limits de Man imposes on his discussion do have serious consequences. First, de Man omits all reference to the whole of the first part of Derrida's book. In the Preface, Derrida had described the first part of his book as its 'theoretical matrix', which the second part was supposed to illustrate. This matrix indicated certain significant historical moments and proposed certain critical concepts: the interpretation of Rousseau's text 'follows implicitly the propositions ventured in Part I' (G 7/1xxix). These go unexamined in 'The Rhetoric of Blindness'.[14] Secondly, de Man virtually neglects the opening chapter of Part II, 'The Violence of the Letter: From Levi-Strauss to Rousseau', except to endorse the contrast Derrida draws between Rousseau and Lévi-Strauss (BI 115). This is particularly unfortunate because it is in this chapter that Derrida indicates the immediate political motivation that provoked his reading of Rousseau. Derrida's readings are almost always occasioned by a contemporary interpretation or recent doctrine which calls for a response. Derrida sets out to expose Lévi-Strauss's ethnocentrism, as well as his logocentrism, precisely because of the dominance of structuralism in France at that time (G 148/99). Given that Lévi-Strauss acknowledges his debt to Rousseau, Derrida can show that a more rigorous reading of Rousseau would have redirected him elsewhere. As new dogmas, or more likely new variations, come to prominence, 'the strategic analysis must be constantly readjusted'.[15] Derrida, who in *Memoires* defends de Man against the charge of being unpolitical in his readings,[16] might have had some cause for complaint against de Man precisely on those grounds. Finally, de Man fails to explore the brief but important introduction to the second part, where Derrida explains what he means when he says he is not just reading Rousseau, but 'the "epoch" of Rousseau' (G 145/97). De Man, as we shall see, simply dismisses this schema of periodization as arbitrary.

On the surface it looks as if de Man virtually ignores half of Derrida's book. Could this silence be understood as strategic? The argument would be that de Man's reticence was necessary in order to portray a version of Derrida which he believes can, with relatively minor modifications, be salvaged from certain difficulties which otherwise threaten to engulf it. It is possible that the distortions which arise from bypassing so much of the book's theoretical underpinnings arise from de Man's attempt to provide a generous reading. But the consequence of this selectivity for the reader is a certain indeterminacy about how de Man actually reads Derrida, not to mention the suspicion of partiality. Did de Man–could de Man– have incorporated this or that passage into his reading? Is his reading guided by the guardrails of a doubling commentary of Derrida? Some of the uncertainties generated by de Man's reticence will emerge as I examine de Man's criticisms of Derrida's reading of Rousseau. These criticisms extend much further than one might at first imagine. His characteristic procedure is to argue by implication, as at one point he grants explicitly: 'we are saying by implication . . . ' (BI 138). This is in keeping with the fact that 'the discrimination that concerns us' is that of 'the mode of knowledge governing the implicit as opposed to the explicit statement' (BI 118). Because de Man's criticisms are often only implicit, they lack the precision which they might have possessed had they been expressly formulated. This exposes de Man to the accusation that he remains within the tradition of philosophical critique because he disdains to address directly the question of the nature of philosophical criticism. Indeed, de Man himself is quite specific throughout 'The Rhetoric of Blindness' that Derrida's contribution to literary criticism cannot be separated from his 'rigour and intellectual integrity' as a philosopher (BI 110).

De Man selects for his scrutiny the second part of *Of Grammatology* out of admiration for both Rousseau and Derrida, whom he characterizes as Rousseau's 'best modern interpreter' (BI 135). This is not to say that de Man underwrites Derrida's reading of Rousseau. According to de Man, Derrida 'had to go out of his way *not* to understand him [Rousseau]' (BI 135), albeit that the misreading was prepared for by Rousseau, who left open 'the possibility of misunderstanding' (BI 136). What is surprising is not the fact that de Man and Derrida disagree about Rousseau so much as the terms in which they both couch their interpretations. First, de Man: remarkably, he refers at one point to 'the "real" Rousseau' (BI 140). The scare quotes, as well as certain comments elsewhere in *Blindness and Insight*, suggest that there is nothing naive about his use of the phrase. What provokes suspicion is the ease with which he slips between understanding the 'real' Rousseau as a text and as an author. It is true that towards the end of his essay de Man makes the transition from Rousseau, the author, to his language, explaining that the former was introduced only as a heuristic device, but the comment runs counter to much of his essay (BI 137).[17] Furthermore, the phrase is employed in a question-begging way insofar as it is used to accuse Derrida, who, as much as anyone, has provided the intellectual resources which enable us to dispense with such a notion and its attendant difficulties.

De Man writes of the 'real' Rousseau in part because of the privileged role he wants to give him. The 'real' Rousseau is introduced as a counter to the dismissive critiques of Rousseau, amongst which de Man incautiously includes *Of Grammatology*. But the phrase is also employed against a schema that is particular to Derrida's account and resides in the ambivalent 'knowledge' which Derrida attributes to Rousseau. De Man correctly points out that Derrida does not only employ the language of fatality where Rousseau is commanded by a logic of which he is unaware. Derrida also writes as if Rousseau 'chose to remain blind to this knowledge' and so introduces the ethical overtone of deceit into his discussion (BI 116). One might add that *Of Grammatology* seems to offer further authorization for the concept of a 'real' Rousseau insofar as it corresponds to Derrida's own equally problematic employment of the phrase 'what Rousseau wants to say'. Derrida employs this phrase frequently throughout *Of Grammatology* and contrasts it with 'what Rousseau says'. What Rousseau wants to say, which Derrida equates with what Rousseau declares in contrast to what he describes, seems to be attributed to the 'real' Rousseau, at least on one understanding of the phrase. As this phrase is in many ways the key to what is most original in *Of Grammatology*, as well as being responsible for what is most questionable in it, I shall at this point put de Man to one side and make a few schematic remarks about Derrida's reading of Rousseau's *Essay on the Origin of Languages*.

III

Derrida introduces the *Essay* in the context to which it was at that time most familiar to Rousseau scholars, the debate about its date of composition. Derrida shows that much of that debate revolved around whether the *Essay* could be reconciled with the *Discourse on the Origin and Foundations of Inequality among Men*. In other words, the *Essay* was, if possible, to be dated to a period which would save Rousseau from contradicting himself: saying A and not-A *at the same time*. But Derrida quickly shifts attention to the contradictions which threaten the internal consistency of the *Essay*. Is one to have recourse to the same device, attributing different parts of the *Essay* to different periods of Rousseau's development? At this point, Derrida goes back on himself and takes the direction which will eventually mark the separation between deconstruction and other ways of reading. It begins innocently enough. Derrida finds reference to the second *Discourse* 'indispensable', specifically for the vexed task of reconciling what Rousseau says in the *Essay* on the relation of passions and needs (G 319/223). Rousseau himself had warned that, 'if I am not to contradict myself, I must take time to explain my argument'.[18] Derrida, in a clear echo of Rousseau's warning, accepts the challenge of continuing the explanation: 'If one does not want Rousseau to contradict himself at all, one must use a great deal of analysis and sympathy' (G 331/232). Derrida will say that the contradictions are only apparent and that what appears contradictory can be reconciled at a deeper level: 'the concept of the supplement . . . should allow us to say the contrary at the same time without contradiction' (G 254/179). It should not be forgotten that Rousseau courts paradox but denies contradiction.[19] Nevertheless, Derrida's attempt to 'organize' (G 348/245) or 'regulate' (G 332/233 and 349/245) the contradiction leads him to put in question the ultimacy of a logic that is readily taken for granted, and not just by Rousseau scholars. The contradictions remain only so long as one's reading of the text is governed by what Derrida calls the logic of identity. They can be resolved if another logic, which Derrida–drawing on a word of Rousseau's–calls the logic of supplementarity, is taken into account. This is Derrida's route in reading Rousseau. He neither dismisses Rousseau for contradicting himself, nor saves him from contradiction by dividing the various works and parts of works into separate parcels. Rather, he attempts to identify a structure which organizes Rousseau's texts.

The initial, somewhat tentative, structure which Derrida identifies as underlying the *Essay* takes the form of a series of oppositions: speech versus writing, liberty versus servitude, presence versus absence (G 239/168). These oppositions–and Derrida adds to the list as his reading proceeds–are linked, although that does not mean that they all function in the text in the same way. The overall pattern, however, is that Derrida regards Rousseau as always *wanting* to opt for the chain of concepts that bears the mark of presence. In the examples given, therefore, this would also leave speech and liberty privileged. Rousseau is thus understood in terms of a contemporary discourse, deriving largely from Heidegger, that identifies Western metaphysics with the priority of presence.

Nevertheless, it soon becomes apparent that this schema cannot be sustained as it stands. So, for example, speech does not always bear the positive significance of full presence. One can read in the first chapter of the *Essay* how, following his introduction of the division between gesture and speech, Rousseau contrasts the power of speech for moving the heart and inflaming the passions with the very different emotion provoked by the presence of the object itself, visible as it is at a single glance (E 35/242). In this case it is pantomime, the language of gesture rather than that of the voice, which bears the mark of presence. The scheme must therefore be complicated to accommodate this instance. This one can do by introducing another opposition, one between intuitive presence and speech. In consequence, speech is found occupying the place of presence only at certain moments. Drawing on an examination of the chapter 'Of Writing', Derrida explains that, when the desire of immediate passion is better represented by the range offered by voice, then Rousseau praises living speech. 'When the immediacy of presence is *better represented* by the proximity and rapidity of the gesture and the glance, he praises the most savage writing, which does not represent oral representation: the hieroglyph' (G 338/237).

Having introduced the oppositional system as an explanatory principle, Derrida argues that it is not adequate of itself to account for the vagaries of Rousseau's text. Only the addition of another schema can save it. It is the system of supplementarity and Derrida introduces it as supplementary to the system of oppositions. Derrida finds this word 'supplement' not only in the *Essay*, but also in the *Confessions*. In particular, Derrida points to a passage in the *Confessions* where Rousseau tells how in society he shows himself 'completely different from what I am'. This leads him to absent himself–'writing and hiding myself'–in an effort to show what he is worth (G 205/142). Rousseau thereby gives testimony to a concealment or non-presence which is felt in speech (G 237/166). Derrida understands that Rousseau's experience of language undermines the ideal of presence in terms of which he interprets it, but the praise of living speech is faithful to only one motif in Rousseau (G 203/141). As in the *Essay*, therefore, speech cannot be identified with presence, but is found to be marked by absence (G 334/234). Rousseau has recourse to writing in order to achieve what speech was supposed to accomplish. It is an addition which, originally conceived as simply exterior to speech, comes to substitute for it.

This model by which the supplement is both addition and substitute is what Derrida understands as the logic of supplementarity (G 208/144–5). What is added to take the place of a lack or default is itself a lack: 'the logic of supplementarity, which would have it that the outside be inside, that the other and the lack come to add themselves as a plus that replaces a minus, that what adds itself to something takes the place of a default in the thing, that the default, as the outside of the inside, should be already within the inside, etc.' (G 308/215). Such is the movement of the desire to recapture a presence which never existed. The paradoxical formulation is required by the claim that no ontology can think the operation of the supplement (G 442/314). But it answers to the problem posed by the state of nature tradition to which Rousseau belongs and whose limits he transgresses. Rousseau has to explain the break with nature–nature's departure from itself–on the basis of 'natural causes alone' (E 27/240). How else could this be done except by positing a lack in nature?

Nevertheless, the *Essay* is still determined by the ideals of nature, presence and origin. According to Derrida, Rousseau attempts a reconstruction (*reconstitution*) of presence as the source of language (G 204/141). 'Rousseau would like the absolute origin to be an absolute South' (G 311/217). This conforms to the oppositional schema organized in terms of the priority of presence. But Derrida then proceeds to show that, in spite of Rousseau's declarations to this effect, Rousseau's account follows another course. This means to Derrida that Rousseau cannot sustain his intentions throughout the course of his argument, so leading his declarations into conflict with his descriptions. It is this conflict which gives rise to the contradictions to be found within the text, and which the logic of supplementarity is called upon to explain, as in the so-called double origin of languages, where the resources referred to the languages of the North are called upon to accomplish what the South alone was supposed to perform but could not in isolation. The languages of the North cannot in consequence be dismissed as secondary or merely derivative, simply because they are introduced with reference to need rather than passion. This is said to be illustrated by the way Rousseau found it impossible to efface need from the description of the languages of the South.

The complex structure of supplementarity can be illustrated by returning to the case of the relation of gesture and speech. I have already cited the point where speech was introduced as 'a substitute for gesture' (G 335/235). But, in the *Discourse*, gesture takes its place as a supplement to speech. According to Rousseau, 'They multiplied the inflexions of the voice, and added gestures, which are in their nature more expressive . . . ' (DI 27/155). This passage, which would otherwise have to be taken as evidence of the difficulty of reconciling the *Essay* and the *Discourse on the Origin of Inequality*, proves in Derrida's hands an invaluable resource for the interpretation of the *Essay*. Derrida writes of the passage just quoted, 'Gesture is here an adjunct of speech, but this *adjunct* is not a supplementing by artifice, it is a re-course to a more natural, more expressive, more immedite sign' (G 334–5/235). The juxtaposition of the two places assigned to gesture in Rousseau's scheme gives rise to the recognition that 'Everything in language is substitute, and this concept of substitute precedes the opposition of nature and culture: the supplement can equally well be natural (gesture) and artificial (speech)' (G 335/235). In a text on the origin of languages, the concept of origin loses its hold. According to a system which recalls some of the claims to be found in the first part of *Of Grammatology*, Derrida writes: '. . . beyond and behind what one believes can be circumscribed as Rousseau's text, there has never been anything but supplements, substitutive significations which could only come forth in a chain of differential references . . . ' (G 228/159). The apparent contradiction is regulated, but by the logic of supplementarity and not according to the oppositional schema from which Derrida set out.

What is of particular interest in terms of the present essay is the way Derrida shows the logic of supplementarity operating within Rousseau's text. Derrida refers to those moments in which Rousseau undermines the priority or presence as 'what Rousseau says' or as 'what Rousseau describes'. These phrases are contrasted with 'what Rousseau wants to say' or 'what Rousseau declares'. These terms take Derrida's reading a stage further and are problematic. They clearly relate to his account of critical reading, mentioned earlier, where Derrida draws a contrast between what Rousseau does and does not command of the logic and language that he uses. Rousseau writes in a language and a logic whose proper system he cannot dominate absolutely (G 227/ 158). What Rousseau says, he says without saying. Rousseau follows the system of supplementarity 'with the sure foot of the sleepwalker' (G 290/203). I shall be returning later to the question as to whether this 'diagram' or ordering does not introduce problems of its own.

However, it is important to emphasize at this stage that it is the juxtaposition of the two readings which is Derrida's contribution. He does not simply add a reading to an account of Rousseau's intentions which is already in place. The two readings are not independent, but require each other. The second reading is therefore to be understood as supplementary in the complex sense with which Derrida invests the word. Description and declaration are themselves 'structural poles rather than natural and fixed points of reference' (G 318/216). The two readings belong together 'in one divided but coherent movement' (G 204/132).

Deconstructive or double reading (not to be confused with doubling commentary) is not an attempt to provide a reading of Rousseau which goes further than previous readings in exhausting the texts. Rather, its concern is with the *relation* between the 'new' reading and the readings which preceded it. Indeed, the 'new' reading emerges in the attempt to see what commands the dominant reading: logocentrism does not show itself as such except from elsewhere. In this way, Derrida regularly engages with and in that way keeps alive the memory of previous–and to his mind one-sided–interpretations of the texts he examines. His reading of Rousseau is no exception. It is no accident that he begins his discussion of the *Essay on the Origin of Languages* by entering into the controversy about the date of its composition. Previous interpretations cannot be ignored. On Derrida's account, those readings come to belong to the text; they are interwoven into it. In consequence the text is to be defined as the history of its various readings. A new reading which 'holds' is not only added to the previous interpretations it addresses, but supplements them, in Derrida's Rousseauian sense of adding *and* substituting. Hence commentators on Derrida who focus only on the new interpretation that Derrida adds, fail to recognize the more complex juxtaposition which constitutes double reading as 'one divided but coherent movement'. Does de Man fall into that bracket? It is time to look more closely at the way de Man reads Derrida.

IV

De Man is surely correct when he portrays Derrida as an ungenerous reader of Rousseau–or, to use de Man's own term, an 'ungracious' reader (BI ix–x). This lack of generosity is already marked by Derrida's use of the terms 'what Rousseau wants to say' and 'what Rousseau says' to distinguish the two readings. The first of these phrases–'what Rousseau wants to say'–seems to identify Rousseau with his intentions according to a familiar model which one usually understands Derrida as challenging. In order to sustain the distinction, Derrida must refuse to attribute to 'what Rousseau wants to say' statements that Rousseau clearly meant. In other words, there are passages which express Rousseau's intentions, but which Derrida finds obliged to refer simply to what Rousseau 'says without saying'. Take, for example, Rousseau's explicit claim in the Preface to the *Discourse on the Origin and the Foundations of Inequality among Men* that 'it is no light undertaking . . . to know accurately a state which no longer exists, which perhaps never did exist, which probably never will exist, and about which it is nevertheless necessary to have exact Notions in order accurately to judge of our present state.'[20] Derrida refers to this passage only once in *Of Grammatology*, and then only in parentheses, even though one suspects that a reading of Rousseau's texts could be organized around this passage, which would be much closer to the reading that Derrida adds than it would be to the dominant reading of Rousseau (G 358/253). This shows the problem of Derrida's decision to identify the dominant reading with 'what Rousseau wants to say'. And no doubt this encourages de Man to claim, against Derrida, that, unlike the literary critics who did not say what they meant to say, Rousseau did indeed say what he meant to say.

But de Man goes too far. When he recalls, without referring to it directly, Derrida's statement that 'blindness to the supplement is the law' (G 213/149), he picks up on Derrida's account of critical reading as aimed 'at a certain relationship, unperceived by the writer, between what he commands and what he does not command of the patterns of the language that he uses' (G 227/158). De Man transforms this into a claim that deconstruction is 'to bring to light what had remained unperceived by the author and his followers' (BI 116), thereby assimilating it to a familiar hermeneutic model, one which remains determined by the idea of a 'real' Rousseau. That phrase seems to suggest something definitive to which one could approximate, so that, for example, one reading might supplant all previous readings, rendering them dispensable. In that way, de Man overlooks the character of double reading.

One does not have to understand Derrida's use of the phrase 'what Rousseau meant to say' as naive. The fact that Derrida scarcely ever appeals to what an author 'meant to say' after de Man's essay leads one to ask if de Man's criticisms–and misunderstandings–of the phrase helped Derrida to understand its limitations. This at least would be one way in which Derrida could have been given much to think about, but was unable to agree or simply disagree with what de Man says. But it is also possible to ask if Derrida's use of the phrase was as simple as it seems. What led Derrida to employ the phrase in this text? Why make it one of the terms of the deconstruction? Perhaps it is wrong to consider it as Derrida's phrase. Perhaps he only borrows it, employing it parasitically according to a law which I will elucidate later. Reference to Starobinski's book on Rousseau, which is so important to understanding the first part of the chapter called '. . . That dangerous supplement . . .', might illustrate the point. Starobinski already remarks upon the discrepancy between Rousseau and his language. So, for example, he writes in his book that 'he [Rousseau] is no more master of his tongue than of his passions. What he says almost never corresponds to what he truly feels: words elude him and he eludes his words.'[21] And in a 1962 article included in the second edition of his book, Starobinski confirms the role of intentions in Rousseau's texts: 'He [Rousseau] asks us to consider his intentions not merely as justification for his ideas but as something more fundamental.'[22] Is Derrida borrowing from Starobinski here or submitting his terms to examination? Perhaps it is even more important to recognize the role of Lévi-Strauss in forming the phrase 'what Rousseau wants to say'. The praise of living speech with which Derrida begins his account of Rousseau corresponds to what Lévi-Strauss finds in Rousseau (G 203/141). 'What Rousseau wants to say' amounts to 'what Lévi-Strauss wants Rousseau to say'. This understanding of the phrase would seem to have the merit of justifying Derrida's use of it in the second part of *Of Grammatology*.

In any event, de Man can be understood as submitting the phrase 'what Rousseau wants to say' to scrutiny and seems to imply that it cannot readily be revised or reinscribed in a way which would salvage it. In an effort to show that Derrida's attempt to portray Rousseau as strictly orthodox with respect to traditional ontology cannot be sustained, de Man selects Rousseau's discussions of representation and of metaphor. These are important moments within de Man's argument because, 'on the two points involving rhetoric, Derrida goes the tradition one better' (BI 123). Hence, if de Man successfully makes his case, it is not possible to save Derrida's account of 'what Rousseau wants to say' by understanding it as a reinscription of the tradition of Rousseau interpretation: 'possibly . . . he substitutes Rousseau's interpreters for the author himself . . .' (BI 139). De Man grants that, 'on the questions of nature, of self, of origin, even of morality, Derrida starts out from the current view in Rousseau interpretations and then proceeds to show how Rousseau's own text undermines his declared philosophical allegiances' (BI 123). It seems that, on these topics at least, de Man would be content to have Derrida's double reading rewritten as divided between what the tradition of Rousseau interpretation has made him say and the 'real' Rousseau. Because of de Man's concentration on rewriting the terms of Derrida's discussion in favour of the 'real' Rousseau, one could be forgiven for thinking that that is the main thrust of 'The Rhetoric of Blindness'. But that would be to overlook his argument that this rewriting of *Of Grammatology* breaks down when it comes to the passages on representation and metaphor. Because the two discussions follow a similar course, the point can be illustrated simply by following de Man's discussion of the priority of figural language as it is proposed in the third chapter of the *Essay on the Origin of Languages*.

In a statement which he italicizes in 'On Reading Rousseau', de Man writes, 'The only literal statement that says what it means to say is the assertion that there can be no literal statements' (BI 133). This is de Man's somewhat Nietzschean undertaking of Rousseau's chapter heading, 'That the first language must have been figural', once he has freed it of its narrative rhetoric. Rousseau's story is that, when a savage encounters other human beings for the first time, he will in fear call them 'giants'. The chapter embarrasses Derrida, according to de Man, because Derrida reads Rousseau as a representational writer and thus understands him as maintaining the priority of literal meaning over metaphorical meaning: 'And since Rousseau explicitly says the opposite, Derrida has to interpret the chapter on metaphor as a moment of blindness in which Rousseau says the opposite of what he means to say' (BI 133). De Man explains that, for Derrida, the word 'giant' is metaphorical in respect of the people seen by the savage, but it is literal in respect of the passion which the sight of them arouses in the savage.

The first thing which has to be said is that de Man's brief rehearsal of Derrida's discussion fails to capture its extraordinary complexity in a number of ways. For example, we hear nothing of the fact that the sign 'represents the affect literally only through representing a false representer' (G 293/277). That the sign is indirect with regard to the affect, expressing emotion only through the false sign, distances this sense of original literality from the conventional sense. The question is whether this complexity is a function of a certain embarrassment arising from an analysis on the brink of collapse or whether it reflects the richness of Derrida's scrutiny of the text. Let me repeat some of the central points, while not forgetting that Derrida's discussion at this juncture is somewhat concentrated, not least because it is found at the beginning of the final chapter and thus after the basic schema of Derrida's reading has already been set out. First, Derrida introduces Rousseau's adherence to the proposition that language is originally metaphorical in the context of a discussion of the natural progress of writing towards literalness and hence non-metaphoricity.[23] Next, Derrida proceeds to refer

Rousseau to the tradition on the basis of the fact that, contrary to literary modernity, he repeats the traditional gesture of subjugating literary specificity to the poetic (G 383/272). But Rousseau is not assimilated to the tradition in a blanket way. Derrida proceeds to show how Rousseau construes the proposition concerning the figural character of the first language in an original way which differentiates him from Vico, Warburton and Condillac.

Derrida makes these points in the course of setting out Rousseau's intentions. On this account, literal meaning is derivative and the task is to see what renders it possible. All of this belongs to a long consideration of what, had one relied on de Man for a guide, one would have supposed that Derrida had ignored. When Derrida does depart from this account to give another reading, he signals it as follows: 'But in spite of his intentions and all appearance to the contrary, he also *starts*, as we shall see, *from the literal meaning. And he does so because the literal must be both at the origin and at the end.* In a word, he resorts to the *expression of emotions* a literalness whose loss he accepts, from the very origin, in the *designation of objects*' (G 289/275). De Man cites this last sentence without giving any hint that he has read the previous one, which shows that it belongs to a reading of Rousseau specifically contrasted with Rousseau's alleged intentions. De Man proceeds as if the interpretation of Rousseau attached to it was to be attributed to Derrida's version of a logocentric Rousseau. An explanation for his mistake might run as follows. As Derrida concedes and de Man noted, Rousseau couches his discussion in terms of knowledge and truth, guided by 'an entire naive philosophy of the idea-sign' (G 392/277). But Derrida does not seem to be attempting to convert Rousseau's account of the first language from an account of figurative language to one of literal language, which is what de Man understands. He is trying to show both accounts as operating simultaneously in Rousseau's text.[24] The question is their relation. Because de Man's focus is on rhetoric, and particularly the question of figurative language, it seems that he could not conceive of Derrida attributing the priority of literal language except to logocentrism. Derrida, whose focus is largely elsewhere, whose scheme has been determined by other texts, and who is guided by a more complex idea of literality, does not see the problem quite as de Man does. If Derrida had to underwrite this reading with his own signature, as if he were somehow committed to its propositions on his own behalf, he would no doubt have been more careful to determine its meaning. In this context he seems content to show that the passage is not simple and conforms to the schema of a double reading. But, particularly given the difficulties that the third chapter presents for any reading of the *Essay*, Derrida could surely grant that, at least in principle, another reading of Rousseau could be offered which would take its starting-point in those very difficulties.

However one judges Derrida's reading, de Man's response to it is surprising. In the course of trying to establish that Rousseau says what he means to say, de Man dismisses Rousseau's selection of the example of fear as ill-chosen. Rousseau does not say what de Man thinks he 'should have' said: 'The third chapter of the *Essai*, the section on metaphor, should have been centered on pity, or its extension: love (or hate)' (BI 135). And elsewhere Rousseau obliges. One might add that de Man was not satisfied with his own response for very long. He soon wrote another essay which presented an alternative interpretation.[25]

V

I suggested earlier that de Man selects Rousseau's discussions of representation and of metaphor in an attempt to argue that Derrida's phrase 'what Rousseau wants to say' could not be rendered less problematic by being rewritten as 'what the dominant tradition of Rousseau wants Rousseau to say'. De Man's argument is that, in these two discussions, 'Derrida goes the tradition one better' and so he cannot disown the reading by ascribing it to the tradition any more than he could to Rousseau. However, there are other possible ways, which de Man does not consider, in which Derrida might have rewritten this phrase so as to serve his purpose better. Derrida need not be confined to what the standard Rousseau interpretation has already said. Derrida could, for example, be engaged in producing a reading that corresponds to what a logocentric reading of Rousseau *would need to say* to deal with certain points which the tradition of Rousseau scholarship has nevertheless hitherto neglected. (In this regard, one should not forget that before Derrida the *Essay on the Origin of Languages* was itself largely ignored.) Perhaps one reason why de Man did not pursue that question was because, like many of Derrida's other readers, he too readily assumes that Derrida is intent on diminishing his subject. It is, of course, an impression sustained in part by the very terms Derrida employs to produce his double reading. Indeed there was a time when many readers of Derrida confused deconstruction with a way of dismissing the tradition altogether, criticism in its simplest, bluntest form. The account of Rousseau in *Of Grammatology* appears to be as responsible for this misapprehension as any of Derrida's writings could be responsible for so distorted an understanding. Paul de Man wrote a letter to Derrida in July of 1970 in which he said: 'I do not yet know why you keep refusing Rousseau the value of radicality which you attribute to Mallarmé and no doubt to Nietzsche' (M 129). In the letter, de Man speculates as to how Derrida might respond: 'I believe that it is for hermeneutic rather than historical reasons, but I am probably wrong'. One suspects that Derrida would not have accepted the alternatives.

De Man, by contrast to Derrida, gives a privileged position to Rousseau. We have seen how he seems to think that Derrida could have said what he had to say without resorting to a double reading of Rousseau. It is even more important to de Man that Rousseau could have said what he meant without contradicting himself. In a sentence which has fully taxed de Man's most sympathetic readers, he claimed: 'There is no need to deconstruct Rousseau' (BI 139). Derrida in *Memoires* provides his own attempt to explain this notorious phrase, but not without making clear that de Man's other references to deconstruction greatly complicate the issue.[26] He does not acknowledge that nowhere is the distance separating him from de Man more apparent than when the latter employs the word deconstruction in an apparent effort to establish some common ground. Why, according to Derrida, might de Man believe that there is no need to deconstruct Rousseau? Because Rousseau has already done it himself. Derrida explains further, 'This was another way of saying: there is always already deconstruction at work *in* works, especially in *literary* works. Deconstruction cannot be applied, after the fact and from the outside, as a technical instrument of modernity. Texts deconstruct *themselves* by themselves, it is enough to recall it or to recall them to oneself' (M 123). But if one recalls the context of de Man's phrase, Derrida's interpretation of it appears less plausible. Derrida appropriates it to himself by imposing the sense that deconstruction does not tolerate any exceptions: all texts can and must be exposed to it, or, more precisely, already incorporate it according to a necessity which deconstruction relies upon. (For this reason, the sense of the 'especially' in respect of literary works needs further interrogation.) De Man is not saying that there is no role for deconstruction in the context of literary writing. He is drawing a distinction between Rousseau, whom there is no need to deconstruct, and 'the established tradition of Rousseau', which 'stands in dire need of deconstruction'. Or, in a passage one part of which I have already discussed, de Man writes, 'Instead of having Rousseau deconstruct his critics, we have Derrida deconstructing a pseudo-Rousseau by means of insights that could have been gained from the "real" Rousseau' (BI 139–40). The problem lies with de Man's image of the 'real' Rousseau as 'the non-blinded author' (BI 141), a phrase he employs in the course of using Derrida's own terms to deny the distinction on which Derrida's double reading of Rousseau hinges. Would not a non-blinded author have to mimic the ideal of a luminous 'self-present substance, conscious and certain of itself at the moment of its relationship to itself' (G 146/97)?

Even if one takes one of de Man's more careful formulations, which refers not to the author but to the text, problems still arise. 'Rousseau's text has no blind spots: it accounts at all moments for its own rhetorical mode' (BI 139). The term 'blind spots' here picks up on a discussion at the end of Derrida's section on method. Returning to the notion of reading as a production which does not 'simply duplicate what Rousseau thought' but which 'does not leave the text', Derrida writes: 'The concept of the supplement is a sort of blind spot in Rousseau's text, the not-seen that opens and limits visibility' (G 234/163). With the discovery of the logic of the supplement, which does not conform to the logic of identity, Derrida moves into the realm of the relation, 'unperceived by the writer', between what Rousseau does and does not command of the patterns of the language that he uses. But de Man sees a difficulty in the way in which Derrida construes this relation.

De Man makes his point in the context of the question of Derrida and literature. He is surely right to think that deconstruction must have a different relation to those texts that present themselves as literature from those that present themselves as philosophy. Derrida himself offers some indications of this in the section on method in the second chapter of Part II, and it is no doubt to these pages that de Man refers when he deems Derrida 'right' on the nature of literary language (BI 138). Derrida's emphasis, at least in this place, is on the need to distinguish the variety of projects within the history of literary forms. For example, there is the way in which the philosophical text has the task of effacing itself (G 229/160). By the same token, one might add, philosophy for most of its history has not tolerated ambiguity, whereas literature cultivates it, which is perhaps why double reading is more disruptive for the study of philosophy than of literature. There is some reason for thinking that Derrida's strategies work best on philosophy texts, not just because of their presuppositions about language, but also because of the way in which, in the works of, for example, Hegel, Nietzsche and Heidegger, philosophy has characterized its own history. De Man seems to support this when he insists that Rousseau does not need to be deconstructed, having escaped the logocentric fallacy 'precisely to the extent that his language is literary', that is to say, to the extent that his language 'implicitly or explicitly signifies its own rhetorical mode and prefigures its own misunderstanding as the correlative of its rhetorical nature' (BI 136).

De Man spells out his claim in the following way: 'we are saying by implication that the myth of the priority of oral language over written language has always been demystified by literature' (BI 138). This implication itself seems to imply that there is a question as to whether deconstruction, at least as Derrida understands it, is to be applied to literary texts. To be sure, the implication is lost sight of behind the claim that 'Derrida's work is one of the places where the future possibility of literary criticism is being decided' (BI 111). But, of course, this Derrida, the one who is so important for the future of literary criticism, is not the same Derrida who, according to de Man, 'remains unwilling or unable to read Rousseau as literature' (BI 138). It would be possible to develop a reading of de Man's essay which would be organized around the difference between these two Derridas, but there are drawbacks in doing so. One is that it would leave open the way for the construction of a blind Derrida and an insightful one, each implicated in the other. This would amount to a false compromise, failing to penetrate the genuine difference between De Man and Derrida. Another is that it would distract from the fact that, contrary to the impression de Man gives, in the section on method which he selects for praise, Derrida does indeed focus on Rousseau's literary writing (G 229–30/160). It is therefore necessary to make the issue more precise. De Man identifies Derrida's failure to read Rousseau as literature as a failure to grant to Rousseau's language what he allows his own: 'Why does he have to reproach Rousseau for doing exactly what he legitimately does himself?' (BI 138). In other words, it returns to the theme of Derrida's lack of generosity towards Rousseau. It is around this issue therefore that de Man's critique of Derrida culminates.

VI

De Man seems confident that Derrida's chronological scheme is only a narrative convention, although at the same time he is aware that some of Derrida's 'more literal-minded followers' might be distressed by this claim (BI 138).[27] He is therefore puzzled that Derrida takes Rousseau's chronological scheme so literally. De Man's question to Derrida is why postulate within Rousseau a metaphysics of presence which can then be shown 'not to operate, or to be dependent on the implicit power of a language which disrupts it and tears it away from its foundation' (BI 119). De Man does not directly pose the question of whether there is a link between Derrida's literality with respect to Rousseau's history and what de Man understands as the fictional character of Derrida's own history. This is because de Man is convinced that Derrida could have recognized the literary quality of Derrida's writing. De Man's response is to intersperse his challenge to Derrida's reading of Rousseau's text with incomprehension, when he recognizes, as indeed he must, that nobody is more aware of these possibilities of Rousseau's text than Derrida. Nowhere is this more apparent than in Derrida's discussion of Rousseau's expression 'primitive times'.[28] Derrida writes, 'The expression "primitive times", and all the evidence which will be used to describe them, refer to no date, no event, no chronology. One can vary the facts without modifying the structural invariant. It is a time before time' (G 357/252). He adds later in the paragraph, 'recourse to factual illustration, even to events distant from the origin, is purely fictive. Rousseau is sure of that.' Rousseau makes a problem of history throughout the *Discourse on the Origin of Inequality* and the *Essay on the Origin of Lanugages* in a way in which previous state of nature theorists did not. Derrida seems readier to release Rousseau from history than almost all of his previous commentators, although not as far as de Man would have him go. Furthermore, de Man in his turn extends the principle to Derrida himself.

According to de Man, Derrida is, like Rousseau, not writing history, but fiction. He is telling a story. This means that Derrida is freed from responsibilities which might otherwise inhibit him. Derrida can be released from the task of being fair to Rousseau and can give free rein to his narrative skills. 'Derrida's story of Rousseau's getting, as it were, a glimpse of the truth but then going about erasing, conjuring this vision out of existence, while also surreptitiously giving into it and smuggling it within the precinct he was assigned to protect, is undoubtedly a good story' (BI 119).

The phrase, 'a good story', might be understood to be somewhat condescending, like de Man's attempted joke that here the gamekeeper is doing the poaching. How does de Man understand the word 'good'? Gasché, in a justly famous article, cites the opening phrase of the sentence–'Derrida's story of Rousseau'–and ignores or otherwise discounts its closing phrase–'a good story'–with the result that he understands de Man to be saying of Derrida's reading that 'this story is a bad story as opposed to the good story of Rousseau'.[29] Gasché suspects de Man of issuing a value judgement against Derrida, one which arises from Derrida's confusion, by which he attributes to Rousseau what properly belongs only to 'the established tradition of Rousseau criticism'. But the whole value to de Man of the category of the story is that stories do not compete to supplant each other: 'We should perhaps not even ask whether it is accurate, for it may well be offered as parody or fiction, without pretending to be anything else. But, unlike epistemological statements, stories do not cancel each other out, and we should not let Derrida's version replace Rousseau's own story of his involvement with language' (BI 119). In other words, de Man proposes that, even if they conflict, the two stories–Rousseau's and Derrida's–may coexist.

It is now clear what is at stake when Derrida begins his *Memoires for Paul de Man* by saying 'I have never known how to tell a story'. Derrida resists de Man's thought-provoking criticisms of *Of Grammatology* by denying the central conclusion of de Man's essay on which everything else hangs, the claim that Derrida is offering a story. Derrida does this so discreetly that the response seems to have gone unnoticed. However, the delicacy of the gesture fits not only the occasion of a memorial to de Man, given so soon after the latter's death, but also the tone of a thinker like Derrida who, for the most part, does not defend his philosophy according to the time-honoured procedure of attacking every other position in sight. When acknowledging in *Memoires for Paul de Man* that he lacked the gift of story-telling, Derrida explained that this required him to turn to myth. In other words, he borrowed stories from elsewhere. This was his practice in *Of Grammatology* also. He relies on a story which he nevertheless disowns. The story of logocentrism is not his. It is drawn from a variety of sources. This is an example of what is now commonly known as the parasitic character of Derrida's writing.[30] He rarely claims to speak, as one says, in his own voice, not least because he is more aware than anyone of the virtual impossibility of doing so. One finds oneself obliged to employ a borrowed–and thus metaphysical–vocabulary (G 148/99). The main contributor to Derrida's borrowed narrative is Heidegger, whose account of metaphysics in terms of presence is applied by Derrida to language with reference to the prejudice in favour of speech, where the speaker presents him- or herself in support of what is said, as the writer cannot. The application, as Derrida shows, recoils on Heidegger in places (G 36/22), but it is the account of metaphysics in terms of presence which, more than anything else, governs Derrida's account of logocentrism and thus his determination of 'what Rousseau wants to say'. There are also contributions from other contemporary thinkers and discourses, particularly linguistics and psychoanalysis. Derrida explores these contributions in the first part of *Of Grammatology* and relies on this account implicitly when he begins the second part with the 'Introduction to the "Age of Rousseau"'.

De Man was fully aware of Derrida's debts, but gave them a different significance when he relied on the notion of fiction to do the work of complicating Derrida's commitments. 'Throughout, Derrida uses Heidegger's and Nietzsche's fiction of metaphysics as a *period* in Western thought in order to dramatize, to give tension and suspense to the story of language and of society by making them pseudo-historical' (BI 137). If one understands this in terms of Rousseau's declaration in the Preface to the *Second Discourse*, this would mean that metaphysics no longer exists, perhaps never did exist, and probably never will exist. This is probably an accurate summary of Derrida's position. Has not Derrida come close to saying this on a number of occasions? For example, in 'Interpreting Signatures': 'And likewise, who has said or decided that there is something like a Western metaphysics, some think that would be capable of being gathered up under this name and this name only?'[31] The story undoes itself. It is self-deconstructing, which does not mean that it can be dispensed with altogether. The reference to metaphysics is necessary, even though it is found to be impossible to sustain. Derrida has, since employing Heidegger's history in such works as *Of Grammatology*, submitted that history and the assumptions on which it depends to the most careful scrutiny.[32] It is not always recognized that in so doing Derrida is engaging in a re-examination of the starting-point of his own early works.

Although de Man recognized Derrida's debt to Heidegger and Nietzsche, he conceived Derrida's use of them as necessary only for rhetorical effect. What they had to say about metaphysics he dismissed as fiction–mere stories–and so, at most, merely pseudo-historical. That is why it is important for Derrida to deny not only that *he* tells the story, but also that what is told is a *story* or a fiction. It is sustained by historical evidence, just as Derrida's readings rely on doubling commentary to establish the limits on what it is possible to hold. This does not make it an historical novel either.

Derrida's text escapes the categories de Man tries to impose on it. This can best be shown by returning to 'Rhetoric and Insight'. As the essay approaches its close, de Man returns to the question of the rhetorical resemblance between the *Essay on the Origin Languages* and *Of Grammatology*: both tell stories.[33] A provisional reading of de Man's essay would leave one with the impression that his attempt to correct Derrida's interpretation of Rousseau is the main thrust of his essay. But de Man himself concludes from the rhetorical status of their works that 'it would seem to matter very little whether Derrida is right or wrong about Rousseau' (BI 137). In consequence, de Man is no longer as troubled as he was at the beginning by the apparently arbitrary way in which Rousseau is enclosed in the epoch of metaphysics that bears his name. 'If Rousseau does not belong to the logocentric "period", then the scheme of periodization used by Derrida is avowedly arbitrary' (BI 138).[34] And yet it is characteristic of de Man that this gesture, which appears to be so conciliatory to Derrida, in fact distorts the character of double reading and thus what is most characteristic of Derrida's approach to the text. Derrida is intent on showing that Rousseau both reflects and exceeds the epoch that bears his name. This explains the tension which de Man finds in Derrida's reading of Rousseau. Rousseau is and is not contained within logocentrism. Derrida refers to the metaphysical Rousseau when he employs the phrase 'what Rousseau wants to say' or 'what Rousseau declares'. He refers to the non-metaphysical Rousseau when he employs the phrase 'what Rousseau says' or 'what Rousseau describes'. De Man thinks of the latter pair as Derrida's contribution and seems surprised that what Derrida says is so close to Rousseau.[35] But what is important to Derrida is that the two Rousseaus cannot be separated. For him a simply non-metaphysical Rousseau would be a nonsense. The non-metaphysical can be sustained only in conjunction with the metaphysical, which is why I sometimes employ the organic metaphor and write of the two limbs of a double reading. This schema is not unique to Derrida. He sets it out in a variety of places, often with reference to Heidegger.[36] So, for example, Derrida writes in a recent essay, 'At the very moment of affirming the uniqueness of Nietzsche's thinking, he [Heidegger] does everything he can to show that it repeats the mightiest (and therefore the most general) schema of metaphysics.'[37] It is important to recognize that Derrida finds this pattern not only in those thinkers who are identified with the tradition, but also with those who are recognized as the most innovative. It would therefore apply to Derrida himself.

Derrida returns to the question of the story in 'Like the Sound of the Sea Deep within a Shell: Paul de Man's War'. This essay was Derrida's response to the furore provoked by the discovery of de Man's wartime journalism. He makes it clear that he believed he had no choice but to write the article, following a telephone call from *Critical Inquiry*, which issued a 'warm invitation that also resonated like a summons'.[38] In the course of the essay, Derrida quotes the opening words of his *Memoires for Paul de Man*: 'I have never known how to tell a story', and poses the following questions: 'How could I then have imagined that it would be from the friend, from him alone, singularly from him, that would one day come the obligation to tell a story? And that this injunction would come to me from the one who always associated narrative structure with allegory, that discourse of the other that always says something still other than what it says?'[39] What is important in the context of this essay is not de Man's history, but the fact that Derrida recognizes, in the face of the accusations levelled against de Man, certain obligations falling on himself, as his friend and former colleague, to defend the latter. These obligations override any theoretical need to renounce story-telling, a move which now is in danger of looking like a ruse, except if it had been a ruse, then nothing would have been easier to sustain it. It would not have been beyond Derrida's ingenuity to persuade us that the story he was telling was not his, but that of his dead friend, and so on. But Derrida goes out of his way to mark the fact that *he* is telling a story and that it is a *story* that he is telling: for example, 'Before going to the end of my story . . .'[40] The parasitic status of the language of deconstruction cannot be maintained in the face of ethico-political constraints.

Another way of measuring the importance of Derrida's gesture in offering to tell the story of de Man's war is to recall that the strength of Derrida's position, its inviolability, lies in large measure in its capacity to disclaim the language it employs. But this, the parasitic character of deconstructive discourse, is renounced in order that he can take responsibility for the language he employs in this ethical situation. Of course, things are not exactly that simple. If it is indeed true, as I suspect could be established, that in recent years ethics has become an ever more prominent concern of Derrida's writings, perhaps even as prominent as the theme of metaphysics, as the priority of presence, was in the early works, this discourse also employs a vocabulary borrowed from a number of sources. One thinks inevitably of a debt to Levinas in this regard, although the debt is by no means one-sided.

Derrida can and cannot tell stories. He does and does not write in his own name.

VII

I have focused on de Man's essay on *Of Grammatology* on the grounds that it would serve as a useful introduction to some of the problems of criticizing Derrida. I have been able to confirm what Derrida writes in 'Paul de Man's War' that, when de Man began to talk about deconstruction, in the essays of *Blindness and Insight*, 'it was *first of all in a rather critical manner*, although complicated as always'.[41] The complications into which de Man is led are instructive for understanding Derrida. The chief difficulty de Man faces in presenting his criticisms of Derrida is in pinning his target down. It is very much to de Man's credit that his essay reflects the movement of Derrida's thought. He does not reduce Derrida's work to a proposition which then serves proxy for that work. Perhaps it is because de Man is ready, unlike so many of Derrida's critics, to follow the course of one of Derrida's readings that he looks as if he is constantly changing ground in the course of his critique. It is perhaps for that reason also that Derrida found de Man's criticism easy to accept, prior to and independent of any question of agreement or disagreement.

More generally there are times when it seems that the problems of criticizing Derrida can for the most part be divided between criticizing him from a position which he has already put under suspicion, and so begging the question, and criticising him for not having recognized what in fact he has already anticipated. Almost all of the criticisms of Derrida of which I am aware fall into one or the other of these categories, although of course this would have to be shown in detail. The difficulty of finding the point from which to criticize Derrida, the sense that he has always circumscribed any riposte to which he might otherwise fall victim, gives rise to speculation that he might have no blind-spots. But if Derrida's text is as well protected as this, it would give rise to a new criticism. Derrida would be vulnerable precisely for occupying such a position of total control. The objections raised earlier against the mastery de Man attributes to Rousseau would come into force against Derrida. Although there is a danger that it might prove just another manifestation of Derrida's mastery, it is striking to find that he himself emphasizes deconstruction's vulnerability. 'Operating necessarily from the inside, borrowing all the strategic and economic resources of subversion from the old structure, borrowing them structurally, that is to say without being able to isolate their elements and atoms, the enterprise of deconstruction always falls prey to its own work' (G 39/24).

De Man focuses most of his criticisms of *Of Grammatology* on the reading of Rousseau which Derrida adds. He tends to refer this reading not to Rousseau, but to Derrida, as if the latter had produced an entirely new text. This tendency is not unusual among Derrida's readers. I have suggested that they would do better to look at the juxtaposition of the two readings 'what Rousseau wants to say' and 'what Rousseau says'. The latter cannot be considered in isolation from the former. In the case of *Of Grammatology* there is the additional problem of the very formula 'what Rousseau wants to say', which I have already discussed, but the problem extends much further than this. In general, one is ill-advised to regard the 'dominant' reading from which Derrida begins as simply given. This is most obvious in the case of texts where no established reading is yet in place. Derrida's early essay on Levinas, 'Violence and Metaphysics', provides a good illustration of this. But the issue is a structural one. Double reading arises as a necessity because there is no simple exit from metaphysics and no simple adherence to it. Derrida shows both the extraordinary resilience of the metaphysical tradition and how resolute attention to any of its moments leads one to encounter what exceeds the tradition. Hence the attempt to bind a metaphysical reading with a reading which metaphysics cannot contain.

The problem of the dominant reading is that it must borrow from an account of the metaphysical tradition and that account can always be subjected to further scrutiny. In *Of Grammatology* the story is not rendered problematic in the way it is in later works, where deconstruction's capacity for self-questioning is more in evidence. When Derrida takes up the account of metaphysics in terms of the priority of presence and applies it to Rousseau, both the application and the model have to be submitted to the same kind of scrutiny as is the reading which Derrida adds. Formally speaking, deconstructive discourse is sustained parasitically, as I have suggested above. But the selection of the dominant reading from which the deconstruction starts has more than a 'simply' philosophical basis. Even if deconstruction can claim in principle to operate on any discourse, one cannot regard as either neutral or arbitrary the decision of a starting-point in any given case.

I have offered two examples of this. One was the case where, from friendship and collegiality, Derrida himself took responsibility for telling a story which was not his–de Man's story. Derrida's recognition of responsibility in this case recoils on other texts that he has written. It seems that, in *Of Grammatology*, Derrida failed to provide the required justification to support his designation of the initial reading of Rousseau as 'what Rousseau wants to say'. But on closer examination–and this is my second example–another explanation presents itself. It is no longer sufficient to say, as one used to be tempted to do, that the occasionality of deconstruction meant that Derrida's starting-point was selected for him. In the occasionality of deconstruction resides its ethico-political character. Derrida sets out in the second part of *Of Grammatology* to put in question the ethnocentrism of Lévi-Strauss by re-examining the language of Rousseau on which it relies for support, and finding other possibilities there. This gives a political motivation to Derrida's writing over and beyond questions of the generosity or 'graciousness' with which he approaches Rousseau's texts. It is important to do justice to the texts one considers, but that is not the only way in which justice intervenes in interpretation. Every interpretation is motivated. And yet, apart from a brief reference to Lévi-Strauss at the end of *Of Grammatology* (G 426/301), Derrida allows the ethico-political motivation to disappear. Furthermore, and this is more important, Derrida does not indicate how he might take responsibility for his ethico-political starting-point. When he employs the language of ethics it is most often in the idiom of Nietzsche and Heidegger, as in his enigmatic reference to 'annulling the ethical qualification and to thinking of writing beyond good and evil' (G 442/314), which is how at the end he characterizes his difference from Rousseau. In which case, how might deconstruction provide itself with the resources to justify or take responsibility for making the charge of ethnocentrism the starting-point of a critical reading? There are very few hints in *Of Grammatology* as to how Derrida might answer such a question.[42] In his most recent works–for example, some of the essays in *Psyche*–Derrida can be seen turning towards this task. Has Derrida once again anticipated the riposte? Or can deconstruction only speak in its own voice by denying the parasitical character from which its strength derives? Is it sufficient for Derrida simply to draw on other languages which appear to have the resources he lacks–Levinas's, for example? These are some of the questions–critical questions, perhaps–which are suggested by a re-reading of one of Derrida's earlier works, and they might provide a starting-point from which to approach the works of the last few years and the works to come.

NOTES

1 Jacques Derrida, *Memoires for Paul de Man* (New York: Columbia University Press, 1986), p. 3. Henceforth M.
2 See, for example, Paul de Man, *Allegories of Reading* (New Haven, CT: Yale University Press, 1979), p. 119.
3 'The Time of a Thesis: Punctuations', trans. Kathleen McLaughlin, *Philosophy in France Today*, ed. Alan Montefiore (Cambridge: Cambridge University Press, 1983), p. 37. See also *La dissémination* (Paris: Seuil, 1972), pp. 203 and 253; trans.

Barbara Johnson, *Dissemination* (Chicago: University of Chicago Press, 1981), pp. 177 and 223.

4 Paul de Man, 'The Rhetoric of Blindness', *Blindness and Insight* (2nd rev. edn, London: Methuen, 1983), p. 111. Henceforth BI.

5 *L'écriture et la différence* (Paris: Seuil, 1967), p. 132; trans. Alan Bass, *Writing and Difference* (Chicago: University of Chicago Press, 1978), p. 88. See also *De l'esprit* (Paris: Galilée, 1987), 64n; trans. G. Bennington and R. Bowlby, *Of Spirit* (Chicago: University of Chicago Press, 1989), pp. 118–19.

6 A thorough examination of this question would no doubt have to consider what Kant and Heidegger have to say about *critique*, not least because this would be the route one would expect Derrida himself to take. Recall, for example, Heidegger's discussion of it as separating out what is superior from what is inferior (*Wegmarken*, Frankfurt: Klostermann, 1976, p. 334) and lifting out what is special, *das Besondere herausheben* (*Die Frage nach dem Ding*, Niemeyer: Tübingen, 1962, p. 93; trans. W. B. Barton and Vera Deutsch, *What is a Thing?*, Chicago: Regnery, 1970, p. 119).

7 For example, *La voix et le phénomène* (Paris: Presses Universitaires de France, 1967), p. 26n; trans. David Allison, *Speech and Phenomena* (Evanston, IL: Northwestern University Press, 1973), p. 25n.

8 J. Derrida, *De la grammatologie* (Paris: Minuit 1967), p. 7; trans. G. Spivak, *Of Grammatology* (Baltimore: Johns Hopkins University Press, 1976), p. lxxxix. Henceforth G.

9 *De la grammatologie*, p. 227; trans. *Of Grammatology*, p. 158. On the word 'production', see J. Derrida, *Limited Inc.* (Evanston, IL: Northwestern University Press, 1988), p. 148, and the reference there to *Positions*, trans. Alan Bass (Chicago: University of Chicago Press, 1981), pp. 86, 104 n. 31.

10 *Limited Inc.*, p. 143.

11 *Limited Inc.*, p. 144. There is inevitably something disingenuous about quoting so early in the essay these later comments of Derrida which postdate de Man's reading. But how could my reading of Derrida not be determined by Derrida's later texts, which are now inextricably interwoven with our understanding of the early works? Is it clear that, except when histories are being written or accounts are being drawn up, neither of which is the case here, chronological considerations must determine the presentation? In any event, I have tried not to forget in reading on de Man on Derrida that even in 1970 much which seems obvious today was not clear then. Part of the value of returning to de Man's essay is to be reminded of this. One measure of the distance which has been travelled since de Man first published his chapter is provided by Richard Klein's essay 'The Blindness of Hyperboles: The Ellipses of Insight', *Diacritics* 3, Summer 1973, pp. 33–44. Klein calls de Man's essay on Derrida, which today seems striking for its reticence and sobriety, 'the most uncanny, the most insane, the most bizarrely interesting critical encounter imaginable' (p. 34).

12 *Dialectical Anthropology* 2, 1977, pp. 1–18.

13 On the importance of the omitted opening pages for understanding the second part of Derrida's essay, or, as one might say, on the importance of 'The Rhetoric of Blindness' for understanding 'On Reading Rousseau', see Wlad Godzich, 'The

Domestication of Derrida', *The Yale Critics: Deconstruction in America*, ed. Jonathan Arac and Wlad Godzich (Minneapolis: University of Minnesota Press, 1983), pp. 20–40.

14 In his review of *De la grammatologie* for the *Annales de la Société J.-J. Rousseau*, de Man actually challenges Derrida's claim that the reading of Rousseau is a 'simple illustration' of the theoretical first part. De Man pronounces it the book's 'centre'. *Annales de la société J.-J. Rousseau* 37, 1966–8, p. 285.

15 *La dissémination*, p. 236n; trans. *Dissemination*, p. 207n.

16 *Memoires*, p. 148.

17 De Man's focus on the author is confirmed, for example, by his phrase 'the pattern is too interesting not to be deliberate' (BI 140). By contrast, one might expect Derrida to write of a pattern as too interesting to be deliberate, that is, too interesting to belong to someone. However, in subsequent essays de Man is much more consistent when it comes to questioning the role of language as 'an instrument in the service of a psychic energy' (*Allegories of Reading*, p. 299).

18 *Essai sur l'origine des langues*, ed. Charles Porset (Paris: Nizet, 1970), p. 111; trans. Victor Gourevitch, *The First and Second Discourses and Essay on the Origin of Languages* (New York: Harper & Row, 1986), p. 267 (translation adapted). Henceforth E.

19 See, for example, 'Narcisse ou l'amant de lui-même', *Oeuvres complètes* II (Paris: Gallimard, Bibliothèque de la Pléiade, 1964), p. 973; trans. 'The Preface to Narcissus', *The First and Second Discourses*, pp. 109–10.

20 J.-J. Rousseau, *Discours sur l'origine et les fondements de l'inegalité*, *Oeuvres complètes* III (Paris: Gallimard, Bibliothèque de la Pléiade, 1964), p. 123; trans. *The First and Second Discourses*, p. 130.

21 Jean Starobinski, *J.-J. Rousseau: la transparence et l'obstacle* (Paris: Gallimard, 1971), p. 149; trans. Arthur Goldhammer, *Jean-Jacques Rousseau: Transparency and Obstruction* (Chicago: University of Chicago Press, 1988), p. 122.

22 Ibid. p. 323; trans. p. 275.

23 Derrida carefully marks this progress which is simultaneously a regression by employing the neologism 'pro-regresses' (G 383/271). De Man earlier in 'The Rhetoric of Blindness' took Derrida to task for 'bypassing' (BI 120) Rousseau's complexities on this score. According to de Man, Derrida had Rousseau wanting to say that 'progress, however ambivalent, moves either toward deterioration, or toward improvement, the one or the other', but had Rousseau describing 'what he does not want to say: that progress moves in both directions, toward good and evil at the same time' (G 320/229; de Man's translation). In de Man's view, Rousseau 'always' asserts the latter.

24 Derrida's claim, that 'even while apparently affirming that the original language was figurative, Rousseau upholds the literal: as arche and as telos' (G 392/277), could be understood as contradicting this, but it should be read in terms of claim, already quoted that Rousseau 'also starts . . . , from the literal meaning' (G 389/275).

25 Paul de Man, 'Theory of Metaphor in Rousseau's *Second Discourse*', *Studies in Romanticism* 12, 1, Spring 1973, pp. 475–98. Repr. as the chapter on Metaphor in *Allegories of Reading*. De Man is here much more conciliatory to Derrida than he was in *Blindness and Insight*. For example, 'Derrida is certainly right in stating that

the act of denomination that follows–calling the other man a giant, a process that Rousseau described as a figural use of language–displaces the referential meaning from an outward, visible property to an "inward" feeling' (*Allegories* p. 150). Nevertheless, he is still far from agreeing with Derrida, and equally far from stating his disagreement directly. For a discussion of the apparent development in de Man's interpretation, see Suzanne Gearhart, 'Philosophy before Literature: Deconstruction, Historicity, and the Work of Paul de Man', *Diacritics* 13, 4, 1983, pp. 63–81.

26 De Man's use of the term 'deconstruction' has been examined by Rodolphe Gasché in '"Setzung" and "Übersetzung": Notes on Paul de Man', *Diacritics* 11, 4, 1981, pp. 306–58, and by Barbara Johnson in 'Rigorous Unreliability', *Critical Inquiry* 11, 1984, pp. 278–85.

27 It should not be forgotten that, within de Man's schema, being 'literal-minded' is low on the scale of his values. By contrast, the term 'blindness' does not record a value-judgement (BI 141). Indeed, as will emerge, much of de Man's text amounts to a plea not to take Derrida literally.

28 Rousseau, *Essai sur l'origine des langues*, p. 39; trans. *The First and Second Discourses*, p. 260.

29 Rodolphe Gasché, 'Deconstruction as Criticism', *Glyph* 6 (Baltimore: Johns Hopkins University Press, 1979), p. 206.

30 See, for example, John Llewelyn, *Derrida on the Threshold of Sense* (London: Macmillan, 1986), chap. 5, pp. 60–82.

31 'Interpreting Signatures (Nietzsche/Heidegger)', *Dialogue and Deconstruction*, ed. R. Palmer and D. Michelfelder (New York: State University of New York Press, 1989), p. 67.

32 See, for example, 'Envoi', *Psyché* (Paris: Galilée, 1987), pp. 109–43; trans. Peter and Mary Ann Caws, 'Sending: On Representation', *Social Research* 49, 2, 1982, pp. 294–326. This is one of the places where Derrida complicates the relation between *Historie* and *Geschichte* which is alluded to in *De la grammatologie*, p. 43; trans. p. 37.

33 The story Derrida tells is, according to de Man, that of 'the repression of written language by what is here called the "logocentric" fallacy of favouring voice over writing . . . narrated as a consecutive, historical process' (BI 137). De Man, like so many others before and since, takes Derrida's reference to writing literally when he claims that 'the myth of the priority of oral language has always been demystified by literature' (BI 138).

34 This, if anything, is confirmed by de Man when, in a footnote attached to this statement in 'The Rhetoric of Blindness', he speculates on whether Derrida would accept the change in historical periodization that would be required if Rousseau was given the credit he deserves (BI 138 n50). In 'The Ellipses of Insight', Richard Klein suggests that this footnote provides the answer to the question of why de Man takes forty pages to set the record straight on Rousseau, when the issue appears to be of only archaeological question (p. 41). Perhaps this was enough to persuade de Man to make it one of the footnotes omitted from 'The Rhetoric of Blindness' when it was reprinted as 'On Reading Rousseau'.

35 In his attempt to isolate Derrida, de Man assumes that what Rousseau describes is

to be identified with what 'Derrida here proclaims' (BI 120). De Man can say this because he neglects double reading.

36 See, for example, 'Ousia and Gramme': 'every text of metaphysics carries within itself, for example, *both* the so-called vulgar concept of time *and* the resources that will be borrowed from the system of metaphysics in order to criticize that concept.' *Marges de la philosophie* (Paris: Minuit, 1972), p. 70; trans. Alan Bass, *Margins of Philosophy* (Chicago: University of Chicago Press, 1982), p. 61.

37 'Interpreting Signatures', p. 65.

38 *Critical Inquiry* 14, Spring 1988, p. 596.

39 Ibid., p. 595.

40 Ibid., p. 637.

41 Ibid., p. 649.

42 At the end of the chapter on Lévi-Strauss, Derrida offers some important reflections on ethics which could be of value in this regard, in spite of remaining undeveloped (G 201/139–40). I have not introduced them here because out of context their meaning is far from clear. Only a careful reading of the chapter can establish the parameters for their interpretation.

8

Christopher Norris

Deconstruction, Postmodernism and Philosophy: Habermas on Derrida

In this essay I propose to contest some of the arguments that Habermas brings against Derrida in *The Philosophical Discourse of Modernity*.[1] It seems to me that he has misread Derrida's work, and done so moreover in a way that fits in too readily with commonplace ideas about deconstruction as a species of latter-day Nietzschean irrationalism, one that rejects the whole legacy of post-Kantian enlightened thought. In short, Habermas goes along with the widely held view that deconstruction is a matter of collapsing all genre-distinctions, especially those between philosophy and literature, reason and rhetoric, language in its constative and performative aspects. This is all the more unfortunate since Habermas's book (which I shall henceforth refer to as *PDM*) is by far the most important contribution to date in the ongoing quarrel between French post-structuralism and that tradition of *Ideologiekritik* which Habermas has carried on from Adorno and earlier members of the Frankfurt School. So I will be criticizing *PDM* from a standpoint which might appear squarely opposed to Habermas's critical project. That this is not at all my intention—that in fact I concur with most of what Habermas has to say—will I hope become clear in the course of this article. His book makes out a very strong case for re-examining the character and historical antecedents of post-modernism, and for seeing it not on its own professed terms as a radical challenge to the outworn enlightenment paradigm, but rather as the upshot of a widespread failure to think through the problems bequeathed by that tradition. Where Habermas goes wrong, I shall argue, is in failing to acknowledge the crucial respects in which Derrida has distanced his own thinking from a generalized 'post-modern' or post-structuralist discourse.

More specifically, Habermas misreads Derrida in much the same way that literary critics (and apostles of American neo-pragmatism) have so far received his work: that is to say, as a handy pretext for dispensing with the labours of conceptual critique and declaring an end to the 'modernist' epoch of enlightened secular reason. I have no quarrel with Habermas's claim that the 'post-' in post-modernism is a delusive prefix, disguising the fact that theorists like Foucault, Lyotard and Baudrillard are still caught up in problems that have plagued the discourse of philosophy at least since the parting of ways after Kant. He is right to point out how their work recapitulates the quarrels that emerged between those various thinkers (left- and right-wing Hegelians, objective and subjective idealists) who attempted— and failed— to overcome the antinomies of Kantian critical reason. One need only look to Lyotard's recent writings on philosophy, politics and the 'idea of history' to remark this resurgence of Kantian themes (albeit deployed to very different ends) in the discourse of post-modern thought.[2] And the same applies to Foucault's genealogy of power/knowledge, as Habermas brings out very clearly when he traces its various intellectual antecedents in the line of counter-enlightenment philosophies running fron Nietzsche to Bataille. In each case, he argues, thought has suffered the disabling effects of an irrationalist doctrine that can only take hold through a form of self-willed amnesia, a compulsive repetition of similar episodes in the previous (post-Kantian) history of ideas. *PDM* is in this sense an exercise of large-scale rational reconstruction, an essentially therapeutic exercise whose aim is to provide a more adequate understanding of those episodes, and thus to recall the present-day human sciences to a knowledge of their own formative prehistory.

All this will of course be familiar enough to any reader moderately versed in Habermas's work over the past two decades. Where these lectures break new ground is in specifying more exactly the terms of his quarrel with French post-structuralism, deconstruction and other such varieties as Habermas would have it—of militant latter-day unreason. To some extent the ground had already been prepared by debates on and around his work in journals like *Praxis* and *New German Critique*. One could summarize the issues very briefly as follows. To his opponents it has seemed that Habermas's thinking belongs squarely within the enlightenment tradition of oppressive, monological reason. That is to say, he has sought a means of reinstating the Kantian foundationalist project—the belief in transcendental arguments, truth-claims, critique of consensual values and so forth—at a time when that project has at last been shown up as a mere historical dead-end, a discourse premised on false ideas of theoretical mastery and power. In support of this argument they point to such instances as the reading of Freud that Habermas offers in *Knowledge and Human Interests*, a reading that interprets psychoanalysis as a therapy designed to overcome the blocks and distortions of repressed desire by bringing them out into the light of a conscious, rational self-understanding.[3] To this they respond by drawing on Lacan's very different account of the 'talking cure', namely his insistence that language is *always and everywhere* marked by the symptoms of unconscious desire, so that any attempt to escape or transcend this condition is deluded at best, and at worst a technique of manipulative reason in the service of a harsh and repressive social order.[4]

These opposing viewpoints can each claim a warrant in Freud's notoriously cryptic statement: 'where id was, there shall ego be'. For Habermas, on the one hand, this sentence should be read as signalling an alignment of interests between psychoanalysis and the wider project of enlightened or emancipatory thought. For the Lacanians, conversely, it enforces the message that the ego is always a plaything of unconscious desire, and that therefore any version of ego-psychology (to which doctrine, in their view, Habermas subscribes) is necessarily a hopeless and misguided endeavour. On their reading the sentence should be paraphrased: 'wherever reason thinks to explain the unconscious and its effects, there most surely those effects will resurface to disrupt such a project from the outset'. In this case there would seem little to choose between Habermas's talk of 'transcendental pragmatics', 'ideal speech-situations', etc., and those previous modes of foundationalist thought (the Cartesian *cogito*, the Kantian transcendental subject or Husserl's phenomenological reduction) whose claims–or so it is argued–have now been totally discredited. The fact that he has been at some pains to distance himself from that tradition apparently counts for nothing in terms of the current polemical exchange. So these thinkers bring two main charges against Habermas: firstly that he attempts the impossible (since reason is in no position to legislate over effects that exceed its furthest powers of comprehension), and secondly that his project is politically retrograde (since it clings to a form of enlightenment thinking whose covert aim is to repress or to marginalize everything that falls outside its privileged domain). And their criticisms will no doubt find ample confirmation now that Habermas has offered his response in the form of these recent lectures. He will still be treated as a last-ditch defender of the strong foundationalist argument, despite the very clear signals that Habermas–no less than his opponents–wants to find a basis for the conduct of rational enquiry that will not have recourse to anything resembling a Kantian epistemological paradigm.

It seems to me that Habermas goes wrong about Derrida mainly because he takes it for granted that deconstruction is one offshoot–a 'philosophical' offshoot–of this wider post-modernist or counter-enlightenment drift. In what follows I shall point to some crucial respects in which Derrida's work not only fails to fit this description but also mounts a resistance to it on terms that Habermas ought to acknowledge, given his own intellectual commitments.

In fact I shall argue that deconstruction, properly understood, belongs within that same 'philosophical discourse of modernity' that Habermas sets out to defend against its present-day detractors. But it may be useful to preface that discussion with a brief account of the very different readings of Derrida's work that have now gained currency among literary theorists and philosophers. This will help to explain some of the blind-spots in Habermas's critique, based as it is on a partial reading which tends to privilege just one of these rival accounts.

I

Commentators on deconstruction are divided very roughly into two main camps: those (like Rodolphe Gasché) who read Derrida's work as a radical continuation of certain Kantian themes,[5] and those (like Richard Rorty) who praise Derrida for having put such deluded 'enlightenment' notions behind him and arrived at a postmodern-pragmatist stance relieved of all surplus metaphysical baggage.[6] Nevertheless they are agreed in thinking that we can't make sense of Derrida without some knowledge of the relevant intellectual prehistory. Where they differ is on the question whether those debates are still of real interest–'philosophical' interest–or whether (as Rorty would have it) they have failed to come up with any workable answers, and should therefore be regarded as failed candidates for Philosophy Honours and awarded nothing more than a Pass Degree in English, Liberal Studies or Comp. Lit.

On Rorty's view we can still put together an instructive *story* about the way that thinkers from Descartes and Kant on down have so misconceived their own enterprise as to think they were offering genuine solutions to a range of distinctively 'philosophical' problems. But we shall be wrong–simply repeating their mistake–if we try to give this story an upbeat conclusion or a Whiggish meta-narrative drift suggesting that we have *now*, after so many errors, started to get things right. The story is just that, a handy little pragmatist narrative, and the most it can do is stop us from believing in all those grandiose philosophical ideas. For Gasché, on the contrary, Derrida is still very much a philosopher, if by this we understand one whose work is both committed to an ongoing critical dialogue with previous thinkers (notably, in this case, Kant, Hegel and Husserl), and centrally concerned with issues in the realm of truth, knowledge and representation. This dialogue may take an unfamiliar or disconcerting form, as when Derrida questions the categorical bases of Kantian argument and sets out to demonstrate what Gasché calls the 'conditions of impossibility' that mark the limits of all philosophical enquiry.

But even so his work remains squarely within that tradition of epistemological critique which alone makes it possible to raise such questions against the more accommodating pragmatist line espoused by thinkers like Rorty. These different readings of Derrida are also, inseparably, different readings of the whole philosophical history that has led up to where we are now. And in Hegel's case likewise there is a conflict of interpretations between those (again including Rorty) who would accept a kind of 'naturalized' Hegelianism, a story of philosophy that includes all the major episodes but dispenses with the vantage-point of reason or truth, and those who reject this compromise solution and regard the dialectic as something more than just a species of edifying narrative.

One could make the same point about all those philosophers whose work has come in for revisionist readings as a consequence of the currently widespread scepticism as regards truth-claims and foundationalist arguments of whatever kind. On the one hand it has led to a new intellectual division of labour, a situation where thinkers like Rorty feel more at home in humanities or literature departments, while the 'real' (analytical) philosophers tend to close ranks and leave the teaching of Hegel, Nietzsche, Heidegger, Derrida, etc., to their colleagues with less exacting standards of argument. On the other, it has persuaded literary theorists that philosophy has no good claim to monopolize the texts of its own tradition, since the current guardians seem overly zealous to protect their canon from any form of unauthorized reading (which is to say, any reading that treats it on rhetorical, hermeneutic or 'literary' terms). And so it has come about that 'theory' now denominates an area (not so much a 'discipline') which straddles the activities of philosophy and literary criticism, taking charge of those figures (the Hegel–Nietzsche–Derrida line) who lend themselves to just such a non-canonical approach. But even within this camp one finds disagreements (as between Rorty and Gasché) concerning the extent to which philosophy may yet be conserved as a discipline with its own distinct mode of conceptual or analytic rigour. Thus 'theory' is construed as post-philosophical *either* in the sense that it dissolves philosophy into a textual, rhetorical or narrative genre with no distinctive truth-claims whatsoever (the Rorty argument), *or* in the sense (following Gasché) that it presses certain Kantian antinomies to the point where they demand a form of analysis undreamt of in the mainstream tradition. Both sides have an interest in claiming Kant since he stands at precisely the cardinal point where their histories will henceforth diverge. On the one hand there is the line that leads from Kant, via Hegel, to the various speculative systems and projects that make up the 'continental' heritage. On the other it is clear that Kant provides the basis for most of those debates about language, logic and truth that have occupied the analytic schools.

One reason why *PDM* seems blind to certain aspects of Derrida's work is that it more or less identifies deconstruction with the Rortyan-postmodern-pragmatist reading, and thus tends to perpetuate the view of it as a species of literary-critical activity, an attempt to colonize philosophy by levelling the genre-distinction between these disciplines. Now of course this corresponds to one major premise of Derrida's thought: namely, his insistence that philosophy is indeed a certain 'kind of writing', a discourse which none the less strives to cover its own rhetorical tracks by aspiring to an order of pure, unmediated, self-present truth. Thus a deconstructive reading will typically fasten upon those moments in the philosophic text where some cardinal concept turns out to rest on a latent or sublimated metaphor, or where the logic of an argument is subtly undone by its reliance on covert rhetorical devices. Or again, it will show how some seemingly marginal detail of the text–some aspect ignored (not without reason) by the mainstream exponents–in fact plays a crucial but problematic role in the entire structure of argument.[7] One result of such readings is undoubtedly to challenge the commonplace assumption that philosophy has to do with concepts, truth-claims, logical arguments, 'clear and distinct ideas', etc., while literary criticism deals with language only in its rhetorical, poetic or non-truth-functional aspects. What Derrida has achieved–on this view at least–is a striking reversal of the age-old prejudice that elevates philosophy over rhetoric, or right reason over the dissimulating arts of language.

This is the reading of Derrida's work that Habermas offers in his 'Excursus on Levelling the Genre-Distinction between Philosophy and Literature' (*PDM*, pp. 185–210). That is to say, he takes it as read that Derrida is out to reduce all texts to an undifferentiated 'freeplay' of signification where the old disciplinary borderlines will at last break down, and where philosophy will thus take its place as just one 'kind of writing' among others, with no special claim to validity or truth. More specifically, Derrida makes a full-scale programme of ignoring those different kinds of language-use that have separated out in the modern (post-Kantian) discourse of enlightened reason. He has privileged just one of these uses (language in its poetic, rhetorical or 'world-disclosive' aspect) and failed to see how the others demand a quite different mode of understanding. Thus, according to Habermas,

> [t]he rhetorical element occurs *in its pure form* only in the self-referentiality of the poetic expression, that is, in the language of fiction specialized for world-disclosure. Even the normal language of everyday life is ineradicably rhetorical; but within the matrix of different linguistic functions, the rhetorical elements recede here. . . . The same holds true of the specialized languages of science and technology, law and morality, economics, political science, etc. They, too, live off the illuminating power of metaphorical tropes; but the rhetorical elements,

which are by no means expunged, are tamed, as it were, and enlisted for special purposes of problem-solving. (*PDM*, p. 209)

It is the main fault of Derrida's work, as Habermas reads it, that he has failed to observe these essential distinctions and thus over-generalized the poetic (rhetorical) aspect of language to a point where it commands the whole field of communicative action. The result is to deprive thinking of that critical force which depends on a proper separation of realms, and which has come about historically–so Habermas contends–through the increasing specialization of language in its threefold social aspect. By extending rhetoric so far beyond its own legitimate domain Derrida has not only collapsed the 'genre-distinction' between philosophy and literature but also annulled the emancipating promise that resides in the poetic (or 'world-disclosive') function of language. For this promise is likewise dependent on the existence of a 'polar tension', a sense of what specifically differentiates literature from 'everyday' communicative language on the one hand, and those specialized problem-solving languages on the other. Derrida, says Habermas, 'holistically levels these complicated relationships in order to equate philosophy with literature and criticism. He fails to recognize the special status that both philosophy and literary criticism, each in its own way, assume as mediators between expert cultures and the everyday world' (*PDM*, p. 207).

Now I think that these criticisms apply not so much to what Derrida has written but to what has been written about him by various (mostly American) commentators. Or more accurately–on the principle 'no smoke without fire'– they find some warrant in certain of his texts, but can then be made to stick only through a very partial reading, one that sets out quite deliberately to level the distinction between philosophy and literature. The favoured texts for this purpose would include Derrida's response to John Searle on the topic of speech-act theory;[8] the closing paragraph of 'Structure, Sign and Play', with its apocalyptic overtones and Nietzschean end-of-philosophy rhetoric;[9] and more recently the 'Envois' section of *La Carte postale*, where Derrida goes about as far as possible towards undermining the truth-claims of logocentric reason by recasting them in fictive or mock-epistolary form.[10] One could then go back to Derrida's earliest published work–his Introduction to Husserl's essay 'The Origin of Geometry'–and cite the well-known passage where he appears to encounter a moment of choice between 'philosophy' and 'literature', or the quest for some pure, univocal, self-present meaning (Husserl) as opposed to the prospect of a liberating 'freeplay' of the signifier glimpsed in such writings as Joyce's *Finnegans Wake*.[11] In so far as he has confronted this choice–so the argument goes–Derrida has come out firmly on the side of a literary approach to the texts of philosophy, one that pays minimal regard to their truth-claims or structures of logical argument, and which thus frees itself to treat them as purely rhetorical constructs on a level with poems, novels, postcards or any other kind of writing.

So it might seem that Habermas's arguments are fully warranted by the 'levelling' or undifferentiating character of Derrida's generalized rhetoric. What drops out of sight is the complex and highly-evolved relationship between (1) everyday communicative language, (2) the mediating discourses of philosophy and criticism, and (3) the various forms of 'expert' or specialized enquiry ('art, literature, science, morality') which would otherwise tend to float free in a conceptual universe of their own creating. Criticism can only perform this essential task so long as it maintains a due sense of its own distinctive role *vis-à-vis* those other disciplines. Where philosophy occupies the middle ground between 'ordinary language' and specialized questions of ethics, epistemology, metaphysics, theory of science, etc., criticism stands in much the same relation to everyday language on the one hand and artistic or literary innovation on the other. And it is also imperative that criticism and philosophy should not become mixed up one with another and thus produce the kind of hybrid discourse that Habermas thinks so damaging in Derrida's work.

The point is best made by quoting him at length, since this is the passage where the charge is pressed home with maximum force.

> Literary criticism and philosophy . . . are both faced with tasks that are paradoxical in similar ways. They are supposed to feed the contents of expert cultures, in which knowledge is accumulated under one aspect of validity at a time, into an everyday practice in which all linguistic functions are intermeshed. And yet [they] are supposed to accomplish this task of mediation with means of expression taken from languages specialized in questions of taste or of truth. They can only resolve this paradox by rhetorically expanding and enriching their special languages. . . . [Thus] literary criticism and philosophy have a family resemblance to literature–and to this extent to one another as well–in their rhetorical achievements. But their family relationship stops right there, for in each of these enterprises the tools of rhetoric are subordinated to the discipline of a *distinct* form of argumentation. (*PDM*, pp. 209–10)

What is presented here is a qualified version of Kant's doctrine of the faculties. It is qualified mainly by Habermas's wish to avoid any kind of a Kantian foundationalist legacy by reasoning in terms of the different languages–'everyday', 'expert', 'specialized', etc.–which between them mark out the range of communicative options. He can thus maintain a critical attitude towards Derrida's 'levelling' of genre-distinctions without having to argue that philosophy has access to some privileged realm of a priori concepts or uniquely self-validating truth-claims. We can afford to give up that outworn tradition, he argues, just so long as we grasp that *language* itself is oriented towards a better understanding of those blocks, aporias, misprisions and so forth which get in the way of our (everyday or specialized) communicative acts.[12] But on Derrida's account–so Habermas believes–this process could never make a start, let alone achieve the levels of complexity and sophistication required by the various present-day arts and sciences.

This follows from Derrida's extreme form of contextualist doctrine, that is, his argument–enounced in the debate with John Searle–that (1) meaning is entirely a product of the various contexts in which signs play a part; (2) that such contexts can in principle be multiplied beyond any possible enumerative grasp; and (3) that therefore meaning is strictly undecidable in any given case. But we are simply not obliged to accept this conclusion if–as Habermas suggests–we drop the idea of an open-ended general 'context' and recognize the various *specific* normative dimensions that exist within the range of communicative action. For Derrida, in short,

> linguistically mediated processes within the world are embedded in a *world-constituting* context that prejudices everything; they are fatalistically delivered up to the unmanageable happening of text-production, overwhelmed by the poetic-creative transformation of a background designated by archewriting, and condemned to be provincial. (*PDM*, p. 204)

'Provincial', one supposes, in the sense that it seeks to reduce all language to a single paradigm, and thereby annexes every form of communicative action to the province of poetic or literary language. Thus Habermas cites Roman Jakobson and the Prague Structuralists by way of insisting that the poetic function be defined more specifically, that is, in terms of those features (like self-reflexivity or lack of informative content) that set it apart from other uses of language. Where Derrida has gone wrong (he argues) is in failing to perceive the constitutive difference between speech-acts engaged in the normative activities of problem-solving, theorizing, giving information, etc., and speech-acts that are not so engaged, and can therefore be construed as fictive, non-serious, parodic or whatever. Otherwise Derrida would not have been misled into extending the poetic function so far beyond its proper reach, or discounting those normative constraints upon language that save it from the infinitized 'freeplay' of an open-ended contextualist account. 'The frailty of the genre distinction between philosophy and literature is evidenced in the practice of deconstruction: in the end, *all* distinctions are submerged in one comprehensive, all-embracing context of texts–Derrida talks in a hypnotizing manner about a "universal text"' (*PDM*, p. 190). The result of this confusion is to give language up to the effects of an infinite regress (or 'unlimited semiosis') which excludes all possibility of rational understanding.

II

The first point to note about Habermas's critique of Derrida is that it more or less re-states John Searle's position with regard to the supposedly self-evident distinction between 'serious' and other (deviant) kinds of speech-act.[13] That is, it assumes that Searle has both common sense and reason on his side of the argument, while Derrida is content to make 'literary' play with certain marginal or merely rhetorical aspects of Austin's text. In which case Searle would be the serious, the faithful or properly authorized exponent of Austin's ideas, while Derrida would stand to Austin in much the same relation as the sophists to Socrates: a gadfly rhetorician merely anxious to display his own ingenuity and wit, and lacking any regard for wisdom or truth. But this ignores several important points about the three-sided debate between Austin, Derrida and Searle. It fails to register the extent to which Austin invites and solicits a deconstructive reading by himself putting up all manner of resistance to the project of a generalized speech-act theory. I have written at length on this topic elsewhere–as have a number of other commentators, including Jonathan Culler and Shoshana Felman–so there is no need to rehearse the details over again here.[14] Sufficient to say that Austin, like Derrida, shows a fondness for marginal or problematic cases, speech-acts which cannot be securely assigned to this or that typecast category. Thus he often comes up with supposedly deviant instances which then turn out to be typical of the kind, or to indicate features that necessarily pertain to all possible varieties of speech-act. Or again, he will pause to illustrate a point with some odd piece of anecdotal evidence, only to find that it creates real problems for his classificatory system.

What is distinctive about Austin's approach–aligning it with Derrida as against Searle–is this readiness to let language have its way with him and not give in to the systematizing drive for method and clear-cut theory.[15] Partly it is a matter of the 'Oxford' ethos, the attitude of quizzical detachment mixed with a passion for linguistic detail that Derrida encountered on his trip to Oxford (narrated in *La carte postale*). But we would be wrong to see this as a downright rejection of philosophical 'seriousness', an opting-out in favour of stylistic 'freeplay' or the possible worlds of his own fictive devising. Certainly Derrida goes a long way towards deconstructiong the terms of this old opposition. Thus *La carte postale* takes up a great variety of philosophic themes, among them the relationship of Plato and Socrates, the Heideggerian questioning of Western metaphysics, the status of truth-claims in the discourse of Freudian psychoanalysis, and the way that all these topics return to haunt the seemingly detached, almost clinical idiom of Oxford linguistic philosophy. But it does so by way of a fictional *mise-en-scène*, a correspondence carried on by postcard, and specifically through a series of fragmentary love-letters inscribed on numerous copies of a card that Derrida discovered in the Bodleian Library. This card reproduces an apocryphal scene which apparently has Plato dictating his thoughts to Socrates and Socrates obediently writing them down at Plato's behest. It thus stages a comic reversal of the age-old scholarly assumption: namely, that Socrates was the thinker who *wrote nothing*–whose wisdom prevented him from entrusting his thoughts to the perilous medium of writing–while Plato, his disciple, gave in to this bad necessity in order to preserve Socrates' teaching for the benefit of later generations. So one can see why this postcard so fascinated Derrida. What it offered was a kind of zany confirmation of his own thesis (in *Of Grammatology* and elsewhere) that writing is the 'exile', the 'wandering outcast' of Western logocentric tradition, the repressed term whose disruptive effects are none the less everywhere manifest in the texts of that same tradition.[16]

So *La carte postale* is undoubtedly a work of 'literature' in so far as it exploits the full range of fictive possibilities opened up by this scandalous reversal of roles between Socrates and Plato. From here it goes on to develop various other counter-factual, extravagant or apocryphal themes, along with a running debate among the scholars as to the authenticity or otherwise of Plato's letters, a 'correspondence' (by postcard, what else?) between Heidegger and Freud, a quizzical commentary on Ryle, Austin and the Oxford tradition of linguistic philosophy, and a whole series of anachronistic swerves and redoublings which enable Derrida to play havoc with accredited notions of history and truth. His point in all this is to show how philosophy has excluded certain kinds of writing–letters, apocrypha, 'unauthorized' genres of whatever sort–while allowing them a place on the margins of discourse from which they continue to exert a fascination and a power to complicate received ideas. And there is something of this even in the Oxford tradition–for all its analytical 'seriousness'–when thinkers like Austin cite (or invent) their various speech-act examples, and then find their argument beginning to get out of hand. 'I adore these theorizations, so very "Oxford" in character, their extraordinary and necessary subtlety as well as their imperturbable ingenuousness, "psychoanalytically speaking"; they will always be confident in the law of quotation marks.'[17] Derrida's reference here is to the problem of naming, and more specifically the difference between *using* and *mentioning* a name, as theorized by Russell and Ryle among others. But where this distinction serves analytical philosophers as a technique for avoiding trouble—for resolving the kinds of paradox that emerge when the two linguistic functions are confused—its appeal for Derrida has more to do with the undecidability of names in general, their tendency to migrate across the borderlines of authorized genre, history, etc., and thus to create all manner of intriguing fictive scenarios.[18] 'Psychoanalytically speaking', it is by no means certain that philosophy can control these potential aberrations of language, or lay down rules for the proper conduct of logical debate.

Thus Derrida cites a 'very good book' by one such analytical thinker, a book which advises us not to be misled by the seeming identity of names-as-used and names as merely cited, mentioned or placed between quotation-marks. To which Derrida responds by asking: what kind of *de jure* regulation can back up this confident policing operation, designed to cure language of its bad propensity for conjuring up phantom nominal presences? The 'law of quotation-marks' could achieve this purpose only on condition that language be treated as *already having attained* what Habermas describes as an 'ideal speech-situation', that is, a transparency of meaning and intent that would admit no impediment to the wished-for meeting of minds. But this condition is impossible—so Derrida implies—for reasons that return us to Freud, Lacan and the arguments of French (post-structuralist) psychoanalysis. That is to say, it ignores the effects of a 'structural unconscious' that forever divides the speaking self ('subject of enunciation') from the self spoken about ('subject of the enounced'). Thus:

> [t]he author of the book of which I am speaking, himself, not his name (therefore he would pardon me for not naming him) is himself reserved as concerns the very interesting 'position of Quine' ('a word-between-quotation-marks is the proper name of the word which figures between the quotation marks, simultaneously an occurrence of the word which is between the quotation marks and an occurrence of the word-between-the-quotation-marks, the latter including the former as a part'—and it is true that this logic of inclusion perhaps is not very satisfying in order to account for the 'simultaneously', but small matter here), and making an allusion to a 'forgetting', his word, a forgetting 'evidently facilitated by the resemblance that there is between a word and the name of this word formed by its being placed between quotation marks', he concludes, I quote, 'But one must not let oneself be abused by this resemblance, and confuse the two names . . .'. Okay, promised, we won't any more. Not on purpose anyway. Unless we forget, but we will not forget on purpose, it's just that they resemble each other so much . . .[19]

This passage is typical of *La carte postale* in the way that it picks up numerous themes, cross-references, cryptic allusions and so forth, among them the 'correspondence' between philosophy and psychoanalysis (or Socrates and Freud), staged as a kind of running encounter where reason confronts its own 'structural unconscious' in the form of a promiscuously generalized writing that circulates without origin or proper addressee. Hence the link that Derrida perceives between philosophy as a 'serious', responsible discourse and the postal service (in its 'grand epoch') as a smoothly functioning system of exchange which ensures that letters arrive on time and at the right destination. But there is always the residue of mail that hasn't been correctly addressed, that bounces back and forth between various recipients and ends up in the dead-letter office. Or, again, those items that arrive out of the blue with some intimate yet wholly undecipherable message, and thus give rise to all manner of pleasing conjecture. So it comes about that 'the guardians of tradition, the professors, academics, and librarians, the doctors and authors of theses are terribly curious about correspondences . . . , about private or public correspondences (a distinction without pertinence in this case, whence the post card, half private half public, neither the one nor the other, and which does not await the post card *stricto sensu* in order to define the law of the genre, of all genres . . . ').[20]

It is on this level that the 'Envois' can be read as relating to the essays on Freud and Lacan that make up the remainder of *La carte postale*. For here also Derrida is concerned with the status of a certain theoretical enterprise (psychoanalysis) which attempts to secure itself on the basis of an authorized truth passed down from founder to disciple, but which runs into all manner of speculative detours and swerves from origin. In each case there is a strong *proprietary* interest at work, a tendency to anathematize those various distortions, misreadings or perversions of the Freudian text that would compromise its original (authentic) meaning. In Freud himself, this takes the form of an obsessive desire to keep psychoanalysis 'in the family', to save it from the egregious falsehoods put about by his erstwhile colleagues and disciples.[21] With Lacan, it produces an allegorical reading of Poe's story 'The Purloined Letter', treated as a virtual *mise-en-scène* of the dialogue between analyst and patient, a dialogue whose meaning can never be fully brought to light, caught up as it is in the shuttling exchange of transference and counter-transference, but which none the less points to an ultimate truth identified with the 'letter' of the Freudian text.[22] In both instances, so Derrida argues, this desire takes the form of a putative master-discourse that attempts to put a frame around the various episodes, case-histories, speculative ventures, correspondences and so forth that make up the proper, self-authorized legacy of Freud's life and work. But these projects cannot reckon with the undecidability of all such narrative frames, or the way that events from 'outside' the frame–whether textual events, as in Poe's short story, or episodes from the life, as in Freud's troubled correspondence with Fliess–

may always return to complicate the record beyond all hope of a straightforward, truth-telling account. Here again, it proves impossible for thinking to master the effects of a generalized writing (or 'structural unconscious') some of whose canniest adepts–like Freud and Lacan–may yet be caught out by its uncanny power to disrupt their projects at source.

Now it might well seem–from what I have written so far–that Habermas is absolutely right about Derrida, since *La carte postale* is a 'literary' text which exploits various philosophical themes merely as a springboard for its own extravagant purposes. This is certainly the reading that most appeals to a postmodern pragmatist like Rorty, one for whom philosophy is in any case a dead or dying enterprise, best treated (as Derrida apparently treats it here) with a fine disregard for the protocols of truth and an eye to its fictive potential or entertainment-value. Thus if Rorty has problems with the 'early' Derrida–too serious by half, too argumentative, too much inclined to take a term like *différance* and give it the status of a privileged anti-concept–these problems disappear with *La carte postale*, where philosophy receives its final come-uppance at the hands of literature. But Rorty's reading is open to challenge, as indeed is Habermas's assumption (in *PDM*) that Rorty has read Derrida aright, and therefore that the two of them must be saying much the same kind of thing. What this ignores is the extent to which a text like *La carte postale* continues to engage with philosophical problems which don't simply disappear when approached from a fictive, apocryphal or 'literary' standpoint. After all, philosophers in the mainstream tradition–from Plato to Austin–have often had recourse to invented case-histories, parables, counter-factual scenarios and so forth, in order to make some critical point about our language or commonplace habits of thought. Hence one of the problems that Derrida remarks in connection with Austin's procedure: namely, his exclusion of 'deviant' or 'parasitical' speech-acts (for example, those merely cited, placed between quotation-marks, uttered in jest, on the stage, in a novel, etc.) as not meriting serious philosophical attention. For it is surely the case that (1) *all* speech-acts must perform, cite or rehearse some existing formulaic convention (since otherwise they would carry no recognized force); (2) this creates a real problem for Austin's distinction between 'serious' and 'non-serious' cases; and (3) the majority of Austin's own examples are speech-acts contrived specifically for the purpose of illustrating speech-act theory. Once again, the 'law of quotation-marks' turns out to have effects far beyond those allowed for on the standard, unproblematical account.

My point is that Habermas mistakes the character of deconstruction when he treats it as having simply *given up* the kinds of argument specific to philosophy, and opted instead for the pleasures of a free-wheeling 'literary' style. It is true that Derrida's writings can be roughly divided–as Rorty suggests–into two main categories. On the one hand there are texts (like the essays collected in *Margins of Philosophy*) that argue their way through a rigorous and consequential treatment of the various blind-spots, aporias or antinomies that characterize the discourse of philosophic reason. On the other there are pieces (like the 'Envois' section of *La carte postale* or Derrida's prolix and riddling response to John Searle) where undoubtedly he is making maximum use of 'literary' devices in order to provoke or to disconcert the more self-assured guardians of that mainstream tradition. But we should be wrong to suppose–as Rorty does–that Derrida has gone over from the one kind of writing to the other, renouncing 'philosophy' and its self-deluded claims for the sake of a henceforth uninhibited devotion to 'literature'. This ignores the extent to which 'Envois' and 'Limited Inc.' (the rejoinder to Searle) continue to work within the same problematics of writing, language and representation that Derrida addresses more explicitly elsewhere. And it also fails to recognize the distinct kinship between deconstruction and those passages of offbeat, speculative musing in Austin's text ('so very "Oxford" in character, their extraordinary and necessary subtlety, as well as their imperturbable ingenuousness, "psychoanalytically speaking"') which Derrida singles out for attention in *La carte postale*.

III

There are, I think, several reasons for Habermas's inability to grasp the philosophical pertinence of Derrida's work. One is the fact that he (Habermas) clearly doesn't have much concern for the finer points of style, writing as he does in a manner that surpasses even Hegel in its heavyweight abstractions, its relentless piling-up of clause upon clause, and the sense it conveys that strenuous thinking is somehow incompatible with 'literary' arts and graces. One can therefore understand why he (like Searle) might regard Derrida's stylistic innovations with a somewhat jaundiced eye. But the antipathy goes much deeper than that, as can be seen from those passages in *PDM* where Habermas sets out his reasons for opposing any attempt to level the genre-distinction between philosophy and literature. Again, I shall need to quote at some length since–at risk of labouring the point–Habermas's style doesn't exactly lend itself to concise summary statement.

Derrida and Rorty are mistaken about the unique status of discourses differentiated from ordinary communication and tailored to a single validity dimension (truth or normative rightness), or to a single complex of problems (questions of truth or justice). In modern societies, the spheres of science, morality, and law have crystallized around these forms of argumentation. The corresponding cultural systems of action administer *problem-solving capacities* in a way similar to that in which the enterprises of art and literature administer *capacities for world-disclosure*. Because Derrida over-generalizes this one linguistic function–namely, the poetic–he can no longer see the complex relationship of the ordinary practice of normal speech to the two extraordinary spheres, differentiated, as it were, in opposite directions. The polar tension between world-disclosure and problem-solving is held together within the functional matrix of ordinary language; but art and literature on the one side, and science, morality, and law on the other, are specialized for experiences and modes of knowledge that can be shaped and worked out within the compass of *one* linguistic function and *one* dimension of validity at a time. (*PDM*, p. 207)

It is clear from this passage that Habermas is still working within a broadly Kantian architectonic, a doctrine of the faculties that insists on maintaining the distinction between theoretical understanding, practical reason and aesthetic judgement. In this respect his arguments in *PDM* are continuous with the project set forth in an early work like *Knowledge and Human Interests*, despite what is presented as a crucial shift of emphasis, from an overtly Kantian ('epistemological' or 'foundationalist') approach to one that takes its bearings from speech-act theory, pragmatics and the study of communicative action. The continuity can be seen clearly enough in Habermas's way of separating out those uses of language 'specialized' for the purposes of problem-solving, argument or rational critique. It is likewise evident in the distinction that Habermas maintains between 'ordinary' and 'extraordinary' language-games, or those that have their place in 'normal speech' and those that belong more properly to art, literature and the 'world-disclosive' function of aesthetic understanding. Here we have the nub of Habermas's case against Derrida: the charge that he has effectively *disenfranchised* critical reason by allowing this promiscuous confusion of realms within and between the various linguistic orientations.

What this argument cannot countenance is any suggestion that *one and the same text* might possess both literary value (on account of its fictive, metaphorical or stylistic attributes) and philosophic cogency (by virtue of its power to criticize normative truth-claims). Thus Habermas would need to reject as non-philosophical not only a text like *La carte postale*, but also those numerous borderline cases–among them Plato, Augustine, Hegel, Kierkegaard, Austin, Borges, Calvino–where fiction and philosophy are closely intertwined. And if the list were then extended to philosophers who had once in a while made use of fictive devices or analogies, then it would also include Aristotle, Kant, Husserl, Frege, Quine, Searle and just about every thinker in the

Western tradition. So Habermas is pretty much out on a limb when he seeks to demarcate the types and conditions of language according to their various specialized roles. And this applies even more to his argument that literary criticism–at least as that discipline has developed since the eighteenth century–should also be regarded as a language apart from those texts that constitute its subject-domain. Thus:

> it [criticism] has responded to the increasing autonomy of linguistic works of art by means of a discourse specialized for questions of taste. In it, the claims with which literary texts appear are submitted to examination–claims to 'artistic truth', aesthetic harmony, exemplary validity, innovative force, and authenticity. In this respect, aesthetic criticism is similar to argumentative forms specialized for propositional truth and the rightness of norms, that is, to theoretical and practical discourse. It is, however, not merely an esoteric component of expert culture but, beyond this, has the job of mediating between expert culture and everyday world. (*PDM*, p. 207)

This last sentence might appear to qualify Habermas's rigid demarcation of realms by allowing that criticism (like philosophy) must have contact with 'ordinary language', at least to the extent of being understood by persons outside the 'expert culture' specifically devoted to such questions. But the passage makes it clear that Habermas conceives this alignment of interests as basically a two-term relationship, holding between 'ordinary language' on the one hand and aesthetics, art-criticism and literary theory on the other. That is to say, he excludes the possibility that this semi-specialized or mediating discourse might also respond to stylistic innovations in literary language, of the kind most strikingly exemplified in Derrida's texts. For Habermas, such developments have exactly the opposite effect. As literature becomes more 'autonomous'–more preoccupied with matters of style, form and technique– so criticism has to insist more firmly on the distance that separates its own language ('specialized for questions of taste') from the language of poetry or fiction. For otherwise–so Habermas implies–criticism will be in no position to claim a knowledge of the text that the text itself has not already made explicit. Only in so far as it maintains this stance can criticism adjudicate in those questions of 'aesthetic harmony, exemplary validity, innovative force, and authenticity' which constitute its own proper sphere of understanding. And in order to do so it will need to be aligned not so much with 'literature' as with 'philosophy', since it is here that such normative validity-claims are most thoroughly tried and tested.

I have already perhaps said enough to indicate just how remote these arguments are from Derrida's practice of a 'philosophical criticism' (for want of any better term) that deliberately mixes the genres of literature and theory. But we should not be misled into thinking that he has thereby renounced philosophy and given himself up to a mode of 'extraordinary' language that severs all links between itself and critical reason on the one hand, or itself and the interests of communal understanding on the other. What Habermas fails to recognize is the extent to which so-called 'ordinary' language is in fact shot through with metaphors, nonce-usages, chance collocations, Freudian parapraxes and other such 'accidental' features that cannot be reduced to any normative account. Henry Staten makes the point well when he describes how Wittgenstein, like Derrida, develops a style that is 'radically errant', one which effectively 'unlids all the accidence concealed by "normal" uses of words in order to show how many different routes it would be possible to take from any given point in the discourse'.[23] Staten is here arguing specifically against those mainstream readings of Wittgenstein which fasten on his talk of 'language-games' and 'forms of life', and use it as a warrant for confining authentic, serious or meaningful discourse to the range of usages sanctioned within some existing cultural community. On the contrary, says Staten: Wittengenstein is just as much concerned as Derrida with the radical 'accidence' of language, the way that it can open up unlooked-for possibilities of meaning precisely through the absence of such binding communal constraints. And the same applies to Derrida and Austin if their texts are read with sufficient regard to these innovative byways of language, routes which 'we had simply not thought of because we were bemused by normality'.[24]

Staten argues a convincing case for Derrida as one who has pushed the project of post-Kantian critical reason to the point of acknowledging its covert involvement in a general problematics of language, writing and representation. This is why his book pays careful attention to Derrida's reading of Husserl, and more specifically those passages where the claims of transcendental phenomenology are subject to a certain dislocating pressure brought about by the effects of linguistic *différance*. It is here, Staten writes, that Derrida most decisively 'wrests the concept of meaning away from the moment of intuition in order to attach it *essentially* to the moment of signification'. Thus language (or writing, in Derrida's extended sense of the term) cannot be confined to its traditional role as a mere vehicle for thoughts and intuitions that would otherwise exist in a state of ideal self-presence or intelligibility. Rather, it is the signifying structure of language–that system of differential marks and traces 'without positive terms'–that constitutes the very possibility of meaning, and thus creates all manner of problems for Husserl's philosophical enterprise.[25] But again we should be wrong to see in this encounter a straightforward instance of philosophy's undoing at the hands of literature, writing or rhetoric. As Staten says,

[w]hat is both original and problematic about Derrida's own project is that it does *not* pursue Joyce's path, but remains faithful to the problematic of that 'univocity' that Derrida sees as underlying Joyce's equivocity, while yet opening out the univocal language in which he works, the language of philosophy, to that spread of meaning Joyce explored.[26]

It is precisely this possibility that Habermas excludes when he takes it that Derrida's levelling of the genre-distinction between philosophy and literature deprives thinking of its critical force and thus betrays the very project of enlightened thought.

One could offer many instances from Derrida's work that would count strongly against this reading. Thus his essay on Foucault ('Cogito and the History of Madness')[27] makes exactly the point that Habermas is making when he asks what kind of *argumentative* force could possibly attach to Foucault's critical genealogies. More specifically: what is the status of a discourse that reduces all truths to the level of an undifferentiated power-knowledge; that denounces reason as merely an agency of ever-increasing surveillance and control; and that claims not only to speak on behalf of that madness which reason has constructed as its outcast other, but moreover to speak the very language of madness from a standpoint beyond any rational accountability?[28] For Habermas, this serves to demonstrate the sheer dead-end that runs into when it follows the line of reactive counter-enlightenment rhetoric that leads from Nietzsche to Bataille, Foucault and other such present-day apostles of unreason. It also goes to show how much they have in common with that one-sided view of modernity and its discontents adopted by an earlier generation of Frankfurt theorists (notably Adorno and Horkheimer in their book *Dialectic of Enlightenment*). For them, as for Foucault, 'modernity' is more or less synonymous with the advance of an instrumental reason that subjugates everything–nature, social existence, art, philosophy, language–to its own homogenizing drive. Thus 'Foucault so levels down the complexity of societal modernization that the disturbing paradoxes of this process cannot even become apparent to him' (*PDM*, p. 291). And he can do so only by ignoring the crucial distinction between instrumental reason–as developed in the service of scientific mastery and power–and those other forms of reason (communicative, critical or emancipatory) which point a way beyond this deadlocked condition.

Derrida is arguing to similar effect when he remarks on the strictly *impossible* nature of Foucault's undertaking and the fact that any such discourse on madness will necessarily have resort to a different order of language, logic and validity-claims. Thus:

if discourse and philosophical communication (that is, language itself) are to have an intelligible meaning, that is to say, if they are to conform to their essence and vocation as discourse, they must simultaneously in fact and in principle escape madness. They must carry normality within themselves. . . . By its essence, the sentence is normal . . . whatever the health or madness of him who propounds it, or whom it passes through, on whom, in whom, it is articulated. In its most impoverished syntax, logos is reason and, indeed, a historical reason.[29]

Where this differs from Habermas's reading is in its argument that Foucault has *not* in fact achieved what he thinks to achieve, that is, a decisive break with the protocols of reason and truth. Since no such break is possible— since every sentence of Foucault's writing betrays an opposite compulsion— Derrida can acknowledge the critical force of his writing *despite and against* its avowed purpose. 'Crisis of reason, finally, access to reason and attack of reason. For what Michel Foucault teaches us to think is that there are crises of reason in strange complicity with what the world calls crises of madness.'[30] For Habermas, conversely, Foucault exemplifies that levelling of the difference between reason and unreason which heralds the 'post-modern condition' and the ultimate betrayal of enlightenment values. In short, Habermas takes Foucault at his word as having left behind all the rational criteria, normative truth-claims, standards of validity, etc., which constitute the 'philosophical discourse of modernity'. And this despite his clear recognition elsewhere that 'Foucault only gains this basis [that is, the explanatory matrix of power-knowledge] by not thinking genealogically when it comes to his *own* genealogical historiography and by rendering unrecogniz- able the derivation of this transcendental-historicist concept of power' (*PDM*, p. 269). For ultimately Habermas cannot conceive that Foucault's project, deriving as it does from the Nietzschean counter-enlightenment lineage, might yet possess a power of demystifying insight that works against its own professed aims and interests.

Derrida can allow for this ambivalence in Foucault's work because (unlike Habermas) he doesn't draw a firm, juridical line between reason and rhetoric, philosophy and literature, the discourse of enlightened critique and the capacity of language (even 'extraordinary' language) to reflect on the inbuilt limits and aporias of that same discourse. But it is simply not the case, as Habermas asserts, that Derrida has thereby abandoned the ground of post-Kantian critical thought, or gone along with that 'drastic levelling of [the] architectonic of reason that results from the Nietzsche-inspired reading of Kant' (*PDM*, p. 305). On the contrary: several of his recent essays are concerned with questions in precisely this sphere. They include Derrida's writings on the modern university and its division of intellectual labour, especially as this relates to Kant's doctrine of the faculties and their role *vis-à-vis* the cardinal distinction between 'pure' and 'applied' forms of knowledge.[31] Here, as in Habermas, philosophy is assigned to its proper place as the discipline that legislates in questions of validity and truth, while the other, more practical or research-oriented disciplines have their separate domains marked out according to their own specific ends and interests. Certainly Derrida calls this system into question, remarking on the various conflicts, aporias or boundary-disputes that arise within and between the faculties. Moreover, he does so by way of a rhetorical reading that suspends the privileged truth-claims of philosophy and asks more specifically what *interests* are served by this policing of the various faculty limits. But there is no question of simply revoking the Kantian paradigm and declaring a break with that entire heritage of enlightened critical thought. In fact Derrida repeatedly insists on the need to keep faith with this 'vigil' of enlightenment, a vigil whose term is not ended (as 'post-modern' thinkers would have it) on account of these constitutive blind-spots in its own project. Those who profess to deconstruct Kant's doctrine of the faculties 'need not set themselves up in opposition to the principle of reason, nor need they give way to "irrationalism"'.[32] While questioning the modern university system and its forms of self-authorized knowledge, they can nevertheless assume, 'along with its memory and tradition, the imperatives of professional rigor and competence'.

IV

Perhaps the most interesting text in this regard is Derrida's essay 'Of an Apocalyptic Tone Recently Adopted in Philosophy'.[33] The title is adapted from an essay of Kant's–a piece of philosophical polemics against those who saw fit to reject the dictates of enlightened reason, and who relied instead on their own unaided intuition as to questions of truth and falsehood or right and wrong. Kant has nothing but scorn for these enthusiasts, these adepts of the 'inner light', imagining as they do that one can bypass the critical tribunal of the faculties and arrive at truth without benefit of reasoned debate. And of course their presumption has religious and political overtones, laying claim to a freedom of individual conscience that goes far beyond Kant's prescription for the exercise of citizenly virtues in a liberal-democratic state. In short, this text bears a close resemblance to Habermas's critique of Derrida, especially those passages where he locates the origins of deconstruction in a 'subject-centred' pre-enlightenment discourse which in turn goes back to the 'mysticism of being', and which thus provides a starting point for Heidegger and Derrida alike. 'If this suspicion is not utterly false, Derrida returns to the historical

locale where mysticism once turned into enlightenment' (*PDM*, p. 184). On
this reading, deconstruction is the upshot of a fateful error in the history of
thought, a path wrongly chosen at precisely the point where philosophy
might have set out on the high road of rational self-understanding.

Thus Habermas takes Derrida to task–just as Kant once chastized the fake
illuminati and apostles of unreason–for rejecting that alternative, far
preferable course that led *through and beyond* Kant and Hegel to the theory of
communicative action. In short, Derrida's deconstructive reading of Heidegger
'does not escape the aporetic structure of a truth-occurrence eviscerated of all
truth-as-validity' (*PDM*, p. 167). And again:

> unabashedly, and in the style of *Ursprungsphilosophie*, Derrida falls
> back on this *Urschrift* [viz, *arche-écriture*] which leaves its traces
> anonymously, without any subject. . . . As Schelling once did in
> speculating about the timeless temporalizing inter-nesting of the past,
> present and future ages of the world, so Derrida clings to the dizzying
> thought of a past that has never been present. . . . He too [like
> Heidegger] degrades politics and contemporary history to the status of
> the ontic and the foreground, so as to romp all the more freely . . . in
> the sphere of the ontological and arche-writing. (pp. 179–81)

This passage tends to confirm the impression that Habermas has based his
critique on a very partial knowledge of Derrida's work. It is a reading that
conspicuously fails to take account of his more recent texts on the 'principle
of reason', the politics of representation and the role of the modern university
system as a site where Kant's doctrine of the faculties is both reproduced and
subjected to forms of destabilizing pressure and critique. But the point can be
made more specifically with reference to Derrida's essay 'Of an Apocalyptic
Tone', and the way that it rehearses not only Kant's quarrel with the
mystagogues but also–at least by implication–the issue between Habermas
and Derrida.

For it is simply not the case (or *not simply* the case) that Derrida here
'deconstructs' the pretensions of enlightenment discourse in order to gain a
hearing for those sophists, rhetoricians or purveyors of an occult wisdom
whose extravagant teachings Kant holds up to ridicule in the parliament of
plain-prose reason. Thus when Derrida offers his own free paraphrase of
Kant's case against the mystagogues it could easily be taken for a passage
from one of Habermas's chapters on Derrida in *PDM*. 'This cryptopolitics is
also a cryptopoetics, a poetic perversion of philosophy' (*AT*, p. 14). And
again: 'this leap toward the imminence of a vision without concept, this
impatience turned toward the most crypted secret sets free a poetico-
metaphorical overabundance' (p. 12). For Kant, 'all philosophy is indeed

prosaic', since it is only by submitting to the democratic rule of reason–to the various 'faculties' duly assembled in parliament, along with all their delegated powers and provisions–that thinking can avoid the manifest dangers of a direct appeal to individual conscience or naked, self-advocating will. Hobbes is a warning presence in the background here, as he is in those passages where Habermas reproaches Foucault for abandoning the ground of enlightened critique, as evolved through the various forms and procedures of civil-administrative reason. What is most to be feared is a wholesale levelling of the faculties which would deprive reason of its moderating role and thereby reduce history, philosophy and politics to a mere force-field of contending interests or rhetorical strategies. And according to Habermas deconstruction is complicit in this process, since it over-extends the province of rhetoric to the point of annulling reason itself, along with all those crucial distinctions that emerged in the sphere of socio-political debate.

Again, these are arguments that Derrida rehearses–and the term seems just right in this context–when he speaks up for Kant and the values of enlightenment, as against the purveyors of a false knowledge vouchsafed by mere intuition. Thus the mystagogues 'scoff at work, the concept, schooling. . . . To what is given they believe they have access effortlessly, gracefully, intuitively or through genius, ouside of school' (AT, p. 9). Where these characters offend most gravely is in 'playing the overlord', in 'raising the tone' of philosophy (or pseudo-philosophy) to such a pitch that it rejects all rational obligations, all the rules of civilized exchange among equals that make up an emergent and developing public sphere. In so doing they seek 'to hoist themselves above their colleagues or fellows and wrong them in their inalienable right to freedom and equality regarding everything touching on reason alone' (AT, p. 11). And the signs of this attitude are there to be read in the various forms of *rhetorical* over-reaching–hyperbole, multiplied metaphor, prosopopeia, apostrophe and other such tropes–whose effect is to disrupt the parliament of faculties by giving voice to a language that respects none of its agreed-upon rules and protocols. As Derrida writes, again paraphrasing Kant: 'they do not distinguish between pure speculative reason and pure practical reason; they believe they *know* what is solely *thinkable* and reach through feeling alone the universal laws of practical reason' (p. 12). Hence their resort to an 'apocalyptic tone' that takes effect through its sheerly *performative* power, its use of an oracular, 'inspired' or prophetic style of speech where the truth-claims of reason (or of language in its constative aspect) have no part to play.

Now it is clear that Derrida is not unambiguously taking Kant's side in this attack on the pretensions of any philosophy that thinks to place itself above or outside the jurisdiction of plain-prose reason. For one thing, his essay is itself shot through with apocalyptic figures and devices, among them various

mystical injunctions from Jewish and Christian source-texts. To this extent
Derrida is asking us to see that the ethos of Kantian civilized reason has sharp
juridical limits; that it has only been able to impose its rule through a
constant policing of the border-lines between reason and rhetoric, concept
and metaphor, 'genuine' philosophy and a discourse that lays false claim to
that title. But we should be wrong to conclude that the essay comes out
squarely *against* Kant, or that Derrida's use of an apocalyptic tone signals yet
another 'post-modern' break with the discourse of enlightened reason. What
sustains this project, he writes, is the 'desire for vigilance, for the lucid vigil,
for elucidation, for critique and truth' (AT, p. 22). Of course it may be said
that Derrida is here not speaking 'in his own voice'; that this essay is a kind of
ventriloquist performance, mixing all manner of citations, intertextual
allusions, contrapuntal ironies and so forth, so that anyone who instances this
or that passage as evidence for their own preferred reading is surely missing
the point. But this objection is itself wide of the mark in so far as it ignores
the distinctly Kantian form of Derrida's argument, namely, his questioning
of enlightenment values and truth-claims through a debate whose terms are
inescapably set by that same Kantian tribunal. That is to say, Derrida is
asking what might be the *conditions of possibility* for the exercise of a critical
reason that thinks to keep itself pure by excluding or denouncing all other
forms of discourse.

To regard this essay as a mere assemblage of 'literary' tricks and devices is
to make the same error that Habermas makes when he criticizes Derrida for
supposedly levelling the genre-distinction between philosophy and literature.
It involves the kind of typecast binary thinking that refuses to see how a
'literary' text–or one which exploits a wide range of stylistic resources–might
yet possess sufficient *argumentative* force to unsettle such deep-laid assumptions.
Derrida belongs very much with those philosophers (Wittgenstein and
Austin among them) who resist this habit of compartmentalized thinking.
He wants to keep open the two-way flow between 'ordinary' language
and the various extra-ordinary styles, idioms, metaphorical usages, 'expert'
registers and so forth, which help to defamiliarize our commonplace beliefs.
But he also sees–unlike Habermas or Searle–that 'ordinary language' is a
gross misnomer, since there is no possibility of laying down rules (or
extracting a generalized speech-act theory) that would separate normal from
deviant instances. It is the idea that such rules *ought* to be available–and that
philosophy is the discipline specialized (as Habermas would say) for the
purpose of producing them–that actually prevents philosophy from perceiving
how manifold, inventive and remarkable are the varieties of 'ordinary'
language. The result of such thinking is to isolate philosophy in a realm of
meta-linguistic theory and principle where it can have no contact with those
energizing sources.

Derrida's point–to put it very simply–is that philosophy is indeed a 'kind of writing', but a kind which (contrary to Rorty's understanding) cannot be collapsed into a generalized notion of rhetoric or intertextuality. It is unfortunate that Habermas takes his bearings in *PDM* from a widespread but none the less fallacious idea of how deconstruction relates to other symptoms of the so-called post-modern condition. What Derrida gives us to read is *not* philosophy's undoing at the hands of literature but a literature that meets the challenge of philosophy in every aspect of its argument, form and style.

NOTES

1 Jürgen Habermas, *The Philosophical Discourse of Modernity: Twelve Lectures*, trans. Frederick Lawrence (Cambridge: Polity Press, 1987). Hereafter cited in the text as *PDM*.

2 See for instance Jean-Francois Lyotard, 'The Sign of History', *Post-Structuralism and the Question of History*, ed. Derek Attridge, Geoff Bennington and Robert Young (Cambridge: Cambridge University Press, 1987), 162–80.

3 Habermas, *Knowledge and Human Interests*, trans. Jeremy J. Shapiro (London: Heinemann, 1972).

4 For a useful account of these differences, see Rainer Nägele, 'Freud, Habermas and the Dialectic of Enlightenment: on Real and Ideal Discourses', *New German Critique*, 22 (1981), 41–62.

5 See Rodolphe Gasché, *The Tain of the Mirror: Derrida and the Philosophy of Reflection* (Cambridge, MA: Harvard University Press, 1986).

6 Richard Rorty, 'Philosophy as a Kind of Writing', *Consequences of Pragmatism* (Minneapolis: University of Minnesota Press, 1982), 89–109. See also Rorty, 'Deconstruction and Circumvention', *Critical Inquiry*, 11 (1984), 1–23.

7 See especially Jacques Derrida, *Margins of Philosophy*, trans. Alan Bass (Chicago: University of Chicago Press, 1982).

8 Derrida, 'Limited Inc. abc', *Glyph*, 2 (1977), 162–254.

9 Derrida, 'Structure, Sign and Play in the Discourse of the Human Sciences', *Writing and Difference*, trans. Alan Bass (London: Routledge and Kegan Paul, 1978), pp. 278–93.

10 Derrida, *The Post Card: From Socrates to Freud and Beyond*, trans. Alan Bass (Chicago: University of Chicago Press, 1987). I have slightly modified Bass's translation in some of the passages cited.

11 Derrida, *Edmund Husserl's 'Origin of Geometry': an Introduction*, trans. John P. Leavey (Pittsburgh: Duquesne University Press, 1978).

12 In this connection see especially Habermas, *Communication and the Evolution of Society*, trans. Thomas McCarthy (London: Heinemann, 1979).

13 John Searle, 'Reiterating the Differences', *Glyph*, 1 (1977), 198–208.

14 See Norris, *Derrida* (Cambridge, MA: Harvard University Press, 1987), 172–93; also Jonathan Culler, 'Convention and Meaning: Derrida and Austin', *New Literary History*, (1981), 15–30, and Shoshana Felman, *The Literary Speech-Act:*

Don Juan with J. L. Austin, or Seduction in Two Languages, trans. Catherine Porter (Ithaca, NY: Cornell University Press, 1983).

15 See J. L. Austin, *How to Do Things with Words* (London: Oxford University Press, 1962), and *Philosophical Papers* (London: Oxford University Press, 1961), especially the essay 'A Plea for Excuses', pp. 123–52.

16 Derrida, *Of Grammatology*, trans. Gayatri C. Spivak (Baltimore: Johns Hopkins University Press, 1976).

17 Derrida, *The Post Card*, p. 98.

18 On this topic see also Derrida, *Signsponge*, trans. Richard Rand (New York: Columbia University Press, 1984).

19 Derrida, *The Post Card*, p. 99.

20 Ibid. p. 62.

21 Derrida, 'To Speculate–on "Freud"', in *The Post Card*, pp. 257–409.

22 Jacques Lacan, 'Seminar on "The Purloined Letter"', trans. Jeffrey Mehlman, *Yale French Studies*, 48 (1972), 38–72. Derrida's essay, 'Le Facteur de la vérité', appears in *The Post Card*, pp. 411–96.

23 Henry Staten, *Wittgenstein and Derrida* (Lincoln and London: University of Nebraska Press, 1984), p. 75.

24 Ibid. p. 75.

25 See Derrida, *'Speech and Phenomena' and Other Essays on Husserl's Theory of Signs*, trans. David B. Allison (Evanston, IL: Northwestern University Press, 1973).

26 Staten, p. 48.

27 Derrida, 'Cogito and the History of Madness', in *Writing and Difference*, pp. 31–63.

28 Michel Foucault, *Madness and Civilization: a History of Insanity in the Age of Reason*, trans. Richard Howard (New York: Pantheon, 1965). Foucault responded to Derrida's essay in his appendix to the second edition of *Folie et déraison* (Paris: Gallimard, 1972), 583–603.

29 Derrida, 'Cogito and the History of Madness', pp. 53–4.

30 Ibid. p. 63.

31 See for instance Derrida, 'The Principle of Reason: the University in the Eyes of its Pupils', *Diacritics*, 19 (1983), 3–20.

32 Ibid. p. 17.

33 Derrida, 'Of an Apocalyptic Tone Recently Adopted in Philosophy', trans. John P. Leavey, *Oxford Literary Review*, 6, 2 (1984), 3–37. Hereafter cited in the text as AT.

9

Irene E. Harvey

Derrida and the Issues of Exemplarity

In some respects one could argue that Derrida's work has from its inception never been concerned with anything *other* than exemplarity. From the earliest deconstructive analysis of Rousseau, through the tortured machinations of *Glas* to his more recent work on the 'hand' of Heidegger, Derrida's vision of philosophy has insistently raised the spectre of this problematic underpinning of the discourse itself. The example, the choice of examples, the series of examples, the Exemplary example, the non-exemplary example, the unique example, the impossible example could be the titles of his numerous essays on the subject. But if these possible titles were not chosen, but rather shifted into the often unthematized backgrounds for ostensibly 'other' issues, it is not because exemplarity as an issue has been treated, resolved, subdued or conquered. On the contrary, the more it has been analysed, the more the need to analyse it further has made its appearance.

Let us consider for a moment three readers of Derrida who have also named the issue of exemplarity as central and forbidding, if not foreboding. Gasché's article entitled 'God For Example'[1] situated the 'exemplarity' issue within the debate over the theological implications–both negative and positive–of Derrida's work. In naming God, for example, Gasché claims, one locates the difference between God and Being, and allows the privilege of the latter to come to light. This despite Heidegger's claim to the contrary, which Gasché also cites. Furthermore, in being the Example, *par excellence*, Gasché says, God is unique, he is exemplary of exemplarity itself. Yet this notion of 'exemplarity itself' is again not Gasché's concern here. Instead he uses the term 'example' as a case or instance, as an Exemplar (model) and as an analogy synonymously. What is at stake for Gasché is 'the impossibility of giving an example of the trace', yet at the same time its revelation via God for example. Thus 'God', for Gasché, can function–in the discourse of Derrida, for example–as an example of this non-exemplificatory relation. An example of the impossibility of example. It is here that Gasché ends his analysis despite the enigmatic demand that has himself raised: what makes exemplarity possible (and impossible, he might add) and thus what is occurring in the process of the constitution of examples? Thus Gasché presents us with–re-presents for us–the very terms of the problem, not its solution, if that were possible. Further, by insisting on the 'limits' of the relation between the trace (supplementarity, differance) and God as inscribed in 'the structure of exemplarity', Gasché contributes to the occultation of exemplarity rather than its obverse. Far from clarifying the issue, Gasché assumes a notion of exemplarity based on the tradition of metaphysics–'an example is after all an instance of a universal', he says–and thus he forecloses further analysis of the issue as such. It is this stricture on the possibility of analysis which we will question in what follows, as well as the assumptions that Gasché's analysis, for example, leaves unquestioned and firmly in place.

Another attempt to review Derrida's work on the example comes from Ulmer's text on deconstruction,[2] in particular in the chapter entitled 'Models'. He surveys much of the corpus of Derrida's work with respect to this issue, but his own use of the terms 'example' and 'exemplarity' shifts from example as frame, as 'the defeat of conceptual closure', to a horizontal displacement, a type of lateral *Aufhebung* that drifts from homonym to homonym, and finally to the notion of example as an autobiographical fetish. How these various structures and motifs are related is reminiscent of a pure metonymy, if not homonymy itself in Ulmer's reading. Far from unifying his wide-ranging survey of Derrida on exemplarity–from context to context– Ulmer leaves open the gaps, *en abyme*, as undecidable and, hence, decidedly lacking in clarification. He summarizes the analyses in *Glas*, the issues of dialectics, and those of a psychoanalytic orientation referring to Kant, Lacan and others via the fetish/example connection. Yet, Ulmer ultimately relies on a notion of 'the detail' (or idiom) that would 'escape conceptual closure' by sheer defiance. Why or how a detail, an instance, after all, could 'escape' from the usurpation of the Concept is not at all clear in Ulmer's account. That it does or can, by resisting is enough from his standpoint. The notion of the autobiographical signature effect as exhibited by examples again opens up the dialectic of closure but again is left as sheer evidence in Ulmer's account. Why this is not again another instance of yet another law is not explicated or analysed by him, though it is by Derrida, as we shall see.

Our third instance of the attempt to extend Derrida's work on exemplarity comes in the form of two readings of Hegel on the example by Warminski.[3] Taking the insights of Derrida, and finding further evidence elsewhere, he shows in detail how the term *Beispiel* functions for Hegel in the first chapter of the *Phenomenology of Spirit* as a marker–between the 'figurative and literal' readings of 'Sense-Certainty'. How *Beispiel* does this, *how* it relates to the constitution of the difference between literal and figurative, is not analysed by him, however. We are left again with the evidence that example shows, functions, performs in this way. It functions as a marker (a pure signifier, he might have said) in the discourse which in turn conceals this function. In his second reading of example, Warminski locates the place where Hegel re-reads Aristotle's example (of wax) and opens the question concerning the ways examples can be read otherwise. What makes Hegel's re-reading possible is precisely his own theory which in turn allows him to interpret the example in a different light. What Warminski illustrates is the excess within any example that always opens it to the possibility of other readings. What makes this possible is not, however, asked by Warminski, nor Hegel, but rather is located only via the term 'excess'. Reading the 'more' that examples are is what is at stake for Warminski inasmuch as he locates the Heideggerian unthought here. Why here? Why via and through examples? Because they have taken on the function of a micro-text—of the paradigm of textuality itself. How and why these assumptions can be justified is not, however, addressed.

In order to thematize more precisely the issue raised by current work on exemplarity, we must now turn to the most systematic and sustained of efforts: the work of Derrida. We shall pursue only the most detailed and intensive of his analyses here in an effort to reach the limits of his position from its depths rather than from an extensive overview. What is needed at this point, we suggest, is an analysis of the way in which the exemplarity issue has been raised by Derrida and yet also left in suspension between 'dialectics and non-dialectics', between the unique idiom and that most general concept which is not a concept—both possible and impossible via exemplarity—namely, God.

From his work on Hegel, notably in *Glas*, Derrida has sought to relocate the 'remainders' of the *Aufhebung*. Beginning with the place of the Jews, in relation to the family, the State, Christianity and philosophy, Derrida traces the ways in which Hegel excludes the Jews only in order to 'include' them 'at a higher level'; namely, not as Jews, but as proto-Christians, as on-the-way-to being what they are not. If not historical or literal, Hegel's analysis does at least contribute to and reaffirm that analogous movement in history as such. Derrida's concern with the example of the Jews as a non-example is multiple and cannot be summarized in full here. What is at stake for him, though, is to articulate this simultaneous inclusion and exclusion of the *non-example*—in every sense of the term—within the Hegelian system. The Jews and their non-place are but one example of this way of being in relation to the *Aufhebung*. As excluded they can be included; yet as radically other, they must be excluded as such. Furthermore, the machinery of philosophy as the including of examples–indeed the constitution of examples (their creation, production, identification and control) is revealed here such that the non-exemplary would violate the spirit (if not the letter) of philosophy as such. Hence, we have the onto-theological foundations which again revolve around the Christian God/son, and the philosophical Concept/example.

Derrida cites another example of this idiomatic non-example again within Hegel's text; namely, the brother–sister relation which is decidedly non-dialectical. The issue one might well ask here, and it is Derrida's work that raises it, is how can an 'example', albeit a non-example, or an example of a non-example, resist the law? Stay outside the law? Or, better, trouble the lawfulness of the law? Following this question, Derrida traces the brother–sister relation Hegel's own letters to his sister exhibit, and thus the signature effect of the ancient Antigone scene is revealed. The latter non-example is revealed as an example of another non-example in Hegel's own autobiography which makes its appearance–another non-example–in the text of philosophy. Far from revealing *non-exemplarity* as radically other than exemplarity, which would therefore be eminently dialecticizable, he reveals that non-exemplarity–the Jews, Antigone, the signature–*obeys* *another law*: the law of the Other, one might call it. In this way, as instance of the trace of differance, these non-examples are precisely what they are not: examples. Has metaphysics ever done anything else? Namely, is metaphysics itself not constituted by the very process of turning the non-example into an example (of something else ostensibly more general)? What is at stake for Derrida here, however, is the simulacre of metaphysics–it is Abraham here, it is circumcision, it is the prosthesis, it is the feigned repetition which is a mark of difference here; not a pure reptition, not another example. The issue then, for Derrida, would seem to be not how to avoid the law–of metaphysics, and hence of exemplarity–but how to use it otherwise. How to double the process, to double the law, to double the double, as he says, which would make the relation between the two laws, on the one hand, dialectical (from Hegel's and philosophy's point of view) and, on the other hand, undecidable (from Derrida's and the differential point of view). Thus exemplarity can be used, as Derrida's analysis exhibits, to double the law and thereby keep open the space for the truly non-exemplary example. That this can always be dialecticized again, transformed into what it is not, is not denied by such an analysis, but that violence is thereby done in the process is what is revealed.

From the signature effects in Hegel–the two brothers and the two sisters–Derrida's pursuit of the exemplarity issue turns to Kant and the *choice* of his examples in the *Third Critique*. Here the notion of example as framed and framing, the issue of the *series* of examples, their laws (inside and outside the series) re-emerges. Derrida's analysis again turns towards the 'law' of the examples, though in a different sense and from a different origin than the explicit law which Kant himself suggests. Far from simply illustrating an argument or theory, the examples themselves re-orient the text around them, according to Derrida. Furthermore, they entail the possibility of being read otherwise such that they do not simply support or clarify the stated argument, but rather exhibit another level and, hence, law operating within the text. By applying what Kant calls 'reflective judgement'–using examples without laws or concepts preceding them–rather than determinant judgement, Derrida claims to find more in the example than Kant could have intended or controlled. Thus the excess is revealed in their being read otherwise, but, more than this, this 'more' is systematic and *lawful*. Examples betray the text they inhabit insofar as they exhibit this other law. In turn we have found in and through Kant's examples yet another instance of the signature effect insofar as Kant's assumptions–not thematized as such by the *Third Critique*– are revealed in and through the 'logic' of the choice of his examples. Thus apparently parasitic and dependent, hermeneutically and hermetically sealed by the text around them, examples betray this same context in which they are found. They tell too much, they betray their own 'law' of appearance by revealing–under Derridean scrutiny at least–an other law which governs them. Far from being simply mutinous, simple excesses, examples thus for Derrida reveal another *allegiance*, another legality, which can be seen as illegitimate only within the system that only apparently governs them.

What is at stake here is again that examples can be found to function in this para-metaphysical manner, and that they do so incessantly. Name an example, one can find its 'law' and its 'other law', from a Derridean standpoint. The issue for us is not that Derrida's analysis is refutable or challengable, but rather: what makes this analysis *possible*? What else is taking place in these relations between example–text–example such that (a) they can *always*–even after Derrida–be read otherwise; (b) that examples relate to the texts in which they are embedded in parasitic, hermeneutical and yet treasonous ways; (c) that there is a relation of example to law which is not singular; and so forth. In short, Derrida's analysis here, as elsewhere on this issue, seems to stop short–at the brink–and turn back to feigning metaphysical forms, laws, and machinations at the very moment when some other articulation–not mimetic, not doubling, not castrating or circumcizing– becomes possible. To this point we have examined Derrida's work on the subject as positive content of a theory that could in principle be worked out. It is now time to turn the above articulation on its head, as it were, in order to show not only what Derrida does not do, but what it is in what he does that he must assume–unthematized–in order to do what he does. This is not a deconstruction of Derrida, though it may appear analogous in some respects. We will not juxtapose what Derrida declares and describes, thematizes and leaves unthematized, in what follows. Rather, we aim to show that, despite the radicality (indeed, perhaps because of it, in the sense of rootedness, the 'radical' side) of Derrida's analysis of the problem of exemplarity, he remains tied to assumptions which not only limit his analysis but blind him to any further articulation. Let us return, then, first to his reading of the example, indeed, the non-example, in Hegel, and then in turn to the Kantian examples of the *Third Critique* in order to locate in detail–by example–what is at stake here.

THE HEGELIAN EXAMPLES OF NON-EXEMPLARITY

Derrida outlines what is at stake in what follows, though he offers no criticism at this point of this ontological structure:

> At least it can no longer play *the role of an example*, if the example is a particular case in a whole or a homogeneous series. It can be an example if the example is the *exemplary ideal*, the absolute sense of which the finite examples are precisely only approximating samples [*exemplaires*]. This passage from the example to the exemplariness of the example, this passage from the finite to the infinite can sometimes be given aspects of rhetoric and of the mode of exposition. This is *in truth* the *ontologic of the passage, the reason of the finite* that posits itself as such only by passing into the infinite. In the finite the examples (*Beispielen*) can be substituted for each other, and that is *why they are examples*, particular cases classed according to the general law. [my emphasis][4]

What this description entails is the classical notion of exemplarity whereby an example is understood to be a particular case of a general law, and as such the former entails a process of substitutability whereas the latter claims uniqueness and idiomaticity. Derrida notably does not question this *passage*– this relation of relatability–between the general and the particular, between the example and the Exemplar. He himself uses it in his effort to show *not* that this passage is problematic, but that the passage is always already double. The example leads us both towards its *law*, via reason and the dialectic, and also towards its 'other law', via différance and the trace. But *that* this passage is problematic, is not a ready translation or translatable, is not raised by Derrida. Instead he reaffirms the very gesture of metaphysics which conceals the conditions of the possibility of exemplarity as such.

That examples, once constituted as such, can replace each other is reaffirmed by Derrida and again left unquestioned and unanalysed. For instance:

This substitution is the freedom of play, of the play among the examples. This freedom is finite. Play here is made possible by finitude, but finitude relieves itself [*se relève*].[5]

What is at issue here is the inessentiality that is attributed to examples insofar as they all equally re-present the law. In this manner, examples in a series re-place and displace each other such that each in principle could stand by itself–in place of the series–and stand in for the law. Derrida's own analysis of the series in Kant's use of examples belies this very substitutability and its implied commutative principle of non-essential ordering. This notion of the 'easy transition' from finitude to the infinite via examples is, however, not questioned by Derrida in either case. What he adds to the issue is yet another law–that of the first in a series–but this addition in no way problematizes the lawfulness of the relation of example to law itself. Further, that examples are particular cases is again reaffirmed by Derrida's omission here, and it is clear that he himself relies on this idea.

As he turns to the issues of other examples of the non-example, the Jews and Judaism as such in Hegel, Derrida describes the place of the non-example as yet another example. Insofar as the Jews are cited, excluded explicitly, the dialectical inclusion and the machinery of the infinite is still in place, Derrida claims. Thus the non-example, a remainder, is also subsumable within exemplarity for Hegel and for Derrida. This leads to the issue of the idiomatic as somehow–perhaps outside the law of the law as–a true non-example. Yet the further outside, exterior and radical, one moves here, the more inside the law and readily assimilable by the dialectic is our position: a true opposite. Derrida's analysis thus searches for the idiomatic as the impossible example, as that which would not be dialectically digestible, and this becomes a certain plurality–a doubleness–that has no ultimate singularity. But, in such a move, again Derrida relies on all that we would question–the very passage from the idiomatic to the general, from the finite to the infinite, from the case to its law. Derrida's analysis ends up in an ontology of duplicity–of two laws–that cannot be subsumed one within the other. Each defies the other; each is illegal with regard to the other; each supplants the other. Yet, they subsist–co-exist, one might argue. What this claim leaves unchallenged is the constitution of the example itself, the other possible relations between examples, and the *foreclosure* produced by the very assumption of exemplarity as the passage between the finite and the infinite. In short, Derrida re-produces the same occlusion that he describes in Hegel, though he leaves open a duplicity in the law as a result. Nonetheless, the passage itself is not placed in question by him.

In an effort to locate what he claims remains outside the *Aufhebung*, however, Derrida locates what he calls '*deux foyers*' (in lieu of two 'examples',

perhaps): the sepulchre and the relation between the brother and sister in the
Phenomenology of Spirit. In each case what he finds in Hegel's analysis is a
remainder, an exclusion, an 'example' whose unity divides itself. As he says:

> For example (the uniqueness of the example is destroyed by itself,
> immediately elaborates the power of a generalizing organ), the very
> moment we would claim to recapture there, in a determined text the
> work of an idiom, bound to a chain of proper names.[6]

Thus in analysing these examples *otherwise*, Derrida finds that though they
fall outside of the dialectical machine, in a sense, as bad examples, or non-
examples of the law, they thereby *fall inside* another law–the law of the
Other–and a law that they do indeed thereby exemplify. Furthermore, the
status of the brother–sister case is, as Derrida says: 'Exemple unique dans le
système'. A unique example? An example not of uniqueness, though that is
also the same from Derrida's point of view, but an example that stands alone,
outside of the dialectical sets of oppositions, yet is placed *inside* the text of the
same story. Thus Derrida searches for why [*pourquoi?*]–for what–this
'unique example' has been chosen. Its 'law', its reason–and all examples have
a reason or law, for Derrida–connects with Hegel's own life and biography as
we have shown earlier. What is at stake for us here is again the frame of
analysis that organizes Derrida's 'own' reading of examples–a simple
doubling of the metaphysical foreclosure–which at most and in every case
shows us that *examples obey more than one law at the same time*. What is the
relation between these two laws? This is precisely what deconstruction has
always and ever anew sought to reveal: in a word, it is an opposition from the
dialectical standpoint, and undecidable, in interminable abyssal oscillation,
from the deconstructive standpoint. Derrida sums it up this way:

> But this nondialecticalness, this ahistoricity can always be interpreted
> as negativity, as resistance proper to the dialectic economy, and
> consequently interned in the speculative process. A certain undecidability
> of the fetish lets us oscillate between a dialectics (of the undecidable and
> the dialectical) or an undecidability (between the dialectical and the
> undecidable).[7]

Thus examples are caught once again–foreclosed by a certain non-analysis–
within the rupture or passage, depending on the point of view (Christian/
Judaic; Hegelian/Derridean) between two laws. Far from opening up a new
articulation of exemplarity, Derrida's analysis reaffirms the most strictly
confined notion of exemplarity that metaphysics has always assumed: an
example is nothing more than a particular instance or case of a more general

law. The only issue here would be which law? That Derrida repeats Hegel's most inclusive gesture of dialectical ingestion is a striking paradox resulting in the mimetic retracing of his analysis over Hegel's. Derrida's foci of the indigestibles has managed, perhaps indeed by the cunning of reason, to relocate these non-examples within another economy of passage from the particular–the example of non-exemplarity–to its law.

The limit case of Derrida's re-writing/re-reading of Hegel is the case of the Holocaust [*le brûle-tout*]. This example, this limit, Derrida insists has no essence; it is a pure play/game [*jeu*] without law. As he says:

> The all-burning is "an essenceless by-play, pure accessory of the substance that rises without ever setting . . ."
>
> A pure essenceless by-play, a play that plays limitlessly, even though it is already destined to work in the service of essence and sense. But as such, supposing that 'as such' can be said of something that is not something. . . . The word itself (*Beiherspielen*) plays the example (*Beispiel*) beside the essence. Here the pure example plays beside the essence so much, holds itself so diverted from [*à l'écart de*] the essence, that it has no essence: pure example, without essence, without law. Therefore without example, like God about which Hegel says that an example cannot be made, but because he, God merges with the pure essence, pure essence is also without example.[8]

Thus we have at least one case, Derrida claims, of the signifier without signified–when God and the Holocaust meet–when two limits are structurally indistinguishable.[9] Can this non-exemplarity be maintained? Only at the limit of deconstruction, one might argue, since we have already seen via Gasché's analysis of Derrida on the law that God again falls back into being an Example; indeed, an example of Exemplarity as such in the pure passage from finitude to infinitude (and vice versa). This, of course, is the named God, the Hegelian-philosophic-Christian God, from Derrida's standpoint. The Holocaust, on the other hand, is without essence, without law; it is the idiom again repeated here in its absolute form. In turn, it becomes an example of the non-example, and we have re-placed this non-essential instance, this unique uniqueness, back into an economy of exemplarity; indeed, the economy of exemplarity which is here as elsewhere isomorphic (if not identical in substance as well) with that of metaphysics.

In turn, even with God and the Holocaust, the two limits of exemplarity from Derrida's point of view, we find another law, indeed the law of the other appears as the double of the law of the same, but otherwise not troubling the traditional economy of exemplarity as such.

THE KANTIAN EXAMPLES OF (NON-) REFLECTIVE
JUDGEMENT

Derrida claims to authorize, or legalize, his reading of Kant's examples in the *Third Critique* by utilizing what Kant terms 'reflective judgement' as distinct from determinant judgement. These two forms of judgement can be distinguished by their usage of the example, or the case, as Derrida also calls it, as, on the one hand, following its law (in order of presentation) and, on the other, as preceding, if not pre-empting its (their) law(s). As he says:

> When the generality is given first, the operation of judgment subsumes and *determines* the particular. It is determinant (*bestimmend*), it specifies, narrows down, comprehends, tightens. In the contrary hypothesis, the *reflective* judgment (*reflectirend*) has only the particular at its disposal and must climb back up to, return toward generality: the example (this is what matters to us here) is here given prior to the law and, in its very uniqueness as example, allows one to discover that law. Common scientific or logical discourse proceeds by determinant judgments, and the example follows in order to determine or, with a pedagogical intention, to illustrate. In art and in life . . . according to Kant . . . the *example precedes*.[10]

In turn Derrida asks if the *Third Critique* could not be considered a work of art–an object of its own theory–and thus the examples could be shown both to follow and to precede two very different laws. On the one hand, they follow Kant's law–his frame around them, illustrating and giving instances of his more general theory. On the other, Derrida will claim these same (but internally divided) examples will be shown to exhibit, again, an other law–to precede an unsaid rule to which they nonetheless adhere. Thus Derrida's analysis accepts the notion of example as (a) a particular; (b) exhibiting, whether prior or antecedently, a law; and (c) an instance of something more general which governs it. He does not ask, and indeed cannot ask, given the above metaphysical determination of 'the example', what makes this *re-reading* of the example (otherwise) possible. He does not ask *whether* examples are always and necessarily lawbound–by one law or another. He does not ask what other structures might be operating *between* examples, and between the examples and the theory, than those of metaphysics. Rather, he suggests that the inclusion/exclusion demarcation between frame and the framed is itself an abyssal structure. Thus the example and its law relate in a parasitic rather than an external way; that is, the law, the frame, is never totally outside the example, nor is the example ever outside or independent of its frame. What this troubling of the boundaries–between example and law–shows, however, is that différance (that other law) operates between the law and its instance such that neither is purely what it is, neither subsists independently of the other. But again, rather than disturbing the traditional metaphysical translatability assumed between example and exemplified, Derrida massively reaffirms it. The example is always already intrinsic, constitutive and law-abiding. It is never arbitrary, from Derrida's point of view. Nor does it only obey one law–the thematized frame. Rather, again, it (they) can be shown to obey at least two laws–and, one might add, only two laws, from Derrida's perspective. The relation between these two laws–undecidable, ontologically double–parallel but other. Why only two laws? This is a question that Derrida does not raise, though de Man focused on the issue as a central one resulting from deconstruction. His answer relied on another type of foreclosure of the analysis of exemplarity as well inasmuch as he claimed the duplicity–blindness and insight, undecidability and dialectics–to be part of, perhaps the ground of, the ontological structure of language itself. Thus ontologized one can only repeat the findings with each new deconstruction, as de Manians, if not de Man himself, were wont to do.

Returning to Derrida's reading of Kant, and the former's unasked questions concerning his own reading and its possibilities, we find that only a few examples are selected from Kant's text. Why these? No reason is given, by Derrida at least. Rather a confession of partiality, to a non-encyclopedic, non-all-inclusive reading:

> I shall not even cite all the examples, but only some of them, and I shall provisionally leave to one side the very complicated theory of colours and sounds, of drawings and composition, which is unfolded between the two fragments I translate here.[11]

Such is the confession of partiality, which will paradoxically not lessen the strength or extent of his findings as a result. Rather, what is found with some examples will be enough to claim that (some) examples exhibit other laws. Indeed, Derrida's movement towards partiality here is precisely what is at stake in his analysis of Kant. That some examples reveal more than others does not detract from the Derridean enterprise; on the contrary, it reaffirms the very partiality that all theories entail; otherwise termed, the signature effect, the fetish, or the autobiographical elements that all ostensibly non-autobiographical discourses entail. What organizes Derrida's choice, however, is still the question. According to his own 'logic of examples' (parallel if not identical to that of classical metaphysics) his choices should in principle exhibit, implicitly if not explicitly, their own laws. It is evident, though no conclusive positive evidence could be given, that Derrida's choice plays with an erotic metaphorics from the clothes on the statue to the colossal nature of the sublime and Kant's choice of the 'all-too-large', rather than the minute, as his example of the sublime. Only suggestive, never explicit, Derrida moulds his discourse around these pillars of potential eroticism. Why these examples, why these metaphorics? One can only speculate, and this is not our purpose here. Rather, what is at stake for us is that Derrida's analysis, however original and rich it may be, nonetheless does not question the fundamental structures of exemplarity he inherits from the metaphysical tradition.

Another tactic used skilfully and fruitfully by Derrida in his work on Kant's examples entails the questioning of the *order of the series* of examples. Why is the first in the series first? What does the ordering betray or expose which is not thematized or admitted by Kant's theory? Again, the first in the series will be shown by Derrida to be the law of the series. The first is the rule by which the others are selected. In turn, one can step back from this first case, to its law–which in turn will be the law of the law of the series. Thus, far from being substitutable, the list of examples (given by Kant at least) can be shown to be a hierarchical stacking of far from equal or substitutable cases. Some cases (examples) are thus more equal than others. Though significant and revealing, this analysis again reaffirms the traditional view that examples are examples insofar as and only insofar as they are examples of a law. Again we have the translation complete, without questions, between the finite and the infinite–the case and its law. The only issue here, for Derrida, is *where* to locate this law–this *ergon* of the *parergon*, which itself turns into a *parergon* itself.

It must be said that the traditional rhetoric of exemplarity locates the importance of examples as 'merely supplementary' to a theory, insofar as the theory (law) comes first–determinant judgement. In addition, the order of appearance of examples is also neutralized inasmuch as it is claimed and assumed that examples simply exhibit their law in a progressively narrowing and increasingly precise manner with the extension of the series. Thus one example can be vague, whereas six examples will narrow down the precise sense of the law they are said to exemplify. Derrida's reading challenges this traditional notion by showing that the order is not insignificant (lawless) but instead reveals some other organizing principle. Again Derrida uses metaphysical determinations here in order to find yet more laws for those aspects of a theory which had hitherto been designated as arbitrary–or at least insignificant (lawless). Finding yet more laws of exemplarity does trouble the ubiquity of the rhetoric of metaphysics–one law for all–but it does not alter the fundamental structure and foreclosure or the understanding (as misunderstanding) of exemplarity itself. Although Derrida claims this is 'his issue' concerning Kant here, and Hegel elsewhere, he does not challenge what we take to be fundamentally questionable here. The results of his analysis of Kant are summed up in the following claim, which we suggest sustains the metaphysical closure of the issue of exemplarity rather than dislocates it:

> The reflective operation which we have just allowed to make itself writing on the frame or have itself written on the frame (this is–writing/ written on the frame): a general law which is no longer a mechanical or teleological law of nature, of the accord or the harmony of the faculties (etc.) but a certain *repeated dislocation, a regulated,* irrepressible dislocation, which makes the frame in general crack, undoes it at the corners in its quoins and joints [*l'abîme en coin dans ses angles, et ses articulations*] . . . [my emphasis][12]

Despite the metaphorics of liberation, opening, cracking, deterioration, Derrida's analysis reinstates and reaffirms precisely the problems of the metaphysical determination of exemplarity as such. Examples for him do nothing more than exhibit other laws. He opens no new territory here, but rather multiplies the traditionally univocal territory that metaphysics claims for itself. That we have many laws, or at least two here revealed in and through examples, does little to open the space to any other vision of exemplarity other than either the lawless or lawful. Both options simply determine exemplarity via the law and thus, ultimately, with indifference.[13]

That examples can be disruptive in a text or a theory, if not also in a classroom or any pedagogical setting, is acknowledged by Kant and Derrida in his turn. But what makes this disruption or dis-rupture, as potential rupture in the text–in its reading, in its closure–which would not support the theory as described but undermines it, is not analysed by Derrida. He admits:

> Thus they can invert, unbalance, incline the natural movement into a parergonal movement, divert the energy of the ergon, introduce chance and the abyss into the necessity of the *Mutterwitz* not a contrary order but an aleatory sidestep [*écart*] . . . [14]

Again we have the metaphorics of a destabilizing, disrupting and chance event–if not the eventfulness of the event itself as unforeseeable, uncontrollable in advance–but without an analysis of what makes this possible. In addition, it is ironically Derrida's own analysis that, far from affirming this 'chance' event which would de-stabilize by its illegality, instead reaffirms the (albeit hidden) lawfulness of the seemingly lawless examples. That this hidden other law de-stabilizes the official, thematized 'ergonized' law is

Derrida's further contention, yet there is little evidence for this. Instead, again we have two laws: the law of the work as it controls (or attempts to control) the examples imported for clarification, and the law of the frame (paradoxically not of the work but of the example as frame) which are shown to relate in a regulated, if not systematic, way. The rule of this rule? De-stabilization, for Derrida. But though he may find this identification and elucidation of yet another law de-stabilizing, one could argue that, instead, he has re-instated, perhaps without ever having left it, the laws of metaphysics as such which govern his analysis of examples no less than Kant's (double) usage of them. In a sense, we end up with two laws–perhaps the same two that we began with from Kant's point of view: determinant (using Kant's text as a theory which uses examples to clarify itself) and reflective (using Kant's text as an example of a law to come: Derrida's). That the results of these two types of judgement are quite different should not surprise us. After all, translations are not the same from the particular to the general and from the general to the particular. No one ever claimed they could be.

A final case needs to be addressed here concerning Derrida's relation to the issue of exemplarity, and this takes us back to his early treatment of Rousseau. In *Of Grammatology* he seeks to justify his choice of Rousseau as an example: to give it a rule, a law, and thereby justify his findings as more extensive, more significant than a mere analysis of Rousseau. His analysis itself is given the status of an example (of something else), and it is this transformation which we will analyse here in what follows. It is the way Derrida reveals the problems of such an inflation at the very moment he seeks to solve them that we shall reveal. In the end, he confesses that no ultimate justification is possible and in turn offers us this as the law of the law of the example. We are concerned here ultimately with the paradoxes Derrida's own attempts exhibit concerning the controlling of his Rousseau example.

DERRIDA'S IMPOSSIBLE TASK: JUSTIFYING THE EXAMPLE

Keenly aware of the dangers of such an enterprise, Derrida opens the second half of *Of Grammatology* with the recognition that *if* he is to use Rousseau *as* an example, then he must make a case for his choice. That is, he must, as he says, 'justify his choice' of Rousseau as an example. Note that it is not the *usage of exemplarity* itself as justifying his approach here that is at issue, but rather an assumption of (a certain type of) exemplarity (that passage from the finite to the infinite, in principle, if not in fact) that is in place in order then to raise the question of the *choice* of *this* particular rather than another. Derrida frames the issue in the following manner:

> Since I am about to deal with what, using the same language and with as much caution, I will call an 'example', I must now *justify my choice*. [my emphasis][15]

Thus he opens and closes the doors on the issue of exemplarity itself by concealing at the very moment of seeming to reveal the problematics of exemplarity as such. In turning to the issue of choice, of some antecendent decision having been made in advance of the text, Derrida does *not question*, nor can he question the strategy of exemplarity itself. Instead, he relies here and in what follows, as we shall show, on the need for an example–some example–and therefore does not attempt to justify this move, but rather why this example rather than another. What he never asks in his reading of Rousseau is: why exemplarity itself? Why transform Rousseau, and in particular his reading, *into* an example in the first place? This transformation is given and concealed in the focus on 'this choice' paradoxically. Yet this move too is in line with the tradition of classical metaphysics, as we shall see.

Seeming to raise the issue of 'the example', Derrida asks the question concerning what is *at stake* in using Rousseau, indeed the 'age of Rousseau' as an example. He says:

> Why accord an 'exemplary value' to the 'age of Rousseau'? [Note that exemplarity now means more than one particular among others–it has switched to the other side of the metaphysical determination of exemplarity in general; namely, to the locus of rule, general or law.] What privileged place does Jean-Jacques Rousseau occupy in the history of logocentrism? What is meant by that proper name? And what are the relationships between that proper name and the texts to which it was underwritten?[16]

That Rousseau occupies a 'privileged' and therefore 'exemplary' place is not in question here, but what that privilege entails is Derrida's question. He attempts to answer it in a number of ways, each time undermining, though attempting to underwrite, the earlier version. Let us trace this movement of Derrida's attempt to 'justify' the *value* he accords to Rousseau *as* an example– an Exemplary example in more senses than one–in order not to show a series of contradictions but rather the increasingly problematic display of the impossibility of 'justification' of examples as such. Far from finding the example simply unjustifiable–lawless–and thereby threatening the claims Derrida wishes to make 'based on the case of Rousseau', he finds the example at least partially justifiable.

Initially, the justification takes the form of *locating* Rousseau's work in an exemplary–and thereby singular–position within the history of 'logocentrism', otherwise known as philosophy. As Derrida puts it: 'Rousseau's work seems to me to occupy, between Plato's *Phaedrus* and Hegel's *Encyclopedia*, a singular position.'[17] What is at stake here is the uniqueness, or singularity, of Rousseau, which at the same time situates him in a tradition within which he is merely a member. Thus Rousseau is already seen here as both a mere example–one case among others–hence, justifiable, and at the same time, and necessarily so, an Exemplar–unique, singular, and therefore the best, indeed, the only, *choice*. The choice here is thus divided by two laws to which it seems to adhere simultaneously: the law of uniqueness, indeed, the 'idiom' as Derrida will later call it in *Glas*, and the law of substitutability, which is overcome, *Aufgehoben*, as Derrida will again later refer to it. Thus we have not one law here but two revealed in the process of justification. Rousseau-as-an-example is justifiable as unique, on the one hand, and not unique, on the other. And this is no contradiction, as we shall see, but the two sides of the same metaphysical foreclosure of exemplarity itself.

This justification is, however, not satisfactory to the rigours of Derrida, and he pursues the problem in an effort to justify this justification. Rather than merely situated between Plato and Hegel–as unique and a member at the same time–Rousseau is now re-situated between Descartes and Hegel. He now represents, insofar as he is the example, the best example, again a certain uniqueness and a certain membership, but these are now determined within a somewhat different matrix of issues.

> Within this age of metaphysics, between Descartes and Hegel, Rousseau is *undoubtedly* the only one *or* the first one to make a theme *or* a system of the reduction of writing profoundly implied by the entire age. [my emphasis][18]

'This age of metaphysics' has now been redefined as stretched between Descartes (not Plato) and Hegel, yet it is an age which did not, until Rousseau, thematize its most profound cohering principle–its law, one might call it. Rousseau is thus now to be seen as 'the only one' *or* 'the first one' to have thematized the unthematized of this 'entire' age. What is the status of this hesitating 'or' within Derrida's attempt at justification here? Why hesitate? Whether Rousseau was the only one OR the first one, it would seem he could not have been both. The 'or' is not only a mark of the hesitation here in Derrida's attempt to find the *law* of his own discourse and thematize it, but also a mark of his withdrawal at the very moment of his justificational exergue. The 'or' takes back the initial determination and re-situates it in the second, less extensive, less exemplary locus such that it re-marks the first justification as unjustified. Thus at the very moment of finding, or at least naming, the law, Derrida takes back what he gives forth: the law, the name, the justification. At least Rousseau must be seen as 'the first one, if not the only one', from this second, or is it third, point of view. Thus Rousseau's law–the law of his choice– will be that he originated, inaugurated, was the first in what will become a series. Rousseau is the law inasmuch as he was the first to 'make a theme', Derrida tells us, 'of the reduction of writing'. Plato's *Phaedrus* is now disqualified from such a place, though earlier, in Derrida's discourse, it marked the inaugural point of 'the entire age'. It was after all the *Phaedrus* which sought to 'reduce writing', privilege the voice, exclude the sign from the philosophic enterprise itself, and that thematically.

We find another hesitating 'or' surfacing at the very point that Derrida seems to offer us the law of the law–why Rousseau would be the law here. He was the first to make a 'theme or a system' of this reduction of writing, Derrida claims. Again one might ask which did Rousseau do for us, since surely a theme is not the same as a system. To discuss an issue thematically is not tantamount to organizing a system around it or through it. Thus the theme gives way, via the 'or' of hesitation, to a system. Before we extend this analysis any further it must be noted that, in the original French text, Derrida uses the term 'et', not 'ou', at this juncture. Thus a slight though important translator's error has replaced the 'and' of Derrida's text with an 'or' in the English version. Let us then turn to the French and presumably 'original' version here. That Derrida uses the term 'and' to relate the notion of a theme and a system only compounds the problem explicated above, however. Now we must unite or at least relate the theme–of the reduction of writing–and the system–of the reduction of writing. Again Derrida does not make the choice but rather shifts from one demarcation to the other, this time seemingly without acknowledging the differences between theme and system. Did Rousseau simply thematize this reduction, name it, make it explicit, or did he systematize this reduction? We are not told and Derrida does not choose, though it would appear that the 'and' of the original does after all function as an 'or' in precisely the way the translator transformed the sentence. A good error on her part, clearly. Returning to our issue, it would seem that now the example-of-Rousseau, as unique and a member at the same time, seems to have been justified. Yet, Derrida returns to the original demarcation to re-establish Rousseau's relation to the original pillars that frame the history of metaphysics as a structure of logocentrism. Why this return? What is the hesitation over the Plato/Rousseau relation here? How are they related by implication to the above? Plato's *Phaedrus* would seem to be inaugural yet in an unthematized or, better, non-systematic way, whereas Rousseau, it would seem, thematized and/or systematized what Plato merely mentions. But rather than take this step, Derrida re-orients the two inaugural moments in the following way:

> He [Rousseau] *repeats* the inaugural movement of the *Phaedrus* and of
> *De Interpretatione* but starts from a new model of presence: the subject's
> self-presence within consciousness or feeling. What he *excluded more*
> *violently* than the others must, of course, have fascinated and tormented
> him more than it did others. [my emphasis][19]

Now we have the law of the law of the law: why Rousseau, rather than Plato,
for instance, as the good example here? Because he *repeats* what Plato began
but from a new model. Why is this model chosen? No answer is given. Why
is this more exemplary than Plato, or Aristotle, who is now also invoked. No
law. No reason. Now the issue turns on the problem of presence, as located
within the subject's sense of him/herself. One could well ask: why not choose
Descartes if this is the law of the law of the law? Does René Descartes not
exemplify, indeed inaugurate, this new model of presence which in turn
Rousseau will simply adopt from his predecessor as such? Derrida is ahead of
us and now focuses on this issue as in need of justification (another law) when
he says:

> But neither Descartes nor Hegel grappled with the problem of writing.
> The place of this *combat* and crisis is called the eighteenth century . . .
> Before Hegel and in explicit terms, Rousseau condemns the universal
> characteristic . . . because it seemed to suspend the voice. [my
> emphasis][20]

We now have Rousseau's uniqueness re-instated, on the one hand, since he
did what *neither* Descartes nor Hegel managed to do: 'grapple with the
problem of writing'. Yet, if this is the law, then we could well invoke Plato
and Aristotle as having done the same. But clearly this is not and cannot be
the law of the law—the reason for the choice of Rousseau— since Rousseau
exemplifies, evidently, something more which only a thinker from the
eighteenth century could represent. *That* is 'the place of this combat and
crisis', Derrida insists, and thus *this* is the reason for his choice. Which crisis,
and which combat? The debates over the 'universal characteristic' exemplified
on the one side by Leibniz, as its defender, and evidently by Rousseau on the
other, as its opponent.

The scene of the law is now a scene of violence, a scene of opposition, but
with only one side of the combat to serve as an example. Derrida certainly
mentions Leibniz in this connection, but only to return to his primary and
indeed only, unique, example of Rousseau and '*his* treatment of writing'.
This uniqueness is now to be seen *not* in terms of an inaugural system, or the
first reduction of writing, or even the first to discuss the presence of a
subject's consciousness to itself (Descartes), but as the *one* who 'excluded

writing more violently' than others, and the one for whom this indicates that the problem (of writing) 'fascinated and tormented him more than it did others'. Thus the *law* now surfaces for Derrida's choice. The scene here is of a combat and a crisis, located only in the eighteenth century and more precisely withinn Rousseau's *feelings* and consciousness, whose conflicting relations to the pen, to writing, to the voice (his own and others) and, of course, consciousness are exemplified by his writings. *This* is the law here-but why? Why is Derrida 'fascinated and tormented', as he seemingly is, with Rousseau's fascination and torment? What other reason is implied here, if any?

At just this moment Derrida returns us to classical metaphysics and a denial of the relevance of biography and autobiography. The law slips away again as he now claims that Rousseau's work indicates nothing more than a 'historical structure'. His texts are to be seen as *symptoms* of something much more general-the overall *disease* of traditional metaphysics insofar as it manifests and maintains logocentrism.

Derrida makes this shift back to the most general level by insisting that the proper name has no particular significance for him-especially that of Rousseau, who is precisely under scrutiny here as the example *par excellence*, and named as such.

> The names of authors or of doctrines have here no substantial value. They indicate neither identities nor causes . . . The indicative value that I attribute to them [proper names] is first the name of a problem.[21]

So, Rousseau-as-an-example becomes 'the name of a problem'-otherwise called logocentrism-from Plato to Hegel. But we have already located a number of problems that this proper name, Jean-Jacques Rousseau, could be naming. Which problem? The problem of inaugurating the systematic reduction of writing, would be Derrida's ready response. It is this that 'Rousseau' exemplifies and better than any other. Yet now this law is taken away from us when Derrida himself pursues the problem in the following way:

> If I provisionally authorize myself to treat this historical structure [not exemplarity but logocentrism] by fixing my attention on philosophical or literary texts, it is not for the sake of identifying in them the origin, cause or equilibrium of the structure.[22]

Now it is *not* that Rousseau or his texts inaugurate anything-they are not the 'origin, cause or equilibrium' of the structure in question here. Thus the law we had found is withdrawn and in no uncertain terms. 'It is not this', Derrida tells us, and though this claim exhibits the form of a denial in traditional Freudian terms, let us take him at his word, so to speak, for the moment. If it is not the inauguration that is at stake, not the uniqueness of the case, the example, of Rousseau that authorizes the choice, what, we may well repeat, is it? So far, each law that has been instated as the justification for the choice has been, if not simultaneously, very soon after its presentation, withdrawn.

What is this *fort/da* movement all about that Derrida's text, if not his justification as such, is manifesting again and again.[23] He approaches the law, even states it, at times and then withdraws and takes the claims just made (the law) with him. What is it that cannot be said here, and that at each moment when it is pronounced, written, inscribed must be denied. We shall see.

Derrida's re-approach to the question of the relation between 'these texts' (Rousseau's) and the structure they exemplify, but do not create, takes the form of a preliminary step. He insists now that this approach must be seen as 'provisional'–providing and enabling but non-essential; indeed, unlawful, we might conclude. As he says:

> But as I do *not* think that these texts are the simple effects of structure, in any sense of the word; . . . *the primordial and indispensable phase*, in fact and in principle, of the development of this problematic, consists in questioning the *internal structure of these texts as symptoms*; as that is the *only condition* for determining these symptoms themselves in the totality of their metaphysical appurtenance. I draw my argument from them in order to isolate Rousseau, and in Rousseauism, the theory of writing. Besides, this abstraction is partial and it remains, in my view, provisional. [my emphasis][24]

The demands are now in place as absolute pre-conditions which Derrida's project will adhere to and follow. That is the law. This step is 'primordial and indispensable' (translate as 'necessary' and 'lawful') in fact and in principle– from the finite to the infinite standpoints; it is 'the only condition' and so forth. Thus Derrida's tone has shifted from the hesitancy of 'or' to the absolutism of necessity, primordiality, and this in principle as well as in fact. What accounts for this shift, and this re-enactment of the necessity of necessity, if not its justification? In this case Derrida says it is the 'internal structure' that is at stake in reading Rousseau, not the thematic or systematized reduction that he earlier insisted upon. The thing in question has slipped away here back into the shadows, as Derrida simultaneously asserts the open necessity of his own method. The tension is increasing here in the attempt to justify the example of Rousseau, and the ground itself has shifted. Rousseau's texts are to be seen as symptoms–symptomatic–of something much larger. Again, we have lost the uniqueness of the case–the exemplary status of Rousseau as opposed to Descartes, Plato, Aristotle and Hegel, to name a few–and we have Rousseau as merely one case among others. Thus the oscillation takes place between Rousseau as a member and Rousseau as unique: the two traditional poles of the range of exemplarity itself. Derrida's justification and incessant search for the law of his justification here moves from one side of the coin to the other without questioning the value of the coin or coinage of exemplarity itself. Are these sovereigns or blanks? The question does not and cannot come up. Derrida's concerns are elsewhere inasmuch as he accepts the metaphysical demands of justification as such. Not questioning this, he strives again and again to find the law of the law here, without, it seems, realizing that its necessity is internal, tautological, and thus this pursuit cannot but lead to an infinite regress to other laws, and yet other laws, each time undermining the very findings one claims to have manifest. Derrida's abyssal search here manifests this very impossibility.

Yet, he also chooses Lévi-Strauss as an example in this same section of his text, as a point of departure for his analysis of the writing problem, and paradoxically seems to have no trouble in justifying his choice straight away and straightforwardly. As he says:

> If I have chosen the *example* of the texts of Claude Lévi-Strauss, as points of departure and as a springboard for a reading of Rousseau, it is for *more than one reason*; for the theoretical wealth and interest of those texts, for the animating role that they currently play, but also for the place occupied in them by the theory of writing and the tone of fidelity to Rousseau.[25]

And, with this, Derrida leaves the issue of justification of the Lévi-Strauss example as finished. There is the law, he tells us; indeed, more than one law. What satisfies him here will be of importance since it does not satisfy him, or he does not find it for the case/example of Rousseau. There is no struggle here, no repetition, no re-instatement of the law. Rather, Derrida claims that the texts of Lévi-Strauss provide him with a certain 'wealth' of 'interest' (capital, one might call it) to trade on. They 'currently' (in the 1960s in France, more precisely) 'play an animating role' (spawning lively debate) but they are also 'inhabited by' 'the theory of writing' and a certain 'fidelity' to Rousseau. Thus we have many laws, many reasons to have picked Lévi-Strauss. Why not make the same claims for Rousseau as the example? Because, first, he is not current, not playing an animating role, and the issue of fidelity in Lévi-Strauss falls back and depends upon the import of the

Rousseau example. Thus one example justifies, is the law for, another. Far from a justification of Lévi-Strauss as an example, here we actually have a detour and a deferral of the issue—or a compounding of the problem. Now we have another example depending on the first, but the first has still to be justified. Thus everything again and still stands or falls on the justification of the Rousseau-example.

Derrida confesses as much in a later section of the same text, which he entitles 'The Exorbitant: Question of Method', Ex-orbitant entails for him something outside the orb of metaphysical circularity—outside the law, one might say. But far from overcoming the problem of the justification of the example in this way, Derrida reaffirms the initial difficulty. This affirmation here takes the form not of a hesitation, not of an absolute dictum, but rather of a confession, as if this issue must finally be put to rest in what follows:

> No doubt Rousseau, as I have already suggested, has only a very *relative privilege* in the history that interests us. . . . We wish to identify a *decisive articulation* of the logocentric epoch. For purposes of this *identification*, Rousseau seems to us to be most revealing. . . . No other trace is available. . . . We must begin wherever we are and the thought of the trace, which cannot not take the scent into account, has already taught us that it was *impossible to justify a point of departure absolutely.* [my emphasis][26]

There we have it: there is no law, but, then again, this law, that of the example of Rousseau, is now an example of another law. The law of the law here is therefore that absolute laws of inauguration cannot be found, named, articulated, thematized or presented. Why not? Why is it impossible to justify a point of departure absolutely? Why has Derrida incessantly tried to do the impossible in all of the above? Why does he now insist that this impossibility is itself a law, and thus he obeys it and manifests it, and therefore, finally, can justify his choice of example as unjustifiable justifiably. Thus the law of the lawless is invoked such that legitimacy can be maintained. What is at stake here and what has been admitted in Derrida's apparent confession of the impossibility of his task? It is not that examples are lawless; far from it. But rather, that the choice itself obeys two laws at the same time, and conflicting ones, mutually exclusive ones, at that. The choice must be *one of many*: substitutable, replaceable, repeatable by others in a series—in principle and in fact. Yet the choice must also be unique: one of a kind, not part of a series, but idiomatic. Can anything be *the one and the many* at the same time? Can anything not be?, would be the metaphysical answer to such a dilemma. Thus the example and its law, from the Derridean point of view here, can never be justified according to one law, but are always and

always already justified according to another. Why does Derrida not say this? He performs it instead.

Lest one conclude here that Derrida has made some mistake, or chosen a 'bad' example, let us end the analysis of the concealment of the problematics of exemplarity with the following ultimate law that Derrida invokes as the 'real reason' for his choice of Rousseau. What was at stake was to locate 'textuality itself', as a structure, as a symptom, an example yet also thereby as exemplary. Where can we find 'textuality itself'–everywhere, by Derrida's own admission. 'All is text', as he was wont to say in the early days until Foucault severely mocked and ridiculed such a claim.[27] Why Rousseau as the bearer of 'textuality itself'? Why not? Indeed, why not. What law would mitigate against choosing Rousseau? None. Why would Rousseau be an exception to the law–the 'law' of *différance* now–since Derrida insists and will insist more and more in the later years that *différance* inhabits the texts of metaphysics from one end to the other, despite its occlusion and foreclosure. It inhabits Rousseau, and his texts exhibit it just as much as any other. Again, this admission cuts two ways for Derrida. On the one hand, it allows him to say that this is the law of his choice. 'Why Rousseau?' has now been definitively answered. He *is* an example, that is why he has been chosen *as* an example. On the other hand, why not someone else? This has not been satisfied and this is the question that haunts Derrida's choice like a shadow of doubt and hesitation that he cannot, for reasons of essence, eradicate. The more he aims to reveal the law, the more this shadow comes along with him to conceal it, or at least place any choice of law he makes in question. The point here is that, by not questioning his desire for the law, Derrida's incessant quest to 'justify' his choice reveals what he must admit in the end: that no absolute law can be found. But *why not* is not the focus of analysis here, nor could it be, since the desire is *for the law*, before the law, towards the law, governed by this incessant tropism. That examples function otherwise or could function in a variety of ways that are not incessantly bound or re-bound between the universal (laws) and particular (cases) seems never to have crossed Derrida's mind here or elsewhere in the later works. Thus it can only be with a heightened sense of irony that one reads the following climactic admission in *Of Grammatology* concerning the choice of Rousseau as the best man for the job:

> The concept of the supplement is a sort of blind spot in Rousseau's text, the not-seen that opens and limits visibility.[28]

We might equally well claim that the notion of the example functions, with irony to be sure, in just this way in the texts of Derrida–from the early to the later works–though that he has thematized, indeed systematized, the issue certainly more than anyone else in the history of philosophy cannot be doubted here. But that he remains tied to that metaphysics in a way that blinds him to the very problematic in question–exemplarity–can also not be doubted at this point. He forecloses the question of exemplarity at the very moment when he seems to reveal it as an issue, as a problem. By finding its law, by succumbing to the desire for the law as such, the 'as such' of the law, of justification, Derrida re-instates exemplarity as the blind spot of his own work.

NOTES

1 Rodolphe Gasché, 'God, for Example', *Phenomenology and the Numinous* (Pittsburgh: Duquesne University Press, 1988), 43–66.

2 Gregory Ulmer, *Applied Grammatology* (Baltimore: Johns Hopkins University Press, 1985).

3 Andrzej Warminski, 'Reading for Example: "Sense-Certainty" in Hegel's *Phenomenology of Spirit, Diacritics*, 83–96; 'Pre-Positional By-Play', *Glyph* 3, 1978, 98–117.

4 Jacques Derrida, *Glas* (Paris: Galilée, 1974), 37–8; *Glas*, trans. John P. Leavey, Jr. and Richard Rand (Lincoln and London: University of Nebraska Press, 1986), 29.

5 *Glas*, p. 38 (French), p. 30 (English).

6 *Glas*, p. 169 (French), p. 149 (English).

7 *Glas*, p. 232 (French), p. 207 (English).

8 *Glas*, p. 266 (French), p. 238 (English).

9 Derrida's text entitled *Feu la cendre* (Paris: Des Femmes, 1987) focuses extensively on the relations of the Holocaust (*le brûle-tout*) and the ashes, the remains, as they relate to the notion of the trace. As Derrida himself remarks, these have been abiding themes in his work and now for the first time are gathered together in this text. Concerning the structure of the Holocaust, as it relates to the earlier mention in *Glas* of the 'all burning', Derrida says: 'c'est que l'incineration suit son cours et la consumation va de soi, la cendre même. Trace destinée, comme toute, à disparaître d'elle-même pour égarer la voie autant que pour rallumer une mémoire. La cendre est juste: parce que sans trace, justement elle trace plus qu'une autre, et comme l'autre trace' (p. 41).

10 Jacques Derrida, 'Parergon', *La Vérité en peinture* (Paris: Flammarion, 1978), 60; *The Truth in Painting*, trans. Geoff Bennington and Ian McLeod (Chicago: University of Chicago Press, 1987), 51 (*TP*).

11 *TP*, 61 (French), p. 52 (English).

12 *TP*, p. 85 (French), p. 73 (English).

13 In Foucault's text entitled *La Volonté de savoir* (Paris: Gallimard, 1976); *The History of Sexuality*, Vol. 1: *An Introduction*, trans. Robert Hurley (New York: Vintage Books, 1980), he claims that the desire for the law in psychoanalysis as much as philosophy and the political is a desire for the King, the monarchy, for

the sovereign power, the sovereignty of power. In his critique of this notion as a historical phenomenon, Foucault claims to relativize philosophic and psychoanalytic explanations of the same. In turn he seeks to examine the manifestation of powers as a heterogeneous plurality and thus open up the closure that traditional philosophical analysis and psychoanalysis have engendered in their investigations of power. From this point of view Derrida's quest for the law, albeit 'that other law', falls into this same problematic and leaves unquestioned the fundamentally monarchical assumptions concerning the theory of power as sovereign or legalistic alone. As Foucault says concerning the psychoanalytic assumptions of this traditional notion of power: 'whence the Freudian endeavor . . . to ground sexuality in the law–the law of alliance, tabooed consanguinity, and the Sovereign-Father, in short, to surround desire with all the trappings of the old order of power' (p. 150). Though Foucault does not explicitly analyse Derrida's assumptions concerning the law here, one could, we suggest.

14 *TP*, p. 92 (French), p. 79 (English).

15 Jacques Derrida, *De la grammatologie* (Paris: Editions de Minuit, 1967); *Of Grammatology*, trans. Gayatri C. Spivak (Baltimore: Johns Hopkins University Press, 1974), 145 (French), p. 97 (English). (*OG*).

16 Ibid.

17 Ibid.

18 *OG*, 147 (French), p. 98 (English).

19 Ibid.

20 Ibid.

21 *OG*, p. 147–8 (French), p. 99 (English).

22 Ibid.

23 Derrida has written extensively on this phenomenon as it occurs in Freud's text of the same theme; namely, *Beyond the Pleasure Principle*. In his analysis in *La Carte postale* (Paris: Aubier-Flammarion, 1980), Derrida shows how the movement of the text itself performs the fort/da movement that Freud is describing therein. Our claim here is that this movement also characterizes Derrida's text in his analysis of Rousseau. The oscillating process of repetition which shifts upon its own return, leaving a re-marked position in its wake, is punctuated in the Rousseau analysis by the issue of exemplarity and the demands for justification.

24 *OG*, pp. 147–8 (French), p. 99 (English).

25 Ibid.

26 *OG*, p. 232–3 (French), p. 162 (English).

27 Foucault's response to Derrida came in two instalments: 'Une petit pédagogie', *Le Monde*, 14 June 1973, p. 23; and 'Mon corps, ce papier, ce feu', Appendix to *Histoire de la folie à l'âge classique*, new edn (Paris: Gallimard, 1972), 583–603.

28 *OG*, p. 233 (French), p. 163 (English).

10

Manfred Frank

Is Self-Consciousness a Case of *présence à soi*? Towards a Meta-Critique of the Recent French Critique of Metaphysics

Among the attempts to salvage Heidegger's critique of metaphysics by conceptual clarification, the most successful was the suggestion that 'metaphysics' meant 'objectifying thinking'. In the light of this premise, the basic thesis that Being (*Sein*) is not beings (*Seiendes*) can be made comprehensible as the rejection of the attempt, with Aristotle, to narrow down philosophy, under the name 'metaphysics', into a theory of objects. Although the artificial expression 'ontology' arose only in the seventeenth century, one can identify the author of the *Metaphysics* as its founder. At the beginning of book IV[1] he explains his new conception of philosophy with the words: 'There is a science which considers being (*das Seiende*) as being . . .'. What distinguishes this science from other particular sciences is supposed to be that each of the latter investigates a single realm of beings (geologists investigate stones, botanists plants, philologists texts, etc.), but not being as being. The concept of being (*Seiendes*) for Aristotle is distinguished by the fact that it is thought along with every other concept and, as such, is universal:[2] clearly one can say of anything and everything that it is, by which Aristotle means: that it is a being. Being (*Seiendes*), object, and something (*tóde ti*) are synonymous.[3]

Heidegger passionately opposed the view that he had introduced this particular version of the theme of Being (*Sein*) into philosophy.

> We maintain (. . .) *Being is the real and only theme of philosophy*. This is not our invention, instead the setting of this theme comes alive with the

beginning of philosophy in antiquity and has its most grandiose effect in Hegel's Logic. Now we just assert that Being is the real and only theme of philosophy. Put negatively that means: philosophy is not the *science of* beings (*Seienden*) but of Being (*Sein*) or, as the artificial Greek expression terms it, *ontology*.[4]

Heidegger reformulates the basic question of Aristotle 'what is being as being?' as the question 'what is the Being of beings (*Sein des Seienden*)?' and defends this reformulation by asserting that we can only experience and understand something as a being 'if we understand it as *Being*'.[5] The precedence of the understanding of Being before the discoverability of the concrete being as 'this or that'[6] (flower or stone) forms the basic conviction of his own philosophizing, which believes itself thereby to be in solidarity with Aristotle. However, neither Aristotle nor Heidegger succeeded in clearly explaining by which epistemological operation one ascends to the concept of being as the most universal concept and what constitutes the specific nature of this universality.

Ernst Tugendhat first drew attention to this deficiency and at the same time proposed a positive alternative suggestion. Being (*das Seiende*) as such, in relation to its Being (*Sein*): the concept 'being' ('*Seiendes*'), is not reached by progressive abstraction from positive attributes, for what is concrete (e.g., this red rose) is just as much in being (*seiend*) as the most universal thing to which I can ascend in the chain of abstraction: namely 'spatially and temporally extended thing'. With the last terms of the chain of abstraction I have therefore not grasped being (*das Seiende*) in its Being (*Sein*). I achieve this only if I reflect upon the manner in which beings become accessible to me, in this case upon the use of that class of linguistic expressions via which beings are disclosed to me as beings. We have always already thematized beings (objects, whatever their degree of abstraction) under the category of beingness (*Seiendheit*) or objectivity, and it is not the case that we only find out inductively, after the event and via abstraction, that it is a question of objects. That also seems to be what Heidegger means when he says: 'A being can only be discovered, whether it be via perception or some other kind of access to it, if the Being (*Sein*) of the being (*Seiendes*) is already disclosed, if I understand it',[7] and explains the expression 'Being of the being' by 'familiarity with the kind of Being (*Seinsart*) of the discovered being, namely its presence at hand (*Vorhandenheit*)' (that is Heidegger's artificial expression for 'objectivity' (*Gegenständlichkeit*)).[8] Tugendhat calls this procedure, along with Donald Davidson (but not in the same sense), 'formal semantics'. It consists–in the reformulation of traditional ontological questions characteristic of linguistic analysis–in turning to the type of usage of the underlying classes of linguistic expression. For there it becomes apparent that we use some expressions in such a way that we disclose objects as objects by them. These are singular terms, which take the subject position in singular predicative propositions, and which we characterize more exactly by predicates.

The question is now: what about the predicate expressions themselves? How is an understanding of Being given in them? Aristotle had already pointed out that every predicate can be reformulated into an expression which contains an 'is', for example, 'A suspects B' into 'A is suspicious of B'.[9] Now Aristotle likewise classified the copulative 'is' in the category of beings–of objects.[10] Indeed, via this 'is', that being is to be designated, or rather 'co-designated' (*prossemaínetai*), for which the predicate stands. But even an innocuous reflection on the use of language makes it clear that 'is suspicious' could not stand for an object at all. For this it was necessary first to nominalize the predicate expression and transfer it into the expression 'suspicion'. 'Is suspicious' is, then, supposed to stand for 'suspicion' as an object. (That this information is meaningless becomes clear if one inserts the nominalized phrase into the originally predicative phrase and sees that now a well-formed statement no longer results.) The meaning of 'is such and such' must, then, be understood differently from the meaning of singular terms which relate to objects. A classificatory expression does not stand for a being and therefore does not come under the jurisdiction of ontology as a theory of objects. The world is not the totality of objects, but rather of what can be established in statements about these objects: the totality of states of affairs (Heidegger says, with a pragmatic expression: of involvements (*Bewandtnisse*)). The basic structure of understanding is the 'something as something', and that is also the structure of the proposition;[11] the real sense of 'Being'–its core meaning–is, then, the meaning of being-true (*Wahrsein*).[12]

Tugendhat has just explicated this basic Heideggerian thought. One arrives at the meaning of the 'is' in the simple predicative proposition only by pointing out the formal-semantic basic characteristic of all predicative statements–for statements are the primary units of meaning of all under-standing. Only by them can one give someone something to understand. Tugendhat formulates a universal formal law via the Aristotelian principle of contradiction in the version: 'It is impossible that something is and is not at the same time'.[13] If one understands the 'is' in this formulation as the copula, then the formulation is identical with the more well-known: 'It is impossible that one and the same predicative determination should at the same time be attributed and not be attributed to the same object and in the same respect'.[14] But we can also–and Aristotle points this out himself–understand the 'is' in the further sense, in the sense of 'it is the case'. For one can put the phrase 'It is the case that . . . ' in front of every proposition, followed by the proposition, without changing the meaning. If we orient ourselves by the first cited version of the principle of contradiction, then it would now, in the light of this sense of 'is', have to be: 'It is impossible that something is and is not at the same time, namely "is at the same time the case and not the case". Or, "It is impossible to affirm and deny something at the same time"'.

Aristotle himself sometimes calls this sense of 'is' *tò einai hôs tò alethés*, thus 'Being in the sense of being true'.[15] It belongs to the form of every negatable proposition and is the real core meaning of 'is', to the extent to which not only a subject- and a predicate-expression can be 'copulated' with it, but above all to which a truth claim can be made. It is impossible to relate to a state of affairs as to a fact, without connecting a truth claim to the 'is' of the proposition. If one means by 'be' ('*sein*') the act of affirmation (in the sense of the raising of a validity claim), then one can now see quite clearly that, and why, Being (*Sein*) is not a being (*Seiendes*). Aristotle, who nevertheless subsumes it under the category of beings–under ontology–has overlooked the ontico-ontological difference, and thereby taken Western philosophy onto the wrong track, from which both analytical philosophy and Heidegger's 'fundamental ontology' have tried to divert it. This wrong track is called 'metaphysics'. Metaphysics would therefore be the name for objectifying thinking; and the thesis of the ontico-ontological difference could be appropriately translated into the terminology of 'formal semantics'.[16]

To begin with we can again follow Heidegger. He was the first to show, in exemplary textual analyses, that from the Greeks to Kant (and Husserl) European thinkers have interpreted 'Being' in the temporal form of 'presence' (*Praesenz*).[17] 'Being as presence (*Anwesenheit*)'[18] assumes that the indeterminately ambiguous verbal expression 'be' ('*sein*') should not be understood as the theme of the understanding of statements, but rather as the object of direct intuition (*Anschauung*). For the Greeks, 'Being' is what presents itself in '*intuiting coming across (Vorfinden)*' to a *noein* or *theorein*.[19] For Kant, being perceived is still the only attribute of reality.[20] If disclosed via the spectacles of the model of sense perception (or intuition), Being has no other possibility than to present itself as an object for an awareness (*Vernehmen*)–as presence–therefore as beings. Heidegger showed this in his various interpretations of Parmenides as the decisive setting of the course for metaphysics.[21] The progenitor and 'real founder of ancient ontology'[22] repeatedly wished to explicate the structure of perception (*noein*) via the structure of speaking (*légein, phánai, phrásai*). Both bring an intentional object with them: I see something, and I say something. The fact that the parallelism is deceptive shows itself above all in the problem of negation. While not-*seeing* and *not-see*ing coincide, a similar conjunction does not take place between not-*saying* and *not-say*ing (for it is always possible to say that something is *not*). That is connected to the fact that perception is directed straight at a being (*Seiendes*) while the structure of speech (of the statement) is the 'something as something'. The object of a *nóesis* (of an intuition) is a spatio-temporal object, the object of a *lógos*, however, is a state of affairs (represented by a proposition: an object as determined in such and such a way). If Being is thought of as the object of an awareness and the difference from the structure of what is intended in a statement is overlooked, then Being is mistaken for beings (the act of affirmation or negation of a state of affairs with the posting of an object). The optical model of the spiritual eye reduces 'Being' to being an object.

The replacement of the ancient and medieval paradigm of ontology by the modern philosophy of consciousness makes no difference to this. If, for example, Kant says: 'Ontology is that science (as part of metaphysics) which constitutes a system of all concepts and principles of the understanding, but only as far as they are concerned with objects given to the senses and can therefore be confirmed by experience' and adds '[Ontology] is called transcendental-philosophy because it contains the conditions and first elements of all our a priori *cognitions*',[23] then the fixation on objects is not overcome, but only given a new foundation by transcendental philosophy. An active constituting ray (*konstitutiver Aktstrahl*) falls on the object from the subject, and Being itself offers itself to perception alone. The world is one of present objects and representations (*Vorstellungen*), and states of affairs must be thought of as syntheses of representations (*Repräsentationen*). The core-meaning of 'be' as 'being true' disappears behind the (subjective) certainty of the awareness of beings that are present at hand (*vorhandenem Seiendem*).

A future candidature of the subject is already prepared by the announcement of the optic model (Being discloses itself in its truth to an ideational gaze): if being true depends upon the 'view' (*idéa*), upon awareness (*noein*), then it is only one more step to the subjectivization of philosophy; the view must be thought as self-reflexive and attributed to a subject as its owner. This is the step taken by Descartes.[24] For him, thinking (*cogitare*) is the deed of a thinker: of an I that thinks. Thinking acquires the indubitable evidence which is peculiar to it only in the first person singular form of inflection: *cogito*. For Kant and his successors, 'thinking' and 'being-able-to-be-accompanied-by-an-I' are still synonyms. Thus the subject—originally the Latin translation of *hypokeimenon*—becomes the ground of the intelligibility of the world (thought of as the totality of objects): it becomes *fundamentum inconcussum* of all thinking which is capable of truth. Hegel's Preface to the *Phenomenology of Spirit* will put the seal on this shift in meaning with the phrase that the substance is really to be thought of as subject.[25] The nominalization of the first person pronoun is to be found for the first time in Leibniz: '*ce moy*'.[26] The subject is identified as *that* I with which Fichte will concern himself. The thought of the self-reflexivity of thinking makes evident the transition from the subject of thinking to the nominalized I, as

Foucault rightly saw.[27] Leibniz's definition of *aperception* as 'the Consciousness, or the reflexive knowledge of this interior state',[28] makes the first step, Kant, who always identified egoity with self-reflexivity, took over this definition.[29] If one further notes that Kant was convinced that no representation (*Vorstellung*) was possible without the active intervention of the understanding, which brings the multiplicity of the representation into unified points of view, one encounters the phrase of the 'I think' which must be able to accompany all my representations.[30] Thus consciousness (in the Leibnizian sense, as apperception or self-reflexivity of the capacity for representation) is equally unifying spontaneity and self-awareness of this spontaneity.

Kant's conception of the essence of subjectivity remained definitive for the philosophy of his successors–not only the Hegelians, but also the neo-Kantians and phenomenologists (with the exception of Brentano, Schmalenbach and Sartre). Even the critics of subjectivity–for example, Heidegger and Derrida–have never seriously questioned the notion that the state of affairs 'subjectivity' is correctly described as the auto-reflexivity of thinking (*des Vorstellens*).

In *Being and Time* Heidegger tried to deduce the phenomenon of our familiarity with ourselves from the supposedly more original phenomenon of the project (as understanding or care): *Dasein* is not initially familiar with itself, but becomes familiar only in the light of the reflection which its projects leave behind on things and which shines back on itself. Sartre already revealed the equivocation in this position: for a project a consciousness is required, but then it is a *petitio principii* to make consciousness into something which is derived from the disclosure of the world.[31]

This equivocation is intensified in Heidegger's lecture of 1927. There it is admittedly stressed that the self is given to *Dasein* 'without reflection and without inner perception [that is, of course, a critical swipe at the theory of self-consciousness of the Husserl of the *Logical Investigations*[32]], *before* any reflection'.[33] The fact that there is no thought of a real pre-reflexivity of consciousness as 'co-revealedness of the self in the self-directedness at beings which understands Being'[34] is clear from the explanation which follows:

> Reflection in the sense of 'turning back on' is only a mode of self-*grasping*, but not the manner of primary self-disclosure. The manner in which the self is revealed to itself in the facticity of Dasein can nevertheless accurately be called reflection, but one must not understand thereby what one commonly understands by this expression: a self-observing which is bent back onto the I, but rather a structure of the kind which is announced by the optical significance of the expression 'reflection'. Reflecting here means: refracting itself on something,

shining back from there, i.e. showing itself in the reflection back from something.[35]

This formulation does not only cite–*expressis verbis*–the optical metaphor of the reflection that shines back from the world onto the self, which, of course, depends on the model of representation (*Vorstellungmodell*) which Heidegger had rejected as metaphysical.[36] It is also completely unsuitable for explaining the familiarity of *Dasein* with itself as itself (and not just with a bundle of anonymous world reflexes). The view that the self owes the knowledge (*Kenntnis*) in which it carries itself (*in der es sich hält*) to a reflection, which shines back to it from the *intentum* of a self-thematization, uses precisely the justifiably criticized model of representation according to which a subject puts an object before itself, whereby in this particular case the *intentum* is, exceptionally, the subject itself. According to this model we would have self-consciousness in analogy to the (for example, perceptive) consciousness of physical objects. That is obviously wrong and the argument attached to it is circular. A contemporary analytical author summarizes the critique of the mirror-model of self-consciousness as follows:

> The latter point is especially important; it shows that the knowledge in question is radically different from perceptual knowledge. The reason one is not presented to oneself 'as an object' in self-awareness is that self-awareness is not perceptual awareness, i.e. is not the sort of awareness in which objects are presented. It is an awareness of facts unmediated by awareness of objects. But it is worth noting that if one were aware of oneself as an object in such cases (as one is in fact aware of oneself as an object when one sees oneself in a mirror), this would not help explain one's self-knowledge. For awareness that the presented object was ϕ would not tell one that one was oneself ϕ, unless one already had some self-knowledge, namely the knowledge that one is the unique possessor of whatever set of properties of the presented object one took to show it to be oneself. Perceptual self-knowledge presupposes non-perceptual self-knowledge, so not all self-knowledge can be perceptual.[37]

As Heidegger does not know the difference between reflexive self-representation (*Selbstvorstellung*) and the feeling of self which does not rest on representation, the point of his critique of the subject as the most extreme sharpening of metaphysical interpretation of Being (*Seinsauslegung*) as presence becomes strangely blunt. On the one hand he has not noticed that modern philosophy since Fichte no longer found it necessary to think subjectivity as the relationship of one being (*eines Seienden*) to itself–therefore as self-presence[38]–on the other hand the positive counter-suggestion via which he challenged the West is a particularly helpless example of the position criticized. Strangely, Heidegger–with his orientation via the 'as-structure of understanding'–did not even think that his explanatory model for self-consciousness could already be questionable because what 'shines back' 'relucently' to *Dasein* from the world are not reflexes of objects, but are rather states of affairs and involvements, from which a 'radiance' ('*Leuchten*') can be gained only be means of an extreme catachresis.[39] These complaints have not stopped Heidegger's neo-structuralist pupils–I shall confine myself to Jacques Derrida as their only philosopher–from blindly adopting both Heidegger's thesis about the end of metaphysics in the subject and his model of explanation of subjectivity. For this reason, as I wish to show in conclusion, their so-called deconstruction of subjectivity–as a mistaken path oriented to the presence-model of 'Being'–shares the whole dividedness (*Zwiespalt*) of the Heideggerian position. It consists in the fact that they have nothing to oppose to the deconstructed model. As modernity has at the same time developed such a counter-model, the diagnostic force of deconstruction remains without any bite, and without sufficient philological support in the texts diagnosed.

Recent French thought–rather like Tugendhat–has wanted to give a new direction to the tack of the ontico-ontological difference. Heidegger's critique of the confusion of Being and beings is omnipresent in Derrida's writings, and the artificial expression *différance*, which stood for a time in the centre of his deconstructive reflections, is an undisguised allusion to Heidegger. (Of course the neologism 'deconstruction' is also indebted to the Heideggerian talk of the 'destruction of Western metaphysics'.) This omnipresence of Heidegger in Derrida, for instance, unfortunately does not mean that the appropriation of his basic thought–as is the case in Tugendhat–has become the object of an explicit and comprehensible reflection. If it appears relatively easy to inform oneself about Derrida's descent from and rejection of Husserl (or even Hegel), precisely the opposite is the case in his relationship to Heidegger. We must therefore reconstruct it from indirect evidence.

Like that of Tugendhat, Derrida's outbidding of Heidegger results from a (here admittedly specifically French) variant of the linguistic turn. Its progenitor is not Ludwig Wittgenstein but rather Ferdinand de Saussure. That explains why Derrida's language philosophy is not oriented via the paradigm of the proposition (and of truth), but rather the paradigm of the single linguistic sign and its distinctness. In the wake of this tradition (which he does not reflect upon sufficiently) he distances himself with the first steps of his Heidegger reception from Heidegger's insistence on the 'as-structure of understanding', on the proposition and the critique of the subject-object schema which asserts that the objects of statements are states of affairs (*Sachverhalte*) and not things (*Sachen*).

This orientation via the single sign and the turning away from Heidegger's reconstruction of the original (Greek) meaning of Being as being true is particularly clear in a text which bears the title *The Supplement of the Copula, Philosophy before Linguistics*[40] and which would have offered an opportunity to study the function of 'is' in the proposition. After the Aristotelian categories have been defined as 'ways for "Being" to say or signify itself, i.e. to open language to its outside, to that which is in as much as it is or such as it is, to truth',[41] Aristotle's talk of the use of Being as being true is invoked only once (following *Metaphysics* E 2 1026a 33) and then does not occur again.[42] Instead, in constant proximity to the essay of Benveniste's on *Categories of Thought and Categories of Language*,[43] the connection of thinking and speaking is reflected upon, as is also the apparent special place of 'be/to be' (*sein*) in Indo-European as opposed to other languages which, for example, do not have the so-called copula. But the function of the copula, the conclusion states, is 'supplemented' in these other languages by an empty space which is, so to speak, pregnant with sense, in whose functioning Derrida thinks he can identify a relative of what he himself will call *la différance*:

> Thus it happens that the lexical absence is only supplemented by an absence pure and simple, the grammatical function of 'be/to be' (*être*) being then assured by the whiteness of a space, by a punctuation which is in some way erased, by a *pause*: oral interruption, that is to say a stopping of the voice (is this then an *oral phenomenon*?), which no *graphic* sign, in the current sense of this word, which no plenitude of writing comes then to mark. The absence of 'be/to be' (*être*), the absence of this singular lexeme, is absence itself. Does not the semantic value of absence in general depend upon the lexical-semantic value of 'be/to be'?[44]

This function of the copula which is itself a-semantic, generating sense and meaning (of which Aristotle himself said that in itself it meant nothing and only carries out the synthesis in the judgement)[45] symptomatically replaces for Derrida the category-generating but itself transcategorial (thus transcendental) place of the indefinite ambiguous verbal expression 'be/to be' ('*sein*') in Greek and related languages.[46] Since its beginning it tends to obliterate itself; and the fact that Heidegger is driven by the will to '*restore the verb "be/to be"* ("*être*") *its whole force and its authentic function*',[47] can be noted only in terms of regret.

In spite of this–that is, despite this turning away from Heidegger's original orientation via the sense of Being as being true–Derrida holds on to

Heidegger's conviction that, even as far as the modern theory of the subject, Western ontology interprets Being according to the schema of presence. The critique of presence is, then, not that of the false reifications of propositions, but of untenable fixing of the sense of individual signs, in whose inexhaustible texture world is disclosed to us. Like Heidegger, Derrida outbids the fixation upon presence of metaphysics[48] by a return to the original structure of temporalization, which for him is admittedly no longer that of the project of *Dasein* and also not that of the sending of Being, but is rather the 'temporization' of the articulation of signs.[49] Subjectivity is not excepted from this either. For, like the analytical philosophers and Peirce, to whom he refers on occasion,[50] Derrida is also convinced that reference to mental phenomena can take place only via the mediation of signs.[51] Meaning (*Sinn*), including the meaning in whose light the phenomena of consciousness come to grasp themselves, is dependent upon signs. Derrida supports this conviction with a radical outbidding of Saussure's principle of differentiality, according to which every sign mediates its identity via the exclusion of its embodiment as a sign from all other such embodiments. The reference (*Bedeutung*) of the sign *a* would therefore be mediated by relations of being-other-than the signs *b, c, d, e, f,* etc. Now according to Derrida there is no compelling reason to assume that the chain of the oppositional terms which are to be negatively separated from the first sign should be finite, or that I could not shift the semantics of each of them by new contextual constellations. Therefore the boundaries of the semantic identity of a term are functions of an open system of permanent new differentiations, without the possible presence of a term with itself. Subjectivity is not unaffected by this:

> Subjectivity–like objectivity–is an effect of *différance*, an effect inscribed in a system of *différance*. That is why the *a* of *différance* also recalls the fact that spacing is *temporisation*, detour, delay via which intuition, perception, consumption, in a word the relationship to the present, the reference to a present reality, to a *being (étant)*, are always deferred. Deferred precisely because of the principle of difference, which means that an element only functions and signifies, only takes or gives 'meaning' ('*sens*') by referring to another past or future element in an economy of traces.[52]

This thought of the non-presence of a verbal sign to itself (and, because subjects only have access to themselves mediated by meaning (*sinnvermittelt*), also of the non-presence of consciousness to itself) can be made clearer by the following consideration: if meaning (*Sinn*) and significance (*Bedeutsamkeit*) arise in the being-related to each other of differing expressive substances, then the identity of a term could be guaranteed only by a state of closure ('*clôtur*') and of the unchangeability of the system. The model which underlies the classical structuralist theory of language–and still underlies Searle's 'taxonomy of speech-acts'–is not by chance the crystal lattice, in which, if the temperature is low enough, all the molecules are immobilized in their places, both separated from all the others and bound to them as well. Now the world of symbolic interaction, as opposed to that of the elements, cannot be cooled down to absolute zero. It only flourishes in a certain heat, which permits the flow, the exchange and re-ordering, of the signs. Texts, Derrida says, are always transformations of other preceding texts,[53] in the same way as signs are always transformations of other preceding signs. And why? Because–via the thought of differentiality–it is at the same time agreed that no sign is immediately and a-temporally present to itself, because it must take the detour through an unforeseeable and changing configuration of other signs before it identifies itself. If one additionally makes it clear to oneself that this detour cannot be predicted because it goes through infinity, then one has revoked the scientistic idea that there is an original, a-temporal presence or familiarity of at least *one* meaning with itself which can be reconstructed by linguistic analysis (as is suggested by Greimas's talk of '*sens total*' or '*sens central*' of a text): a presence of the kind that I am always certain to find my way back to, whatever paths I may take via the signs. Such a central meaning which is withdrawn from the play of the structure would be the principle of the structure–Derrida says: 'the transcendental signified'.[54]

But the certainty of this Archimedian locus is always already lost; none of the many paths that I take through the web of relationships of language, in order to establish its single meanings or its total meaning (*Gesamtsinn*), leads reliably back to the point of departure. For this value is, of course, a function of the infinitely open row of all its opposing elements. The paradigm of reflection (or of the speculative return to the point of departure), which one also recognizes in the classical hermeneutic talk of the 'reconstruction of the original meaning of the word (*Wortsinn*)', cannot stand up to the experience of the de-limited economy of semantic oppositions.

This consequence must–following the first of the two premises, according to which meaning is mediated by signs–also be applied to the meaning in whose light *subjectivity* is disclosed to itself. However, as a result of the second premise–according to which the de-limited differentiality of the '*marques*' deprives every sign of its identity–self-consciousness can then no longer be thought of classically (as in Descartes, Hegel or Husserl) as 'self-presence' ('*présence à soi*') (that is, the traditional formula for the reflection model).

In the depths of what ties these two decisive moments of the description together, an irreducible non-presence is recognised as a constitutive value and with it a non-life or a non-presence or non-belonging to itself of the living present, an ineradicable non-originarity.[55]

Derrida considers this to be an immediate consequence of the reflection-model of consciousness. Certainly: reflection (*Reflexion*) means mirroring back (*Widerspiegelung*). The model would like to guarantee the unity of the split consciousness, by unmasking the Other as the Other *of itself*. But in order to achieve this reflection it must–temporarily–take the reality of the opposition, of the splitness and non-simultaneity of the related aspects of consciousness, in its own hands. Once exposed to the medium of reality, of temporal sequence and of differentiality, there is no way back for consciousness into the sphere of pure ideality and instantaneity, to the extent to which this is understood (as it sometimes is in Husserl) as pure, incorporeal and supra-temporal self-affection (*Selbstberührung*):

> . . . a pure difference divided self-presence. It is in this pure difference that the possibility of everything which one thinks one can exclude from auto-affection takes root: space, the outside, the world, the body, etc. As soon as one admits that auto-affection is the condition of self-presence no pure transcendental reduction is possible. But one has to go via it to recapture difference as it is closest to itself: not to its identity, nor to its origin. It does not have one. But to the movement of *différance*.
>
> This movement of *différance* does not happen to a transcendental subject. It produces it [the transcendental subject]. Auto-affection is not a modality of experience which characterises a being (*étant*) which would already be itself (*autos*). It produces the Same as a relation to itself in the *différance* from itself, the Same as the non-identical.[56]

Here the artificial expression *différance* (with an *a*) emerges again. Admittedly the context is slightly changed: *différance* no longer serves to explain the non-identity of meaning in the framework of an uncloseable sign-system, but now appears as condition of possibility of self-consciousness. Derrida arrives at this consequence via an at first sight insignificant re-interpretation of the (Husserlian) reflection-model: instead of the play of reflection attesting or confirming the identity of what is reflecting with what is reflected, the detour through reflection is sufficient to deprive the self of its identity for ever:

> The present does not present itself as such except by relating itself to itself, it does not say itself as such except to divide itself, folding itself to itself in the angle, in the break (break: 'fault' and 'articulation', by a hinge in a piece of locksmithing. *Littré*). In the unlocking (*déclenchement*).

Presence is never present. The possibility–or the power–of the present is only its own limit, its interior fold, its impossibility–or its impotence. . . . What is true here of the present is equally true of 'history', of 'form', of the form of history, etc., as well as of all meanings which, in the language of metaphysics, are indissociable from the meaning 'present'.[57]

Indeed: once one moves in the epistemological frame of the model of reflection one cannot escape its logic. If, namely, the self does not originally know itself, but first needs the mirror of reflection to gain knowledge of itself, then one can distinguish three temporal moments in the movement of self-understanding: a first moment of still unconscious inwardness, a second of going-out-of-self and reflecting-self, and a third of re-internalization of the mirror image in the self. One can as little talk of an instantaneity of what happens as one can of a 'living present'. Self-consciousness can then no longer vouch for its unity, which transforms itself into an 'idea in the Kantian sense', as Husserl says. For Derrida it thereby becomes simply 'undecidable'.[58] The reflection-model implies, of course, that the ray which consciousness directs at itself also arrives there. Not so in Derrida's deconstructed model. In the last longer quotation there was talk of a folding, '[of a folding of the present] to itself in the angle'. 'Now, the fold is not a reflexivity.'[59] The fold bends back on itself, without, however, completely reaching itself. The reflection-model, on the other hand, implies

that the mirror unites the self (*moi*) to its image . . . , deliberately and unilaterally closes the fold, interprets it as coincidence with itself, makes the opening the condition of *adequation* to itself, reduces everything in the fold which also marks dehiscence, dissemination, spacing, temporisation, etc.[60]

Elsewhere Derrida speaks of the barricaded street of reflection.[61] The comparison expresses the fact that a criterion is lacking which would guarantee the identity of the gaze which is directed at the mirror and of the image which comes back to the eye from the mirror. Indeed nothing about the mirror (and nothing about a description of my physical and psychic attributes, however exhaustive it may be) betrays that it really is a mirror and that it is reflecting *me*. I could only assert the sameness (*Selbigkeit*) of my mirror image with myself if I had a pre-reflexive or non-specular knowledge of myself at my disposal: but that is a thought that Derrida does not consider for a moment in his critique of the reflection-model, and which he seems never to have encountered in the rich literature on the phenomenon of self-consciousness. Instead he tries by uncanny metaphors to move his reader into a Hoffmannesque nocturne: what, he ponders, if the mirror of reflection has no tain, if it threw an uncontrollable alterity back to me?[62] The aporia is always the same: consciousness identifies itself via its mirror image; but the mirror image does not have a criterion which makes re-identification possible; therefore the mirror image could indeed be the Other of consciousness, *without* which one the one hand *consciousness* would not be as such, *via* whose mediation on the other hand the *identity* of consciousness is threatened and is made something undecidable. (It is clear that this alterity, following Derrida's first premise, is the delimited differentiality of language: 'A language has preceded my presence to myself. Older than consciousness, than the spectator, anterior to any presence (*assistance*), a sentence was waiting for "you", looks at you, observes you, everywhere concerns you.'[63]

Now one must, even if one concedes the dependence of meaning upon the sign, challenge whether Derrida could maintain at all in the framework of his own model that there *is* (even if not in the manner of self-presence) subjectivity.[64] First, because one cannot see how familiarity with oneself could arise from the delimited play of differential '*marques*', if a consciousness had not already attributed a meaning to them in a hypothetical judgement. But then the thesis that this meaning is for its part the result of oppositional relations between signs is circular (predicates from the sphere of consciousness have already gone into the description of that from which consciousness was supposedly deduced: signs are not meaningless lines or natural noises). Second, because Derrida's attack on the metaphysical thought of the present self-relation is so radical that minimal conditions of the phenomenon of our familiarity with ourselves can no longer be explained by it. But a theory which can only sustain itself against the phenomenon it is to explain is absurd: it would only be right if the phenomenon were to disappear. Finally: without a moment of relative self-identity differentiation (shift of meaning, metaphorical redescription of meaning, change of psychic states) could not be established at all, differentiation would lack a criterion and would be indistinguishable from complete inertia: but terms can only be opposed to each other which agree with each other with regard to at least one moment of significance, in the same way as terms can only be identified with each other which diverge from each other with regard to at least one moment of significance. Derrida saw that when he admitted in his reply to Searle's criticism:

> Iterability requires a minimal remaining (*restance*) (like an, albeit limited, minimal idealisation) for identity to be repeatable and identifiable *in*, *through*, and even *with a view to* alteration. For the structure of iteration—another decisive trait—implies *at the same time* identity *and* difference.[65]

But Derrida cannot account for this minimal 'remaining' of the meaning of the sign (and of the self-consciousness which is mediated by it) by means of his theory–it remains just an assumption whose necessity can be admitted only if one relinquishes his position.

In short: Western metaphysics is not endangered by Derrida's deconstruction of the subject. Admittedly the author succeeds in demonstrating the absurdity of the reflection-model; strangely, though, it does not cross his mind for a moment that this model is simply wrong (inappropriate for the phenomenon) and should be replaced by another. Instead he just gives up 'subjectivity'–which he, in Heidegger's footsteps, considers to be the most extreme intensification of the Western repression of Being or *différance*–and with it gives up the gesture [*Gestus*] of traditional philosophizing altogether.

But all that would have been necessary here was a reflection on the essential difference between the instantiation of mental phenomena from the I- and from the he-perspective. If I am in love with V, I do not need any self-identification to attribute the corresponding predicate to myself, neither via a mirror, nor via a list of necessary and sufficient conditions, nor via any information based on observation: I have consciousness of it in a manner which is immune to error. Derrida, on the other hand, describes subjectivity, in the logic of the reflection-model, from the perspective of an other (subject) which relates to the subject from outside, and there it is admittedly the case that, as in all non-trivial identifications and as in all cognitions (which are fallible in principle), mistakes and even indeterminacies can crop up. But once one has made it clear that self-consciousness–unlike the linguistic form in which it articulates itself–is not something relational at all, then one can no longer believe it is possible to get closer to the phenomenon with descriptions like '*identité à soi*' or even '*présence à soi*'. It would–at the very least–be overhasty to wish to say farewell to the West for the sake of this simple insight, or to believe oneself to be in a nameless space 'beyond metaphysics'. '*Lieb' Abendland, kannst ruhig sein*', ('Dear West, worry not'–an ironic reference to '*Lieb' Vaterland, magst ruhig sein*'.)

NOTES

1 1003 a 22–5, 1025 b 7–10.
2 998 b 20 f.
3 Cf. Ernst Tugendhat, *Vorlesungen sur Einführung in die sprachanalytische Philosophie*, (Frankfurt am Main, 1976) 3rd and 4th lecture.
4 Martin Heidegger, *Die Grundprobleme der Phänomenologie* (Marburger Vorlesung, 1927, Gesamtausgabe Band 24, Frankfurt am Main, 1975), 15.
5 l. c., 13–14, 18, 23, 27.

6 *Die Grundbegriffe der Metaphysik* (Freiburger Vorlesung 1929–30, Gesamtausgabe Bd. 29–30. Frankfurt am Main, 1983), 65.

7 Gesamtausgabe Bd. 24, 102.

8 l. c. 102/2.

9 The example might appear inappropriate because it contains a relation, thus an expression with two places about an ordered pair of subject-terms, and has to be formalized differently from a simple predicative statement. But this difference does not matter for what I have in mind here.

10 Cf. Tugendhat, *Vorlesungen . . .* , l. c. 44.

11 Cf. Heidegger, *Die Grundbegriffe der Metaphysik*, l. c., 416f.

12 L.c. 481; as well as in: *Die Grundprobleme der Phänomenologie*, l.c. §18, = pp. 304ff.

13 *Metaphysik* 1006 a 3; Tugendhat, l. c., 58.

14 1005 b 19f.

15 E.g., *Peri hermeneias* 1051 b 33, *Metaphysik*, E2 1026 a 33, passim.

16 Theunissen's simultaneous reconstruction of Hegel's *Logic* as a critique of metaphysics as an objectification of 'being' ('*Sein*') and its transfer into a theory of the speculative proposition stays completely within this framework and is original only in its application to Hegel: *Sein und Schein: die kritische Funktion von Hegels Logik*, (Frankfurt am Main, 1978) cf. above a; 66–7 and pp. 95ff.

17 *Die Grundprobleme der Phänomenologie*, l. c., 431ff.

18 L. c., 448.

19 L. c., 154.

20 *Critique of Pure Reason*, B p. 273.

21 And Tugendhat has again specified his ideas in terms of formal semantics: '*Das Sein und das Nichts*', in *Durchblicke, Martin Heidegger zum 80 Geburtstag*, ed. Vittorio Klostermann (Frankfurt am Main, 1970) 132–61, 134–46.

22 Heidegger, *Die Grundprobleme der Phänomenologie*, 154.

23 *Welches sind die wirklichen Fortschritte . . .* In Theorie-Werkausgabe, ed. W. Weischedel (Frankfurt am Main, 1958) VI, 590.

24 Cf. *Holzwege* (Frankfurt am Main, 1950) 80ff., 100ff.

25 Ed. von Joh. Hoffmeister (Hamburg, 1956), 19, 24.

26 §34 of the *Discours de la Métaphysique*.

27 Cf. my *Ein Grundelement der historischen Analyse der Diskontinuität: die Epochenwende von 1775 in Foucaults 'Archäologie' in Das Sagbare und das Unsagbare* (Frankfurt am Main, 1989), pp. 362ff, especially 382–3 and 392ff.

28 §4 of *Principes de la Nature de la Grace*.

29 Cf. Refl. Nr. 3929 and *Vorlesungen über die Metaphysik*, ed. K. H. L. Pölitz (Erfurt, 1821), 135.

30 *Critique of Pure Reason*, B 132.

31 *L'être et le néant* (Paris, 1943), 115f., 128.

32 II/1 354f.

33 *Die Grundprobleme der Phänomenologie*, l. c., 226.

34 L. c., 224.

35 L. c., 226

36 In *Being and Time* Heidegger had spoken of 'relucence' (*Reluzenz*) (Tübingen,

1967), 21; cf. 16 'ontological shining back of the understanding of the world onto the interpretation of *Dasein*'.

37 Sidney Shoemaker, 'Personal Identity: A Materialist's Account', in Sidney Shoemaker and Richard Swinburne, *Personal Identity* (Oxford, 1984), 104–5.

38 I have demonstrated this in more detail in *Die Unhintergehbarkeit von Individualität, Reflexionen über Subjekt, Person und Individuum aus Anlass ihrer 'postmodernen' Toterklärung* (Frankfurt am Main, 1986 [2nd edition 1988]).

39 Tugendhat also tried to make good this inconsistency by the suggestion that self-consciousness does not thematize an object called self, but rather articulates itself as a cognitive relationship of a person to propositions, which represent in this case mental states like 'I am in love'. Tugendhat's position is, though, unconvincing for other reasons. Cf. *Die Unhintergehbarkeit von Individualität*, l.c. 67ff.

40 In *Marges de la philosophie* (Paris, 1972), 209–46.

41 L.c., 218.

42 L.c., 219.

43 L.c. 214. (Essay of 1958, reprinted in *Problèmes de linguistique générale* (Paris, 1966), 63ff.).

44 L.c., 241.

45 L.c., 234/5.

46 L.c., 232ff.

47 L.c., 246.

48 'Of course, to return to Heidegger, the point which is no doubt the most decisive and the most difficult remains that of meaning, of the present and of presence' (*Positions*, Paris, 1972), 75.

49 Cf. l.c. 40 in context.

50 *De la grammatologie* (Paris, 1967), 70ff.

51 Saussure spoke in chapter IV of the version of the *Cours de linguistique générale*, which was compiled by his students in 1915, of the fact that before its articulation by the 'phonic chain' mind resembled a 'nebulous amorphousness'.

52 *Positions*, l. c., 40.

53 *Positions*, l. c., 39, 46–7.

54 L. c., 61f., 88; cf. *L'écriture et la différence* (Paris, 1967), 409ff.

55 *La voix et le phénomène* (Paris, 1967), 5.

56 L.c., 92.

57 *La dissémination* (Paris, 1972), 349–50.

58 L.c., 248ff.

59 L.c., 302.

60 L.c., 302.

61 L.c., 299.

62 L.c., 349–50, 39, 359.

63 L.c., 378–9.

64 Derrida does in fact stress that his counter-thesis did not wish to explain away 'the effects of ideality, of signification, of meaning and of reference', but only wished to explain them differently ('what we need is to determine them *in another way*, according to a differential system'). (*Positions*, l.c. 89–90). Subjectivity is included among these phenomena, as the context makes clear.

65 *Limited Inc abc* (Baltimore: Johns Hopkins University Press, 1977), pp. 24–5.

Translated by Andrew Bowie

11

Richard Rorty

Is Derrida a Transcendental Philosopher?

For years a quarrel has been simmering among Derrida's American admirers. On the one side there are the people who admire Derrida for having invented a new, splendidly ironic way of writing about the philosophical tradition. On the other side are those who admire him for having given us rigorous arguments for surprising philosophical conclusions. The former emphasize the playful, distancing, oblique way in which Derrida handles traditional philosophical figures and topics. The second emphasize what they take to be his results, his philosophical discoveries. Roughly speaking, the first are content to admire his manner, whereas the second want to say that the important thing is his matter–the truths which he has set forth.

Geoffrey Hartman's *Saving the Text* set the tone for the first way of appropriating Derrida. At the same time that I was picking up this tone from Hartman, and imitating it, Jonathan Culler was criticizing Hartman for light-mindedness. The term 'Derridadaism', Culler said, was 'a witty gesture by which Geoffrey Hartman blots out Derridean argument'.[1] I weighed in on Hartman's side, claiming that Culler was too heavy-handed in his treatment of Derrida, too anxious to treat him as having demonstrated theorems which literary critics might now proceed to apply.[2] I thought it too much to ask of 'deconstruction' that it be, in Culler's words, *both* 'rigorous argument within philosophy and displacement of philosophical categories and philosophical attempts at mastery'.[3] Something, I claimed, had to go. I suggested we jettison the 'rigorous argument' part.

This suggestion was contested by Christoper Norris.[4] Norris was concerned to show that Derrida has arguments, good solid arguments, and is not just playing around. Like Culler, he was also concerned to block my attempt to analogize deconstruction to pragmatism. Whereas a pragmatist view of truth, Culler said, treats conventionally accepted norms as foundations, deconstruction goes on to point out that 'norms are produced by acts of exclusion'. 'Objectivity', Culler quite justly pointed out, 'is constituted by excluding the views of those who do not count as sane and rational men: women, children, poets, prophets, madmen'.[5] Culler was the first to make the suggestion, later taken up and developed in considerable detail by others,[6] that pragmatism (or at least my version of it) and deconstruction differ in that the one tends towards political conservatism and the other towards political radicalism.

In his recent book on Derrida, Norris repeats this suggestion, and reaffirms that to read Derrida in Hartman's and my way is

> to ignore the awkward fact that Derrida has devoted the bulk of his writings to a patient working-through (albeit on his own, very different terms) of precisely those problems that have occupied philosophers in the 'mainstream' tradition, from Kant to Husserl and Frege. And this because those problems are indubitably *there*, installed within philosophy and reaching beyond it into every department of modern institutionalized knowledge.[7]

The quarrel about whether Derrida has arguments thus gets linked to a quarrel about whether he is a private writer–writing for the delight of us insiders who share his background, who find the same rather esoteric things as funny or beautiful or moving as he does–or rather a writer with a public mission, someone who gives us weapons with which to subvert 'institutionalized knowledge', and thus social institutions. I have urged that Derrida be treated as the first sort of writer,[8] whereas most of his American admirers have treated him as, at least in part, the second. Lumping both quarrels together, one can say that there is a quarrel between those of us who read Derrida on Plato, Hegel and Heidegger in the same way as we read Bloom or Cavell on Emerson or Freud–in order to see these authors transfigured, beaten into fascinating new shapes–and those who read Derrida to get ammunition, and a strategy, for the struggle to bring about social change.

Norris thinks that Derrida should be read as a transcendental philosopher in the Kantian tradition–somebody who digs out hitherto unsuspected presuppositions. 'Derrida', he says, 'is broaching something like a Kantian transcendental deduction, an argument to demonstrate ("perversely" enough) that *a priori* notions of logical truth are *a priori* ruled out of court by rigorous reflection on the powers and limits of textual critique.'[9] By contrast, my view of Derrida is that he nudges us into a world in which 'rigorous reflection on the power and limits . . .' has as little place as do '*a priori* notions of logical truth'. This world has as little room for transcendental deductions, or for rigour, as for self-authenticating moments of immediate presence to consciousness.

On my view, the only thing that can displace an intellectual world is another intellectual world–a new alternative, rather than an argument against an old alternative. The idea that there is some neutral ground on which to mount an argument against something as big as 'logocentrism' strikes me as one more logocentric hallucination. I do not think that demonstrations of 'internal incoherence' or of 'presuppositional relationships' ever do much to disabuse us of bad old ideas or institutions. Disabusing gets done, instead, by offering us sparkling new ideas, or utopian visions of glorious new institutions. The result of genuinely original thought, on my view, is not so much to refute or subvert our previous beliefs as to help us forget them by giving us a substitute for them. I take refutation to be a mark of unoriginality, and I value Derrida's originality too much to praise him in those terms. So I find little use, in reading or discussing him, for the notion of 'rigorous argumentation'.

I

Culler and Norris have now been joined, on their side of the quarrel I have been describing, by Rodolphe Gasché. Gasché's *The Tain of the Mirror* is by far the most ambitious and detailed attempt to treat Derrida as a rigorous transcendental philosopher. Gasché says that

> [i]n this book I hope that I have found a middle ground between the structural plurality of Derrida's philosophy–a plurality that makes it impossible to elevate any final essence of his book into its true meaning–and the strict criteria to which any interpretation of his work must yield, if it is to be about that work and not merely a private fantasy. These criteria, at center stage in this book, are, as I shall show, philosophical and not literary in nature.[10]

Just as in the case of Culler I doubted that one could displace philosophical concepts while still having rigorous philosophical arguments, so in Gasché's case I doubt that one can eschew the project of stating Derrida's 'true meaning' while still judging him by 'strict criteria'. I do not think that one should try to pay good old logocentric compliments to enemies of logocentrism.

In what follows, I shall try to spell out why the compliments Gasché offers Derrida seem to me to be misapplied. To my mind, 'private fantasy' is, if not entirely adequate, at least a somewhat better compliment. Many responsibilities begin in dreams, and many transfigurations of the tradition begin in private fantasies. Think, for example, of Plato's or St Paul's private fantasies–fantasies so original and utopian that they became the common sense of later times. Someday, for all I know, there may be some social changes (perhaps even changes for the better) which retrospection will see as having originated in Derrida's fantasies. But the *arguments* which Derrida can be read as offering on behalf of his fantasies seem to me no better than the ones Plato offered for his. Anybody who reads through Plato in search of rigorous arguments is in for a disappointment. I think that the same goes for Derrida.

I can begin quarrelling with Gasché by taking up his distinction between philosophy and literature. On my view, 'philosophy' is either a term defined by choosing a list of writers (for example, Parmenides, Plato, Aristotle, Kant, Hegel, Heidegger) and then specifying what they all have in common, or else just the name of an academic department. The first sense of the term is hard to apply to a writer who, like Derrida, is trying to extricate himself from the tradition defined by such a list. But the second sense of the term is not much help either, for in this sense 'philosophy' is just an *omnium gatherum* of disparate activities united by nothing more than a complicated tangle of genealogical connections–connections so tenuous that one can no longer detect even a family resemblance between the activities.[11] Only if one buys in on the logocentric idea that there just *must* be an autonomous discipline which adjudicates ultimate questions would 'philosophy' have a third sense, one appropriate for Gasché's purposes. It is only by reference to some such idea that it makes sense to worry, as he does, about the lines between philosophy and literature.

For my purposes, the important place to draw a line is not between philosophy and non-philosophy but rather between topics which we know how to argue about and those we do not. It is the line between the attempt to be objective–to get a consensus on what we should believe–and a willingness to abandon consensus in the hope of transfiguration. Gasché, by contrast, thinks that we can separate the philosophical books (or, at least, the important philosophical books of recent centuries) from other books by a fairly straightforward test. The former are the books in which we find a specifically *transcendental* project–a project of answering some question of the form 'what are the conditions of the possibility of . . . ?'–of, for example, experience, self-consciousness, language, or philosophy itself.

I have to admit that asking and answering that question is, indeed, the mark of a distinct genre. But, unlike Gasché, I think that it is a thoroughly self-deceptive question. The habit of posing it–asking for non-causal, non-empirical, non-historical conditions–is the distinctive feature of a tradition which stretches from the *Critique of Pure Reason* through Hegel's *Science of Logic* to *Being and Time* (and, if Gasché is right about the early Derrida's intentions, through *Of Grammatology*). The trouble with the question is that it looks like a 'scientific' one, as if we know how to debate the relative merits of alternative answers, just as we know how to debate alternative answers to questions about the conditions for the *actuality* of various things (for example, political changes, quasars, psychoses). But it is not. Since that for which the conditions of possibility are sought is always *everything* that any previous philosopher has envisaged–the whole range of what has been discussed up to now–anybody is at liberty to identify any ingenious gimmick that he dreams up as a 'condition of possibility'.

The sort of gimmick in question is exemplified by Kantian 'transcendental synthesis', Hegelian 'self-diremption of the concept', Heideggerian *Sorge*, and (on Gasché's intepretation) Derridean *différance*. These suggestions about transcendental conditions are so many leaps into the darkness which surrounds the totality of everything previously illuminated. In the nature of the case, there can be no pre-existent logical space, no 'strict criteria' for choosing among these alternatives. If there were, the question about 'conditions of possibility' would automatically become merely 'positive' and not properly 'transcendental' or 'reflective'.[12] Once again, I would want to insist that you cannot have it both ways. You cannot see these leaps in the dark as the magnificent poetic acts they are and still talk about 'philosophical rigour'. Rigour just does not come into it.

This insusceptibility to argument is what makes 'the philosophy of reflection'–the tradition of transcendental inquiry within which Gasché wishes to embed Derrida–the bête noir of philosophers who take public discussability as the essence of rationality. Habermas's polemic against the late Heidegger and against Derrida has the same motives as Carnap's attack on the early Heidegger.[13] Like Carnap, Habermas thinks that philosophy ought to be argumentative. He thinks that Heidegger and Derrida are merely oracular. My own view is that we should avoid slogans like 'philosophy ought to be argumentative' (or any other slogan that begins 'philosophy ought to be . . .') and recognize that the writers usually identified as 'philosophers' include both argumentative problem-solvers like Aristotle and Russell and oracular world-disclosers like Plato and Hegel–both people good at rendering public accounts and people good at leaping in the dark.

But this conciliatory ecumenicism still leaves me hostile to those who, like Gasché, think that one can synthesize world-disclosing and problem-solving into a single activity called 'reflection'. In particular, I object to the idea that one can be 'rigorous' if one's procedure consists in inventing new words for what one is pleased to call 'conditions of possibility' rather than playing sentences using old words off against each other. The latter activity is what I take to constitute argumentation. Poetic world-disclosers like Hegel, Heidegger and Derrida have to pay a price, and part of that price is the inappropriateness to their work of notions like 'argumentation' and 'rigour'.[14]

Habermas differs with me and agrees with Gasché in thinking that philosophy ought to be argumentative, but he agrees with me and differs from Gasché in refusing to see the transitions in Hegel's *Logic*, or the successive 'discoveries' of new 'conditions of possibility' which fill the pages of *Being and Time*, as *arguments*. Habermas and I are both in sympathy with Ernst Tugendhat's nominalist, Wittgensteinian rejection of the idea that one can be non-propositional and still be argumentative. Tugendhat sees the attempt of a German tradition stemming from Hegel to work at a sub-propositional level, while nevertheless claiming the 'cognitive status' which people like Carnap want to deny them, as doomed to failure.[15] By contrast, Gasché explicitly rejects Tugendhat's 'theoretical asceticism', his self-confinement to 'linguistic and propositional truth'.[16] Gasché thinks that such confinement will forbid one to do something which needs to be done, and which Derrida may in fact have accomplished.

Whereas Gasché thinks that words like 'différance' and 'iterability' signify 'infrastructures'–structures which it is Derrida's great achievement to have unearthed–I see these notions as merely abbreviations for the familiar Peircean-Wittgensteinian anti-Cartesian thesis that meaning is a function of context, and that there is no theoretical barrier to an endless sequence of recontextualizations. I think the problems with taking this Derridean jargon as seriously as Gasché does are the same as those which arise if one takes the jargon of *Being and Time* as a serious answer to questions of the form 'How is the ontic possible? What are its *ontological* conditions?' If one thinks of writers like Hegel, Heidegger, and Derrida as digging down to successively deeper levels of non-causal conditions–as scientists dig down to ever deeper levels of causal conditions (molecules behind tables, atoms behind molecules, quarks behind atoms . . .)–then the hapless and tedious metaphilosophical question 'How can we tell when we have hit bottom?' is bound to arise. More important, so will the question 'Within what language are we to lay out arguments demonstrating (or even just making plausible) that we have *correctly* identified these conditions?'

The latter question causes no great embarrassment for physicists, since they can say in advance what they want to get out of their theorizing. But it *should* embarrass people concerned with the question of what *philosophical* vocabulary to use, rather than with the question of what vocabulary will help us accomplish some specific purpose (for example, splitting the atom, curing cancer, persuading the populace). For either the language in which the arguments are given is itself an antecedently given one or it is a disposable ladder-language, one which can be forgotten once it has been *aufgehoben*. The former alternative is impossible if one's aim is to cast doubt on *all* final vocabularies previously available–an ambition common to Hegel, Heidegger and Derrida. Seizing the latter horn of the dilemma, however, requires admitting that the arguments which one uses must themselves be thrown away once they have achieved their purpose. But that would mean, on the normal understanding of the term, that these were not *arguments*, but rather suggestions about how to speak differently. Argumentation requires that the same vocabulary be used in premises and conclusions–that both be part of the same language-game. Hegelian *Aufhebung* is something quite different. It is what happens when we play elements of an old vocabulary off against one another in order to make us impatient for a new vocabulary. But that activity is quite different from playing old beliefs against other old beliefs in an attempt to see which survives. An existing language-game will provide 'standard rules' for the latter activity, but *nothing* could provide such rules for the former. Yet Gasché tells us that 'Derrida's work is a genuinely philosophical inquiry that takes the standard rules of philosophy very seriously'.[17]

On my view, it is precisely *Aufhebung* that Derrida is so good at. But one could only think of this practice as *argumentative* if one had a conception of argument as sub-propositional–one which allowed the unit of argumentation to be the word rather than the sentence. That is, indeed, a conception of argumentation which, notoriously, we find in Hegel's *Logic*–the text to which Gasché traces back 'the philosophy of reflection'. Hegel tried to give a sense to the idea that there are inferential relations among individual concepts which are not reducible to inferential relations among sentences which use the words signifying those concepts–that there is a 'movement of the concept' for the philosopher to follow, not reducible to the reweaving of a web of belief by playing beliefs off against each other. Hegel thought that he followed this movement as he went from 'Being' at the beginning of the *Logic* to 'the Absolute Idea' at its end.

Nominalists like myself–those for whom language is a tool rather than a medium, and for whom a concept is just the regular use of a mark or noise– cannot make sense of Hegel's claim that a concept like 'Being' breaks apart, sunders itself, turns into its opposite, etc., nor of Gasché's Derridean claim that 'concepts and discursive totalities are already cracked and fissured by necessary contradictions and heterogeneities'.[18] The best we nominalists can do with such claims is to construe them as saying that one can always make an old language-game look bad by thinking up a better one–replace an old tool with a new one by using an old word in a new way (for example, as the 'privileged' rather than the 'derivative' term of a contrast), or by replacing it with a new word. But this need for replacement is *ours*, not the concept's. *It* does not go to pieces; rather, we set it aside and replace it with something else.

Gasché is quite right in saying that to follow Wittgenstein and Tugendhat in this nominalism will reduce what he wants to call 'philosophical reflection' to 'a fluidization or liquefaction (*Verflüssigung*) of all oppositions and particularities by means of objective irony'.[19] Such liquefaction is what I am calling *Aufhebung* and praising Derrida for having done spectacularly well. We nominalists think that all that philosophers of the world-disclosing (as opposed to the problem-solving) sort can do is to fluidize old vocabularies. We cannot make sense of the notion of discovering a 'condition of the possibility of language'–nor, indeed, of the notion of 'language' as something homogeneous enough to have 'conditions'. If, with Wittgenstein, Tugendhat, Quine and Davidson, one ceases to see language as a medium, one will reject *a fortiori* Gasché's claim that '[language] must, in philosophical terms, be thought of as a totalizing medium'.[20] That is only how a certain antinominalistic philosophical tradition–'the philosophy of reflection'–must think of it.

If one does think of it that way, to be sure, then one will have to worry about whether one has got hold of a true or a false totality. One will worry about whether one has burrowed deeply enough (whether, for example, Derridean infrastructures, though doubtless deeper than mere Heideggerian *Existentiale*, may not conceal still deeper and more mysterious entities which underlie *them*). But if, with Wittgenstein, one starts to think of vocabularies as tools, then totality is no longer a problem. One will be content to use lots of different vocabularies for one's different purposes, without worrying much about their relation to one another. (In particular, one will be more willing to accept a private-public split: using one set of words in one's dealings with others, and another when engaged in self-creation.) The idea of an overview of the entire realm of possibility (one made possible by having penetrated to the conditionless conditions of that realm) seems, from this Wittgensteinian angle, crazy. For we nominalists think that the realm of possibility expands whenever somebody thinks up a new vocabulary, and thereby discloses (or invents–the difference is beside any relevant point) a new set of possible worlds.

Nominalists see language as just human beings using marks and noises to get what they want. One of the things we want to do with language is to get food, another is to get sex, another is to understand the origin of the universe. Another is to enhance our sense of human solidarity, and still another may be to create oneself by developing one's own private, autonomous, philosophical language. It is possible that a single vocabulary might serve two or more of these aims, but there is no reason to think that there is any great big meta-vocabulary which will somehow get at the least common denominator of all the various uses of all the various marks and noises which we use for all these various purposes. So there is no reason to lump these uses together into something big called 'Language', and then to look for its 'condition of possibility', any more than to lump all our beliefs about the spatio-temporal world together into something called 'experience' and then look, as Kant did, for *its* 'condition of possibility'. Nor is there any reason to lump all attempts to formulate great big new vocabularies, made by people with many different purposes (for example, Plato, St Paul, Newton, Marx, Freud, Heidegger), into something called 'the discourse of philosophy' and then to look for conditions of the possibility of that discourse.

II

How does one go about deciding whether to read Derrida my way or Gasché's way? How does one decide whether he is really a much-misunderstood transcentental 'philosopher of reflection', a latter-day Hegel, or really a much-misunderstood nominalist, a sort of French Wittgenstein?[21] Not easily. Derrida makes noises of both sorts. Sometimes he warns us against the attempt to hypostatize something called 'language'. Thus early in *Of Grammatology* he says 'This inflation of the sign "language" is the inflation of the sign itself, absolute inflation, inflation itself' (6). But, alas, he immediately goes on to talk in a grandiloquent, Hegel-Heidegger, 'destiny of Europe' tone about how 'a historico-metaphysical epoch *must* finally determine as language the totality of its problematic horizon'.[22]

Derrida himself, I have to admit, used to use words like 'rigorous' a lot. There is a lot in his early work which chimes with Gasché's interpretation.[23] But as he moves along from the early criticisms of Husserl through *Glas* to texts like the 'Envois' section of *The Post Card*, the tone has changed. I should like to think of Derrida as moving away from the academic, 'standard rules of philosophy' manner of his early work to a manner more like the later Wittgenstein's. Indeed, I should like to see his early work as something of a false start, in the same way that *Being and Time* seems to me, in the light of Heidegger's later work, to have been a false start, and as Wittgenstein thought his *Tractatus* had been a false start.

But perhaps it is just too soon for a judgement to be rendered on whether Gasché or I am looking at Derrida from the right angle, or whether we both may not be somewhat squinty-eyed. For Derrida is, to put it mildly, still going strong. Still, it may be a service to those coming to Derrida for the first time to have a choice between opposed readings at their disposal.

NOTES

1 Jonathan Culler, *On Deconstruction* (Ithaca, NY: Cornell University Press, 1982), 28.
2 See my 'Deconstruction and Circumvention', *Critical Inquiry*, 11 (1984), 1–23.

3 Culler, 85.

4 See Norris's 'Philosophy as *not* just a "kind of writing"': Derrida and the claim of reason' and my 'Two senses of "logocentrism": a reply to Norris', both in *Redrawing the Lines: Analytic Philosophy, Deconstruction and Literary Theory*, ed. Reed Way Dasenbrock (Minneapolis: University of Minnesota Press, 1988).

5 Culler, 153.

6 For a partial list of those who make this sort of charge, and my attempt to reply to it, see my 'Thugs and Theorists: A Reply to Bernstein', *Political Theory* 15 (November 1987), 564–80. A fuller reply can be found in my *Contingency, Irony and Solidarity* (Cambridge: Cambridge University Press, 1988). In that book I claim that 'theory' cannot do much to bring the excluded in from the margins–to enlarge the community whose consensus sets the standards of objectivity–but that other kinds of writing (notably novels and newspaper stores) can do quite a lot.

7 Christopher Norris, *Derrida* (Cambridge, MA: Harvard University Press, 1987), 156.

8 See, especially, chapter 6 ('From Ironist Theory to Private Allusions: Derrida') of *Contingency, Irony and Solidarity*. The original title of this chapter, which I sometimes wish I had retained, was 'From Ironist Theory to Private Jokes'.

9 Norris, 183. also: '[D]econstruction is a Kantian enterprise in ways that few of its commentators have so far been inclined to acknowledge' (94).

10 Rodolphe Gasché, *The Tain of the Mirror* (Baltimore: Johns Hopkins University Press, 1986), 8.

11 There is no interesting least common denominator of, for example, Rawls, Croce, Frege, Nietzsche and Gödel–no feature which makes them all representative of the same natural kind. One can only explain why all six are studied within a single academic department by developing a complicated historico-sociological story.

12 Another way of putting this point is to note that each successive figure in the tradition in question has had to invent his own 'central problem of philosophy' rather than work on some issue previously agreed to be problematic. Consider, in this light, Gasché's claim that 'Arche-writing is a construct aimed at resolving the philosophical problem of the very possibility (not primarily the empirical fact, which always suffers exceptions), of the usurpation, parasitism and contamination of an ideality, a generality, a universal by what is considered its other, its exterior, its incarnation, its appearance, and so on' (274). Nobody knew *that* was a 'philosophical problem' before Derrida came along, any more than we knew that 'the conditions of the possibility of synthetic a priori judgments' was a problem before Kant came along.

13 See Jurgen Habermas, *The Philosophical Discourse of Modernity* (Cambridge, MA: MIT Press, 1987); Rudolf Carnap, 'The Overcoming of Metaphysics through the Logical Analysis of Language' in *Logical Positivism*, ed. A. J. Ayer (Glencoe, IL: Free Press, 1963).

14 Consider Gasché's claim that Derrida has 'demonstrated' that 'the source of all being beyond being is *generalized*, or rather *general*, writing' (176). This is just the sort of claim which inspired the logical positivists to say that metaphysics lacked 'cognitive status'. Their point was that such a claim cannot be 'demonstrated', unless 'demonstration' means something very different from 'can be argued for on the basis of generally shared beliefs'.

15 For Tugendhat's Wittgensteinian working-through of Frege's holistic dictum ('only in the context of a sentence does a word have meaning') see his *Traditional and Analytic Philosophy* (Cambridge, MA: MIT Press, 1984) and my review of that book in *Journal of Philosophy* 82 (1985), 220–9. For his use of the resulting repudiation of the non-propositional to criticize 'the philosophy of reflection', see his *Self-Consciousness and Self-Determination* (Cambridge, MA: MIT Press, 1986), especially the claim that 'the phenomenon of justification and the question of justifying what is considered true is actually nowhere to be found in Hegel' (294). On the attempts of 'the philosophy of reflection' to work at a sub-propositional level, to get behind sentences to 'the conditions of possibility' of sentences, see my 'Strawson's Objectivity Argument', *Review of Metaphysics* 24 (December 1970), 207–44. In that paper I try to show how Kant's search for 'conditions of the possibility of experience' requires him to violate his own claim that we cannot know anything that is not a possible experience. I argue that the temptation to go transcendental (i.e., to search for non-causal conditions of possibility) is lessened (though not, alas, eliminated) once the 'linguistic turn' is taken. Gasché, by contrast, believes that 'the method of reflection' (the one common to Hegel, Heidegger and, on his view, Derrida) can survive the linguistic turn; he claims, for example, that Austin 'hinged the entire representational function of language . . . on a constituting self-reflexivity of the linguistic act' (76). I criticize the idea of transcendental argumentation at greater length in 'Verificationism and Transcendental Arguments', *Nous* 5 (1971), 3–14, and in 'Transcendental Argument, Self-Reference, and Pragmatism' in *Transcendental Arguments and Science*, ed. Peter Bieri, Rolf-P. Horstman and Lorenz Kruger (Dordrecht: Reidel 1979), 77–103.

16 'For Tugendhat, and the analytic tradition he represents, knowledge and truth can only be propositional. . . . [But] by eliminating altogether the ontological dimension of self-identity in self-consciousness (and, for that matter, in absolute reflection), one deprives oneself of the possibility of thinking the very foundations of propositional knowledge and truth, as well as of the very idea of epistemic self-consciousness. . . . Without the presupposition of ontological or formal-ontological identity of being and thought, of subject and object, of the knower and what is known, there is no ground for any propositional attribution whatsoever' (Gasché, 77). On the 'analytic' view I share with Tugendhat and Habermas, the very idea of a 'ground' for 'propositional attribution' is a mistake. The practice of playing sentences off against one another in order to decide what to believe–the practice of argumentation–no more requires a 'ground' than the practice of using one stone to chip pieces off another stone in order to make a spear-point.

17 Gasché, 122.

18 Gasché, 136.

19 Gasché, 139. Gasché thinks that the confusion of Derrida's enterprise with such a *Verflüssigung* is one of the 'dominant misconceptions' of deconstruction. He views American Derrida-fans as especially prone to such misconceptions, in particular to the misconception that Derrida 'literarizes' philosophy.

20 Gasché, 45. For a discussion of Davidson's work as a break with the notion of language as medium, see the first chapter of my *Contingency, Irony and Solidarity*.

21 See Henry Staten, *Wittgenstein and Derrida* (Lincoln: University of Nebraska

Press, 1984: 'The deconstructive critique of language could even be phrased as a *denial that there is language*' (20).

22 I have criticized Derrida's tendency to adopt this tone in 'Deconstruction and Circumvention'. For a more general criticism of the Heideggerian, un-'playful' side of Derrida, see Barbara Herrnstein Smith, 'Changing Places: the Transformation of Deconstruction' in her *Contingencies of Value* (Cambridge, MA: Harvard University Press, 1988). Smith argues that '"the metaphysics of Western thought" *is* thought, all of it, root and branch, everywhere and always' and that 'as figure and ground change places, the unravelling of Western metaphysics weaves another Western metaphysics'. I agree, and take the point to be that each generation's irony is likely to become the next generation's metaphysics. Metaphysics is, so to speak, irony gone public and flat—liquefaction congealed, providing a new ground on which to inscribe new figures. From my angle, the attempt to make Derrida into somebody who has discovered some 'philosophical truths' is a premature flattening-out of Derrida's irony. I think that he ought to be kept fluid a while longer before being congealed (as eventually he must be) into one more set of philosophical views, suitable for doxographic summary.

23 Gasché himself expresses doubt (page 4) that his way of reading Derrida works for some of Derrida's later writings.

Albert Leventure with Thomas Keenan

A Bibliography of the Works of Jacques Derrida

BOOKS

1962

1 Introduction to *L'origine de la géométrie* by Edmund Husserl. Epiméthée, Essais Philosophiques, Collection fondée par Jean Hyppolite (Paris: Presses Universitaires de France, 1962). Eng. trans. (of the 2nd French edn) and preface by John P. Leavey, Jr., *Edmund Husserl's 'Origin of Geometry': An Introduction* (Stony Brook, NY: Nicolas Hays, 1978; Brighton: Harvester Press, 1978). Repr. University of Nebraska Press, 1989, with a new afterword by the translator.

1967

2 *La voix et le phénomène: introduction au problème du signe dans le phénoménologie de Husserl* (Paris: Presses Universitaires de France, 1967). Eng. trans. and introduction by David B. Allison, *Speech and Phenomena: And Other Essays on Husserl's Theory of Signs*; preface by Newton Garver (Evanston, IL: Northwestern University Press, 1973). Also contains two other essays: 'La forme et le vouloir-dire: note sur la phénoménologie du langage'/'Form and Meaning: A Note on the Phenomenology of Language', and 'La différance'/'Differance'. Chap. 1, 'Sign and Signs', and other material incorporated into the book, was published as 'Jacques Derrida's Husserl interpretation: text and commentary', in *Philosophy Today*, 11, 2/4, 1967, pp.106–23. This text has been condensed from the 130 pages that Derrida prepared, but did not deliver, for the American Phenomenology Society at Pennsylvania State Univesity in October 1966. Material selected and trans. F. Joseph Smith, who also supplied the commentary. An extract from the book also appears in *A Derrida Reader* (see Books, no. 30).

3 *De la grammatologie* (Paris: Editions de Minuit, 1967). Eng. trans. and preface by Gayatri Chakravorty Spivak, *Of Grammatology* (Baltimore: Johns Hopkins

University Press, 1976). In her preface (see especially pp. lxxix–lxxxv) Spivak delineates some of the emendations performed by Derrida between the first appearance of the work as a two-part review article (see Texts no. 9) and its publication in book form. Eng. trans. of pt 1, chap. 2, 'Linguistics and Grammatology', pubd in *Sub-Stance*, 10, 1974, pp. 127–81. Opening section of pt 1, 'The End of the Book and the Beginning of Writing', repr. in *Philosophy Looks at the Arts: Contemporary Readings in Aesthetics*, ed. Joseph Margolis (Philadelphia: Temple University Press, 1986). Extracts anthologized in *Critical Theory Since 1965*, ed. Hazard Adams and Leroy Searle (Tallahassee: University Presses of Florida and Florida State University Press, 1986); *The Theory of Criticism: from Plato to the Present*, ed. Raman Selden (New York and London: Longman, 1988); *Contemporary Critical Theory*, ed. Dan Latimer (New York: Harcourt Brace Jovanovich, 1989); *A Derrida Reader* and *Acts of Literature* (see Books, nos. 30, 32).

4 *L'écriture et la différence* (Paris: Seuil, 1967). Eng. trans. with introduction and additional notes by Alan Bass, *Writing and Difference* (Chicago: University of Chicago Press, 1978; London: Routledge & Kegan Paul, 1978).
   'Force et signification'/'Force and Signification'
   'Cogito et histoire de la folie'/'Cogito and the History of Madness'
   'Edmond Jabès et la question du livre'/'Edmond Jabès and the Question of the Book'
   'Violence et métaphysique: essai sur la pensée d'Emmanuel Levinas'/'Violence and Metaphysics: An Essay on the Thought of Emmanuel Levinas'
   '"Genèse et structure" et la phénoménologie'/'"Genesis and Structure" and Phenomenology'
   'La parole soufflée'
   'Freud et la scène de l'écriture'/'Freud and the Scene of Writing'
   'Le théâtre de la cruauté et la clôture de la représentation'/'The Theatre of Cruelty and the Closure of Representation'
   'De l'économie restreinte à l'économie générale: un hégélianisme sans réserve'/ 'From Restricted to General Economy: A Hegelianism without Reserve'
   'La structure, le signe et le jeu dans le discours des sciences humaines'/ 'Structure, Sign, and Play in the Discourse of the Human Sciences'
   'L'ellipse'/'Ellipsis'
   Excerpts from *L'écriture* have been published in *Panorama des idées contemporaines*, ed. Gaëtan Picon (Paris: Gallimard, 1968) and in *La philosophie contemporaine en cent textes choisis*, ed. D. Huisman and A. Verges (Paris: Ferdinant Nathan, 1973).

1972

5 *La dissémination* (Paris: Seuil, 1972). Eng. trans., with introduction and additional notes, by Barbara Johnson, *Dissemination* (Chicago: University of Chicago Press, 1981; London: Athlone Press, 1981).
   'Hors livre'/'Outwork, Prefacing'
   'La pharmacie de Platon'/'Plato's Pharmacy'

'La double séance'/'The Double Session'
'La dissémination'/'Dissemination'

6 *Marges de la philosophie* (Paris: Editions de Minuit, 1972). Eng. trans. and additional notes by Alan Bass, *Margins of Philosophy* (Chicago: University of Chicago Press, 1982; Brighton: Harvester Press, 1982).
'Tympan'
'La différance'/'Differance'
'*Ousia et Grammé*: note sur une note de *Sein und Zeit*'/'*Ousia* and *Grammé*: Note on a Note from *Being and Time*'
'Le puits et la pyramide: introduction à la sémiologie de Hegel'/'The Pit and the Pyramid: Introduction to Hegel's Semiology'
'Les fins de l'homme'/'The Ends of Man'
'Le cercle linguistique de Gèneve'/'The Linguistic Circle of Geneva'
'La Forme et le vouloir-dire: note sur la phénoménologie du langage'/'Form and Meaning: A Note on the Phenomenology of Language'
'Le supplément de copule: la philosophie devant la linguistique'/'The Supplement of Copula: Philosophy before Linguistics'
'La mythologie blanche (la métaphore dans le texte philosophique)'/'White Mythology: Metaphor in the Text of Philosophy'
'Qual, quelle: les sources de Valéry'/'Qual Quelle: Valery's Sources'
'Signature evénement contexte'/'Signature Event Context'

7 *Positions* (Paris: Editions de Minuit, 1972). Eng. trans. and annotations by Alan Bass, *Positions* (Chicago: University of Chicago Press, 1981; London: Athlone Press, 1981).
'Implications: entretien avec Henri Ronse'/'Implications: Interview with Henri Ronse'
'Sémiologie et grammatologie: entretien avec Julia Kristeva'/'Semiology and Grammatology: Interview with Julia Kristeva'
'Positions: entretien avec Jean-Louis Houdebine et Guy Scarpetta'/'Positions: Interview with Jean-Louis Houdebine and Guy Scarpetta'
Also contains fragments of letters exchanged betwen Derrida and Houdebine, dated, respectively, 15 July and 1 July 1971.

1974

8 *Glas* (Paris: Editions Galilée, 1974); 2 vols. (Paris: Denoël/Gonthier, 1981). Eng. trans. John P. Leavey, Jr., and Richard Rand, *Glas* (Lincoln and London: University of Nebraska Press, 1986). Brief passages of Leavey's trans. pubd as 'Jacques Derrida's *Glas*: A Translated Selection and some Comments on an Absent Colossus', in *Clio*, 11, 4, Summer 1982, pp. 327–37. For the complement to *Glas*, see *Glassary* by John P. Leavey, Jr. (Lincoln and London: University of Nebraska Press, 1986). An extract from *Glas* appears in *A Derrida Reader* (see Books, no. 30).

1976

9 *L'archéologie du frivole: lire Condillac* (Paris: Denoël/Gonthier, 1976). Eng. trans. and introduction by John P. Leavey, Jr., *The Archeology of the Frivolous: Reading Condillac* (Pittsburgh: Duquesne University Press, 1980). Repr. University of Nebraska Press, 1987.

10 *Eperons, Sporen, Spurs, Sproni* (Venice: Corbo e Fiore, 1976); quadrilingual presentation. French version (Paris: Aubier-Flammarion, 1978) as *Éperons: les styles de Nietzsche*; bilingual version (French and English, trans. Barbara Harlow; introduction by Stefano Agosti; drawings by François Loubrieu) (Chicago: University of Chicago Press, 1979) as *Spurs: Nietzsche's Styles*. Extract pubd in *A Derrida Reader* (see Books, no. 30).

1977

11 *Limited Inc* (Baltimore: Johns Hopkins University Press, 1977). This is the French text which originally appeared in *Glyph*, 2, 1977, pubd as a suppl. to its Eng. trans. by Samuel Weber; see Texts, nos. 62, 203, Books, no. 24.

1978

12 *La vérité en peinture* (Paris: Aubier-Flammarion, 1978). Eng. trans. and preface by Geoff Bennington and Ian McLeod, *The Truth in Painting* (Chicago: University of Chicago Press, 1987).
'Passe-Partout'
'Le Parergon'/'Parergon'
'+R (par dessus le marché)'/'+R (Into the Bargain)'
'Cartouches'
'Restitutions de la vérité en pointure'/'Restitutions of the Truth in Pointing'
'Passe-Partout' and an excerpt from '+R' in *Art and Design*, 4, 3–4, 1988, pp. 19–25.

1980

13 *La carte postale: de Socrate à Freud et au-delà* (Paris: Aubier-Flammarion, 1980). Eng. trans. with introduction and additional notes by Alan Bass, *The Post Card: from Socrates to Freud and Beyond* (Chicago: University of Chicago Press, 1987).
'Envois'
'Spéculer–sur "Freud"'/'To Speculate–on "Freud"'
'Le facteur de la vérité'
'Du tout'
Extract from 'To Speculate–on "Freud"' in *On Signs*, ed. Marshall Blonsky (Baltimore: Johns Hopkins University Press, 1985; Oxford: Blackwell, 1985), pp. 236–58. Another version, 'Speculations–on Freud', Ian McLeod, in *Oxford Literary Review*, 3, 2, 1978, pp. 78–97.

1982

14 *L'oreille de l'autre: transferts, traductions, otobiographies: textes et débats avec Jacques Derrida* (Montréal: VLB Editions, 1982). Eng. trans. Peggy Kamuf and Avital Ronell, *The Ear of the Other: Otobiography, Transference, Translation: Texts and Discussions with Jacques Derrida*, ed. with preface, by Christie V. McDonald (New York: Schocken Books, 1985); repubd with new preface and the inclusion of 'Choreographies' (University of Nebraska Press, 1988); –see Texts no. 97. Fragment from 'Otobiographies', 'All Ears: Nietzsche's Otobiography', pubd in *Yale French Studies*, 63, 1982, pp. 245–50. *Otobiographies: l'enseignement de Nietzsche et la politique du nom propre* (Paris: Editions Galilée, 1984), contains only the essay on Nietzsche, which is repr. as 'The Teaching of Nietzsche and the Politics of the Proper Name' in *Modern Critical Views: Friedrich Nietzsche*, ed. Harold Bloom (New York: Chelsea House, 1987), pp. 105–34.

L'oreille de l'autre is the result of a colloquium held at the University of Montreal, 22–4 October 1979. 'Nietzsche's Otobiography' was delivered in spring 1982 at Yale, Emory and the University of Florida.

1983

15 *D'un ton apocalyptique adopté naguère en philosophie* (Paris: Editions Galilée, 1983). Eng. trans. John P. Leavey, Jr., in *Semeia* and *Oxford Literary Review*. See Texts, no. 84.

1984

16 *Feu la cendre/cio'che resta del fuoco* (Florence: Sansoni, 1984; Paris: Editions des femmes, 1987); bilingual presentation; Ital. trans. Stefano Agosti. Eng. trans. Ned Lukacher, *Cinders*, in preparation, to be pubd in a bilingual edn (University of Nebraska Press). See also entry under Recording.

17 *Signéponge/Signsponge* (New York: Columbia University Press, 1984; Paris: Seuil, 1988); bilingual presentation; Eng. trans Richard Rand. A fragment of this text appeared in an earlier translation of Rand's in *Oxford Literary Review*, 5, 1–2, 1982, pp. 102–12; in the same issue, pp. 96–101, appears 'Signsponge 2', trans. Geoff Bennington and Richard Rand. Fragments of *Signéponge* pubd in *Ponge Inventeur et Classique*, ed. Philippe Bonnefis and O. Oster (Paris: Union Générale d'Editions, 1975), pp. 115–44; and in *Digraphe*, 8, April 1976, pp. 17–39; these extracts, and the text pubd in *OLR* as 'Signsponge 2', constitute most of the French text of *Signéponge*. The Columbia University edn includes the introduction (pp. 3–17), fills in two gaps (pp. 135–45, 145–7), adds the postscripts, and deletes the introductory notes and the discussion from the first versions. These missing portions, absent from the UGE and *Digraphe* publications, are to be found in 'Signéponge'. *Cahiers de l'Herne: Francis Ponge* (Paris: Editions de l'Herne, 1986), ed. Jean-Marie Gleize, pp. 438–50.

Part of 'Signéponge' was originally delivered as a lecture at a colloquium on Francis Ponge held at Cerisy-la-Salle in July 1975.

1986

18 *Mémoires for Paul de Man*, trans. Cecile Lindsay, Jonathan Culler and Eduardo Cadava (New York: Columbia University Press, 1986). *Mémoires pour Paul de Man* (Paris: Editions Galilée, 1988) includes Derrida's preface to the work and 'Comme le bruit de la mer au fond d'un coquillage: la guerre de Paul de Man' (see Texts, no. 192) and 'In Memoriam' (see Texts, no. 148). Enlarged edn (New York: Columbia University Press, 1989) includes material hitherto available only in the French version.

Mémoires for Paul de Man was written in January–February 1984, and first delivered (in French) at Yale University, and as the Wellek Library lectures at the University of California at Irvine, in March of that year.

19 *Parages* (Paris: Editions Galilée, 1986). Eng. trans. John P. Leavey, Jr. in preparation (University of Nebraska Press).
    Introduction
    'Pas'
    'Survivre: journal de bord'/'Living On: Border Lines'
    'Titre (à préciser)'/'Title (To be Specified)'
    'La loi du genre'/'The Law of Genre'

20 *Schibboleth, pour Paul Celan* (Paris: Editions Galilée, 1986). Eng. trans. Joshua Wilner of 'Shibboleth', in *Midrash and Literature*, ed. Geoffrey Hartman and Sanford Budick (New Haven, CT: Yale University Press, 1986), pp. 307–47, reproduces Derrida's lecture version (given in Seattle) of the text, which was enlarged for its publication in book form. Part of the Seattle version of 'Shibboleth' repr. in *Cahiers de l'archipel*, 13, April 1985, pp. 140–43, and in *Argumentum e silentio*, ed. Amy D. Colin (Berlin and New York: Walter de Greyter, 1987); an extract from the augmented version appears in *Acts of Literature* (see Books, no. 32). Complete text in *Word Traces*, ed. Aris Fioretis (Baltimore: Johns Hopkins University Press, 1992).

'Shibboleth' was first delivered at a conference on the work of Paul Celan held at the University of Washington, Seattle, on 14 October 1984.

1987

21 *De l'esprit: Heidegger et la question* (Paris: Editions Galilée, 1987). Eng. trans. Geoffrey Bennington and Rachel Bowlby, *Of Spirit: Heidegger and the Question* (Chicago: University of Chicago Press, 1989). Excerpts from the first five chaps, selected by Arnold I. Davidson, in *Critical Inquiry*, 15, 2, Winter 1989, pp. 457–74. Included, with the *'Geschlecht'* texts (see Texts, nos. 112, 175), in *Heidegger et la question: De l'esprit et autres essais* (Paris: Flammarion, 1990). See Texts, no. 190.

22 *Psyche: inventions de l'autre* (Paris: Editions Galilée, 1987).
'Psyché: invention de l'autre'/'Psyche: Invention(s) of the Other'
'Le retrait de la métaphore'/'The *retrait* of Metaphor'
'Ce qui reste à force de musique'
'Envoi'/'Sending: On Representation'
'Moi–la psychanalyse'/'Me–Psychoanalysis'
'En ce moment même dans cet ouvrage me voici'/'At This Very Moment in This Work Here I am'
'Des Tours de Babel'
'Télépathie'/'Telepathy'
'Ex-abrupto'
'Les morts de Roland Barthes'/'The Deaths of Roland Barthes
'Une idée de Flaubert: la lettre de Platon'/'An Idea of Flaubert: "Plato's Letter"'
'Géopsychanalyse–et "the rest of the world"'/'Geopsychoanalysis: "and the rest of the world"'
'Le dernier mot du racisme'/'Racism's Last Word'
'No Apocalypse, Not Now (à toute vitesse, sept missiles, sept missives)'/'No Apocalypse, Not Now (Full Speed Ahead, Seven Missiles, Seven Missives)'
'Lettre à un ami japonais'/'Letter to a Japanese Friend'
'*Geschlecht*: différence sexuelle, différence ontologique'/'*Geschlecht*: Sexual Difference, Ontological Difference'
'La main de Heidegger (*Geschlecht* II)'/'*Geschlecht* II: Heidegger's Hand'
'Admiration de Nelson Mandela: ou les lois de la réflexion'/'The Laws of Reflection: Nelson Mandela, in Admiration'
'Point de folie–maintenant l'architecture'
'Pourquoi Peter Eisenman écrit de si bons livres'/'Why Peter Eisenman Writes Such Good Books'
'52 aphorismes pour un avant-propos'/'52 Aphorisms for a Foreword'
'L'aphorisme à contretemps'/'Aphorism Countertime'
'Comment ne pas parler: dénégations'/'How to Avoid Speaking: Denials'
'Désistance'/'Desistance'
'Nombre de oui'/'A Number of Yes (Nombre de oui)'

23 *Ulysse gramophone: deux mots pour Joyce* (Paris: Editions Galilée, 1987).
'Deux mots pour Joyce'/'Two Words for Joyce'
'Ulysse gramophone: ouï-dire de Joyce'/'Ulysses Gramophone: Hear Say Yes in Joyce'

1988

24 *Limited Inc*, trans. Samuel Weber and Jeffrey Mehlman, ed. Gerald Graff (Evanston, IL: Northwestern University Press, 1988). (See Books, no. 11 and Texts, nos. 62, 203). French edn, trans. Elisabeth Weber (Paris: Editions Galilée, 1990).
'Signature Event Context'

'Limited Inc abc . . .'
'Afterword: Toward an Ethic of Discussion'

1990

25 *Du droit à la philosophie* (Paris: Editions Galilée, 1990).
'Privilège: titre justificatif et remarques introductives'
'Où commence et comment finit un corps enseignant'
'La crise de l'enseignement philosophique'
'L'âge de Hegel'/'The Age of Hegel'
'La philosophie et ses classes'
'Les corps divisés'
'Philosophie des États Généraux'
'Le langage et les institutions philosophiques'/'Languages and Institutions of Philosophy'
'Mochlos–ou le conflit des facultés'
'Ponctuations: le temps de la thèse'/'The Time of a Thesis: Punctuations'
'Les pupilles de l'Université: le principe de raison et l'idée de l'Université'/'The Principle of Reason: The University in the Eyes of its Pupils'
'Éloge de la philosophie'
'Les antinomies de la discipline philosophique'
'Popularités: du droit à la philosophie du droit'
'Qui a peur de la philosophie?'
'Titres'
'Coups d'envoi'/'Sendoffs'
'Rapport de la Commission de Philosophie et d'Épistémologie'

26 *Mémoires d'aveugle: l'autoportrait et autres ruines* (Paris: Réunion des Musées Nationaux, 1990). Extracts, with illustrations, in *Libération*, 24 October 1990, pp. 44–5 ('De l'invisible à l'origine du dessein'); *Les lettres françaises*, 4, December 1990, pp. 3–4 (text untitled); *Art International*, 14, spring/summer 1991 ('Memories of a Blind Man: The Self-Portrait and Other Ruins', trans. Thomas West), pp. 82–7; *Art in America*, 79, 4, April 1991, pp. 47–53 (Meyer Raphael Rubinstein, 'Sight Unseen', trans. Richard Miller).
   Mémoires d'aveugle is the catalogue of drawings chosen by Derrida to accompany an exhibition in the 'Parti pris' cycle, held at the Louvre from 26 October 1990 to 21 January 1991.

27 *Le problème de la genèse dans la philosophie de Husserl* (Paris: Presses Universitaires de France, 1990).

1991

28 *Jacques Derrida* (in collaboration with Geoffrey Bennington) (Paris: Seuil, 1991). Derrida's contribution is entitled 'Circonfession'.

29 *L'autre cap* (Paris: Editions de Minuit, 1991). This includes 'La démocratie ajournée' [see Texts no. 229]. It is translated by Pascale-Anne Brault and Michael Naas as *The Other Heading: Reflections on Today's Europe* (Bloomington: Indiana, forthcoming), and includes 'Call it a Day for Democracy'.

30 *A Derrida Reader: Between the Blinds* ed. with introduction and notes, Peggy Kamuf (New York: Columbia University Press, 1991; Brighton: Harvester Wheatsheaf, 1991).

　Speech and Phenomena (extract)
　Of Grammatology (extract)
　'Différance'
　'Signature Event Context'
　'Plato's Pharmacy' (extract)
　'Tympan'
　'The Double Session' (extract)
　'Psyche: Inventions of the Other' (extract)
　'Che cos'è la poesia?'
　'Des Tours de Babel' (extract)
　'Living On: Border Lines' (extract)
　'Letter to a Japanese Friend'
　'Restitutions of the Truth in Pointing' (extract)
　Glas (extract)
　Spurs: Nietzsche's Styles (extract)
　'*Geschlecht*: Sexual Difference, Ontological Difference'
　'At This Very Moment in This Work Here I Am' (extract)
　'Choreographies' (extract)
　'Le facteur de la vérité' (extract)
　'Envois' (extract)
　'To Speculate–on "Freud"' (extract)
　'Ulysses Gramophone: Hear Say Yes in Joyce' (extract)

31 *Donner le temps I: la fausse monnaie* (Paris: Editions Galilée, 1991). Eng. trans. Peggy Kamuf (University of Chicago Press, forthcoming). Chap. 1, 'Given Time: The time of the King', in *Critical Inquiry* (forthcoming).

32 *Acts of Literature*, ed. Derek Attridge (London and New York: Routledge, 1991).
　'"This Strange Institution Called Literature": An Interview with Jacques Derrida'
　'"That Dangerous Supplement . . ."' (extract from *Of Grammatology*)
　'Mallarmé'
　'The First Session' (extract from 'The Double Session')
　'Before the Law'
　'The Law of Genre'
　'Ulysses Gramophone: Hear Say Yes in Joyce'
　'Psyche: Invention of the Other' (extract)

Signsponge (extract)
'Shibboleth: for Paul Celan' (extract)
'Aphorism Countertime'

1992

33 *Institutions of Philosophy*, ed. Deborah Esch and Thomas Keenan (Cambridge, MA, and London: Harvard University Press, 1992).

34 *Negotiations: Writings*, ed. Deborah Esch and Thomas Keenan (Minneapolis: University of Minnesota Press, 1992).

TEXTS

1963

1 'Force et signification'. *Critique*, 19, 193–4 (1963), pp. 483–99, 619–36. Repr. in *L'écriture et la différence/Writing and Difference*; see Books, no. 4.
2 'Cogito et histoire de la folie'. *Revue de métaphysique et de morale*, 68, 4 (1963), pp. 460–94. Repr. in *L'écriture et la différence/Writing and Difference*; see Books, no. 4). Extract in *Descartes: textes et débats*, ed. Geneviève Rodis-Lewis (Paris: Librarie Générale Française, 1985).
   'With the exception of several notes and a short passage (in brackets), this paper is the reproduction of a lecture given 4 March 1963 at the Collège Philosophique.' Derrida

1964

3 'A propos de Cogito et histoire de la folie'. *Revue de métaphysique et de morale*, 69, 1 (1964), pp. 116–19.
4 'Edmond Jabès et la question du livre'. *Critique*, 20, 201 (1964), pp. 99–115. Repr. in *L'écriture et la différence/Writing and Difference*; see Books, no. 4.
5 'Violence et métaphysique: essai sur la pensée d'Emmanuel Levinas'. *Revue de métaphysique et de morale*, 69, 3–4 (1964), pp. 322–45, 425–73. Repr. with alterations in *L'écriture et la différence / Writing and Difference*; see Books, No. 4. Certain of the revisions made by Derrida between the original appearance of the essay and its subsequent publication in *L'écriture* are recorded by Robert Bernasconi in 'The Trace of Levinas in Derrida', in *Derrida and Differance*, ed. David Wood and Robert Bernasconi (Coventry: Parousia Press, 1985; Evanston, IL: Northwestern University Press, 1988), pp. 13–29.

1965

6 '"Genèse et structure" et la phénoménologie'. *Entretiens sur les notions de genèse et de structure*, ed. Maurice de Gandillac, Lucian Goldmann and Jean Piaget (Paris

and The Hague: Mouton, 1965), pp. 243–60. Derrida also takes part in discussions after other papers: pp. 49, 178, 188, 236, 279, 282–3, 314–15. Repr. (without the discussion, pp. 261–8) in *L'écriture et la différence/Writing and Difference*; see Books, no. 4.
First delivered as a lecture at Cerisy-la-Salle in 1959.

7 'La parole soufflée'. *Tel Quel*, 20 (winter 1965), pp. 41–67. Repr. in *L'écriture et la différence/Writing and Difference*; see Books, no. 4.

8 'De la grammatologie'. *Critique*, 21, 223 (1965), pp. 16–42; 224 (1966), pp. 23–53. Repr. with substantial modifications in *De la grammatologie/Of Grammatology*; see Books, no. 3.

1966

9 'La Phénoménologie et la clôture de la métaphysique: introduction à la pensée de Husserl'. *Epoches*, 7 (February 1966), pp. 181–9.

10 'Freud et la scène de l'écriture'. *Tel Quel*, 26 (summer 1966), pp. 10–41. Repr. in *L'écriture et la différence/Writing and Difference*; see Books, no. 4. Repr. as 'Freud and the Scene of Writing', trans. Jeffrey Mehlman, in *Yale French Studies: French Freud, Structural Studies in Psychoanalysis*, 48 (1972), pp. 74–117, and in *Freud: A Collection of Critical Essays*, ed. Perry Meisel (Englewood Cliffs: Prentice-Hall, 1981), pp. 145–82; both omit the essay's preface and postface.
'This text is a fragment of a lecture given at the *Institute de psychanalyse*'. (At Andre Green's seminar)–Derrida

11 'Le théâtre de la cruauté et la clôture de la représentation'. *Critique*, 22, 230 (1966), pp. 595–618. Repr. in *L'écriture et la différence/Writing and Difference*; see Books, no. 4. Also available in *Theatre*, 9, 3 (1978), pp. 7–19.
Lecture delivered at the Antonin Artaud colloquium, International Festival of University Theatre, Parma, April 1966.

12 'Nature, culture, écriture (de Levi-Strauss à Rousseau)'. *Cahiers pour l'analyse*, 4 (September–October 1966), pp. 1–45. repr. in *De la grammatologie/Of Grammatology*; see Books, no. 3.

13 'La structure, le signe et le jeu dans le discours des sciences humaines'. *L'écriture et la différence/Writing and Difference*; see Books, no. 4. Eng. trans. of a revised version of this paper, as 'Structure, Sign and Play in the Discourse of the Human Sciences', by Richard Macksey, first appeared in *The Languages of Criticism and the Sciences of Man: The Structuralist Controversy*, ed. Macksey and Eugenio Donato (Baltimore: Johns Hopkins Univesity Press, 1970); when published in paperback format in 1972, the book's title and subtitle were reversed, thus becoming *The Structuralist Controversy*. Derrida participates in the discussion following the presentation of his paper (*The Structuralist Controversy*, pp. 265–72), and contributes to the discussions occasioned by Roland Barthes' 'To Write: An Intransitive Verb?' (ibid., pp. 155–6) and Jean-Pierre Vernant's 'Greek Tragedy: Problems of Interpretation' (ibid., p. 294).
'La structure, . . .', trans. Alan Bass, in *Critical Theory Since 1965*, ed. Hazard Adams and Leroy Searle (Tallahassee: University Presses of Florida and

Florida State University Press, 1986), pp. 83–93; *Literary Theories in Praxis*, ed. Shirley F. Staton (Philadelphia: University of Pennsylvania Press, 1987), pp. 390–409; *Debating Texts: A Reader in 20th Century Literary Theory and Method*, ed. Rick Rylance (Toronto and Buffalo: University of Toronto Press, 1987; Milton Keynes: Open University Press, 1987), pp. 123–36; *Twentieth-Century Literary Theory: An Introductory Anthology*, ed. Vassilis Lambropoulos and David Neal Miller (New York: Stony Brook, 1987), pp. 38–58. Extract in *Modern Literary Theory: A Reader*, ed. Philip Rice and Patricia Waugh (New York and London: Edward Arnold, 1989). Excerpts, 'reorganized and renumbered from the original' (*sic*), trans. Macksey, in *Twentieth-Century Literary Theory: A Reader*, ed. K. M. Newton (London: Macmillan, 1988), pp. 149–53. Macksey's trans. also repr. in *Contemporary Literary Criticism: Modernism Through Poststructuralism*, ed. Robert Con Davis (New York and London: (Longman, 1986), pp. 480–98; *Modern Criticism and Theory: A Reader*, ed. David Lodge (New York and London: Longman, 1988), pp. 229–48; *Contemporary Literary Criticism: Literary and Cultural Studies*, ed. Robert Con Davis and Ronald Schleifer (2nd edn, New York and London: Longman, 1989); Charles Kaplan and William Anderson, ed., *Criticism: The Major Statements* (New York: St Martin's Press, 1991) pp. 515–34.

Lecture delivered on 21 October 1966 at the International Colloquium on Critical Languages and the Sciences of Man, held at the Johns Hopkins University, Baltimore.

1967

14 'De l'économie restreinte à l'économie générale: un hégélianisme sans réserve'. *L'arc: Georges Bataille*, 32 (May 1967), pp. 24–44. Repr. in *L'écriture et la différence/Writing and Difference*; see Books, no. 4. Eng. trans. Alan Bass, 'From Restricted to General Economy: A Hegelianism without Reserve', in *Semiotext(e)*, 2, 2 (1976), pp. 25–55.

15 'La forme et le vouloir-dire: note sur la phénoménologie du langage'. *Revue internationale de philosophie*, 21, 81 (1967), pp. 277–99. Repr. in *Marges de la philosophie/Margins of Philosophy*; see Books, no. 6. Trans. David B. Allison, 'Form and Meaning: A Note on the Phenomenology of Language', in *Speech and Phenomena*; see 1967 Book entry.

16 'La linguistique de Rousseau'. *Revue internationale de philosophie*, 21, 82 (1967), pp. 443–62. Repr. with slight alterations as 'Le cercle linguistique de Genève' in *Marges de la philosophie/Margins of Philosophy*; see Books, no. 6. Also available in *Critical Inquiry*, 8 (summer 1982), pp. 675–91.

Lecture given at a colloquium on Jean-Jacques Rousseau held in London, 3–4 February 1967.

17 'Implications: entretien avec Henri Ronse'. *Les Lettres françaises*, 1211 (6–12 December 1967), pp. 6–14. Repr. in *Positions*; see Books, no. 7.

18 'L'ellipse'. *L'écriture et la différence/Writing and Difference*; see Books, no. 4.

1968

19 Comments by Derrida in Tania Bothezat, 'Lecturer to Visit Baltimore'. *Baltimore Sun* (2 February 1968), B3. Includes quotations, apparently from an interview in Paris.

20 '*Ouisia* et *Grammé*: note sur une note de *Sein und Zeit*'. *L'endurance de la pensée: pour saluer Jean Beaufret*, ed. Marcel Jouhandeau (Paris: Plon, 1968), pp. 219–66. Repr. in *Marges de la philosophie/Margins of Philosophy*; see Books, no. 6. Eng. trans. Edward Casey as '"Ousia" and "Grammé": A Note to a Footnote in *Being and Time*', in *Phenomenology in Perspective*, ed. F. Joseph Smith (The Hague: Nijhoff, 1970), pp. 54–93.

21 'Culture et écriture: la prolifération des livres et la fin du livre'. *Noroit*, 130 (August–September 1968), pp. 1, 5–12); [débat with Derrida], 132 (November 1968), pp. 3, 5–14.

22 'Sémiologie et grammatologie: entretien avec Julia Kristeva'. *Information sur les sciences sociales*, 7 (3 June 1968), pp. 135–48. Repr. in *Positions*; see Books, no. 7. Also in *Essays in Semiotics: Essais de sémiotique* (Approaches to Semiotics 4), ed. Julia Kristeva, Josette Rey-Debove and Donna Jean Unicker (Paris: The Hague and Mouton, 1971), pp. 11–27. Extracts in *Panorama des Sciences Humaines* (Paris: Gallimard, 1973), p. 582, as 'L'écriture: grammé et différance', and in *The Theory of Criticism: from Plato to the Present*, ed. Raman Selden (New York and London: Longman, 1988).

23 'La "différance"'. *Bulletin de la société française de philosophie*, 62, 3 (1968), pp. 73–101, and *Théorie d'ensemble*, coll. *Tel Quel* (Paris: Seuil, 1968), pp. 41–66. Repr. with slight alterations in *Marges de la philosophie/Margins of Philosophy*; see Books, no. 6. Also in *Speech and Phenomena*; see Books, no. 2. The discussion which followed the original presentation, although included in the *Bulletin*, is omitted from the four volumes referred to above. Eng. trans. David Wood, Sarah Richmond and Malcolm Barnard in *Derrida and Différance*, ed. David Wood and Robert Bernasconi (Coventry: Parousia Press, 1985; Evanston, IL: Northwestern University Press, 1988), pp. 83–95. The participants in the discussion are Derrida, G. Comtesse, Lucien Goldmann, J. Hersh, P. Kaufmann, Brice Parain, A. Philonenko and Jean Wahl. Trans. Alan Bass in *Deconstruction in Context*, ed. Mark C. Taylor (Chicago: University of Chicago Press, 1986), and in *Critical Theory Since 1965*, ed. Hazard Adams and Leroy Searle (Tallahassee: University Presses of Florida and Florida State University Press, 1986. Extract in *A Derrida Reader*; see Books, no. 30.

   'La "différance"' was first delivered as a lecture at a meeting of the Société française de philosophie, in the Amphithéâtre Michelet on 27 January 1968.

24 'The Ends of Man'. *Philosophy and Phenomenological Research*, 30, 1 (1969), pp. 31–57 (Eng. trans. Edouard Morot-Sir, Wesley C. Puisol, Hubert L. Dreyfus and Barbara Reid of 'Les fins de l'homme'). Repr. in *Marges de la philosophie/Margins of Philosophy*; see Books, no. 6. Also in Eng. trans. in *After Philosophy*, ed. Kenneth Baynes, James Bohman and Thomas Macarthy (Cambridge, MA: MIT Press, 1986).

The essay is dated by Derrida 12 May 1968. Lecture given at a French-American philosophers' conference on 'Philosophy and Anthropology', held on 18–19 October 1968, at the State University of New York Conference Center.

25 'La pharmacie de Platon'. *Tel Quel*, 32 (winter 1968), pp. 3–48; 33 (spring 1969), pp. 18–59. Repr. in *La dissémination/Dissemination*; see Books, no. 5. Also in *Platon: Phèdre*, ed. Luc Brisson (Paris: Flammarion, 1989). Extracts in *Literary Criticism and Theory: the Greeks to the Present*, ed. Robert Con Davis and Laurie Finke (London: Longman, 1989), and in *A Derrida Reader*; see Books, no. 30.

1969

26 'La dissémination'. *Critique*, 25, 261 (1969), pp. 99–139; 25, 262 (1969), pp. 215–49. Repr. in *La dissémination/Dissemination*; see Books, no. 5.

1970

27 'Le puits et la pyramide: introduction à la sémiologie de Hegel'. *Hegel et la pensée moderne*, ed. Jacques d'Hondt (Paris: Presses Universitaires de France, 1970), pp. 27–83. Repr. in *Marges de la philosophie/Margins of Philosophy*; see Books, no. 6. Eng. trans. Alphonso Lingis, as 'Speech and Writing According to Hegel', in *Man and World*, 11, 1–2 (1978), pp. 107–30; no acknowledgement is made that the text is an abridgement, omitting the final section (see Bass, *Margins*, pp. 96–108) and reproducing only two of Derrida's notes.
   Paper first presented at Jean Hyppolite's seminar at the Collège de France on 16 January 1968.

28 'D'un texte a l'écart'. *Les temps modernes*, 25, 284 (1970), pp. 1546–52.

29 'La double séance'. *Tel Quel*, 41 (spring 1970), pp. 3–43; 42 (summer 1970), pp. 3–45. Repr. in *La dissémination/Dissemination*; see Books, no. 5. Extract in *Acts of Literature*; see Books, no. 32.

1971

30 'La mythologie blanche (la métaphore dans le texte philosophique)'. *Poétique*, 5 (1971), pp. 1–52. Repr. in *Marges de la philosophie/Margins of Philosophy*; see Books, no. 6. Also in Eng. trans. by F. C. T. Moore as 'White Mythology: Metaphor in the Text of Philosophy', in *New Literary History*, 6, 1 (1974), pp. 5–74.

31 'Signature evénement contexte'. *La Communication II: Actes du XVe Congrès de l'Association des Sociétés de Philosophie de Langue Française* (Montreal: Editions Montmorency, 1973), pp. 393–431. Repr. (without the discussion, pp. 393–431) in *Marges de la philosophie/Margins of Philosophy*; see Books, no. 6. Eng. trans. Samuel Weber and Jeffrey Mehlman, as 'Signature Event Context', in *Glyph: Johns Hopkins Textual Studies*, 1 (1977), pp. 172–97; repr. in *Limited Inc* (Evanston, IL: Northwestern University Press, 1988; see Books, nos. 11, 24. Also in *A Derrida Reader*; see Books, no. 30. Participants in the round-table

discussion, presided over by René Schaerer, are Derrida, Ernest Joos, Paul Ricoeur, Roland Blume, Gilles Lane, Yvon Gauthier, Claude Pannccio, Clément Légairé, Roger Marcotte, Thomas De Koninck, Henry Declève and Jeanne Parain-Vial.

A communication delivered to the Congrès international des Sociétés de philosophie du langue française in Montréal, August 1971. The theme of the colloquium was 'Communication'.

32 'Positions: entretien avec Jean-Louis Houdebine et Guy Scarpetta'. *Promesse*, 30–1 (autumn–winter 1971), pp. 5–62. Repr., with some omissions, in *Positions*; see Books, no. 7. Eng. trans. Richard Klein in *Diacritics*, 2, 4 (1972), pp. 35–43; 3, 1 (1973), pp. 33–46; 3, 2 (1973), pp. 57–9. Interview with Derrida conducted on 17 June 1971, with 'certain complements' added to the transcription (see Bass, *Positions*, p. 38).

33 'Les sources de Valéry: Qual, Quelle'. *MLN* [Modern Language Notes], 87, 4 (1972), pp. 563–99. Repr. as 'Qual Quelle: les sources de Valéry', in *Marges de la philosophie/Margins of Philosophy*; see Books, no. 6.

Lecture given on 6 November 1971 at Johns Hopkins University on the centenary of Paul Valéry's birth.

34 'Le supplément de copule: la philosophie devant la linguistique'. *Langages*, 24 (December 1971), pp. 14–39. Repr. in *Marges de la philosophie/Margins of Philosophy*; see Books, no. 6. Eng. trans. David B. Allison as 'The Copula Supplement', in *Dialogues in Phenomenology*, ed. Don Ihde and Richard M. Zaner (The Hague: Nijhoff, 1975), pp. 7–48, and as 'The Supplement of Copula: Philosophy *Before* Linguistics', in *Georgia Review*, 30 (fall 1976), pp. 527–64. This trans. was used when the essay formed part of the collection *Textual Strategies: Perspectives in Post-Structuralist Criticism*, ed. Josué V. Harari (Ithaca, NY: Cornell University Press, 1979; London: Methuen, 1980), pp. 82–120.

1972

35 'Tympan'. *Marges de la philosophie/Margins of Philosophy*; see Books, no. 6. Repr. in *A Derrida Reader*; see Books, no. 30.

36 'Jacques Derrida: avoir l'oreille de la philosophie'. *La Quinzaine littéraire*, 152 (16–30 November 1972), pp. 13–16. Lucette Finas' interview with Derrida repr. in Lucette Finas, Sarah Kofman, Roger Laporte, Jean-Michel Rey, *Ecarts: quatre essais à propos de Jacques Derrida* (Paris: Fayard, 1973), pp. 303–12.

37 'Hors livre'. *La dissémination/Dissemination*; see Books, no. 5.

38 *Les nouveaux cahiers*, 31 (winter 1972–3), p. 56. Derrida reconstitutes his first impressions of encountering Edmond Jabès' *Le Livre des Questions*.

1973

39 'La question du style'. *Nietzsche aujourd'hui?* I: *Intensités* (Paris: Union Générale d'Éditions, 1973), pp. 235–87. Repr. in an altered form (among the changes made, Derrida's replies to the series of questions addressed to him have not been

reproduced) in *Éperons: les styles de Nietzsche/Spurs: Nietzsche's Styles*; see Books, no. 10. Selections in Eng. trans. by Ruben Berezdivin in *The New Nietzsche: Contemporary Styles of Interpretation*, ed. David B. Allison (New York: Dell, 1977), pp. 176–89. Excerpts in *Semiotext(e)*, 3, 1 (1978), as 'Becoming Woman', trans. Barbara Harlow, and in *A Derrida Reader*; see Books, no. 30.

'La question du style' was first presented at a colloquium on Nietzsche held at Cerisy-la-Salle in July 1972.

1973

40 'Glas'. *L'arc: Jacques Derrida*, 54 (1973), pp. 4–15. Repr. in *Glas*; see Books, no. 8. Excerpts in *La Quinzaine littéraire*, 172 (1973), pp. 23–36, and in *A Derrida Reader*; see Books, no. 30.

41 'L'archéologie du frivole'. Introduction to Condillac, *Essai sur l'origine des connaissances humaines*, ed. Charles Porset (Paris: Editions Galilée, 1973), pp. 9–95. Repr. as *L'archéologie du frivole: lire Condillac/The Archeology of the Frivolous: Reading Condillac*; see Books, no. 9.

1974

42 'Mallarmé'. *Tableau de la littéraire française: de Madame de Staël à Rimbaud*, ed. Dominique Aubry (Paris: Gallimard, 1974), pp. 368–79. Eng. trans. Christine Roulston in *Acts of Literature*; see Books, no. 32, pp. 110–26.

43 'Le Parergon'. *Digraphe*, 2 (April 1974), pp. 21–57. Expanded version in *La vérité en peinture/The Truth in Painting*; see Books, no. 12. Abbreviated version and 'Le sens de la coupure pure (Le parergon, II) in Eng. trans. by Craig Owens in *October*, 9 (summer 1979), pp. 3–40. 'Le sens de la coupure pure (Le parergon II)'. *Digraphe*, 3 (September 1974), pp. 5–31. Revd in *La vérité en peinture/The Truth in Painting*; see Books, no. 12.

1975

44 'Faut-il défendre l'enseignement de la philosophie?'. *Libération* (11 March 1975), p. 4. Interview with 'GREPH' by Martine Storti.

45 'Economimesis'. Derrida, Sylviane Agacinski, Sarah Kofman, Philippe Lacoue-Labarthe, Jean-Luc Nancy, Bernard Pautrat, *Mimesis des articulations*. (Paris: Aubier-Flammarion, 1975), pp. 55–93. Eng. trans. Richard Klein in *Diacritics*, 11, 2 (1981), pp. 3–25.

46 'Le facteur de la vérité'. *Poétique*, 21 (1975), pp. 96–147. Revd in *La carte postale/The Post Card*; see Books, no. 13. Trans. as 'The Purveyor of Truth' by Marie-Rose Logan, Willis Domingo, James Hulbert and Moshe Ron in *Yale French Studies, Graphesis: Perspectives in Literature and Philosophy*, 52 (1975), pp. 31–113. Also in trans. by Alan Bass in *The Purloined Poe: Lacan, Derrida, and Psychoanalytic Reading*, ed. John P. Muller and William J. Richardson (Baltimore: Johns Hopkins University Press, 1987). Extract in *A Derrida Reader*; see Books, no. 30.

'Le facteur de la vérité' was first delivered as a lecture at Johns Hopkins University in November 1971.

47 '+R (par dessus le marché)'. *Derrière le miroir*, 214 (Paris: Editions Maeght, 1975), pp. 1–23. Revd in *La vérité en peinture/The Truth in Painting*; see Books, no. 12. Extract, consisting of material from the final section on Adami's drawing *Ritratto di Walter Benjamin*, in *La Quinzaine littéraire*, 211 (15 June 1975), pp. 14–16. Also in *Adami* (Paris: Editions du Centre Georges Pompidou, 1985), the catalogue produced in conjunction with the retrospective of Valerio Adami's work held in Paris between 4 December and 10 February 1986.

48 'Pour la philosophie'. *La Nouvelle Critique*, 84 (May 1975), pp. 25–9. Altered to 'Réponses à la Nouvelle Critique' in *Qui a peur de la philosophie?* (Paris: Aubier-Flammarion, 1977), pp. 451–8. [Groupe de recherches sur l'enseignement de la philosophie (GREPH); Derrida wrote many of the unsigned texts in the volume.] Appears as 'Les corps divisés' in *Du droit à la philosophie* (see Books, no. 25).

49 'Lettre'. *La Nouvelle Critique*, 85 (June–July 1975), p. 73.

50 'La philosophie refoulée'. *Le monde de l'éducation*, 4 (March 1975), pp. 14–15. Excerpted as 'La philosophie et ses classes' in *Le Nouvel Observateur*, 541 (24–30 March 1975), pp. 48–9, reprinted in full in *Qui a peur de la philosophie?* (Paris: Aubier-Flammarion, 1977), and in *Du droit à la philosophie* (see Books, no. 25).

51 'Trente-huit réponses sur l'avant-garde. *Digraphe*, 6 (October 1975), pp. 152–3.

1976

52 'Entre crochets: entretien avec Jacques Derrida, première partie'. *Digraphe*, 8 (April 1976), pp. 97–114. Eng. trans. Peggy Kamuf in *Negotiations: Writings*; see Books, no. 34. The interview with Derrida took place during September–October 1975, and was conducted by D. Kambouchner, Jean Ristat and D. Sallenave.

53 'Six philosophes occupés à déplacer le philosophique à propos de la mimesis'. *La Quinzaine Littéraire*, 231 (16–30 April 1976), pp. 19–22. Discussion between Derrida, Roger Dadoun, Philippe Lacoue-Labarthe, Sarah Kofman, Sylviane Agacinski, Christian Descamps, Jean-Luc Nancy, Maurice Nadeau and Jean-Louis Bouttes. Includes an insert by Derrida and Dadoun, 'Qu'est-ce que le GREPH', p. 20.

54 'Pas I'. *Gramma: lire Blanchot*, 3–4 (1976), pp. 111–215. Repr. in *Parages*; see Books, no. 19. Eng. trans. by John P. Leavey, Jr., in preparation.

55 'Où commence et comment finit un corps enseignant'. *Politiques de la philosophie: Châtelet, Derrida, Foucault, Lyotard, Serres*, ed. Dominique Grisoni (Paris: Bernard Grasset, 1976), pp. 60–89. Eng. trans. in *Institutions of Philosophy*; see Books, no. 33.

56 'Où sont les chasseurs de sorcières?' *Le Monde* (1 July 1976), p. 9. Eng. trans. in *Institutions of Philosophy* (see Books, no. 33).

57 'Fors: Les mots anglés de Nicolas Abraham et Maria Torok'. Foreword to Nicolas Abraham and Maria Torok, *Cryptonomie: le verbier de l'homme aux loups* (Paris: Aubier-Flammarion, 1976), pp. 7–73. Eng. trans. Nicholas Rand, *The Wolf Man's Magic Word: A Cryptonymy* (Minneapolis: University of Minnesota

Press, 1986), pp. xi–xlviii. Foreword by Derrida trans. Barbara Johnson as 'Fors: The Anglish Words of Nicolas Abraham and Maria Torok', in *Georgia Review*, 31, 1 (1977), pp. 64–116.

58 'Lettre [à Rogier Munier, 'Aujourd'hui Rimbaud'].' *Archives des Lettres Modernes*, 160 (1976), p. 42.

1977

59 'Ja, ou le faux-bond'. *Digraphe*, 11 (March 1977), pp. 83–121. Second and concluding part of an interview with Derrida (first part is 'Entre crochets'; see Texts no. 62). Eng. trans. by Peggy Kamuf in *Negotiations: Writings*; see Books, no. 34.

60 'L'âge de Hegel'. *Qui a peur de la philosophie?* (Paris: Aubier-Flammarion, 1977), pp. 73–107. Eng. trans. Susan Winnett, in *Glyph Textual Studies 1* (new series), *Demarcating the Disciplines: Philosophy, Literature, Art* (1986), pp. 3–35.

61 'Scribble (pouvoir/écrire)'. Preface to book IV, section 4, of the 2nd edn of Bishop William Warburton's *The Divine Legation of Moses demonstrated, Essai sur les hiéroglyphes des Egyptiens* (Paris: Aubier-Flammarion, 1977), pp. 7–43. In truncated form (it lacks the preliminary section) in Eng. trans. by Cary Plotkin as 'Scribble (writing-power)', in *Yale French Studies*, 58 (1979), pp. 116–47. Repr. in *La Revue des lettres modernes* (1988).

62 'Limited Inc abc . . . ' *Glyph*, 2 (1977), pp. 162–254. Eng. trans. Samuel Weber; see Books, nos. 11, 24.

63 'Prière d'inserer'. In Mathieu Bénézet, *Dits et récits du mortel* (Paris: Flammarion, 1977).

64 'Entretien avec François Laruelle', in Laruelle, *Le déclin de l'écriture* (Paris: Aubier-Flammarion, 1977), pp. 252–61; questions posed by Derrida to Laruelle about his book, pp. 252–3, and Laruelle's answer, pp. 252–61.

1978

65 'Table ronde avec le GREPH: qui a peur de la philosophie?' *Noroit*, 224 (January 1978), pp. 3, 14–23; 225 (February 1978), pp. 8–23; 226 (March 1978), pp. 6–23; 227 (April 1978), pp. 20–3; discussion between Derrida, Roland Brunet, Sylviane Agacinski, Sarah Kofman, A. Phillipon and members of GREPH.

66 'Le retrait de la métaphore'. *Poésie*, 7 (1978), pp. 103–26. Repr. in *The Phenomenology of Man and of the Human Condition*, ed. Anna-Teresa Tymieniecka (Dordrecht: Reidel, 1983), pp. 273–300, and in *Psyché: inventions de l'autre* (see Books, no. 22). Eng. trans. Frieda Gasdner, Biodun Iginla, Richard Madden and William West, 'The *Retrait* of Metaphor', in *Enclitic*, 2, 2 (1978), pp. 5–33.
    Lecture originally presented at a colloquium on Philosophy and Metaphor at the University of Geneva on 1 June 1978.

67 'Legs de Freud'. *Etudes freudiennes*, 13–14, (April 1978), pp. 87–125 ['Présence de Nicolas Abraham']. Incorporated as chap. 2 of 'To Speculate–on "Freud"', in *La carte postale/The Post Card*; see Books, no. 13. An abridgement and

reconstruction of 'Freud's Legacy', trans. James Hulbert, pubd as 'Coming Into One's Own', in *Psychoanalysis and the Question of the Text*, ed. Geoffrey Hartman (Baltimore: Johns Hopkins University Press, 1978) pp. 114–48). The state of this text is attributed by the translator to 'limitations of space'. Extract in *A Derrida Reader*; see Books, no. 30.

'Legs de Freud' is an 'extract of a seminar held in 1975 at *l'Ecole normale supérieure* under the heading *Life death*'.–Derrida

68 'Cartouches'. Gérard Titus-Carmel: *The Pocket Size Tlingit Coffin* (Paris: Centre Georges Pompidou, 1978), pp. 6–71. Catalogue accompanying the Titus-Carmel exhibition, held at the National Museum of Modern Art, Pompidou Centre, 1 March–10 April 1978. Revd version in *La vérité en peinture/The Truth in Painting*; see Books, no. 12.

69 'Le Colossal'. *Erres*, 6–7 (1978). This is the fourth section of 'Le Parergon'; see *La vérité en peinture/The Truth in Painting*; (see Books, no. 12).

70 'Restitutions de la vérité en pointure'. *Macula*, 3–4 (September 1978), pp. 11–37. This is the first part of the essay which was enlarged for inclusion in *La vérité en peinture/The Truth in Painting*; see Books, no. 12. Shortened version, John P. Leavey, Jr., as 'Restitutions of Truth to Size', in *Research in Phenomenology*, 8 (1978), pp. 1–44. Leavey's abridgement reproduces approximately (the first) half of the integral text. Extract, in the Bennington-McLeod translation, in *A Derrida Reader*; see Books, no. 30.

An excerpt from 'Restitutions' was delivered in a seminar on Theory of Literature at Columbia University on 6 October 1977.

71 'Du tout'. *Cahiers Confrontation* I (1978), pp. 63–77. Repr. in *La carte postale/The Post Card*; see Books, no. 13.

'Du tout' is Derrida's response to questions addressed to him by René Major *et al.*, organized by the journal *Cahiers Confrontation* and held in Paris on 21 November 1977.

72 'Passe-Partout'. *La vérité en peinture/The Truth in Painting*; see Books, no. 12.

1979

73 'Me–Psychoanalysis: An Introduction to the Translation of "The Shell and the Kernel" by Nicolas Abraham'. *Diacritics*, 9, 1 (1979), pp. 4–12; Eng. trans. by Richard Klein. 'Moi–la psychanalyse' pubd in *Cahiers Confrontation* 8 (1982), pp. 5–15, and in *Méta*, 27, 1 (1982); repr. in *Psyché: Inventions de l'autre*; see Books, no. 22.

74 'Illustrer, dit-il . . .', *Ateliers Aujourd'hui*, 17 (1979), pp. 2–3; brochure for an exhibition by François Loubrieu in the Salle contemporain of the Centre Georges Pompidou, Paris, 12 September–22 October 1979.

75 'Ce qui reste à force de musique'. *Digraphe*, 18–19 (April 1979), pp. 165–74. Repr. in *Psyché: inventions de l'autre*; see Books, no. 22.

76 'Philosophie des Etats Généraux'. *Les Etats Généraux de la philosophie* (Paris: Flammarion, 1979), pp. 27, 44. Also in *Libération* (20 June 1979), pp. 14–15,

and in *Du droit à la philosophie*; see Books, no. 25. Eng. trans. Peggy Kamuf in *Institutions of Philosophy*; see Books, no. 33.

This communication was the principal address delivered by Derrida as one of the five-member committee formed to examine the diminishing role of philosophy in French education. The debate took place at the Sorbonne on 16–17 June 1979.

77 'La loi du genre'. *Le Genre/Die Gattung/Genre*, Colloque International, Université de Strasbourg, 4–8 Juillet 1979 (Strasbourg: Université de Strasbourg II, Groupe de Recherches sur le Théories du Signe et du Texte, 1979), pp. 183–211; discussion: pp. 212–13 (Derrida also participates in a number of the other discussions: pp. 66–7, 273–4, 311, 403, 477–8, 518–19). Eng. trans. Avital Ronell, in *Glyph* 7 (1980), pp. 176–232. Repr. in *Critical Inquiry*, 7, 1 (1980), pp. 55–81; in *On Narrative*, ed. W. J. T. Mitchell (Chicago: University of Chicago Press, 1981); in *Parages* (see Books, no. 19; Eng. version by John P. Leavey, Jr.); and in *Acts of Literature* (see Books, no. 32).

'La loi du genre' was first delivered as a lecture in July 1979 at the University of Strasbourg, and later at a symposium on 'Narrative: the illusion of sequence' held at the University of Chicago, 26–8 October 1979.

78 'Living On: Border Lines'. *Deconstruction and Criticism* (New York: Seabury Press, 1979; London: Routledge & Kegan Paul, 1979), pp. 75–176. Derrida, Harold Bloom, Paul de Man, Geoffrey H. Hartman, and J. Hillis Miller. As 'Survivre: Journal de bord', in *Parages*; see Books, no. 19. Extract in *A Derrida Reader*; see Books, no. 30.

1980

79 'Qui a peur de la philosophie?' *Esprit*, 38 (February 1980), pp. 52–75. Round-table discussion with Derrida, Roland Brunet, Guy Coq, Vladimir Jankélévitch, and Olivier Mongin. Repr. in *Du droit à la philosophie* (see Books, no. 25) without the contributions by the other participants in the exchange.

80 'Ocelle comme pas un'. Preface to Jos Joliet, *L'enfant au chien-assis* (Paris: Editions Galilée, 1980), pp. 9–43.

81 'An Interview with Jacques Derrida'. *The Literary Review*, 14 (18 April–1 May 1980), pp. 21–2. Derrida interviewed by James Kearns and Ken Newton during his lecture visit to Scotland; his subject: 'Should Philosophy be Taught in Schools?' Aso available in repr. of Antony Easthope's *British Post-Structuralism: Since 1968* (London and New York: Routledge 1991), pp. 236–40.

82 'En ce moment même dans cet ouvrage me voici'. *Textes pour Emmanuel Levinas*, ed. Francis Laruelle (Paris: Jean-Michel Place, 1980), pp. 21–60. Repr. in *Psyché: inventions de l'autre*; see Books, no. 22. Eng. trans. Ruben Berezdivin, 'At This Very Moment in This Work Here I Am', in *Re-Reading Levinas*, ed. Robert Bernasconi and Simon Critchley (Bloomington: Indiana University Press, 1991; London: Athlone Press, 1991), pp. 11–48. Extract in *A Derrida Reader*; see Books, no. 30.

83 'Envois'. *La carte postale/The Post Card*; see Books, no. 13. Extract in *A Derrida Reader*; see Books, no. 30.

1981

84 'D'un ton apocalyptique adopté naguère en philosophie'. *Le fins de l'homme: à partir du travail de Jacques Derrida*, ed. Philippe Lacoue-Labarthe and Jean-Luc Nancy (Paris: Editions Galilée, 1981), pp. 445–79. Pubd in book form with some modifications; see Books, no. 15. Eng. trans. as 'Of an Apocalyptic Tone Recently Adopted in Philosophy', John P. Leavey,Jr., in *Semeia*, 23 (1982), pp. 63–97. In accordance with the revs made by Derrida for its repubn in 1983, Leavey revd his earlier trans. for its inclusion in *Oxford Literary Review*, 6, 2 (1984), pp. 3–37. Reprinted in Harold Coward and Toby Foshay, ed., *Derrida and Negative Theology* (Albany: SUNY Press, 1992). Further revd version in *On the Rise of Tone in Philosophy: Kant and Derrida*, ed. Peter D. Fenves (Baltimore: Johns Hopkins University Press, 1992). Exchanges between Derrida and commentators on his work, while included in *Les fins de l'homme*, have not been reproduced in the Leavey texts. These contain a discussion between Derrida and Jean-François Lyotard (pp. 311–13) and Derrida's response (pp. 675–6) to Jean-Marie Wipf's 'La pratique de enseignement et la figure de la communication'. A further intervention of Derrida's, responding to Sarah Kofman's paper 'Ça cloche', in Eng. trans. by Caren Kaplan, in *Continental Philosophy II: Derrida and Deconstruction*, ed. Hugh J. Silverman (London and New York: Routledge, 1989), pp. 133–8.

'Of an Apocalyptic Tone Recently Adopted in Philosophy' was originally presented at a colloquium occasioned by Derrida's work held at Cerisy-la-Salle, 23 July–2 August 1980.

85 'Titre (à préciser)'. *Nuova Corrente* 84 (January–April 1981), pp. 7–32. Repr. in *Parages*; see Books, no.19. Eng. trans. Tom Conley, as 'Title (tb be specified)', in *Sub-Stance*, 31 (1981), pp. 5–22.

'Titre (à préciser)' was first delivered as a lecture on 14 March 1979 at Saint Louis College in Brussels.

86 'Télépathie'. *Furor* 2 (February 1981), pp. 5–41. Repr. in *Cahiers Confrontation*, 10 (autumn 1983), pp. 201–30, and in *Psyché: inventions de l'autre*; see Books, no. 22. Eng. trans. Nicholas Royle, in *Oxford Literary Review*, 10, 1–2 (1988), pp. 3–41.

87 Comments, in Robert Denoon Cumming, 'The Odd Couple: Heidegger and Derrida'. *Review of Metaphysics*, 34, 13 (1981), pp. 487–521; comments by Derrida on an earlier draft of the paper quoted in the footnotes.

88 'Ex-abrupto'. *Avant-Guerre*, 2 (spring 1981), p. 70. Repr. in *Psyche: inventions de l'autre*; see Books, no. 22.

89 'Géopsychanalyse–"and the rest of the world"'. *Géopsychanalyse: Les Souterrains de l'institution. Recontre franco-latino-américaine, Février 1981*, ed. René Major (Paris: Editions Confrontation, 1981), pp. 11–30. Repr. in *Psyché: invention de l'autre*; see Books, no. 22. Eng. trans. Donald Nicholson-Smith in *American*

Imago, 48, 2 (1991), pp. 199–231. Eng. trans. Peggy Kamuf in *Negotiations: Writings*; see Books, no. 34.

Lecture given at a colloquium on psychoanalysis and Latin America, held in Paris on 12 February 1981.

90 'Une idée de Flaubert: la lettre de Platon'. *Revue d'Histoire littéraire de la France*, 81, 4–5 (1981), pp. 658–76. Repr. in *Cahiers Confrontation*, 12 (1984), and in *Psyché: inventions de l'autre*; see Books, no. 22. Eng. trans. Peter Starr as 'An Idea of Flaubert: "Plato's Letter"', in *MLN*, 99, 4 (1984), pp. 748–68.

'Un idée de Flaubert' was a communication delivered at an international colloquium organized by the Société d'Histoire Littéraire de la France to commemmorate the centenary of Flaubert's death, and held in Paris 28–9 November 1980.

91 'Les morts de Roland Barthes'. *Poétique*, 47 (September 1981), pp. 269–92. Repr. in *Psyché: inventions de l'autre*; see Books, no. 22. Eng. trans. Pascale-Anne Brault and Michael Nass, in *Continental Philosophy I: Philosophy and Non-Philosophy since Merleau-Ponty*, ed. Hugh J. Silverman (New York and London: Routledge, 1988), pp. 259–97.

92 'Éloge de la philosophie'. *Libération*, 163 (21–2 November 1981), pp. 22–4. Derrida is interviewed by Didier Eribon, Robert Maggiori and Jean-Pierre Salgas. Repr. in *Du droit à la philosophie* (see Books, no. 25). The *Libération* text also contains, as an inset box, a short piece by Derrida entitled 'Les propositions du GREPH' (p. 24).

1982

93 Catherine Clément, 'Derrida, liberé à Prague: "un scénario connu et infernal"'. *Le Matin* (4 January 1982), p. 8; interview with Clément on Derrida's arrest in Prague.

See also: Marie Claude Dubin, '"On a caché de la drogue dans ma valise"'. *France-Soir* (2 January 1982), pp. 1, 5; and William Echikson, 'French Professor's Arrest Part of Prague Crackdown on Intellectuals'. *Christian Science Monitor* (8 January 1982), p. 13. Both quote excerpts from press conference after Prague release. For the background and account of the arrest, by the Czech professor who conducted the seminar, see Ladislas Hejdanek, 'L'affaire du philosophe Jacques Derrida'. *Les Temps Modernes*, 429 (April 1982), pp. 1839–43; also, untitled, in *La Quinzaine Littéraire*, 368 (1–15 April 1982), pp. 30–1.

94 'Envoi.' *Actes du XVIIIe congrès des sociétés de philosophie de langue française (Strasbourg, July 1980)* Strasbourg: Association des Publications près les Universités de Strasbourg, 1982, pp. 5–30. Repr. in *Psyché: inventions de l'autre*; see Books, no. 22. Eng. trans. Peter and Mary Ann Caws, with some excisions, as 'Sending: On Representation', in *Social Research*, 49, 2 (1982), pp. 294–326. Also in *Transforming the Hermeneutic Context: From Nietzsche to Nancy*, ed. Gayle L. Ormiston and Alan D. Schrift (Albany: State University of New York Press, 1990), pp. 107–38.

Paper first given in 1980 at the University of Strasbourg.

95 Letter by Derrida to John P. Leavey, Jr. *Semeia*, 23 (1982), pp. 61–2. Derrida's letter (dated 2 January 1981) is a response to the request to submit a contribution to the journal; see Texts, no. 84 ('Of An Apocalyptic Tone').

96 'Jacques Derrida sur les traces de la philosophie'. *Le Monde* (31 January 1982), pp. xiii–xiv. Repr. in *Entretiens avec Le Monde, I: Philosophies*, ed. Christian Delacampagne (Paris: Editions La Découverte/Le Monde, 1984), pp. 78–90. Derrida interviewed by Christian Descamps.

97 'Choreographies'. *Diacritics*, 12, 2 (1982), pp. 66–76; Eng. trans. Christie V. McDonald. Repr. in *The Ear of the Other*; see Books, no. 14 (pp. 163–85). The product of an exchange of letters between Derrida and McDonald during the autumn of 1981. Extract in *A Derrida Reader*; see Books, no. 30.

98 'Pour la création d'un Collège International de Philosophie: une lettre-circulaire de Jacques Derrida'. *La Quinzaine Littéraire*, 374 (1–15 July 1982), p. 29. Derrida's letter (dated 18 May 1982) also in *Sub-Stance*, 35 (1982), pp. 80–1.

99 'Douze leçons de philosophie, 1; Le langage'. *Le Monde* (2 June 1982), p. xi. Reprinted in *Douze leçons de philosophie*, with an introduction by Christian Delacampagne (Paris: Editions La Découverte & Le Monde, 1985), pp. 14–26. Eng. trans. Peggy Kamuf in *Negotiations: Writings*; see Books, no.

100 Letter (dated 15 June 1982) written by Derrida to *Sub-Stance*, 35 (1982), p. 2, commending the journal for its work.

101 'Correspondance: à propos du collège international de philosophie'. *Le Monde* (15 July 1982). Letter concerning an article in *Le Monde* (2 July 1982).

102 *Affranchissement du transfert et de la lettre* ed. René Major (Paris: Editions Confrontation, 1982). Proceedings of a colloquium on *La carte postale/The Post Card* (see Books, no. 13), held in Paris, 4–5 April 1981. Includes Derrida's replies to comments made concerning his book, pp. 46–8, 75–82, 91–6, 105–6, 110–11, 123, 134. Participants in the exchange are Marie Moscovici, Isi Beller, Didier Cohen, Jean-Claude Sempé, Serge Viderman, René Major, Jean Petitot, Irène Diamantis, Gérard Huber, Jean-Paul Chardin, Claude Rabant, Heitor d'Dwyer de Macedo, Patrick Lacoste, Jacques Trilling, Pierre Ickowicz, and Bernard Lemaigire.

103 'Coups d'envoi'. *Collège International de Philosophie: sciences, interscience, arts* (Paris: Collège International de Philosophie, 1982), pp. 105–55. The text is dated 30 September 1982. Selections in *Extraits d'un rapport pour le Collège International de Philosophie* (1983). Further excerpts, as 'Légitimité de la philosophie', in *T.E.L. (Temps Economie Littérature)*, 8 (25 November 1982), pp. 1, 7. Eng. trans. Thomas Pepper (ed. Deborah Esch and Thomas Keenan), as 'Sendoffs', in *Yale French Studies: Reading the Archive: On Texts and Institutions*, 77 (1990), pp. 7–43. 'Coups d'envoi' repr. in *Du droit à la philosophie* (see Books, no. 25) and *Institutions of Philosophy* (see Books, no. 33).

104 'Je n'écris pas sans lumière artificielle'. *Le Fou Parle*, 21–2 (November–

December 1982), pp. 61–3. Derrida interviewed by André Rollin. Repr. in Rollin, *Ils écrivent: où? quand? comment?* (Paris: Mazarine, 1986), pp. 145–52.

105 'Feu la cendre'. *Anima* 5 (December 1982), pp. 47–99; see Books, no. 16.

1983

106 'Mes chances, Au rendez-vous de quelques stéréophonies épicuriennes'. *Tijdschrift voor Filosofie*, 1 (1983), pp. 3–40. Eng. trans. Irene E. Harvey and Avital Ronell as 'My Chances/*Mes Chances*: A Rendezvous with some Epicurean Stereophonies', in *Taking Chances: Derrida, Psychoanalysis and Literature*, ed. Joseph H. Smith and William Kerrigan (Baltimore: Johns Hopkins University Press, 1984), pp. 1–32. Also in *Cahiers Confrontation*, 19 (1988).
  This is a revised version of a text Derrida delivered as the Edith Weigert Lecture, sponsored by the Forum on Psychiatry and the Humanities, at the Washington School of Psychiatry on 15 October 1982.

107 'Ce que j'aurais dit . . . ' *Création et développement: recontres internationale de la Sorbonne, 12–13 February, 1983*, ed. André Larquie (Paris: Ministère de la Culture, 1983), pp. 397–414. Repr. in *Le complexe de Léonard ou la Société de création* (Paris: Editions de Nouvel Observateur/J. C. Lattès, 1984), pp. 77–92. Eng. trans. Peggy Kamuf in *Negotiations: Writings*; see Books, no. 34.

108 Derrida contributes to the discussion occasioned by Thomas Fries's paper 'Critical Relation: Peter Szondi's Studies on Celan'. *Boundary* 2, 11, 3 (1983), pp. 155–67; special issue, ed. Michael Hays, on the criticism of Peter Szondi. Derrida's interventions trans. James G. Hughes. French text in *L'acte critique: un colloque sur l'oeuvre de Peter Szondi*, ed. Mayotte Bollack (Paris: Presses Universitaires de Lille/Editions de la Maison des Sciences de l'Homme, 1985). Includes additional remarks of Derrida's (pp. 255–64) not reproduced in the American journal.
  The colloquium on the work of Peter Szondi was held in Paris, 21–3 June 1979.

109 '*Geschlecht*: différence sexuelle, différence ontologique'. *Les cahiers de l'herne*, ed. Michel Haar (Paris: Editions de l'Herne, 1983), pp. 419–30; issue on Martin Heidegger, uncredited Eng. trans. (Ruben Berezdivin) as '*Geschlecht*: sexual difference, ontological difference', in *Research in Phenomenology*, 13 (1983), pp. 65–83. Repr. in *Psyché: inventions de l'autre* (see Books, no. 22), and in *A Derrida Reader* (see Books, no. 30). Collected with '*Geschlecht* II' (see Texts, no. 172) and *De l'esprit* (see Books, no. 21) in *Heidegger et la question: De l'esprit et autres essais* (Paris: Flammarion, 1990).

110 'The Time of a Thesis: Punctuations'. *Philosophy in France Today*, ed. Alan Montefiore (Cambridge: Cambridge University Press, 1983), pp. 34–50. Eng. trans. Kathleen McLaughlin. Repr. in *Du droit à la philosophie*; see Books, no. 25.

111 'Tout redéfinir'. *Le Matin* (28 July 1983), p. 21. A paraphrase of Derrida's

unsigned response to an inquiry about the debate on 'le silence des intellectuels face au pouvoir.'

112 'Economies de la crise'. *La Quinzaine Littéraire*, 339 (August 1983), pp. 4–5. Eng. trans. Peggy Kamuf in *Negotiations: Writings*; see Books, no. 34.

113 'Derrida, Philosophie au Collège'. *Libération*, 692 (11 August 1983), pp. 15–16. Interview with Derrida conducted by Jean-Loup Thebaud.

114 'Derrida l'insoumis'. *Nouvel Observateur*, 983 (9 September 1983), pp. 62–7. Interview with Derrida conducted by Catherine David in spring 1983 which received 'extensive emendations' prior to its pubn in the *Observateur*. Eng. trans., prepared by members of the Contemporary Texts Seminar of the SUNY-Stony Brook and the Paris-IV Programme in Philosophy and the Social Sciences, in *Derrida and Différance*, ed. David Wood and Robert Bernasconi (Coventry: Parousia Press, 1985; Evanston, IL: Northwestern University Press, 1988), pp. 71–82. 'An interview with Jacques Derrida', in *Graduate Faculty Philosophy Journal*, 10, 1 (1984), pp. 31–45.

115 'Excuse Me, But I Never Said Exactly So: Yet Another Derridian Interview'. *On the Beach*, 1 (Glebe NSW, Australia, autumn 1983), p. 43. From an interview in Paris with Paul Brennan.

116 'The Principle of Reason: The University in the Eyes of its Pupils'. *Diacritics*, 13, 3 (1983), pp. 3–20. Eng. trans. Catherine Porter and Edward P. Morris of 'Les pupilles de l'université, le principe de raison et l'idée de l'université'. Repr. in slightly different form in *Graduate Faculty Philosophy Journal*, 10 (spring 1984), pp. 5–45. Also in *Cahiers du Collège International de Philosophie*, 2 (July 1986), pp. 7–34, and in *Du droit à la philosophie* (see Books, no. 25).
   'The Principle of Reason' was delivered as a lecture in 1983 at the New School for Social Research, Cornell University and the University of Frankfurt.

117 'La langue et le discours de la méthode'. *Recherches sur la philosophie et le langage*, 3 (Grenoble: Université des Sciences Sociales de Grenoble; Paris: Librarie J. Vrin, 1983), pp. 35–51.

118 'Le dernier mot du racisme'. *Art contre/against Apartheid*. pp. 11–35. [Les artistes du monde contre l'apartheid/Artists of the World against Apartheid.] This text appeared in the bilingual (French and English) catalogue accompanying the exhibition which opened in Paris in November 1983. Revd version of 'Racism's Last Word', trans. Peggy Kamuf, in *Critical Inquiry*, 12 (1985), pp. 290–9. Repr. in *Race, Writing and Difference*, ed. Henry Louis Gates (Chicago: University of Chicago Press, 1986), and in *Psyché: inventions de l'autre*; see Books, no. 22. Extract in *L'événement du jeudi* (22–8 August 1985), p. 53, and, as 'Derrida: Racism's Last Word', in *Harper's Magazine*, 1629 (February 1986), pp. 21–2.

119 'Une conversation avec Jacques Derrida'. *Fruits*, 1 (December 1983), pp. 75–91. Derrida in conversation with Anne Berger; the meeting took place on 27 September of that year.

120 'Roger Laporte au bord du silence'. *Libération*, (22 December 1983), p. 28. Conversation between Derrida and Laporte.

1984

121 'Devant la loi'. *Royal Institute of Philosophy Lecture Series 16, Supplement to Philosophy, 1983: Philosophy and Literature*, ed. A. Phillips Griffiths (Cambridge: Cambridge University Press, 1984), pp. 173–88. The editor states: '"Devant la loi" was first read in an English translation prepared by Dr Paul Foulkes. Having done so, the author felt that Dr Foulkes' translation was too English for publication. The article is therefore published in the original French, edited by Dr Foulkes, with some cuts imposed by limitations of space.' Incomplete Eng. trans. by Avital Ronell in *Kafka and the Contemporary Critical Performance: Centenary Readings*, ed. Alan Udoff (Bloomington: Indiana University Press, 1987), pp. 128–49. Complete version, trans. Avital Ronell and Christine Roulston as 'Before the Law', in *Acts of Literature* (see Books, no. 32), pp. 181–220. As 'Préjugés: devant la loi', in *La faculté de juger* (Paris: editions de Minuit, 1985), pp. 87–139. French version also in *Spiegel und Gleichnis: Festschrift für Jacob Taubes*, ed. Norbert W. Bolz and Wolfgang Hübner (Würzburg: Königshausen & Neumann, 1983), pp. 342–66.

   'Devant la loi' was delivered as a lecture at the Royal Institute of Philosophy, London, on 12 February 1982, under the title 'Philosophy and Liteature: Before the Law' and shortly after at the University of Cambridge. It was also presented at the Free University of Berlin and at Cerisy-la-Salle during the summer of that year.

122 'Women in the Beehive: A Seminar with Jacques Derrida'. *subjects/objects* (spring 1984), pp. 5–19. Repr. in *Men in Feminism*, ed. Alice Jardine and Paul Smith (New York and London: Methuen, 1987), pp. 189–203. 2nd edn contains Derrida's 'Reply' (p. 285) to Paul Smith's note of clarification (p. 285), arising over objections made by Derrida concerning Smith's characterization of his work. Repr. in *Discourses: Conversations in Postmodern Art and Culture*, ed. R. Ferguson, W. Olander, M. Tucker and K. Fiss (New York: New Museum of Contemporary Art: Cambridge, MA, and London: MIT Press, 1990), pp. 115–128.

   This text is a 'modified transcript of a seminar given by the Pembroke Center for Research and Teaching on Women at Brown University with guest speaker Jacques Derrida'.

123 'Deconstruction and the Other'. *Dialogues with Contemporary Continental Thinkers: The Phenomenological Heritage*, ed. Richard Kearney (Manchester: Manchester University Press, 1984), pp. 105–26. Dialogue between Derrida and Kearney recorded in Paris in 1981.

124 'Mochlos ou le conflit des facultés'. *Philosophie*, 2 (April 1984), pp. 21–53. Eng. trans. Richard Rand and Amy Wygant as 'The Conflict of the Faculties', in *The Conflict of the Faculties in America*, ed. Rand (Lincoln: University of Nebraska Press, forthcoming). Repr. in *Du droit à la philosophie*; see Books, no. 25.

   Paper originally delivered at a conference at Columbia University on 17 April 1980.

125 'No Apocalypse, Not Now (full speed ahead, seven missiles, seven missives)'. *Diacritics*, 14, (1984), pp. 20–31. Eng. trans. Catherine Porter and Philip Lewis. Repr. in *Psyché: inventions de l'autre*; see Books, no. 22.

'No Apocalypse, Not Now' was delivered at a colloquium at Cornell University in April 1984.

126 'Bonnes volontés de puissance (une réponse à Hans-Georg Gadamer)'. *Revue Internationale de Philosophie*, 38, 151 (1984), facs. 4, pp. 341–3. [Herméneutique et néo-structuralisme: Derrida, Gadamer, Searle. Avant-propos de Manfred Frank.] Eng. trans. Diane P. Michelfelder and Richard E. Palmer as 'Three Questions to Hans-Georg Gadamer', in *Dialogue and Deconstruction: The Gadamer–Derrida Encounter*, ed. Michelfelder and Palmer (New York: State University of New York, 1989), pp. 52–4.

127 'Deux mots pour Joyce'. *Post-Structuralist Joyce: Essays from the French*, ed. Derek Attridge and Daniel Ferrer (Cambridge: Cambridge University Press, 1984), pp. 145–58. Eng. trans. Geoff Bennington as 'Two Words for Joyce'. French text in *Les Cahiers de l'herne*, 50 (1985), and in *Ulysse gramophone*; see Books, no. 23.

'Deux mots pour Joyce' is a transcription of a 'more or less extemporary talk given at the Centre Georges Pompidou, Paris, on 15 November 1982'.

128 'Les événements? quels événements?' *Nouvel Observateur*, 1045 (1984), pp. 83–4. [1964–1984: Les Grands Tournants.] Eng. trans. Peggy Kamuf in *Negotiations: Writings*; see Books, no. 34.

129 'Languages and Institutions of Philosophy'. *RS/SI (Recherches Sémiotiques/Semiotic Inquiry*, 4, 2 (1984), pp. 91–154. Repr. in *Du droit à la philosophie*; see Books, no. 25. Revd version of the four lectures delivered by Derrida at the University of Toronto between 31 May and 25 June 1984 (see 'Les langages et les institutions de la philosophie' in Texts, no. 143); Eng. trans. Sylvia Söderlind, Rebecca Comay, Barbara Havercroft and Joseph Adamson, with revisions by Gabriel Moyal and David Savan.

130 'Les philosophes et la parole. "Passage du témoin" de François George à Jacques Derrida'. *Le Monde Aujourd'Hui* (21–2 October 1984), p. xi. Derrida in conversation with François George; excerpts from transcript of radio interview, hosted by Thomas Ferenczi, broadcast on 'France-Culture', 20 and 24 October 1984.

131 'Plaidoyer pour la metaphysique. "Passage de témoin" de Jacques Derrida à Jean-François Lyotard.' *Le Monde* (28–9 October 1984), p. ix. Derrida in conversation with Jean-François Lyotard. Excerpts from the transcript of a radio interview, hosted by Thomas Ferenczi, broadcast on 'France-Culture', 27 and 31 October 1984.

132 'Voice II . . . ' *Boundary* 2, 12, 2 (1984), pp. 76–93. Derrida's text, dated 25 December 1982 (available in French and English), is a response to a letter addressed to him by Verena Andermatt Conley, pubd in the same issue of the journal; Eng. trans. by Conley.

133 'Artists, Philosophers and Institutions: A Talk with Jacques Derrida'. *Rampike*, 3:3–4:1 (1984–5), pp. 34–6. Extract from a seminar Derrida gave at St Michael's College, University of Toronto, at a conference on semiotics, summer 1984.

1985

134 Interventions by Derrida occasioned by the papers 'La société scientifique, la technologie et la culture', 'L'avenir de la démocratie de masse', 'Coopération franco-japonaise, gouvernements et secteur prive', and 'Discours de clôture'. *L'avenir de la Culture: Sommet Culturel Franco-Japonais, 4–9 May, 1984* (Paris: Ministère de la Culture; Tokyo: Asahi Shimbun, 1985), pp. 34, 76, 135, 141.

135 Comments in Roland Sicard, 'Deconstructionist revisits Yale: Derrida looks at Nationalism and Literature', *Yale Daily News* 107, 114 (5 April 1985, p. 5); quotations from an interview, Yale University, spring 1985.

136 'Épreuves d'écriture'. (Paris: Editions du Centre Georges Pompidou, 1985). Repr. in *Revue Philosophique* (April–June 1990), pp. 269–84. Derrida's contribution is not an autonomous text, but a series of comments arranged alphabetically by term.

   'Épreuves d'écriture' is Derrida's contribution to the exhibition catalogue for 'Les Immateriaux', organized by Jean-François Lyotard and held at the Centre Georges Pompidou, 28 March–15 July 1985.

137 'La philosophie perd une voix'. *Libération* (8–9 June 1985), p. 34. Derrida, along with Bouveresse, Deleuze, Lyotard and others, reacts to the death of Vladimir Jankélévitch.

138 'Le langage'. *Douze leçons de philosophie*, with an introduction by Christian Delacampagne (Paris: Editions La Découverte & Le Monde, 1985), pp. 14–26. Eng. trans. Peggy Kamuf in *Negotiations: Writings*; see Books, no. 34). First appeared as 'Douze leçons de philosophie, 1; Le langage'. *Le Monde* (2 June 1982), p. xi.

139 'Jacques Derrida, la déconstruction du monde'. *Libération* (8 August 1985), pp. 20–1. Interview with Patrick Mauriès.

140 Marie-Françoise Plissart, *Droit de regards; avec une lecture de Jacques Derrida* (Paris: Editions de Minuit, 1985). Eng. trans. David Wills as 'Right of Inspection', in *Art & Text*, 32 (autumn 1989), pp. 19–97. In its original appearance, Derrida's text followed Plissart's photographs; this arrangement has not been observed in the pubd trans., nor have all the photographs been reproduced.

141 'Des tours de Babel'. *Difference in Translation*, ed. Joseph F. Graham (Ithaca, NY: Cornell University Press, 1985), pp. 165–248; bilingual presentation; Eng. trans. Graham. Also in *L'art des confins mélanges offerts à Maurice de Gandillac* (Paris: Presses Universitaires de France, 1985) pp. 209–37, and *Psyché: inventions de l'autre*; see Books, no. 22. Extract in *A Derrida Reader*; see Books, no. 30. Reprinted in Rainer Schulte and John Biguenet, ed., *Theories of Translation: An Anthology of Essays from Dryden to Derrida* (Chicago: Chicago University Press, 1992).

142 'Popularités: du droit à la philosophie du droit'. Preface to *Les Sauvages dans le cité: auto-émancipation de peuple et instruction des prolétaires au XIXe siècle* (Paris: Champ Vallon, 1985), pp. 12–19. Repr. in *Du droit à la philosophie*; see Books, no. 25. Eng. trans. Peggy Kamuf in *Institutions of Philosophy*; see Books, no. 33.

143 'Théologie de la traduction'. *Qu'est-ce-que Dieu? Philosophie/Théologie: hommage à l'abbé Daniel Coppieters de Gibson* (Brussels: Facultés Universitaires Saint-Louis, 1985), pp. 165–84. Also in *Texte*, no. 4 (see Texts, no. 144).

144 'Les langages et les institutions de la philosophie'. *Texte: revue de critique et de théorie littéraire*, 4: Traduction/Textuality–Text/Translatability (1985), pp. 9–41. 'Les langages . . . ' consists of two texts: 'Chaire vacante: censure, maîtrise, magistralité, and 'Théologie de la traduction' (see Texts no. 143). Repr. in *Du droit à la philosophie*; see Books, no. 25.

'Les langages . . . ' was the title for a series of four lectures given by Derrida at the Fifth International Summer Institute for Semiotic and Structural Studies at the University of Toronto, 31 May–25 June 1984 (see Texts, nos. 129, 133).

145 'Ulysse gramophone: l'oui-dire de Joyce'. *Genèse de Babel; etudes présentés par Claude Jacquet* (Paris: CNRS, 1985), pp. 227–64. Collected with 'Deux mots pour Joyce' (see Texts, no. 127) in *Ulysse gramophone*; see Books, no. 23. Trans. Tina Kendall as 'Ulysses Gramophone: Hear Say Yes in Joyce' (revd Shari Benstock), in *James Joyce: The Augmented Ninth*, ed. Bernard Benstock (Syracuse, NY: Syracuse University Press, 1988), pp. 27–75. Repr., in accordance with the French version of the text, in *Acts of Literature*; see Books, no. 32. Extract in *A Derrida Reader*; see Books, no. 30.

'Ulysse gramophone' was first delivered at the Ninth International James Joyce Symposium, Frankfurt am Main, June 1984.

146 'Pas la moindre influence . . . (réponse à la Cinématheque de Toulouse)'. *L'effet Godard*, ed. Carole Desbarats and Jean-Paul Gorce (Toulouse: Editions Milan, [privately circulated, 1985] 1989), p. 110.

147 'Letter to a Japanese Friend'. *Derrida and Différance*, ed. David Wood and Robert Bernasconi (Coventry: Parousia Press, 1985; Evanston, IL: Northwestern University Press, 1988) pp. 1–5; Eng. trans. David Wood and Andrew Benjamin. The letter is dated 10 July 1983. Also in *Le Promeneur*, 42 (October 1985), pp. 2–4; in *Psyché: inventions de l'autre* (see Books, no. 22), and in *A Derrida Reader* (see Books, no. 30). In *Psyché*, the letter carries a note by Derrida, offering a dictionary definition of 'deconstruction'.

148 'In Memoriam: For Paul de Man'. *Yale French Studies*, 69 (1985), pp. 13–16, 323–6; Eng. trans. Kevin Newmark. Also in French edn of *Mémoires* (see Books, no. 18), and in the augmented version (1989) of *Mémoires for Paul de Man*.

A commemorative address delivered by Derrida at the Memorial Service for Paul de Man, held at the Yale University Art Gallery on 18 January 1984.

149 'Deconstruction in America: An Interview with Jacques Derrida'. *Critical Exchange*, 17 (winter 1985), pp. 1–33; Eng. trans. James Creech. Derrida interviewed at Miami University in April 1984 by Creech, Peggy Kamuf and Jane Todd.

150 Comments by Derrida cited in Ellen Carol Jones, 'Introduction: Deconstructive Criticism of Joyce'. *James Joyce: The Augmented Ninth*, ed. Bernard Benstock (Syracuse, NY: Syracuse University Press, 1988), pp. 77–9. Excerpts from Derrida's contributions to the panel on 'Deconstructive Criticism of Joyce' at the Ninth International James Joyce Symposium, Frankfurt am Main, June 1984.

1986

151 'Séquence 2–Scène 2: "quand à la construction, je m'y suis mis à cause de mon psychanalyste" . . .' *Cahiers du CCI*, 1: *Architecture* (Paris: Editions du Centre Georges Pompidou/Centre de Création Industrielle, 1986), pp. 51–4. Discussion between Derrida and Peter Eisenman at CCI.

152 'On Colleges and Philosophy'. *ICA Documents* 4–5 (1986), pp. 66–71. Jacques Derrida in conversation with Geoff Bennington. Repr. in *Postmodernism: ICA Documents*, ed. Lisa Appignanesi (London: Free Association Books; New York: Columbia University Press, 1989). Derrida discusses 'current preoccupations', principally the Collège International de Philosophie, at the Institute of Contemporary Arts, London, on 29 November 1985.

153 'Jacques Derrida (interview)'. *Art Papers* (Atlanta), 10, 1 (1986), pp. 31–5. Derrida interviewed by Jerry Cullum and Robert Cheatham.

154 'Encore un effort'. *Le Matin* (20 February 1986), p. 25. A sort of advertisement for the series of 'Rencontres Franco-Germaniques' which took place at the Centre Pompidou, 20 February–13 March 1986. Comments by Derrida, cited in reports of the opening session, in Rainer Rochlitz, 'The Missed Meeting: a Conference Report on French and German Philosophy', trans. Thomas R. Thorp, in *Telos*, 66 (winter 1985–6), pp. 124–8, and J.-L. de Rambures, 'Le difficile dialogue des intellectuels'. *Le Monde* (12 March 1986), p. 6.

155 Comments by Derrida in Colin Campbell, 'The Tyranny of the Yale Critics'. *New York Times Magazine* (9 February 1986), pp. 20–7, 43, 47–8. Repr. as 'Deconstruction and All That, from Yale's Critical Jungle', in *International Herald Tribune* (14 February 1986), pp. 7–8. Quotations from an interview.

156 'Jacques Derrida on the University'. Interview conducted by Imre Salusinszky. *Southern Review*, 19, 1 (1986), pp. 3–12. Repr. as 'Jacques Derrida' in *Criticism in Society* (New York and London: Methuen, 1987), pp. 9–24. Interview at Yale University, 15 April 1985.

157 'Architetture ove il desiderio può abitare'. *Domus* 671 (April 1986), pp. 17–24. Italian and Eng. trans. of interview with Eva Meyer recorded in Paris, February 1986 (abridged). German text, as 'Labyrinth und Archi/Textur: ein Gespräch mit Jacques Derrida', in *Das Abenteuer der Ideen* (Berlin: Internationale Bauaustellung Berlin, 1987), pp. 95–106.

158 'Pardonnez-moi de vous prendre au mot'. *La Quinzaine Littéraire*, 459 (16–31 March 1986), pp. 20–1. Eng. trans. Peggy Kamuf in *Negotiations: Writings*; see Books, no. 34.

159 'Petite fuite alexandrine (vers toi)'. *Monostiches/One-Line Poems*, organized in 1981 by Emmanuel Hocquard and Claude Royet-Journoud, in *Notes, Publiées Par Raquel*, 1 (May 1986), p. 2.

160 'Declarations of Independence'. *New Political Science*, 15 (summer 1986), pp. 7–15. Eng. trans. Tom Keenan and Tom Pepper. In French edn of *Otobiographies* (see Books, no. 14), but not included in the French-Canadian edition of *L'oreille de l'autre*; it is therefore omitted from the subsequent Eng. trans. as *The Ear of the Other*.

'Declarations of Independence' was first delivered as a lecture at the University of Virginia in Charlottesville in 1976.

161 'Admiration de Nelson Mandela: ou les lois de la réflexion'. *Pour Nelson Mandela*, ed. Jacques Derrida and Mustapha Tlili (Paris: Editions Gallimard, 1986), pp. 13–44. Repr. in *Psyché: inventions de l'autre*; see Books, no. 22. Eng. edn of *For Nelson Mandela* (New York: Seaver Books, 1987), with additional material, includes trans. by Mary Ann Caws and Isabelle Lorenz as 'The Laws of Reflection: Nelson Mandela, in Admiration', pp. 13–42.

162 'But, beyond . . . (Open Letter to Anne McClintock and Rob Nixon)'. *Critical Inquiry*, 13 (autumn 1986), pp. 155–70; Eng. trans. Peggy Kamuf. Repr. in *Race, Writing and Difference*, ed. Henry Louis Gates (Chicago: University of Chicago Press, 1986). Derrida's letter, dated 6 February 1986, with an April postcript, is addressed to McClintock and Nixon's 'response' to 'Racism's Last Word' (see Texts, no. 118).

163 Jacques Derrida and Paule Thévenin, *Antonin Artaud; dessins et portraits* (Paris: Editions Gallimard, 1986), pp. 55–108. Eng. trans. Mary Ann Caws in preparation. Fragment pubd as 'Forcener le subjectile', in *Le Matin* (26 July 1985), pp. 25–6; this text was delivered by Derrida as a lecture at a colloquium on 'Théâtre et philosophie' in Avignon.

164 'Point de folie–maintenant l'architecture'. Bernard Tschumi, *La Case Vide* (London: Architectural Association, Folio VIII, 1986), pp. 4–20; bilingual presentation; Eng. trans. Kate Linker. Repr in *A A Files* (London), 12 (1986), pp. 65–73, and in *Psyché: inventions de l'autre*; see Books, no. 22. Excerpts in *Pratt Journal of Architecture*, 2 (spring 1988), p. 132.

165 Introduction to *Parages*, pp. 9–19; see Books, no. 19.

166 'Proverb: "He that would pun . . . "'. Foreword to John P. Leavey's *Glassary* (Lincoln and London: University of Nebraska Press, 1986), pp. 17–20.

167 'Interpreting Signatures (Nietzsche/Heidegger): Two Questions'. *Philosophy and Literature*, 10, 2 (1986), pp. 246–62; Eng. trans. Diane P. Michelfelder and Richard E. Palmer. This text, with 'Three Questions to Hans-Georg Gadamer' (see Texts, no. 126), in *Dialogue and Deconstruction: The Gadamer-Derrida Encounter*, ed. Michelfelder and Palmer (New York: State University of New York, 1989), pp. 57–71.

'Interpreting Signatures' was delivered at a colloquium organized by Philippe Forget at the Goethe Institute, Paris, on 25 April 1981. Derrida's text originally appeared in German, edited by Forget, in *Text und Interpretation* (Munich, 1984).

168 'L'aphorisme à contretemps'. *Roméo et Juliette* (Paris: Papiers, Théâtre Gérard Philippe de Saint-Denis, 1986), pp. 24–39. Repr. in *Psyché: inventions de l'autre*; see Books, no. 22. Eng. trans. Nicholas Royle, as 'Aphorism Countertime', in *Acts of Literature* (see Books, no. 32), pp. 415–34.

169 'Les antinomies de la discipline philosophique'. Lettre préface à *La grève des philosophes* (Paris: Osiris, 1986), pp. 9–31. Eng. trans. Peggy Kamuf in *Institutions of Philosophy*; see Books, no. 33.

170 'Questions'. Jacques Derrida and Pierre-Jean Labarrière, *Altérités* (Paris: Editions Osiris, 1986), pp. 29–33 70–94. Derrida is responding, with

Labarrière, to texts, collected in the volume, on their work by Francis Guibal and Stanislas Breton.

171 'Deconstruction: a trialogue in Jerusalem'. *Mishkenot Sha'ananim Newsletter* (Jerusalem), 7 (December 1986), pp. 1–3, 6–7. Abridged and ed. version of Derrida in conversation with Geoffrey Hartman and Wolfgang Iser; the whole of the encounter is available on videotape from Mishkenot Sha'ananim.

1987

172 '*Geschlecht* II: Heidegger's Hand'. *Deconstruction and Philosophy: The Texts of Jacques Derrida*, ed. John Sallis (Chicago: University of Chicago Press, 1987), pp. 161–96; Eng. trans. John P. Leavey, Jr. Repr. in *Psyché: inventions de l'autre*; see Books, no. 22. Collected with '*Geschlecht*: sexual difference . . .' (see Texts, no. 119) and *De l'esprit* (see Books, no. 21) in *Heidegger et la question: De l'esprit et autres essais* (Paris: Flammarion, 1990).

'*Geschlecht* II' was originally presented at an international conference on 'Deconstruction and Philosophy: the Texts of Jacques Derrida', held at Loyola University, Chicago, 22–3 March 1985.

173 'Pourquoi Peter Eisenman écrit de si bons lives'. *Psyché: inventions de l'autre*; see Books, no. 22. Bilingual (English and Japanese) version, 'Why Peter Eisenman Writes Such Good Books', in *Architecture and Urbanism* (Tokyo, August 1988), pp. 113–24; [Extra Edition: Peter Eisenman.] Eng. trans. Sarah Whiting. Also in *Threshold*, 4 (spring 1988). Repr. in *Restructuring Architectural Theory*, ed. Marco Diani and Catherine Ingraham (Evanston,IL: Northwestern University Press, 1989), pp. 99–105, and in *Arquitectura* (Madrid), 270 (January–February 1988).

174 'Nombre de oui'. *Michel de Certeau: cahiers pour un temps*, ed. Luce Girard (Paris: Editions Centre Georges Pompidou, 1987), pp. 191–205. Repr. in *Psyché: inventions de l'autre*; see Books, no. 22. Eng. trans. Brian Holmes as 'A Number of Yes (Nombre de oui)', in *Qui Parle*, 2, 2 (1988), pp. 120–33.

175 'Some Questions and Responses'. *The Linguistics of Writing: Arguments Between Language and Literature*, ed. Nigel Fabb, Derek Attridge, Alan Durant and Colin MacCabe (Manchester: Manchester University Press, 1987), pp. 252–64.

This is a 'minimally-edited record' of Derrida's replies to questions addressed to him during a conference on 'The Linguistics of Writing' held at the University of Strathclyde, 4–6 July 1986.

176 '52 aphorismes pour un avant-propos'. *Mesure pour mesure: architecture et philosophie* (Paris: Editions Centre Georges Pompidou/CCI, 1987), pp. 7–13. Preface to a collection of papers dealing with the relationship between philosophy and architecture. Repr. in *Psyché: inventions de l'autre*; see Books, no. 22. Eng. trans. Andrew Benjamin in *Deconstruction*, ed. Andreas Papadakis, Catherine Cooke and Andrew Benjamin (London: Academy Editions, 1989), pp. 66–9.

177 'On Reading Heidegger: An Outline of Remarks to the Essex Colloquium'. *Research in Phenomenology*, 17 (1987), pp. 171–88. At the colloquium 'Reading Heidegger' held at the University of Essex, 16–18 May 1986, Derrida presented some remarks based on conversations with Tom Keenan, Tom Levin, Tom

Pepper and Andrzej Warminski at Yale University in April 1986. This text is an outline of those conversations, prepared by David Farrell Krell. Derrida contributes to the discussions on four of the papers collected in the volume: Krell's 'Daimon Life, Nearness and Abyss: An Introduction to Za-ology' (pp. 47–8); Françoise Dastur's 'Logic and Ontology: Heidegger's "Destruction" of Logic' (pp. 68–71); Robert Bernasconi's 'Descartes in the History of Being' (pp. 95–8); and David Wood's 'Heidegger After Derrida' (pp. 113–14).

178 'Psyché: invention de l'autre'. *Psyché: inventions de l'autre*; see Books, no. 22. Eng. trans. Catherine Porter, as 'Psyche: Inventions of the Other', in *Reading de Man Reading*, ed. Lindsay Waters and Wlad Godzich (Minneapolis: University of Minnesota Press, 1989), pp. 25–66. Extracts in *A Derrida Reader* (see Books, no. 30) and in *Acts of Literature* (see Books, no. 32), where it appears as 'Psyche: Invention of the Other'.

   'Psyché: Inventions de l'autre' was originally presented in two lectures at Cornell University in April 1984.

179 'Chôra'. *Poikilia: Études offertes à Jean-Pierre Vernant* (Paris: Editions de l'EHESS, 1987), pp. 265–96.

180 'Désistance'. *Psyché: inventions de l'autre*; see Books, no. 22. Eng. trans. Christopher Fynsk as the Introduction to Philippe Lacoue-Labarthe's *Typography* (Cambridge, MA: Harvard University Press, 1989), pp. 1–42.

181 'Comment ne pas parler: dénégations'. *Psyché: inventions de l'autre*; see Books, no. 22. Eng. trans. Ken Frieden, as 'How to Avoid Speaking: Denials', in *Languages of the Unsayable: The Play of Negativity in Literature and Literary Theory*, ed. Sanford Budick and Wolfgang Iser (New York: Columbia University Press, 1989), pp. 3–70. Reprinted in Harold Coward and Toby Foshay, ed., *Derrida and Negative Theology* (Albany: SUNY Press, 1992).

   Paper first presented at a conference in Jerusalem in June 1986, and delivered as a lecture in the same year at Cornell University.

182 'Artaud et ses doubles'. *Scènes Magazines* (Geneva), 5 (February 1987), pp. 30–3; interview with Derrida conducted by Jean-Michel Olivier.

183 'Heidegger, l'enfer des philosophes'. *Nouvel Observateur* (6–12 November 1987), pp. 170–4. Derrida is responding to Victor Farias' *Heidegger et le nazisme*. Text available only in the French edn of the *Observateur*, and not its international version. Eng. trans. Richard Wolin as 'Philosophers' Hell: An Interview', in *The Heidegger Controversy: A Critical Reader*, ed. Richard Wolin (New York, Columbia University Press, 1991), pp. 264–73. See Texts, no. 184.

184 'La réponse de Jacques Derrida', *Le Nouvel Observateur* (27 Nov–3 Dec 1987) p. 47. Response to Victor Farias's, 'pas d'accord avec Jacques Derrida' on the same page. See Texts, no. 183.

185 'Fragments of a conversation with Jacques Derrida'. *Precis* (Columbia University Graduate School of Architecture), 6 (spring 1987), pp. 48–9. Excerpts from a discussion between Derrida and the editors of the journal, Yale University, 24 April 1985.

186 'Vers la déconstruction: entretien avec Jacques Derrida'. *Digraphe*, 42 (1987), pp. 9–27. Discussion between Derrida and Didier Cahen, recorded 22 March 1986.

1988

187 'De l'écrit à la parole: table ronde animée par Jacques Munier'. *Théâtre/Public*, 79 (January–February 1988), pp. 36–41. Discussion among Derrida, Maurice Attias, Philippe Lacoue-Labarthe and Pierre-Antoine Villemaine on the staging by the last named of a dramatic version of Blanchot's *L'arrêt de mort* in Paris, January 1987.

188 'Une nouvelle affaire'. *La Quinzaine Littéraire* (16–29 February 1988), p. 31. Letter addressed to Maurice Nadeau on the subject of Paul de Man.

189 'Une lettre de Jacques Derrida'. *Libération* (3 March 1988), p. 7. On Paul de Man.

190 'De l'esprit'. *Heidegger: questions ouvertes* (Le Cahier du Collège International de Philosophie, 6, March 1988; Paris: Osiris), pp. 213–45. Presentation by Eliane Escoubas. Contains only the first part of *De l'esprit*; see Books, no. 21.

   Lecture given at a colloquium on Heidegger held in Paris, 12–14 March 1987.

191 'Heidegger: Derrida–Bourdieu débat'. *Libération* (30 March 1988).

192 'Like the Sound of the Sea Deep within a Shell: Paul de Man's War'. *Critical Inquiry*, 14 (spring 1988), pp. 590–652. Eng. trans. Peggy Kamuf of 'Comme le bruit de la mer au fond d'un coquillage: la guerre de Paul de Man' (see Books, no. 18). Repr. in *Responses: On Paul de Man's Wartime Journalism*, ed. Werner Hamacher, Neil Hertz and Thomas Keenan (Lincoln and London: University of Nebraska Press, 1989). Also in augmented edn of *Mémoires for Paul de Man* (1989).

193 'Les chances de la pensée'. *Légende du siècle*, 5 (19 April 1988), p. 2. Derrida's text is in support of François Mitterand's candidacy for President of the Republic.

194 Derrida interviewed by Jean-Luc Nancy. *Topoi*, 7 2 (1988), pp. 113–21; Eng. trans. Peter T. Connor. Abridgement of 'Il faut bien manger, ou le calcul de sujet', in *Cahiers Confrontation*, 20 (winter 1989), pp. 91–114. Eng. trans. Peter Connor and Avital Ronell of complete version, as '"Eating Well", or the Calculation of the Subject: An Interview with Jacques Derrida', in *Who Comes After the Subject?*, ed. Eduardo Cadava, Peter Connor and Jean-Luc Nancy (New York and London: Routledge, 1991), pp. 96–119.

195 'Controverse sur la possibilité d'une science de la philosophie'. *La Décision philosophique*, 5 (1988), pp. 63–76. Derrida interviewed by François Laruelle.

196 'Le philosophe et les architectes'. *Diagonal*, 73 (August 1988), pp. 37–9. Derrida interviewed by Hélène Viale.

197 'The Derridean View: An Inter-view with Jacques Derrida'. *BM 04* (City University of New York), 1 (September 1988). Derrida interviewed by Edward Marx; Eng. trans. Mary Ann Caws pp. 4–5, 8.

198 'Che cos'e la poesia?' *Poesia*, 1–11 (1988), pp. 5–10; bilingual (French and Italian) presentation; Eng. trans. (with the French text accompanying it) by Peggy Kamuf in *A Derrida Reader* (see Books, no. 30), pp. 221–37. French text repr. in *Po&sie* 50 (1989), pp. 109–12. Quadrilingual (French, English, German and Italian) version, *Was ist Dichtung?* trans. Kamuf, Alexander Garcia Düttman and Maurizio Ferraris, pubd Berlin (Brinckmann und Bose, 1990).

199 'Abus de pouvoir à la Sorbonne'. *Nouvel Observateur* (24–30 november 1988), p. 27. Derrida interviewed by Henri Guirchoun.

200 'Ya-t-il une langue philosophique?' *Autrement*, 102 (November 1988), pp. 30–7. [Issue: *à quoi pensent les philosophes?* Four responses.]

201 Comments by Derrida in Nicole Gauthier, 'Les philosophes sous les fourches caudines de la politique'. *Libération* (24 November 1988), p. 37.

202 'The Politics of Friendship'. *Journal of Philosophy*, 75, 11 (1988), pp. 632–45; Eng. trans. Gabriel Motzkin.

   Text presented at the American Philosophical Association symposium on Law and Society on 30 December 1988.

203 Extract of a letter written by Derrida to the Editors of the *Southern Humanities Review*, 22, 1 (1988), p. iv.

204 'Afterword: Toward an Ethic of Discussion'. *Limited Inc*, ed. Gerald Graff (Evanston, IL: Northwestern University Press, 1988), pp. 111–60 (see Books, no. 24); Eng. trans. Samuel Weber. Derrida's text is a response to questions addressed to him in writing by Graff.

1989

205 "L'école a été un enfer pour moi: conversation avec Jacques Derrida," *Cahiers Pedagogiques* 270 (Janvier 1989) pp. 41–42. Interview with Bernard Defrance (first part). See Texts, no. 207, 213.

206 'La danse des fantômes'/'The Ghost Dance: An Interview with Jacques Derrida'. *Public*, 2 (1989), pp. 61–73. Eng. trans. by 'Jean-Luc Svoboda'; Derrida interviewed by Andrew Payne and Mark Lewis. Conversation in video journal *Diderot*, 3, pubd by the United Media Arts Studies (Toronto). The interview in *Public* carries the bilingual text.

207 'Liberté au present: "La démocratie ajournée"' Abridged version of a conversation with Olivier Salvatori and Nicolas Weill. *Le Monde de la Révolution Française*, 1 (January 1989), p. 27. Full text in *L'autre cap*; see Books no. 29.

208 'Conversation avec Jacques Derrida (2): Libérer la curiosité, susciter du désir'. *Cahiers pedagogiques*, 272 (March 1989), pp. 44–7. Derrida interviewed by Bernard Defrance. See Texts, no. 204, 213.

209 'Jacques Derrida in Conversation with Christopher Norris'. *Architectural Design*, 58, 1–2 (1989), pp. 6–11; see Film and Video Appearances, no. 4. Also in *Deconstruction*, ed. Andreas Papadakis, Catherine Cooke and Andrew Benjamin (London: Academy Editions, 1989), pp. 71–5.

210 'Rhétorique de la drogue'. *Autrement*, 106 (April 1989), pp. 197–214. Derrida's written reply to questions addressed to him by the editors of the periodical. [Issue: L'esprit des drogues.] Eng. trans. in *I-800*, 2 (forthcoming).

211 'Prólogo: ". . . Una de las virtudes más recientes . . ."' Preface to Cristina della Rocca, *Jacques Derrida: texto y deconstrucción* (Barcelona: Editorial Anthropos, 1989), pp. 9–16; Spanish trans. Cristina de Peretti.

212 'Biodegradables: Seven Diary Fragments'. *Critical Inquiry*, 15, 4 (1989), pp. 812–73; Eng. trans. Peggy Kamuf.

213 Comments by Derrida in Scott Malcomson, 'Not Everyone Loves a Parade'. *Village Voice*, 25 (July 1989), pp. 29–32. Excerpts from an interview in Paris.

214 'Une mise au point de Jacques Derrida.' *Cahiers Pedagogiques*, 276 (September 1989), p. 2. Derrida protests against the publication of an unedited interview transcript. See Texts, no. 204, 207.

215 'Interpretations at War. Kant, le Juif, l'Allemand'. *Phénoménologie et politique* (Brussels: Editions Ousia; Paris: Librarie J. Vrin, 1989), pp. 209–92. Introduction by Danielle Luries and Bernard Stevens. [Mélanges offerts à Jacques Taminiaux.] Eng. trans. Moshe Ron in *New Literary History*, 22, 1 (1991), pp. 39–95. Additional text included in note 1 of trans.: 'The Jewish-German Psyche: The Examples of Hermann Cohen and Franz Rosenzweig' (pp. 93–4).
   Paper delivered at the Center for Literary Studies, Hebrew University of Jerusalem, 1988.

216 'Comment donner raison? "How to Concede, with Reasons?"' *Diacritics*, 19, 3–4 (1989), pp. 4–9; bilingual presentation; Eng. trans. John P. Leavey, Jr.

1990

217 'A Discussion with Jacques Derrida'. *Writing Instructor*, 9, 1–2 (1989–90), pp. 7–18. Edited transcript of a discussion held in April 1989 at the University of Southern California between Derrida and a group of students and professors.

218 'Jacques Derrida on Rhetoric and Composition: A Conversation'. *JAC* (Journal of Advanced Composition), 10, (1990), pp. 1–21. Conversation between Derrida and Gary A. Olson. Reprinted in Gary A. Olson & Irene Gale, ed., *(Inter)views: Cross-Disciplinary Perspectives on Rhetoric and Literacy* (Carbondale and Edwardsville: Southern Illinois UP, 1991) pp. 121–41.

219 'Pour Moi, Le Seuil . . .'. *Libération* (22 January 1990), p. 29. Derrida's response to the question 'Le seuil de tolérance, c'est quoi pour vous?'

220 'Some Statements and Truisms about Neo-Logisms, Newisms, Postisms, Parasitisms, and other Small Seismisms'. *The States of 'Theory': History, Art and Critical Discourse*, ed. David Carroll (New York: Columbia University Press, 1990). pp. 63–95; Eng. trans. Anne Tomiche. Excerpts, as 'Interventions', in *Zeitgeist in Babel: The Post-Modernist Controversy*, ed. Ingeborg Hoesterey (Bloomington: Indiana University Press, 1991).
   Delivered at a colloquium organized by the Critical Theory Institute at the University of California, Irvine, spring 1987.

221 'Heidegger's Silence'. *Martin Heidegger and National Socialism*, ed. Günther Neske and Emil Kettering (New York: Paragon House, 1990). pp. 145–8. Excerpts from a talk given at a colloquium on 'Heidegger: portée philosophique et politique de sa pensée', held with Hans-Georg Gadamer and Philippe Lacoue-Labarthe in Heidelberg, 5 February 1988; German trans. Philip Rinke; Eng. trans. Lisa Harries. 'Heidegger's Silence' originally appeared as 'Heideggers Schweigen', in Neske and Kettering's *Antwort: Martin Heidegger im Gespräch* (Pfullingen: Neske, 1988), pp. 157–62.

222 'Droit de réponse: à propos de l'enseignement philosophique, J. Derrida répond à Guy Coq'. *Esprit* (6 June 1990), pp. 168–9.

223 Interview with Derrida conducted by Raoul Mortley. *French Philosophers in*

Conversation: Derrida, Irigaray, Levinas, Le Doeuff, Schneider, Serres (London and New York: Routledge, 1990), pp. 92–108.

224 'Mise au point'. *Figaro-Magazine* (10 March 1990).

225 'Subverting the Signature: A Theory of the Parasite'. *Blast Unlimited* (Boston), 2 (1990), pp. 16–21. Unauthorized transcript of a tape-recorded seminar in Paris.

226 'Un penseur dans la cité: "le philosophe n'a pas à parler comme tout le monde . . ."'. *L'evènement de jeudi* (12–18 April 1990), pp. 114–16. Interview with Yves Roucaute on the French edn of *Limited Inc*.

227 'Force de loi: le "fondement mystique de l'autorite"'/'Force of Law: The "Mystical Foundation of Authority"', *Cardozo Law Review*, 11, 5–6 (1990), pp. 920–1045. Bilingual presentation; Eng. trans. Mary Quaintance.

The first part of 'Force of Law' was delivered in October 1989 at a colloquium on 'Deconstruction and the Possibility of Justice' at the Cardozo Law School, New York. The second part was delivered on 26 April 1990 at the University of California, Los Angeles, as part of the colloquium on 'Nazism and the "Final Solution": Probing the Limits of Representation'.

228 'Privilège: titre justificatif et remarques introductives'. Introduction to *Du droit à la philosophie* (see Books, no. 25), pp. 9–108. Text dated July–August 1990.

229 'A Letter to Peter Eisenman'. *Assemblage*, 12 (August 1990), pp. 7–13; Eng. trans. Hilary P. Hanel. Derrida's letter was written in October 1989.

230 'L'autre cap: mémoires, réponses et responsabilités'. *Liber*, 5 (October 1990), pp. 11–13. *Liber* is an international book supplement to *Le Monde* (issue of 29 September 1990), *L'Indice*, *El Pais*, and the *Frankfurter Allgemeine Zeitung*. See Books, no. 29.

231 'Let Us Not Forget: Psychoanalysis'. *Oxford Literary Review*, 12, 1–2 (1990), pp. 3–7. Eng. trans. Geoffrey Bennington and Rachel Bowlby.

Derrida's text was delivered on 16 December 1988 in the Amphithéâtre Descartes at the Sorbonne, Paris, as part of the forum on 'Thinking at Present', organized by the Collège International de Philosophie. It formed the introduction to René Major's paper 'Reason from the Unconscious' (pubd in the same issue of *OLR*).

232 'Accecato di fronte al disegno', *Il Giornale dell'Arte* 82 (October 1990), pp. 12–13; in English trans. as 'The Philosopher sees (or doesn't see)', *The Art Newspaper* 1, no. 1 (October 1990) p. 9. Interview with Luciana Mottola Colban on 'Mémoires d'aveugle' exhibition at the Louvre.

233 'Videor'. *Passages de l'image*, ed. Raymond Bellour (Paris: Editions du Centre Georges Pompidou; 1990), pp. 158–61. [Response to Gary Hill: *Disturbance (Among the Jars)*, 1988.] Eng. trans. Peggy Kamuf in Raymond Bellour et al, ed., *Passages de l'image*, (Barcelona: Centre Culturel de la Fundació Caixa de Pensions, 1991) pp. 174–79.

234 'Le programme philosophique de Derrida'. *Libération* (15 November 1990), pp. 32–4. Derrida in conversation with Robert Maggiori.

235 'Louis Althusser'. *Lettres françaises*, 4 (December 1990), pp. 25–6. Read by Derrida at Althusser's burial.

236 'La voix de l'ami'. *Recherches sur la philosophie et le langage*, 12 (1990), pp. 163–76. Hommage à Henri Joly. An excerpt from 'L'oreille de Heidegger: Philopolemologie (*Geschlecht* IV)'; see Texts no. 249.

237 'Jacques Derrida ici et ailleurs'. *Le Monde* (16 November 1990), p. 21. Derrida interviewed by Roger-Pol Droit.

238 'Le dessein du philosophe'. *Beaux Arts Magazine*, 85 (December 1990), pp. 88–91. Derrida interviewed by Jérôme Coignard. A partial translation by Lois Grjebine of this interview, titled 'The Philosopher's Riddle', can be found on pp. 158–61 of the same issue.

1991

239 Fragment of a letter (dated July 1989) in Albert Leventure, 'A bibliography of the French and English works of Jacques Derrida'. *Textual Practice*, 5, (1991), p. 94.

240 'La philosophie demandée'. *Bulletin de la Société Française de Philosophie* (January–March 1991), pp. 5–23. Séance du 24 November 1990: 'Réflexion sur l'état actuel et les perspectives de l'enseignement de la philosophie en France'. Discussion, pp. 31–51 following Derrida's presentation and that of Bernard Bourgeois.

241 'Entretien avec Jacques Derrida'. *La Sept* (23–5 March 1991), pp. 12–13. Derrida interviewed by Frédérique Bilbaut-Faillant.

242 'Une "folie" doit veiller sur la pensée'. *Magazine littéraire*, 286 (March 1991), pp. 16–30. Derrida in conversation with François Ewald.

243 'Pour l'amour de Lacan' and 'Après tout: les chances du collège'. *Lacan avec les philosophes* (Paris: Albin Michel, 1991), pp. 397–420, 443–6.

244 Comments by Derrida in Mitchell Stephens, 'Deconstructing Jacques Derrida'. *Los Angeles Times Magazine* (21 July 1991), pp. 12–15, 31. Includes quotations from interviews.

245 '"This Strange Institution Called Literature": An Interview with Jacques Derrida'. *Acts of Literature* (see Books, no. 32), pp. 33–75. Edited transcript of an interview with Derrida conducted by Derek Attridge, recorded in Laguna Beach in April 1989; Eng. trans. Geoffrey Bennington and Rachel Bowlby.

246 'Canons and Metonymies: A Conversation with Jacques Derrida'. *The Conflict of the Faculties in America*, ed. Richard Rand. The interview between Derrida and Rand took place at Irvine, California, 1 May 1988; Eng. trans. Rand and Amy Wygart (Lincoln: University of Nebraska Press, forthcoming).

247 'Summary of Impromptu Remarks', in Cynthia Davidson and Jeffrey Kipnis, ed., *Anyone*, New York: Rizzoli International Publications, 1991, pp. 38–45. Derrida's remarks at a conference on architecture, held in Los Angeles and Santa Monica, CA, 10–11 May 1991. Derrida also contributes to 'Discussion A1' (pp. 78–93), 'Discussion A2' (pp. 164–72), and 'Discussion A3' (pp. 240–1), and a letter from Derrida to the editors, dated 2 August 1991, is reprinted on p. 250.

248 Short excerpts from Derrida's lecture 'The Politics of Friendship' [see Texts, no. 201], delivered at Cornell University in October 1988, in David Lehman, *Signs of the Times: Deconstruction and the fall of Paul de Man* (London: André Deutsch, 1991), pp. 246–52.

1992

249 'Passions: "An oblique offering"'. *Derrida: A Critical Reader* ed. David Wood (Oxford: Blackwell, 1992), pp. 5–35; Eng. trans. David Wood.

250 'Heidegger's Ear: Philopolemology (*Geschlecht IV*)'. *Commemorations: Reading Heidegger*, ed. John Sallis (Bloomington: Indiana University Press, 1992); Eng. trans. John P. Leavey, Jr.

251 'Post-Scriptum', in Harold Coward and Toby Foshay, ed., *Derrida and Negative Theology*, Albany: SUNY Press, 1992.

252 'Nous autres Grecs,' in *Les Stratégies contemporaines d'appropriation de l'Antiquité*, Paris: Seuil, 1992.

BOOK REVIEWS

1 Review of Edmund Husserl's *Phänomenologische Psychologie: Vorlesungen Sommersemester 1925*. *Etudes Philosophiques*, 2, 18 (1963), pp. 203–6.

2 Review of J. N. Mohanty's *Edmund Husserl's Theory of Meaning*. *Etudes Philosophiques*, 18, 1 (1963), pp. 95–6.

3 Review of J. N. Mohanty's *Edmund Husserl's Theory of Meaning*. *Etudes Philosophiques*, 19, 4 (1964), pp. 617–19.

4 Review of Edmund Husserl's *The Idea of Phenomenology*. *Etudes Philosophiques*, 20, 4 (1965), p. 538.

5 Review of Edmund Husserl's *The Paris Lectures*. *Etudes Philosophiques*, 20, 4 (1965), p. 539.

6 Review of Robert Sokolowski's *The Formation of Husserl's Concept of Constitution*. *Etudes Philosophiques*, 20, 4 (1965), pp. 557–8.

7 Review of Eugen Fink's *Studien zur Phänomenologie, 1930–1939*. *Etudes Philosophiques*, 21, 4 (1966), pp. 549–50.

8 Review of Edmund Husserl's *Zur Phänomenologie der inneren Zeitbewusstseins*. *Etudes Philosophiques*, 22, 1 (1967), p. 94.

EHESS COURSE DESCRIPTIONS*

1 'Les Institutions Philosophiques. Nationalité et nationalisme philosophiques', *Annuaire EHESS* (1984–6) pp. 441–3.

2 'Les Institutions Philosophiques. Nationalité et nationalisme philosophiques: Le théologico-politique (langue sacrée, langue séculaire; l'élection, l'alliance, la promesse)', *Annuaire EHESS* (1986–7) pp. 366–8.

3 'Les Institutions Philosophiques. Nationalité et nationalisme philosophiques: Kant, le Juif, l'Allemand', *Annuaire EHESS* (1987–8) pp. 343–4.

4 'Les Institutions Philosophiques. Nationalité et nationalisme philosophiques: politiques de l'amitié', *Annuaire EHESS* (1988–9) pp. 380–2.

5 'Les Institutions Philosophiques. Nationalité et nationalisme philosophiques: politiques de l'amitié (séminaire ouvert)', *Annuaire EHESS* (1989–90) pp. 358–9.

* EHESS/*Ecole des Hautes Etudes en Sciences Sociales* (Paris)

TRANSLATIONS

1962

1 Edmund Husserl's *Die Frage nach dem Ursprung der Geometrie als intentional-historisches Problem*, as *L'Origine de la géométrie*; see Books, no. 1.

1964

2 With Roger Martin, W. V. Quine's 'The Frontiers of Logical Theory', as 'Les frontières de la théorie logique'. *Etudes philosophiques*, 19, 2 (1964), pp. 191–208. [Perspectives sur la philosophie nord-américaine.]
3 Marvin Farber's 'The World of Life and the Tradition of Philosophy', as 'Le monde-de-la vie et la tradition de la philosophie'. *Etudes philosophiques*, 19, 2 (1964), pp. 209–19. [Perspectives sur la philosophie nord-américaine.]

ARCHITECTURE

1986

1 Collaboration with Bernard Tschumi (le Parc de la Villette) and Peter Eisenman (Choral Work), Paris. Documentation of Derrida's project with Eisenman can be found in Jayne Merkel's 'Oeuvre Chorale', in *Parc-Ville Villette*, ed. Isabelle Auricoste and Hubert Tonka (Vaisseau de Pierres 2: Seyssel, Champ Vallon, 1987), pp. 30–5); in 'Choral Works/Parc de la Villette', *Architecture and Urbanism: Peter Eisenman* (August 1988), pp. 136–45; and in Renato Rizzi's 'Eisenman: Porgetto per il Parco "La Villette"', Parigi, 1986', *Domus*, 681 (March 1987), pp. 1–3. Eisenman has discussed the collaboration in 'Peter Eisenman: An *Architectural Design* interview with Charles Jencks', *Architectural Design*, 58, 3/4 (1988), pp. 49–61. *Choral Works* (New York: Rizzoli, forthcoming) will include Derrida's 'Chôra' (see Texts no. 179), 'Fifty-Five Aphorisms on the Aphorism', and a transcript of conversations with Eisenman on the 'Choral Works' project.

FILM AND VIDEO APPEARANCES

1983

1 *L'Appel du Silence* (1983), directed by Philippe Alfonsi, broadcast on 'Résistances', Antenne 2 (French television), 1 December 1983. Artists and writers discuss 'art against apartheid.'

2 *Ghost Dance* (100 min., 1983), produced, written, and directed by Ken McMullen; a Looseyard Production, for Channel 4 (Great Britain) and ZDF (West Germany). Derrida, in a cameo appearance, discusses cinema, mourning, and ghosts, among other things.

1986

3 *Caryl Chessman, l'écriture contre la mort* (57 min., 1985), directed by Jean-Christophe Rosé; produced by I.N.A. for TF 1 (French television). A documentary on death-row prisoner and writer Caryl Chessman, based loosely on a treatment by Derrida, 'Couloirs de la mort: Caryl Chessman, l'écriture ou la vie.'

1987

4 *Big Words . . . Small Worlds*. Derrida is one of the participants filmed at the University of Strathclyde during a conference on 'The Linguistics of Writing', 4–6 July 1986 (comments transcribed and pubd in *The Linguistics of Writing*; see 'Some questions and responses', Texts, no. 175). Programme broadcast on Channel 4 (London), 22 November 1987.

1988

5 *Jacques Derrida, Deconstruction in Art and Architecture: Interview with Christopher Norris*, edited and directed by Marcus Latham. Interview recorded in Paris in March, and made in conjunction with the International Symposium on Deconstruction held at the Clore Gallery, London, 26 March 1988. Transcript in *Architectural Design* (see Texts, no. 208).

1990

6 *The Late Show* (BBC television), broadcast on 5 April 1990. Derrida is one of the contributors discussing the work of Roland Barthes.

RECORDING

1987

Feu la cendre. A cassette recording of Derrida reading the text with Carole Bouquet was issued with the book in France; see Books, no. 16, and Texts, no. 105).

TEXTS ORIGINALLY (AND STILL) AVAILABLE ONLY IN LANGUAGES
OTHER THAN FRENCH OR ENGLISH

1 'Jacques Derrida, Europas "svåraste" filosof: tankarna som rubbar maktens cirklar. *Expressen* Stockholm, (23 April 1981), p. 4. Interview with Horace Engdahl.

2 Interview, *Asahi Journal* 26, (25 May 1984), pp. 6–15.

3 'Une carte postale de l'Amérique: interview met Derrida'. *Krisis* (Amsterdam) 22 (March 1986), pp. 5–18. Interview with Veronica Vasterling.

4 'Leer lo ilegible'. *Revista del Occidente* (Madrid), 62–3 (July–August 1986), pp. 160–82. Interview with Carmen Gonzalez-Marin in Paris, 16 January 1986.

5 'Ist Dekonstruktion kritisierbar?', *Frankfurter Rundschau* 195, 25 August 1986, p. 22. Interview with Florian Rötzer, trans. from French by Christine Pries. Reprinted, with some modifications, in Rötzer, ed., *Französische Philosophen im Gespräch* (München: Klaus Boer Verlag, 1986), pp. 67–87.

6 'Positionen, 14 Jahre später'. *Positionen*, ed. Peter Engelman (Graz and Wien: Böhlau, 1986), pp. 19–30. Interview with Peter Engelman in German, trans. Mathilde Fischer, prefacing the first German translation of *Positions*.

7 'Nacionalidad y nacionalismo filosofico'. Trans. Marie-Christine Peyrrone, in *Diseminario*, ed. Lisa Block de Behar (Montevideo: XYZ Editores, 1987), pp. 27–47.

8 'Antwort an Apel', trans Michael Wetzel, in *Zeitmitschrift* 3, (1987), pp. 76–85. Derrida's reply to Apel at the Collège International de Philosophie, 13 November 1985.

9 'Ma l'ideologia non è azione'. *Panorama* (8 November 1987), p. 144. Interview with Lidia Breda on Farias and *De l'esprit*.

10 'Machtmissbrauch', *Frankfurter Allgemeine Zeitung* (16 March 1988), p. 11. Letter responding to earlier articles in *FAZ* of 10 and 24 February on Paul de Man.

11 'Entrevista con Jacques Derrida', *Política y sociedad* (Madrid), 3 (Spring 1989), pp. 101–6. Interview with Cristina de Peretti.

12 'Istrice 2. Ick bünn all hier: conversation con Jacques Derrida'. *Aut Aut* 235, (January–February 1990), pp. 126–46. Interview with Maurizio Ferraris.

13 '¿Un ser que no habla puede comer?' *Literatura y libros* 2 (11 February 1990), pp. 4–5. Interview with Cristina de Peretti.

14 'Donner le temps (de la traduction)/Die Zeit (der Übersetzung) geben'. *Zeit-Zeichen*, ed. George Christoph Tholen and Michael O. Scholl (Weinheim: VCH Acta Humanoria, 1990), pp. 37–56. German protocol by Elisabeth Weber of a lecture given at a symposium in Kassel, June 1989. See *Donner le temps*; see Books, no. 31.

15 'La amistad está siempre por venir, y sólo Ilegará con el superhombre'," *El Independiente* (24 December 1989), pp. 2–3. Interview with Cristina de Peretti, conducted in Madrid on 2 December 1989.

16 'Entrevista: Del materialismo no dialéctico'. *Diario 16/Culturas*, 69 (3 August 1986), pp. III–V. Interview with Kadhim Jihad.

17 'La visite de Jacques Derrida'. *Vul: Magazine français du Japon* (Tokyo), 38–9 (January 1984).

A Jacques Derrida curriculum vitae, constituted by Geoffrey Bennington, is available in *Jacques Derrida* (see Books, no. 28).

ACKNOWLEDGEMENTS

The brevity of this acknowledgement ought in no way to diminish the importance of the part played by those who contributed to the realization of this bibliography. I offer my warmest thanks to Derek Attridge, Jacques Derrida, Peggy Kamuf, Thomas Keenan, John P. Leavey, Jr., John Llewelyn, Chantal Morel and David Wood.

Albert Leventure

Index

Abraham, Nicholas and Torok, Maria, 109
Adorno, Theodor, 167; and Horkheimer,
  Max, *Dialectic of Enlightenment*, 185
affect, 14, 55, 56, 68, 150; *see also* symbol,
  symbolization
affirmation, affirmative, 14, 26n4, 53, 54,
  59, 68, 92; and confession, 214; and
  denial, 89–90, 93–4; double, 91; of
  language, 90–1; or negation, 222
alterity, 93, 131, 133; speaking, 103;
  vertical and horizontal, distinguished,
  88, 92
apophasis, 20, 33n11
appeal, 40, 42; *see also différance*, demand
argument, 240, 241; philosophy ought to
  be, 239; *see also* Deconstruction
Aristotle, 43, 57, 89, 132, 182, 195, 210,
  213, 218–21, 226, 238, 239
Aufhebung (sublation), 98, 104, 194–5, 199,
  241
Augustine, St, 21, 182
Austin, J. L., 77–8, 79, 81, 83, 90, 93, 94,
  176–7, 181, 182, 184, 190, 245n15; 'How
  to Talk–some simple ways', 87
author, 23, 81, 142, 148–9, 153, 164, 179;
  creative power of, 115; intention, 2, 23,
  149, 151
Autrui, 88, 92

Bataille, Georges, 168, 185
Baudelaire, Charles, 12, 26n3, 33n14, 41

Baudrillard, Jean, 168
being, 52, 54, 63, 68, 193, 218–19, 232,
  241; and beings, 219–22, 225;
  interpretation of (*Seinsauslegung*), 224;
  meaning of, 43, 63, 226; mysticism of,
  187; optical model of, 222; and passion,
  45; potentiality for (*Seinkönnen*), 85; as
  presence (*Anwesenheit*), 221, 227;
  thinking of, 101; -true 220–1, 222, 226;
  -with (*Mitsein*), 24; withdrawal of, 43
Benjamin, Walter, 48
Bennington, Geoffrey, 97–119
Benveniste, Emile, 27n4, 226
Berkeley, Bishop George, 87
Bernal, Martin, 97, 110
Bernasconi, Robert, 4n1, 99–100, 137–66
Blanchot, Maurice, 48, 68, 140; *La Folie du
  jour*, 82, 85, 137
Bloom, Harold, 236
body, the, 45, 60, 126, 132; of language,
  43; lost, 50; philosophical tradition as
  organs of, 39; of the signifier, 129; and
  writing, 50
Borges, Jorge Luis, 182

Calvino, Italo, 182
cannibalism, rhetoric of, 16
Carnap, Rudolph, 239, 240
castration, 107, 197
Catesson, Jean, 44
Cavell, Stanley, 236

ceremony, 5–6; *see also* ritual, sacrifice
citation, 86; *see also* iteration
commentary, 141; *see also* doubling
Condillac, Maurice, 151
confession, 31; *see also* affirmation
consensus, 14, 15
constative: and performative, 77–80, 167
critical: moment, 6; position, 6; reason, 184; *see also* reading
critique, 11, 17, 18, 94, 138, 142, 163n6, 168, 171, 182, 186, 188, 190; auto-, 12; and crisis, (*Krinein*) 6–7, 72, 210, 211; Derrida's relation to, 139–40; enlightened, 189; of metaphysics, 218; and non-critique, 6; phenomenological, 123; textual, 236; and truth, 190; *see also* Enlightenment
Culler, Jonathan, 176, 235–7

Dasein, 24, 41, 68, 223–5, 227
Davidson, Donald, 219, 242
debt, 11, 53; Benveniste on, 27–8n4; economy of, 9, 18, 26–9n4; Malamoud on, 28–9n4
deconstruction, 13, 17, 53, 61, 85, 94, 97, 98, 99, 102–3, 125, 129, 131, 137, 143, 148–9, 152–3, 154, 159, 160, 161, 162, 167, 168, 170, 173, 175, 180, 181, 188, 191, 194, 201, 203, 225, 232, 235–6; Hegelianism of, 99; and irrationalism, 187; and metaphysics, 56; and morality, 14; and rigorous argument, 235, 237–9
de Man, Paul, 104, 137–66, 203; *Allegories of Reading*, 164n17; *Blindness and Insight*, 138, 140, 142, 160; 'On Reading Rousseau', 140–1, 165n34; 'Rhetoric of Blindness', 138–42, 164n23, 165n34; wartime journalism, 159
demand, 48; and appeal, 42; repetition of, 42; and seduction, 40; *see also* appeal
democracy, 27n4; *see also* literature
Derrida, Jacques, 5–35; *Altérités*, 72; *L'Autre cap*, 29n5; 'Cogito and the History of Madness', 185; 'Comment ne pas parler', 87, 88, 90, 91; *De l'esprit*, 88–9, 91, 92; *La Démocratie ajournée*, 29n5; Derridadaism, 235; 'La différance', 53, 87; *Dissemination*, 135n5; 'The Double

Session', 122; 'Ellipsis', 36–51; *La Fausse monnaie*, 33n14; *Feu le cendre*, 93, 216n9; 'Force of Law', 30n7, 96n7; 'Freud et la scène de l'écriture', 113, 118n1; *Glas*, 11, 16, 30n7, 60, 63, 73, 86, 92, 93, 101, 118n1, 193–5, 208, 216n9, 243; *Glassary*, 73, 86, 92; *Of Grammatology*, 31n8, 44, 52, 122–3, 125, 138–66, 177, 206–8, 215, 243; 'La Guerre de Paul de Man', 94, 159; Hegelian and anti-Hegelian view of, 93; 'Hölderlin: Wechsel der Töne', 93; 'Interpreting Signatures', 157; *Introduction to Husserl's "Origin of Geometry"*, 72, 76, 92; 'The Last Word of Racism', 3; 'The Law of Genre', 81, 84; *Limited Inc. abc . . .*, 81, 87, 181; *Margins of Philosophy*, 30n7, 99, 181; *Memoires for Paul de Man*, 137–8, 141, 153, 156–7, 159; 'Mes chances', 30n7; 'Nombre de oui', 91; 'Numbers', 64; *Otobiographies*, 53; *Parages*, 76; 'Plato's Pharmacy', 61, 104; 'The Politics of Friendship', 96n7; on Ponge's 'Par le mot *par . . .*', 80, 82, 90, 93; *Positions*, 98; *The Post-Card*, 24, 93, 173, 176, 178–82, 217n23, 243; *Psyche: Invention de l'Autre*, 76, 78, 79, 162; *Schibboleth*, 66; 'Scribble', 112, 118n1; 'Signature Event Context', 87; *Speech and Phenomena*, 123–4; *Spurs: Nietzsche's Styles*, 53, 54, 93; 'Structure, Sign and Play', 173; 'Supplement of the Copula', 226; *D'un Ton apocalyptique*, 90, 93, 187, 188; as transcendental philosopher, 236; *La Vérité en peinture*, 91; 'Violence and Metaphysics', 103, 138, 161
Descartes, René, 79, 87, 170, 208, 210, 213, 222, 228
dialectic: dialectical, 98
différance, 53, 63, 86, 88, 103, 131, 133, 134, 184, 198, 203, 215, 225–7, 229, 232, 239, 240; as appeal, 39; as infinite repetition of meaning, 39; and laughter, 41–2; and passion, 39
direct (*capitale*), 10, 11; and the oblique, 11–13; *see also* oblique
dissemination, 103

donation: *coup de don*, 54; feminine, 54
double: mark, 123, 125, 135n8; ontologically, 203; origin of languages, 146; reading *see* reading; writing *see* writing
doubling, 120, 197; and commentary, 139, 142, 147; re-, 120–1, 124; retentional and protentional, 133
duty, 8–11, 14, 18, 33n12, 36, 26n4; and the categorical imperative, 31n9

Eckhart, Meister, 91
Egypt: in deconstruction, 97, 99
Einstein, Albert, 79
ellipse: ellipsis, 35–8, 39, 43, 51, 81; of the centre, 49; economy of, 11; of the transcendental *see* transcendental
Emerson, Ralph Waldo, 236
Enlightenment, the, 167, 168, 169, 170, 185, 186, 187, 188, 189; counter-, 169, 186; and critical thought, 187; discourse of, 188; and reason, 190; values, 190
Ereignis, 43, 45
ergon, parergon, 204–5
eschatology: eschaton, 105, 106
ethico-political, 159, 162
ethics: ethical, 3, 10, 26n4, 143; space, 3
exemplarity, 3, 15, 23, 31–2n10, 33–5n14, 85, 87, 88, 140, 193–6, 204–8, 211, 213, 215, 216; economy of, 201; excess within, 195; and exhibition, 202–3, 205; and the fetish, 194, 203; and framing, 196, 202, 205–6, and God, 201; in Hegel (*Beispiel*), 194–5; justifying, 206, 213–14; law of the law of, 206, 209; limits of, 201; misunderstanding of *see* misunderstanding; non-, 196, 198–9; parasitic aspect of, 202
exorbitant: and thirst, 40

Felman, Shoshana, 176
Fichte, Johann, 222, 224
figurative: and literal, 164n24; *see also* language
Fink, Eugen, 64
force, 57–8, 59, 64–5, 66, 69, 74; and the body, 51; and language, 65; language as

the tomb of, 55; as substance, critique of, 65; writing as image of, 65
formal semantics: as reformulation, 219–21
Fort/da, 212
Foucault, Michel, 115, 168, 185, 189, 215, 216–17n13, 223
Frank, Manfred, 218–34
Frege, Gottlob, 81, 182, 236, 245n15
Freud, Sigmund, 8, 53, 73, 74, 97, 98, 106, 107, 108, 109, 113, 115, 116, 168–9, 177–8, 180, 217n23, 236, 243; *Totem and Taboo*, 27n4
friendship, 8–9, 37

Gadamer, Hans-Georg, 2, 4n2
Gasché, Rodolphe, 3, 4n1, 36–7, 118n3, 156, 170–1, 193–4, 201, 237–43, 244n14, 245n16, 246n23; 'God for Example', 193; *The Tain of the Mirror*, 237
Geist, 89, 127, 134
Genette, Gérard, 85
genre, 81, 82–3, 85, 86, 93; deconstructive, marks of, 85; Habermas on the levelling of the genre distinction between philosophy and literature, 172, 174, 178, 181, 184, 190; law of, 36; literary, 84–5
gesture, 126; and speech, 144
gift (*don*), 13, 52, 68, 93; as present, 46
graphematic alterity, 87
graphematics, 78
Greeks, 109; *see also* Jews
Greimas, A. J., 228

Haar, Michel, 52–71
Habermas, Jürgen, 1, 2, 4n2, 167–90, 239–40, 245n16; critique of Derrida, 167–76, 187; *Knowledge and Human Interests*, 168, 182; *The Philosophical Discourse of Modernity*, 167, 172
Handelman, Susan, 115, 118n4
Hartman, Geoffrey, 235–6
Harvey, Irene, 3, 193–217
Hegel, Georg Wilhelm Friedrich, 20, 36, 38, 39, 42, 53, 63, 65, 74, 97, 100–3, 106, 114, 120, 154, 170, 171, 181, 182, 188, 199, 201, 210–11, 225, 228, 236, 237, 238, 239, 243, 245n15;

Encyclopedia, 120, 208; God in, 102; *Logic*, 219, 233n16, 238, 240–1; *Phenomenology of Spirit*, 194, 200, 222

Heidegger, Martin, 2, 24, 43, 44, 45, 52, 53, 59, 60, 64–5, 68, 78, 83, 84, 87, 88, 101, 138, 144, 154, 157, 158, 162, 163n6, 171, 177, 187, 188, 193, 218–19, 220–1, 224–7, 232, 234n48, 236, 238–9, 243, 245n15; *Being and Time*, 27n4, 67, 81, 85, 89–91, 223, 233–4n36, 239, 240, 243; concept of 'earth', 65; *Grundbegriffe der Metaphysik*, 89–90; *Kant and the Problem of Metaphysics*, 133; 'The Nature of Language', 90; 'The Origin of the Work of Art', 91; *The Principle of Reason*, 64; *Time and Being*, 91; *Wass heisst Denken?*, 92

Heraclitus, 64

hermeneutics, 148, 152, 171, 197, 228; and tradition, 100

heteronomy: and autonomy, 101–2

historical reason, 186

history, 45, 48, 98, 103, 108, 156–7, 178; idea of, 168; of ideas, 168; Jewish, 105; of metaphysics, 20, 123; philosophical, 171; of philosophy, 188, 216; *see also* logocentrism

Hobbes, Thomas, 189

Hölderlin, Friedrich, 93, 102

Holocaust (*le brûle tout*), 201, 216n9

hope: Heideggerian, 92

Huizinga, Alvin, *Homo Ludens*, 66

Husserl, Edmund, 2, 24, 48, 72–3, 100, 123–32, 134, 169, 170, 173, 182, 184, 221, 225, 228, 229, 230, 236, 243; *Ideas*, 132; *Logical Investigations*, 124, 223

hybris, 12, 16

hymen, 68, 86

hysteria, 49; and 'hystery', 51; *see also* writing

ideal speech situation, 178

identity: logic of, 144, 154

Ideologiekritik, 167

illocutionary act, 90

il y a, 101; *see also* language

indication and expression, 124–32, 134; Husserl's reduction of, 125; and sense,

131–2, 134; *see also* sign

indicative function, 127–8

intensity, 56–9, 65; and the aphorism, 59

interpretation, 3, 33n12, 34n14, 139–40, 142; concepts of, 53; deconstructive, 53; dream, 112–13; symbolic, 113

intertextuality, 191

irresponsible, 94; and ethics, 94; *see also* undecidability

iterability, 86, 140, 231

iteration, 86

Jabès, Edmond, 36, 40, 102, 114

Jakobson, Roman, 175

Jemeinigkeit (Mineness), 24

Jews, 107, 113, 116, 195–6; as example of the non-example, 199; Hegel's exclusion of, 195; and Greeks, 97, 99, 101–3, 104, 105; and Judaism, 102, 199; Kant and Hegel as Jew and Greek, 104; opposition of Jew and Greek, 104

joining: and fracturing, 40, 42, 45

Joyce, James, 113, 173, 185

judgement: reflective and determinant, 94; *see also* Kant

Kant, Immanuel, 8, 9, 20, 26–27n4, 31n10, 33n12, 37, 50, 80, 100–3, 106, 119n10, 163n6, 168, 170, 171, 174, 182, 186–7, 188, 189, 190, 194, 203, 205, 221, 222, 223, 236, 238–9, 242, 244n12, 245n15; *Critique of Judgement*, 100, 196–8, 202; *Critique of Practical Reason*, 27n4, 32n10; *Critique of Pure Reason*, 14, 114, 238; determinant and reflective judgments, 197, 202, 204, 206; *Groundwork for a Metaphysics of Morals*, 9, 27n4, 32n10; on imagination, 20; on sacrifice (*Auföpferung*), 14; *see also* judgement, sacrifice

Kearney, Richard, 100, 103, 105–6

Kierkegaard, Søren, 20, 31n8, 182

Lacan, Jacques, 169, 178, 180, 194

language: and the body, 57; carnage of, 60, 63; eidetic reduction of, 124; energy of, 52; entropy of, 57; figural and literal, 150–1, 164n24, 165n25, 194–5; music

language (*cont.*):
   and, 56; natural, 74; origin of, 55, 57; of
   the other, 94; and play, 63; of ritual and
   duty, 8; severity towards, 59; signs and,
   125; spoken and written, 56, 59, 122–3;
   structuralist theory of, 228; and the *il y a*,
   42; thirst for, 57; and truth, 42; *see also*
   language games
language games, 241; 'ordinary' and
   'extraordinary', 182, 184, 190
law, 9, 15, 23, 27n4, 32n10, 73, 86, 92, 94,
   101–3, 110, 111, 112, 114–16, 196–206,
   208–16; desire for, 215; of the example,
   196–7; of the frame; Judaic, 112; the
   other, 197, 198, 205; of the other, 196,
   200, 201; moral, 14, 101
Le Carré, John, 74
legislator, 114, 115; and charlatan, 114; *see
   also* state
Leibniz, Gottfried Wilhelm, 210, 222–3
Lévi-Strauss, Claude, 141, 149, 162, 213–
   14
Levinas, Emmanuel, 2, 53, 68, 83, 91, 92,
   94, 101, 103, 110–11, 138, 159 161, 162;
   on Derrida, 91; on Heidegger, 2; *Totality
   and Infinity*, 88; '*Tout autrement*', 91
life: as economy of death, 107
liquifaction, (*Verflüssigung*) 242; and
   deconstruction, 245n19
literature, 22–3, 82, 84–6, 114, 154; and
   democracy, 23; Derrida and, 154;
   jouissance, 34n14; and philosophy, 1, 22,
   34–35n14, 121, 137–8, 154, 167, 173,
   175, 181, 183, 184–5, 186, 190, 191,
   237–8, 245n19; and play, 34n14;
   question of, 138; *see also* secret
Llewelyn, John, 3, 4n1, 72–96
logocentrism, 124, 129, 141, 147, 151, 157,
   158, 177, 207, 109, 211, 237; history of
   207; in Husserl, 124–5
Logos, 98
Lukacs, Georg, 140
Lyotard, Jean-François, 1, 118n6, 168

Malamoud, Charles, 27–28n4
Mallarmé, Stéphane, 79, 152
Marcel, Gabriel, 30n6
Marion, Jean-Luc, 87, 88–9

Marx, Karl, 243
meaning (*sens*), 37–9, 41, 42, 44, 47, 51,
   129, 227; abolition of, 59; of Being, 43;
   dissemination of, 47; ellipsis of, 38–9;
   excess of, 38–9; literal, 151; and passion,
   38; and repetition, 39, 48; and touch, 50
meaning (*vouloir-dire*), 127; and appeal, 38;
   call to, 45; and intention, 126; *see also*
   appeal
metaphor, 55, 56, 134, 149, 150, 152, 172,
   184, 189, 190, 204–5; ontic, 134; optical,
   224; usage of, 190; *see also* being
metaphysics, 157, 161; beginning of, 123,
   128; closure of, 99; tradition of, 194; *see
   also* history
mimesis, 3, 21, 31–32n10, 121–2, 123,
   134, 135n5, 197; and non-mimesis,
   33n12
misreading, 2, 142, 179
misunderstanding, 142, 149, 154; of
   exemplarity, 204; *see also* misreading
Moore, G. E., 83
moralist, 20
morality, 13, 14, 31n10, 149; concept of,
   32n10; imperative, 32n10; and
   moralisms, 14
music: and the life of the drives; 57; *see also*
   language
mythology, 104
mythos, 104

name, 11, 12, 14, 21, 60, 63; proper, 7,
   200, 207, 211; problem of, 177; and
   signatures, 7, 40, 46, 196; *see also*
   undecidables, undecidability
Nancy, Jean-Luc, 3, 36–51
narcissism, 11–12
New Critics, the, 140
Newton, Sir Isaac, 243
Nietzsche, Friedrich Wilhelm, 2, 27n4,
   53–71, 91, 121, 152, 154, 157, 158, 162,
   168, 171, 185, 186; *Genealogy of Morals*,
   59; Heideggerian reading of, 54; 'On
   Truth and Life', 55; *Untimely
   Meditations*, 59; *Thus Spake Zarathustra*,
   59; and writing, 55
non-response, 14–15, 17–18; absolute, 22;
   art of the, 18; and the secret, 23; *see also*

responding, response, responsibility, responsiveness

Norris, Christopher, 167–92, 235–37

obligation, 92

oblique, 24, 60–1; *see also* direct, offering

obliqueness, 24, 30n7

offer, 7

offering, 6, 46; the body, 18; oblique, 16; of the other, 17

ontico-ontological difference, 44, 64, 86, 88, 221, 225, 240

ontology, 43, 49, 145, 149, 198, 219, 220, 222; fundamental, 221; of the text, 3; western, 227

ontotheology, 63, 87, 88, 196

origin, 123, 128, 145, 146, 149, 151; drive to 121, 129; forgetting of, 123; *see also* Passion, Writing

Other, 2, 10, 17, 24, 33n12, 94, 134, 145, 185, 229; consuming the, 16; of the Greek and the Jew, 105; invention of the, 86; name of the, 10; *stigmè* of, 116; *see also* law

paradox, 76, 81, 82, 90; logical and semantic, distinguished, 75; of quasi-analysis, 83, 84; *see also* use

Parmenides, 221, 238

passion, 6, 10, 12, 21, 23, 24–5, 31n8, 38, 39, 40, 45, 49, 58, 144, 146, 150; of the centre 49; concept of, 14; *différance* as, 39; as example, 31–32n10; of language, 46; mechanical, 44; and need, 143, 146; of the origin, 37; sacrificial, 31n10; secret of, 33n12; of sense, 49; of the text, 3; *see also* writing

passivity, 6

Peirce, Charles Sanders, 227

performative and constative, 77–80, 93; contradiction, 83

pharmakon, 61, 86, 100

pharmakos, 6

phenomenological tradition, 100

philosophy: of consciousness, 222; distinction between the empirical and the essential, 114; 'doing' and 'reading', 98; fictive potential or entertainment value

of, 180; and literary criticism, 173, 174, 183; and its other, 100; *see also* history, literature

phonocentrism, 122

physis, 65–7, 69

place: and text, 67; without earth, 66

Plato, 44, 48, 58, 97, 107, 108–10, 121, 123, 176–7, 182, 208–11, 213, 236, 238, 239, 243; *Phaedo*, 121, 123; *Phaedrus*, 104, 109, 208–9; *Republic*, 104, 109; *Sophist*, 104; *Timaeus*, 108

play, 34n14, 57, 64, 67, 199; drive of (*Spieltrieb*), 64–5; free- 73, 172–3, 175, 176; and irresponsibility, 68; and language, 63; of the trace, 63; word, 42; of words, 60; of the world, 67; of writing, 66

pleasure, 37, 41, 47, 55–6, 74; and displeasure, 55–6; as *jouissance*, 34n14; and pain, 47, 56

Poe, Edgar Alan, 6, 25n2, 179

poetic, the, 114

poiesis, 83

politics, 168; crypto-, 186; *see also* ethics, literature

Ponge, Francis, 76–7, 79, 81, 84; 'Fable' 81

postmodernism, 167–91

post-structuralism, 167–8

Poulet, Georges, 140

praxis, 83

presence, 39, 42, 45, 51, 62, 67, 107, 122, 128–31, 134, 145, 159, 230–1, 234n48, 236; and absence, 144; Derrida's critique of, 227; at hand (*Vorhandenheit*), 219, 222; and the *il y a*, 43; and intuition, 130; and the limit, 46; metaphysics of, 53, 144, 155; self-, 55, 126, 128–9, 132–3, 225, 228, 231; as source of language, 145; of the signified, 127

problem, 11; and mystery, 30n6

problema, 10

problem-solving: and world-disclosure, 172–3, 182, 239, 242

provocation, 89, 91–2

psychoanalysis, 115, 157, 168–9, 177, 178; and the law, 216–17n13

puns, 73, 74, 92

quasi-transcendence, 100–1
Quine, Willard van Orman, 178, 182, 242

Ramsay, F. P., 75–6
reader, 81; critical, 19
reading, 34n14, 143; critical, 19, 139–40,
　147–8; deconstructive, 2–3, 172; double,
　122, 123, 147, 148, 150–4, 158, 161,
　166n35; dominant, 247, 148, 161;
　metaphysical, 161; strong, 2–3
re-mark, 82, 116; *see also* double, genre
reflection, reflexivity, 222–4, 230–2, 236,
　239, 241, 243, 245n15; critique of, 230
respect, 22, 32n10; for the law, 31n10; for
　the other, 31n10
responding: without responding, 34n14
response, 11, 13, 16–17, 20; aporia of, 19;
　deferred, 18; elliptical, 18; oblique, 18;
　see also non-response, responding,
　responsibility, responsivity
responsibility, 11, 13–14, 17–18, 20, 90,
　92; ethics of, 23; metaphysical definition
　of, 10; ontological, 91; politics of, 23;
　pre-ethical, 68; and undecidability, 72;
　see also non-response, responding,
　responsivity, rhetoric, space
responsiveness, 13, 24; *see also* non-
　response, responding, responsibility
retention and protention, 131
rhetoric: of responsibility, 9; of war, 18
ritual, 5–9, 19; logic of, 5; *see also*
　ceremony, sacrifice
Roudinesco, Elisabeth, 116
Rousseau, Jean-Jacques, 2, 58, 109, 114,
　119n9, 137–66, 193, 206–15;
　Confessions, 145; *Discourse on the Origin
　and Foundations of Inequality Among
　Men*, 143, 146, 148, 156; *Essay on the
　Origin of Languages*, 143, 144, 145, 146,
　147, 150, 151, 153, 156, 158; *The Social
　Contract*, 111–13
Rorty, Richard, 170–1, 181, 191, 235, 246
Russell, Bertrand, 75, 81, 82, 98, 177, 239
Ryle, Gilbert, 177

sacrifice, 2, 18–19, 33n12, 27n4, 30n6,
　31n9, 32n10, 33n12, 62; of words, 60; *see
　also* ceremony, Kant, ritual

Sallis, John, 3, 4n1, 120–36
Sartre, Jean-Paul, 223
Saussure, Ferdinand de, 2, 123, 124,
　135n7, 225, 227, 234n51
Schiller, Friedrich, 64
Schmalenbach, Herman, 223
Schönberg, Arnold, 107, 111
Searle, John, 86, 94, 173, 175, 176, 181,
　182, 190, 228, 231
secret, the, 7–8, 20–2, 23–4, 25n2, 31n8,
　31–2n10, 34n14; exemplary, 23, 33n14;
　and the name, 21; place of, 22–3; right
　to, 21; and speech, 22; *see also* literature
self-consciousness, 238; *see also* presence
self-reference, 75
Shakespeare, William, 120
sign: and indication, 128; general concept
　of, 125; repression of, 128; question of,
　124; written and sensible, 128; *see also*
　signifier
signature, 20, 151; effect, 196, 203; *see also*
　name
signifier: and signified, 127, 129
Sinn: and *Bedeutung*, distinguished, 227
skin: of the book, 50; passion for, 50
solitude, 25; as the other name of the
　secret, 24
Socrates, 120, 176–7
Sophocles, 10, 30n6
Sorge (care), 223, 239
space: ethical, 3; of philosophy's passion, 3;
　of responsibility, 3; textual, 3
speech, 22, 23, 126–7, 221; and gesture,
　146; of the other, 68; and presence, 144,
　145, 157; and writing, 60, 124, 129, 132,
　144
speech acts, 80–1, 93, 172; parasitical, 180;
　Searle's taxonomy of, 228; theory, 173,
　176, 180, 182, 190
Starobinski, Jean, 149
state: foundation of, 110 and the legislator,
　110
Staten, Hentry, 184–5
Stoppard, Tom, 74
story, 137, 157–9; telling, 139, 157, 159,
　160; good and bad, 156
stricture, 11
subject: of enunciation and subject of the

enounced, distinguished, 178
subjectivity, 132–3, 223, 225, 227, 228, 231–2
sublime, the, 41, 204
supplement, 86, 134, 140, 144, 145, 149, 154; and the law, 148; logic of, 66, 67, 87, 144–6, 147, 215
supplementarity, 105
symbol: symbolization, 56, 75, 113; and the affect, 57, 60

teleology, 64–5
telos, 101, 104, 164n24
text: literary, 82; of metaphysics, 166n36; *see also* genre
theology 86; negative, 20, 87, 88
theoria, 83
thinking: and weighing, 41
thought: impassioned and transcendental, compared, 37
time, 134; production of, 134; and temporality, 133
trace, 12, 24, 25n2, 43, 88, 92, 93, 184, 198; economy of, 227; example of, 193; play of, 63; and touch, 49
traduction: translation, 26n3, 31n9, 87, 89
Trakl, Georg, 89
transcendental, 43, 48; ellipsis of, 47; and the ontological, 43, 50, 51; *see also* thought
transgression, 5, 9
tribunal, 52; philosophical or moral, 11
tribute, 7, 8
truth, 17, 54–5, 77, 78–9, 102, 125; as adequation, 21; desire for, 68; as *homoiosis* 21; of language, 56; letter of, 179; as memory (*aletheia*), 21, 68; and reason, 186; telling, 180; thinking of, 101
Tugendhat, Ernst, 219–20, 225, 233n21, 234n39, 240, 241, 242, 245n15

Ulmer, Gregory, 194
unconscious, the, 20, 86, 178, 180; and desire, 169; structural, 179

undecidability, undecidibles, 14–15, 72, 74–5, 76, 80, 82, 90, 93, 94, 100, 179, 200, 203, 230; and dialectics, 200, 203; and the fetish, 200; and irresponsibility, 93; and meaning, 175; and names, 178
unique: example, 200, 209, 213
uniqueness, 208–9, 212–13
use: and mention, 73–5, 77, 86, 177; paradoxes of, 75

Valéry, Paul, 38
Vico, Giambattista, 151
voice, 45, 129, 132–3, 144, 165n33, 209, 211; of Being, 54; and writing, 165n33

Warburton, William, 97, 112–13, 151
Warminski, Andrzej, 194–5
will: to power, 55, 56, 64; to write, 59
Wittgenstein, Ludwig, 98, 102, 116–17, 184, 190, 225, 241, 242, 243; *Tractatus*, 243
Wood, David, 1–4, 7, 11, 13, 16, 30–1n8
writing (*écriture*), 25n2, 37–9, 41–3, 45, 46, 47, 48, 49, 53, 54, 57, 59, 62, 87, 98, 103, 114, 121, 133, 140, 145, 177, 178, 180, 181, 184, 210–13, 244n14; and the aphorism, 59; as archetype of the voice, 59; archi-, 86, 175, 188, 244n8; as binding joint of the book, 39; classical concept of, 124; contempt for, 58; double-, 61; and doubling, 123, 124, 129–31, 133–4, 135n8; and empiricalness, 48; and hiding, 145; hysteria in, 45; and ideality, 124; and the limit, 40, 48; and metaphoricity, 150; non-subordination of, 55; parasitic character of Derrida's, 157; passion of, 44, 49, 50; as passion of the origin, 37–8; philosophy as a kind of, 172, 191; reduction of, 208–9; and style, 54–5, 57, 58, 60, 93, 181, 183; supplementary god of, 105; transcendental experience of, 38

index compiled by Iain Hamilton Grant